Lecture Notes in Computer Science   11808

More information about this series at http://www.springer.com/series/7412

Marco Cristani · Andrea Prati ·
Oswald Lanz · Stefano Messelodi ·
Nicu Sebe (Eds.)

New Trends in Image Analysis and Processing – ICIAP 2019

ICIAP International Workshops
BioFor, PatReCH, e-BADLE, DeepRetail, and Industrial Session
Trento, Italy, September 9–10, 2019
Revised Selected Papers

 Springer

Editors
Marco Cristani (iD)
University of Verona
Verona, Italy

Andrea Prati (iD)
University of Parma
Parma, Italy

Oswald Lanz (iD)
Fondazione Bruno Kessler
Povo, Italy

Stefano Messelodi (iD)
Fondazione Bruno Kessler
Povo, Italy

Nicu Sebe (iD)
University of Trento
Povo, Italy

ISSN 0302-9743   ISSN 1611-3349   (electronic)
Lecture Notes in Computer Science
ISBN 978-3-030-30753-0   ISBN 978-3-030-30754-7   (eBook)
https://doi.org/10.1007/978-3-030-30754-7

LNCS Sublibrary: SL6 – Image Processing, Computer Vision, Pattern Recognition, and Graphics

This Springer imprint is published by the registered company Springer Nature Switzerland AG
The registered company address is: Gewerbestrasse 11, 6330 Cham, Switzerland

Preface

This volume contains the 39 papers accepted for presentation at the workshops and the industrial session hosted by the 20th International Conference on Image Analysis and Processing (ICIAP 2019), held in Trento, Italy, September 9–13, 2019. ICIAP is the conference series organized every two years by the CVPL, the group of Italian researchers affiliated with the International Association for Pattern Recognition (IAPR). The aim of the conference is to bring together researchers working on image processing, computer vision, and pattern recognition from around the world. Topics traditionally covered are related to computer vision, pattern recognition, and image processing, addressing both theoretical and applicative aspects.

Four individual workshops – one full-day and three half-day – were selected by the workshop chairs Marco Cristani (University of Verona) and Andrea Prati (University of Parma) to complement ICIAP 2019 in Trento:

- Second International Workshop on Recent Advances in Digital Security: Bio-metrics and Forensics (BioFor 2019)
- First International Workshop on Pattern Recognition for Cultural Heritage (PatReCH 2019)
- First International Workshop on eHealth in the Big Data and Deep Learning Era (e-BADLE 2019)
- Workshop on Deep Understanding Shopper Behaviours and Interactions in Intelligent Retail Environments (DeepRetail 2019)

A dedicated industrial session for researchers, practitioners and manufacturers was included in the pre-conference program.

The Second International Workshop on Recent Advances in Digital Security: Biometrics and Forensics (BioFor 2019) organized by Daniel Riccio (University of Naples Federico II, Italy), Chang-Tsun Li (Deakin University, Australia), Francesco Marra (University of Naples Federico II, Italy), and Diego Gragnaniello (University of Naples Federico II, Italy) provided an international forum for scientists and researchers to develop synergies between the biometrics and forensic research areas.

The First International Workshop on Pattern Recognition for Cultural Heritage (PatReCH 2019) organized by Francesco Fontanella (University of Cassino and Southern Lazio, Italy), Mario Molinara (University of Cassino and Southern Lazio, Italy), and Filippo Stanco (University of Catania, Italy) aimed to give an overview of recent advances in Pattern Recognition techniques for data analysis and representation in the cultural heritage field.

The First International Workshop on eHealth in the Big Data and Deep Learning Era (e-BADLE 2019) organized by Tanmoy Chakarboty (Institute of Information Technology Delhi, India), Stefano Marrone (University of Naples Federico II, Italy), and Giancarlo Sperlì (CINI - ITEM National Lab, Naples, Italy) provided a forum to gather recent advances in the biomedical images processing field to help advance the scientific research within the broad field of medical imaging using machine learning, deep learning, and big data techniques.

The Workshop on Deep Understanding Shopper Behaviours and Interactions in Intelligent Retail Environments (DeepRetail 2019) organized by Emanuele Frontoni (Università Politecnica delle Marche, Italy), Sebastiano Battiato (University of Catania, Italy), Cosimo Distante (ISASI CNR, Italy), Marina Paolanti (Università Politecnica delle Marche, Italy), Luigi Di Stefano (University of Bologna, Italy), Giovanni Marina Farinella (University of Catania, Italy), Annette Wolfrath (GFK Verein, Germany), and Primo Zingaretti (Università Politecnica delle Marche, Italy) aimed at encouraging and highlighting novel strategies and original research in computer vision and pattern recognition for shoppers' behavior understanding, to build a network between European universities and industries and a roadmap for future deep learning applications.

The Industrial Session organized by Luigi di Stefano (University of Bologna, Italy), Vittorio Murino (Istituto Italiano di Technologia, Italy), Paolo Rota (University of Trento, Italy), and Francesco Setti (University of Verona, Italy) brought together researchers and practitioners in industrial engineering and computer science interested in industrial machine vision to overview the state of the art and identify the most interesting research lines. It was intended as a joint session for researchers to show recent advancements in research projects on industrial applications and new technologies suitable for industrial environments, for practitioners to bring an applicative point of view on the state of the practice in industry and take inspiration for their use cases, for manufacturers to present the state of the art on technologies and case studies, and challenge researchers and engineers with open problems.

We thank all the workshop organizers and the industrial session organizers who made possible such an interesting program.

August 2019   Marco Cristani
                                                                        Andrea Prati

Organization

General Chairs

Oswald Lanz   Fondazione Bruno Kessler, Italy
Stefano Messelodi   Fondazione Bruno Kessler, Italy
Nicu Sebe   University of Trento, Italy

Program Chairs

Elisa Ricci   University of Trento & Fondazione Bruno Kessler,
     Italy
Samuel Rota Bulò   Mapillary Research, Austria
Cees Snoek   University of Amsterdam, The Netherlands

Workshop Chairs

Marco Cristani   University of Verona, Italy
Andrea Prati   University of Parma, Italy

Tutorial Chairs

Costantino Grana   University of Modena e Reggio Emilia, Italy
Lamberto Ballan   University of Padova, Italy

Special Session Chairs

Marco Bertini   University of Florence, Italy
Tatiana Tommasi   Italian Institute of Technology, Italy

Industrial Chairs

Paul Chippendale   Fondazione Bruno Kessler, Italy
Fabio Galasso   OSRAM, Germany

Publicity/Web Chairs

Davide Boscaini   Fondazione Bruno Kessler, Italy
Massimiliano Mancini   Fondazione Bruno Kessler, Sapienza University
     of Rome, Istituto Italiano di Tecnologia, Italy

Publication Chair

Michela Lecca   Fondazione Bruno Kessler, Italy

Local Chairs

Fabio Poiesi   Fondazione Bruno Kessler, Italy
Gloria Zen   University of Trento, Italy
Stéphane Lathuillère   University of Trento, Italy

Asia Liaison Chair

Ramanathan Subramanian   University of Glasgow, UK

USA Liaison Chair

Yan Yan   Texas State University, USA

Steering Committee

Virginio Cantoni   University of Pavia, Italy
Luigi Pietro Cordella   University of Napoli Federico II, Italy
Rita Cucchiara   University of Modena and Reggio Emilia, Italy
Alberto Del Bimbo   University of Firenze, Italy
Marco Ferretti   University of Pavia, Italy
Gian Luca Foresti   University of Udine, Italy
Fabio Roli   University of Cagliari, Italy
Gabriella Sanniti di Baja   ICAR-CNR, Italy

Invited Speakers

Davide Scaramuzza   University of Zurich and ETH Zurich, Switzerland
Tal Ayellet   Technion Israel of Technology, Israel
Emanuele Rodolà   Sapienza University of Rome, Italy
Alessandra Sciutti   Italian Institute of Technology, Italy

Area Chairs

Video Analysis and Understanding

Andrea Cavallaro   Queen Mary University of London, UK
Efstratios Gavves   University of Amsterdam, The Netherlands

Pattern Recognition and Machine Learning

Battista Biggio   University of Cagliari, Italy
Marcello Pelillo   University of Venice, Italy

Deep Learning

Marco Gori   University of Siena, Italy
Francesco Orabona   Boston University, USA

Multiview Geometry and 3D Computer Vision

Andrea Fusiello   University of Udine, Italy
Alessio Del Bue   Istituto Italiano di Tecnologia, Italy
Federico Tombari   Technische Universität München, Germany

Image Analysis, Detection, and Recognition

Barbara Caputo   Politecnico di Torino and Istituto Italiano di
                              Technologia, Italy
Jasper Uijlings   Google AI, Switzerland

Multimedia

Xavier Alameda-Pineda   Inria, France
Francesco De Natale   University of Trento, Italy

Biomedical and Assistive Technology

Giovanni Maria Farinella   University of Catania, Italy
Roberto Manduchi   UCSC, USA

Digital Forensics

Giulia Boato   University of Trento, Italy
Fernando Pérez-González   University of Vigo, Italy

Image Processing for Cultural Heritage

Andreas Rauber   TU Wien, Austria
Lorenzo Seidenari   University of Florence, Italy

Brave New Ideas

Michele Merler   IBM T. J. Watson Research Center, USA
Concetto Spampinato   University of Catania, Italy

Contents

BioFor: Workshop on Recent Advances in Digital Security: Biometrics and Forensics

EEG-Based Biometric Verification Using Siamese CNNs

Emanuele Maiorana$^{(\boxtimes)}$ (iD)

Roma Tre University, Via V. Volterra 62, 00146 Rome, Italy
emanuele.maiorana@uniroma3.it

Abstract. Cognitive biometric characteristics have recently attracted the attention of the scientific community thanks to some of their interesting properties, such as their intrinsic liveness detection capability and their robustness against spoofing attacks. Among the traits belonging to this category, brain signals have been considered in several studies, commonly focusing on the analysis of electroencephalography (EEG) recordings. Unfortunately, a significant intra-class variability affects EEG data acquired at different times, making it therefore hard for current state-of-the-art methods to achieve high recognition rates. To cope with this issue, deep learning techniques have been recently employed to search for EEG discriminative information, yet only identification scenarios have been so far considered in literature. In this paper a verification context is instead taken into account, and proper networks are proposed to extract features allowing to differentiate subjects which are not available during network training, by resorting to siamese designs. The performed experimental tests, conducted over a longitudinal database comprising EEG acquisitions taken during five sessions spanning a period of one year and a half, show the effectiveness of the proposed approach in achieving high-level accuracy for brain-based biometric verification purposes.

Keywords: Biometrics · Electroencephalography · Deep learning · Convolutional neural networks · Siamese Networks

1 Introduction

Biometric recognition is nowadays a mature technology, with many applications adopted in our daily life, ranging from the use of fingerprint and face traits to access a mobile device, to the exploitation of iris patterns to enter restricted areas in airports. Nonetheless, several issues still have to be properly addressed to guarantee a high security level to the users of such systems. For instance, all the aforementioned biometric traits can be covertly acquired with relative ease to perform a presentation attack at a later time. Integrating liveness detection strategies within the deployed systems can be often hard and costly, thus motivating the research for alternatives based on biometric traits possessing useful properties not available in mainstream solutions.

© Springer Nature Switzerland AG 2019
M. Cristani et al. (Eds.): ICIAP 2019 Workshops, LNCS 11808, pp. 3–11, 2019.
https://doi.org/10.1007/978-3-030-30754-7_1

In this regard, the exploitation of cognitive biometrics [17] has been recently proposed to reduce such security issues. This kind of biometric traits involves the acquisition of biosignals generated by the nervous system while performing a specific task or in response to a given stimulus, such as electrocardiography (ECG), blood pulse volume (BVP), electrodermal response (EDR), or electroencephalography (EEG). Such characteristics inherently perform liveness detection, and are much more difficult to be covertly captured than traditional biometric data.

Unfortunately, due to their nature of being dependent on both physical and behavioral characteristics of an individual, cognitive biometric traits typically show significant intra-class variability, especially when comparing recordings taken at different times. Actually, the considered signals may depend on the placement of the employed recording devices, on the current emotional state of the involved subjects, the specific performed task, as well as the environment surrounding the person to be recognized, thus severely affecting the recognition performance achievable in practical scenarios.

In order to handle such variability, deep neural networks (DNNs) have been recently applied to traits such as ECG [9] and EEG [10] to derive discriminative and stable information from the recorded data. With this line of research still in its infancy, identification is commonly employed as the considered recognition modality, being it the standard supervised framework in which deep learning approaches are designed and evaluated. Yet, it has to be remarked that most of deployed biometric recognition systems works in verification modality, and that this latter is a scenario allowing the estimate of more reliable performance metrics with respect to identification. It is in fact well known that the recognition rates estimated for systems working in identification modality are highly affected by the number N of classes (subjects) available for testing purposes, with a behavior resembling the $log(N)$ law for the associated reliability. Since collecting databases with cognitive biometric traits taken from a large number of subject is a hard task, due to the usually uncomfortable and time-consuming recording procedure, estimating the achievable recognition performance considering a verification modality should represent a preferable choice to properly assess the effectiveness in generating discriminative features from the considered data.

Stemming from these observations, this paper evaluates for the first time the feasibility of performing biometric verification by applying deep learning techniques to EEG traits. Specifically, the effectiveness of siamese designs in learning similar characteristics for acquisitions of the same subject, and different representations for samples taken from different subjects, while not having the possibility of dealing with these users' data during network training, is here investigated. This process is performed while taking into proper account the intra-class variability of EEG data, by exploiting a database collected from 45 users, whose brain signals have been recorded during five distinct sessions spanning a period of approximately one year and a half.

The paper is organized as follows. The state of the art on the use of deep learning techniques for EEG-based biometric recognition is presented in Sect. 2.

Section 3 then outlines the processing applied to the treated EEG signals as well as the employed deep-learning architectures. The database employed for the experimental part, the performed tests, and the obtained results are discussed in Sect. 4, while conclusions are eventually drawn in Sect. 5.

2 Deep Learning Techniques for EEG-Based Biometric Recognition

Although the use of brain signals for people recognition purposes has been postulated almost 40 years ago [20], concrete and reliable studies evaluating the feasibility of exploiting such modality in practical applications have been proposed only in the last decade [2]. Many features have been employed in the attempt of capturing the discriminative information residing in the brain signal recorded from a subject, exploiting for instance auto-regressive (AR) models [1], power spectral density (PSD) coefficients [14], wavelet representations [22], or connectivity measures [6].

More recently, deep learning methods have been also adopted to this aim. For instance, convolutional neural networks (CNNs) have been first applied to brain signals in [10], where two convolutional layers have been used to classify 10 subjects whose traits have been recorded in resting state scenarios with eyes-closed (EC) and eyes-open (EO) conditions. A network with a single convolutional layer has been employed in [7] to classify EEG signals taken from 30 subjects receiving visual stimuli, while event-related potentials (ERPs) from 40 subjects have been used as inputs to a four-convolutional-layer CNN in [4]. A network with three convolutional layers has been used in [13] to discriminate between 100 subjects performing a driving task in a virtual-reality scenario. Three convolutional layers have been also employed in the CNN architectures presented in [3] to deal with EEG signals collected from 50 subjects while performing motor imagery (MI) tasks, and in [19] to process EC and EO signals recorded from the 109 subjects in the Physionet EEG Database. A rapid serial visual presentation (RSVP) protocol has been employed to capture EEG signals from 10 subjects during three sessions in [16], where a network using two losses in an adversarial-like strategy has been designed to maximize classification accuracy while minimizing inter-session variability. Also signals captured using a steady state visual evoked potential (SSVEP) protocol have been processed through DNNs, as in [5] where data taken from 10 subjects is provided as input to six convolutional layers, and in [23] where two large convolutional layers treat EEG acquisitions from 8 users.

As already observed, all the mentioned papers have applied deep learning methods to EEG biometric traits only considering identification scenarios, using standard CNN frameworks to process data recorded from the same set of subjects during both enrolment and recognition phases. Moreover, raw EEG temporal data have been always employed as input of the proposed CNN architectures, with the only exception of [13] where AR and PSD features are instead obtained during a preprocessing step and then fed to the used CNN. Even more importantly, it is worth remarking that only the works described in [3,4,16] and [23] have considered EEG data from disjoint recording sessions, typically spanning a period in the order of days between acquisitions, to separately perform the training and the testing of the proposed networks. Actually, as remarked in [12], this should be the only proper way for conducting experiments on EEG biometric characteristics, since otherwise the resulting recognition performance would be severely affected by the session-specific exogenous conditions differently characterizing every EEG acquisition, therefore greatly overestimating the actual system behavior when it would be applied in practical scenarios.

As it will be described in the following sections, the present paper properly evaluates for the first time the feasibility of using DNN architectures to perform EEG-based biometric verification, resorting to siamese designs for the training phase. Moreover, the usefulness of employing hand-crafted features instead of raw EEG temporal data as inputs of the considered networks, a frequently-used practice in brain-computer interfaces (BCIs) and medical applications [8], is also here evaluated. Eventually, a challenging scenarios consisting of a time distance greater than one year for the EEG signals collected for enrolment and verification purposes from 45 subjects is here taken into account, in order to verify whether EEG-based verification could be performed under very tough conditions.

3   EEG Signal Processing

The preprocessing applied to the collected EEG signals is outlined in Sect. 3.1, which also introduces the data representations provided as inputs to the considered DNN architectures. These latter are then described in Sect. 3.2.

3.1   Preprocessing

The treated EEG signals are assumed to be collected through C electrodes placed on the subjects' scalp, being $C = 19$ in the performed tests as specified in Sect. 4. Leveraging on the outcomes of previous studies regarding EEG signals distinctiveness and permanence [11], the considered data are band-pass filtered limiting their frequencies within the $[\alpha, \beta] = 8 \div 30$ Hz subband, and a downsampling to $S = 64$ Hz is then performed to simplify the subsequent processing without loosing any significant information. A spatial filtering is also applied by means of a common average referencing (CAR) filter [15] to limit the effects of possible incorrect reference positioning.

The obtained signals are then segmented into overlapping epochs, each lasting $H = 5$s with an 80% overlap percentage between consecutive epochs, which are used as inputs to the considered frameworks. Specifically, an EEG sample can be represented as a matrix $\mathbf{M}_T$ with size $C \times (H \cdot S)$, whose rows contain the raw temporal behaviors $\mathbf{m}_{T(c)}$, $c = 1, \ldots, C$, of the EEG signals acquired through the considered C channels. Alternatively, a separate yet identical processing can be applied to the C signals recorded through the employed electrodes, by considering as epoch's representation the set $\mathcal{M}_T = \{\mathbf{m}_{T(1)}, \ldots, \mathbf{m}_{T(C)}\}$, containing

C signals each with length $H \cdot S$. Overlapping epochs are used to learn better representations during training and estimating more reliable performance during testing.

In order to evaluate whether it could be beneficial to fed a DNN with hand-crafted characteristics instead of with raw EEG data, additional representations of the considered epochs are also taken into account. Specifically, mel-frequency cepstrum coefficients (MFCC) are here used for this purpose, having proven the discriminative capabilities of such features in [11]. In more detail, $W = 12$ coefficients are derived from each c-th channel of an EEG epoch producing a vector $\mathbf{m}_{F(c)}$, leading to a sample representation as a matrix $\mathbf{M}_F$ with C rows $\mathbf{m}_{F(c)}$, $c = 1, \ldots, C$, or also as a set $\mathcal{M}_F = \{\mathbf{m}_{F(1)}, \ldots, \mathbf{m}_{F(C)}\}$ of C vectors with length W.

3.2 Employed Siamese Networks

The networks considered in the performed tests are trained by exploiting siamese designs, where two identical CNNs receive as input a couple of EEG epoch representations, and produce outputs which are then fed to a loss function calculating the distance between the two obtained feature vectors. Network training is performed trying to minimize the distance between pairs of inputs belonging to the same user, while maximizing the distance between features extracted from pairs of samples taken from distinct subjects. During this process, the two considered CNNs are simultaneously updated, sharing the same parameters and weights. In more detail, as depicted in Fig. 1, the outputs $\mathbf{x}_P^{(1)}$ and $\mathbf{x}_P^{(2)}$ of two CNNs with P layers $L_1, \ldots, L_P$ are compared through an Euclidean distance $D(\mathbf{x}_P^{(1)}, \mathbf{x}_P^{(2)})$, and a contrastive loss function is then computed as

$$\mathcal{L}(\mathbf{x}_P^{(1)}, \mathbf{x}_P^{(2)}, y) = (1 - y)\frac{1}{2}D^2(\mathbf{x}_P^{(1)}, \mathbf{x}_P^{(2)}) + y\frac{1}{2}[max(0, d - D(\mathbf{x}_P^{(1)}, \mathbf{x}_P^{(2)}))]^2, \quad (1)$$

being y a label associated with the considered pair of inputs, with $y = 0$ in case both samples belong to the same subject and $y = 1$ otherwise, and d is a parameter to be learned while minimizing the loss $L(\mathbf{x}_P^{(1)}, \mathbf{x}_P^{(2)}, y)$.

The CNN configurations used to process the considered EEG epoch representations $\mathbf{M}_T$, $\mathcal{M}_T$, $\mathbf{M}_F$, and $\mathcal{M}_F$ are detailed in Table 1. A batch-normalization is employed after each convolutional (conv) layer, maxpooling (MP) is used to reduce input dimensionality, rectified linear units (ReLus) are used as non-linearities, and dropout (DO) at 50% is exploited for regularization purposes before final fully-connected layers. As can be seen, the conv layers employed to process the matrices $\mathbf{M}_T$ and $\mathbf{M}_F$ use unidimensional filters, as recently suggested to model brain signals in [18] and [16]. Experimental tests performed on the used multi-session database have in fact shown that disentangling the temporal and spatial processing of the recorded signals guarantees a significant improvement in recognition rates, with respect to the use of bidimensional filters like in most of state-of-the-art CNN-based EEG recognition systems [3–5, 7, 10, 13, 19]. Resorting to $\mathcal{M}_T$ and $\mathcal{M}_F$ representations further separates temporal and spatial processing of collected EEG signals, since the employed CNNs

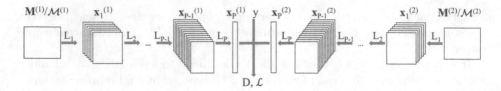

$$\mathbf{M}^{(1)}/\mathcal{M}^{(1)} \quad \mathbf{x}_1^{(1)} \qquad\qquad \mathbf{x}_{P\text{-}1}^{(1)} \quad \mathbf{x}_P^{(1)} \quad y \quad \mathbf{x}_P^{(2)} \quad \mathbf{x}_{P\text{-}1}^{(2)} \qquad\qquad \mathbf{x}_1^{(2)} \quad \mathbf{M}^{(2)}/\mathcal{M}^{(2)}$$

$$D, \mathcal{L}$$

Fig. 1. Siamese design for network training.

Table 1. Employed CNNs, depending on the chosen EEG representation.

(a) input: $\mathbf{M}_T$

#	Layer	Filter	Pad
L_1	Conv	$(1\times5\times1)\times16$	[0,2]
L_2	Conv	$(19\times1\times16)\times16$	-
L_3	ReLu	-	-
L_4	MP	1×3	-
L_5	Conv	$(1\times5\times16)\times32$	[0,2]
L_6	ReLu	-	-
L_7	MP	1×3	-
L_8	Conv	$(1\times3\times32)\times64$	-
L_9	ReLu	-	-
L_{10}	MP	1×3	-
L_{11}	Conv	$(1\times3\times64)\times128$	-
L_{12}	ReLu	-	-
L_{13}	MP	1×3	-
L_{14}	DO	-	-
L_{15}	Conv	$(1\times1\times128)\times256$	-

(b) input: $\mathcal{M}_T$

#	Layer	Filter	Pad
L_1	Conv	$(1\times5\times1)\times16$	[0,2]
L_2	ReLu	-	-
L_3	MP	1×3	-
L_4	Conv	$(1\times5\times16)\times32$	[0,2]
L_5	ReLu	-	-
L_6	MP	1×3	-
L_7	Conv	$(1\times3\times32)\times64$	-
L_8	Relu	-	-
L_9	MP	1×3	-
L_{10}	Conv	$(1\times3\times64)\times128$	-
L_{11}	ReLu	-	-
L_{12}	MP	1×3	-
L_{13}	DO	-	-
L_{14}	Conv	$(1\times1\times128)\times256$	-

(c) input: $\mathbf{M}_F$

#	Layer	Filter	Pad
L_1	Conv	$(1\times5\times1)\times64$	[0,2]
L_2	Conv	$(19\times1\times64)\times64$	-
L_3	ReLu	-	-
L_4	MP	1×2	-
L_5	Conv	$1\times3\times64)\times128$	[0,1]
L_6	ReLu	-	-
L_7	MP	1×2	-
L_8	DO	-	-
L_9	Conv	$(1\times1\times128)\times256$	-

(d) input: $\mathcal{M}_F$

#	Layer	Filter	Pad
L_1	Conv	$(1\times5\times1)\times64$	[0,2]
L_2	ReLu	-	-
L_3	MP	1×2	-
L_4	Conv	$1\times3\times64)\times128$	[0,1]
L_5	ReLu	-	-
L_6	MP	1×2	-
L_7	DO	-	-
L_8	Conv	$(1\times1\times128)\times256$	-

Table 2. EERs (mean and confidence interval, in %) achieved using a single EEG epoch for verification, with and without resorting to siamese designs for network training.

CNN training	Input Representation			
	$\mathbf{M}_T$	$\mathcal{M}_T$	$\mathbf{M}_F$	$\mathcal{M}_F$
Not-siamese	21.70 ± 2.10	16.23 ± 1.65	23.20 ± 1.70	18.68 ± 1.60
Siamese	23.13 ± 1.70	$\mathbf{9.67 \pm 0.90}$	19.52 ± 1.80	14.33 ± 1.10

are applied to unidimensional signals, and fusion of the available information is performed only at the feature level during verification, combining the representations generated by the CNNs applied to the C available signals. This way, the proposed networks avoid the computation of connectivity features, which are instead produced at the second conv layer of the CNNs applied to $\mathbf{M}_T$ and $\mathbf{M}_F$.

Networks are trained using stochastic gradient descend with momentum (SGDM), batches with size 512, 0.001 for learning rate and 0.005 for weight decay, employing the MatConvNet [21] deep learning framework with a Nvidia GeForce GTX GPU.

4   Experimental Tests

The effectiveness of the networks designed for EEG biometric verification has been evaluated using the signals collected in EC conditions from the longitudinal database described in [11]. The employed data comprises recordings taken from 45 subjects during five different recording sessions, indicated in the following as $R_1, R_2, \ldots, R_5$, using a GALILEO BE Light amplifier with $C = 19$

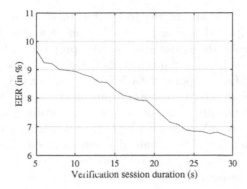

Fig. 2. EERs achievable using the proposed siamese network with $\mathcal{M}_T$ as input.

wet electrodes, working at 256 Hz. The average distances between the first and the other four recordings are $\Delta_{R_1,R_2} = 1$ week, $\Delta_{R_1,R_3} = 1$ month, $\Delta_{R_1,R_4} = 7$ months, and $\Delta_{R_1,R_5} = 16$ months, with the distributions of the time distances Δ_{R_1,R_n}, $n = 2, \ldots, 5$ elapsed between the first and the n-th EEG acquisition of each subject.

A cross-validation approach has been followed by randomly dividing for five times the available subjects into a training set comprising acquisitions from 30 subjects, used for training the designed siamese networks, and a testing set with EEG signals from the remaining users, used to estimate the verification performance achievable though the learned representations. Specifically, in order to test the designed networks in the hardest possible conditions, the verification performance has been evaluated by comparing signals taken during the fifth session of each user against those in the first three ones, therefore putting a temporal distance of 15 months on average between enrolment and verification. The siamese networks have been trained considering pairs of epochs of the same subject, yet from different sessions, as inputs for legitimate comparisons. In more detail, recordings from the first three sessions have been paired with those from the fifth for training purposes, and with epochs from the fourth for validation to decide when training should be stopped. Once the employed CNNs have been trained, they have been used to generate EEG representations for the testing users, taking the minimum of the computed Euclidean distances as score for the comparison between a probe epoch and the enrolment ones.

To report baseline performance, the hand-crafted features $\mathbf{M}_F$ are employed as biometric template, and Euclidean distance used for comparison, as typically done in state-of-the-art EEG-based verification systems [11]. The equal error rate (EER) thus achieved, using a single EEG epoch lasting 5 s as verification probe, is $15.69\% \pm 1.90$.

The EERs obtained through the proposed frameworks are instead reported in Table 2, where they are compared with those attainable in a not-siamese training design, where EEG representations are learned by training the employed CNNs for identification purposes over the considered training subjects, and then used to encode the biometric traits of the test subjects. The same training/testing data allocation is employed to evaluate all the considered methods.

The obtained results show that training the proposed networks with hand-crafted MFCC features $\mathbf{M}_F$ guarantees verification accuracies greater than those achieved using raw EEG temporal data $\mathbf{M}_T$ as inputs of CNNs. Yet, giving up on trying to extract connectivity features from the available data, and processing each electrode independently from the others by resorting to a $\mathcal{M}_T$ representation, CNNs are actually able to learn a EEG representation retaining significant discriminative information. The obtained results suggest that relying on connectivity features to perform EEG-based biometric recognition across different sessions is not a rewarding approach.

The employed siamese design also allows to improve the recognition performance achievable when using MFCC-based representations as CNN inputs, by arranging them as $\mathcal{M}_F$. Such improvement cannot be achieved when considering features learned from MFCC-based representations in an identification scenario, further testifying the effectiveness of the exploited siamese training strategy.

In order to convey additional evidence on the feasibility of using brain signals as biometric identifiers for recognition purposes, Fig. 2 reports the average EERs achieved for increasing lengths of EEG verification probes, using $\mathcal{M}_T$ as input to the proposed network, and applying a score-level fusion strategy to the distances computed over each epoch to determine whether a subject is a genuine user or an impostor. It is worth remarking that the reported recognition rates are obtained by comparing EEG traits taken at an average temporal distance of 15 months between enrolment and verification. Although better results have been reported in literature [2,6], these latter have been obtained only when comparing EEG signals from the same recording session, which is not a proper testing strategy as already pointed out in Sect. 2 [11].

5   Conclusions

Siamese designs have been exploited to train CNNs for EEG-based biometric verification purposes. The performed experimental tests have highlighted the possibility of achieving better recognition results following the proposed approach, with respect to the use of representations learned for identification tasks. More importantly, highly-discriminative EEG features have been derived by applying the designed networks to the raw EEG temporal data, allowing to achieve EER under 7% when comparing brain signals captured at time distances greater than one year, and using acquisitions of only 30s as verification probes.

References

1. Brigham, K., Kumar, B.V.: Subject identification from electroencephalogram (EEG) signals during imagined speech. In: IEEE BTAS (2010)
2. Campisi, P., La Rocca, D.: Brain waves for automatic biometric-based user recognition. IEEE Trans. Inf. Forensics Secur. **9**(5), 782–800 (2014)

3. Das, R., Maiorana, E., Campisi, P.: Visually evoked potential for EEG biometrics using convolutional neural network. In: EUSIPCO (2017)
4. Das, R., Maiorana, E., Campisi, P.: Motor imagery for EEG biometrics using convolutional neural network. In: IEEE ICASSP (2018)
5. El-Fiqi, H., et al.: Convolution neural networks for person identification and verification using steady state visual evoked potential. In: IEEE International Conference on SMC (2018)
6. Garau, M., Fraschini, M., Didaci, L., Marcialis, G.: Experimental results on multimodal fusion of EEG-based personal verification algorithms. In: IEEE ICB (2016)
7. Gui, Q., Yang, W., Jin, Z.: A residual feature-based replay attack detection approach for brainprint biometric systems. In: IEEE WIFS (2016)
8. Hosseini, M.P., Pompili, D., Elisevich, K., Soltanian-Zadeh, H.: Optimized deep learning for EEG big data and seizure prediction BCI via internet of things. IEEE Trans. Big Data **3**(4), 392–404 (2017)
9. Labati, R., Munoz, E., Piuri, V., Sassi, R., Scotti, F.: Deep-ECG: Convolutional neural networks for ECG biometric recognition. Pattern Recogn. Lett. (2018)
10. Ma, L., Minett, J., Blu, T., Wang, W.Y.: Resting state EEG-based biometrics for individual identification using convolutional neural networks. In: IEEE EMBC (2015)
11. Maiorana, E., Campisi, P.: Longitudinal evaluation of EEG-based biometric recognition. IEEE Trans. Inf. Forensics Secur. **13**(5), 1123–1138 (2018)
12. Maiorana, E., La Rocca, D., Campisi, P.: On the permanence of EEG signals for biometric recognition. IEEE Trans. Inf. Forensics Secur. **11**(1), 163–175 (2016)
13. Mao, Z., Yao, W., Huang, Y.: EEG-based biometric identification with deep learning. In: IEEE EMBC (2017)
14. Marcel, S., Millan, J.D.R.: Person authentication using brainwaves (EEG) and maximum a posteriori model adaptation. IEEE Trans. Patt. Anal. Mach. Intell. **29**(4), 743–748 (2006)
15. McFarland, D., McCane, L., David, S., Wolpaw, J.: Spatial filter selection for EEG-based communication. Electroencephal. Clin. Neurophysiol. **103**(3), 386–394 (1997)
16. Ozdenizci, O., Wang, Y., Koike-Akino, T., Erdogmus, D.: Adversarial deep learning in EEG biometrics. IEEE Sign. Proces. Lett. **26**(5), 710–714 (2019)
17. Revett, K.: Cognitive biometrics: a novel approach to person authentication. Int. J. Cogn. Biom. **1**(1), 1–9 (2012)
18. Schirrmeister, R., et al.: Deep learning with convolutional neural networks for EEG decoding and visualization. Hum. Brain Mapp. **38**, 5391–5420 (2017)
19. Schons, T., Moreira, G., Silva, P., Coelho, V., Luz, E.: Convolutional network for EEG-based biometric. In: CIARP (2017)
20. Stassen, H.H.: Computerized recognition of persons by EEG spectral patterns. Electroencephalogr. Clin. Neurophysiol. **49**(1–2), 190–194 (1980)
21. Vevaldi, A., Lenc, K.: MatConvNet - convolutional neural networks for Matlab. In: ACM International Conference on Multimedia (2015)
22. Wang, Y., Najafizadeh, L.: On the invariance of EEG-based signatures of individuality with application in biometric identification. In: IEEE EMBC (2016)
23. Yu, T., Wei, C.S., Chiang, K.J., Nakanishi, M., Jung, T.P.: EEG-based user authentication using a convolutional neural network. In: IEEE EMBS International Conference on Neural Engineering (2019)

On the Cross-Finger Similarity
of Vein Patterns

Emanuela Piciucco⑩, Ridvan Salih Kuzu⑩, Emanuele Maiorana⁽✉⁾⑩,
and Patrizio Campisi⑩

Roma Tre University, Via Vito Volterra 62, 00146 Rome, Italy
{emanuela.piciucco,ridvansalih.kuzu,emanuele.maiorana,
patrizio.campisi}@uniroma3.it

Abstract. Biometric recognition based on finger-vein patterns is gaining more and more attention, as several approaches have been recently proposed to extract discriminative features from vascular structures. In this paper we investigate the similarity between vein patterns of symmetric fingers of the left and right hand of a subject. More in detail, we analyze the performance achievable when using symmetric fingers and geometry- or deep-learning-based feature extraction methods for recognition. A database with acquisitions from left and right index, medium, and ring fingers of 106 subjects is exploited for experimental tests.

Keywords: Biometrics · Finger-Vein Recognition ·
Convolutional neural networks

1 Introduction

Biometric systems are nowadays deployed in many practical applications requiring human recognition with high-level security, such as border controls, smartphone unlocking, ATM cash withdrawals, and e-commerce to cite a few. Among the exploitable biometric traits, vein patterns [9] have recently attracted a significant interest from industrial and academic communities, thanks to the several advantages they can offer with respect to other traditional biometric identifiers. In fact, the acquisition of vein patterns can be performed only in proximity through a near-infrared (NIR) camera, being therefore hard to implement presentation attacks. Moreover, being possible to perform a contactless recording of the interested train, vein-based biometric recognition systems ensure users' comfort and ease of use. Additionally, liveness detection is intrinsically provided.

Different kinds of vein patterns have been analyzed in literature for recognition purposes, namely finger veins [15], palm veins [22], hand dorsal veins and wrist veins [11]. For all the aforementioned traits, state-of-the-art approaches used for extracting representative features from the structure of blood vessels can be categorized into five classes:

This work has been supported by the EU Horizon 2020 Framework for Research and Innovation under Grant Agreement Number 675087 as part of the AMBER (enhAnced Mobile BiomEtRics) Marie Sklodowska-Curie project.

© Springer Nature Switzerland AG 2019
M. Cristani et al. (Eds.): ICIAP 2019 Workshops, LNCS 11808, pp. 12–20, 2019.
https://doi.org/10.1007/978-3-030-30754-7_2

- geometry-based [9,10]: shape or topological structures are extracted from vein patterns and used as discriminative information. Most methods are based on the segmentation of the veins from the background, with features then extracted from the obtained patterns;
- statistical-based [8,13]: statistical features, such as the local binary histogram and moments, are used to generate the employed templates;
- local invariant-feature-based [12]: algorithms such as scale invariant feature transform (SIFT) or speeded-up robust features (SURF) are employed to derive discriminative representations;
- subspace learning-based [17,19]: methods such as linear discriminant analysis (LDA) or principal component analysis (PCA) are used to extract features;
- deep learning-based techniques [2,3]: deep neural networks are exploited to learn discriminative representations from vein patterns. This latter approach has recently attracted a significant interest, being for instance used in [3], where two different light-weight CNNs have been examined for feature extraction from finger vein patterns. Generative adverserial networks (GANs) have been exploited for finger-vein-based biometric recognition in [20], while the Densenet-161 network has been applied to composite samples created from vein images in [16].

In this paper we focus on finger vein biometric traits, and investigate the existence of similarities between vein patterns of symmetrical fingers belonging to left and right hands, in order to explicitly asses whether it could be possible, for recognition purposes, to consider pairs of symmetric fingers of a subjects as a single class. To the best of our knowledge, the aforementioned aspect has not been analyzed so far in literature for finger-vein-based biometric applications, while it has been evaluated when using palmprint [6,18]. The research has highlighted the presence of shared patterns between the palmprints of both hands of a person, allowing a user to be recognized through his/her left palmprint even when only the other one has been recorded during enrolment. In order to perform a comprehensive analysis, the SDUMLA database [21], comprising finger-vein images from 106 users, with six samples for each of the left and right hand index, middle, and ring fingers, has been considered. Moreover, four different methods, belonging to the geometry- and deep-learning-based categories, have been exploited to derive the employed finger-vein feature representations.

2   Experimental Protocol

The purpose of the performed experimental tests is to verify whether finger-vein patterns of different hands of the same subject have a higher degree of similarity than traits belonging to different persons. To this aim, several tests have been performed on the SDUMLA databas, estimating the distributions of scores obtainable by comparing different classes of biometric samples, specifically:

1. *genuine* scores are obtained by comparing vein patterns from the same finger of the same hand of the same subject. For instance, vein patterns of the right index of a subject are compared between themselves;

Table 1. Score distributions evaluated in the performed tests.

Case	Subject	Hand	Finger	Scores
1	same	same	same	genuine
2	different	same	same	impostor
3	same	different	same	genuine CH
4	same	same/different	different	genuine CF
5	different	same/different	different	impostor CF

2. *impostor* scores are obtained by comparing veins from the same finger of the same hand of different subjects. For instance, patterns of the right index of a subject are compared with those of the right index of a different person;

3. *genuine cross-hand (CH)* scores are obtained by comparing veins from the same finger of different hands of the same subject. For instance, the right index of a subject is compared with the left index of the same person;

4. *genuine cross-finger (CF)* scores are obtained by comparing veins from different fingers of the same subject. For instance, patterns of the right index are compared with those of the right/left middle finger of the same person;

5. *impostor cross-finger (CF)* scores are obtained by comparing veins from different fingers of different subjects. For instance, the right index of a subject is compared with the left/right middle finger of another person.

Table 1 summarizes the aforementioned combinations and the required scores. On the basis of the computed distributions, the false rejection rate (FRR) and the false acceptance rate (FAR) related to different scenarios have been evaluated:

1. *Test-1*: standard scenario where each finger from each hand is taken as a separate class, FRR and FAR are derived by considering respectively the aforementioned genuine scores and impostor scores;

2. *Test-2*: a naïve scenario where an impostor uses a finger different from the one enrolled by the legitimate user is taken into account. FRR and FAR respectively from genuine scores and impostor CF scores are evaluated;

3. *Test-3*: in order to verify whether a subject could be recognized by using as authentication probe the same finger of a hand different from the enrolled one, FRR and FAR are derived by considering respectively genuine scores and genuine CH scores;

4. *Test-4*: the feasibility of using interchangeably the same finger of different hands to be recognized is further investigated by evaluating the FRR and FAR computed respectively on genuine CH and impostor scores;

5. *Test-5*: eventually, the possibility of using as authentication probe fingers different from the enrolled one is also evaluated by deriving FRR and FAR respectively from genuine scores and genuine CF scores.

In order to obtain results from which reliable conclusions could be derived, the aforementioned score distributions have been computed according to several distinct processing methods described in the following section.

3   Finger-Vein Recognition Methods

Score distributions have been computed by considering several different recognition methods, belonging to both geometry- and deep-learning-based approaches.

3.1   Geometry-Based Finger-Vein Recognition

Since the original vein images are typically characterized by low contrast, they are first enhanced in order to improve their quality using a contrast limited adaptive histogram equalization (CLAHE) [23]. Finger boundaries are then obtained by filtering the image with a mask [7]. Eventually, the finger is rotated and aligned to the image center as described in [4]. Finger vein patterns are extracted from finger areas using the following feature extraction methods:

1. *Maximum Curvature (MC)* [10]: scores related to veins width and curvature are assigned to positions where vein centers are located, which are then connected using filtering operations. Binary vein images are then obtained by thresholding the computed patterns;
2. *Principal Curvature (PC)* [1]: the image gradient field is computed, and noise components filtered out by means of hard thresholding. Values of principal curvature are first computed by considering the eigenvalue corresponding to the eigenvector of the Hessian matrix related to the maximum curvature, and then binarized to generate the desired template;
3. *Wide Line Detector (WLD)* [4]: vein positions are extracted by considering circular neighborhoods of each pixel, and computing differences between the center and its neighbors. The final binary image is determined by counting the number of pixels inside this neighborhood.

The obtained binary vein patterns are trimmed and then compared using the correlation-based method proposed in [9] and [10], with the maximum correlation used as matching score.

3.2   Deep-Learning-Based Finger-Vein Recognition

Along with standard geometry-based recognition methods, tests have also been performed exploiting convolutional neural networks (CNNs) to obtain discriminative representations from finger-vein images. Since the target of the present study is not proposing a novel network architecture, an effective CNN, namely Densenet-201 [5], has been employed in the tests. Specifically, the final layers of a Densenet-201 architecture, that is, those performing classification after the extraction of discriminative features, have been substituted with:

- a batch-normalization layer, followed by a dropout regularization with 50% of hidden units dropped;
- a fully-connected and a batch-normalization layers producing C outputs, being C the number of unique identities considered for training.

Table 2. EERs (in %) over the SDUMLA database for the performed tests.

Method	Test-1	Test-2	Test-3	Test-4	Test-5
MC	8.94	8.36	9.93	46.73	9.73
PC	11.70	11.07	12.81	46.64	12.95
WLD	13.66	12.72	14.50	45.56	14.66
CNN	1.02	0.54	1.73	32.62	1.69

Densenet's weights have been initialized with those estimated for an image classification task over Imagenet [14], while a unit weight initialization has been adopted for the batch normalization layer, and Glorot uniform initialization preferred for the fully-connected layers. The layers have been then updated using a cross-entropy (CE) loss function for back-propagation, with stochastic gradient descent (SGD) and a batch size of 64. Learning rate has been set to $\epsilon = 0.01$ and divided by 10 after each 30-epoch iteration. Momentum with $\alpha = 0.9$ has been used, as well as an L_2 weight decay regularization penalty with $\lambda = 0.025$. The maximum number of training epoch is set to 90, with early stopping in case the validation loss is minimized. In the testing phase, the features extracted by the employed network from two input finger-vein samples are compared by evaluating a cosine distance as score, to make geniune/impostor verification.

4   Results and Discussion

The equal error rates (EERs) achieved with the considered recognition methods for each of the test conditions presented in Sect. 3 are reported in Table 2. It is worth mentioning that, since the standard approaches in Sect. 3.1 do not require any specific training, the associated performance has been computed considering all the available $106 \times 3 \times 2 = 636$ classes. Conversely, the results regarding the proposed CNN-based approach have been obtained while reserving the first half of the 106 subjects in the SDUMLA dataset for testing purposes, with the remaining 53 subjects used for CNN training. More in detail, two different training methodologies have been considered:

- to compute the scores associated with the distributions employed for Tests 1–3 and 5, the network has been trained with each finger of each hand of 53 subjects representing a different class. A total of $C = 53 \times 3 \times 2 = 318$ finger-vein classes have been therefore taken into account in this case. For each class, five out of the six available samples have been used for model training, with the remaining one employed for model validation;
- the scores of the distributions used for the considered Test 4, where the feasibility of using interchangeably the same finger of different hands to be recognized is analyzed, have been generated considered a network trained with the same fingers of different hands taken as the members of the same class. A total of $C = 53 \times 3 = 159$ classes have been therefore taken into account

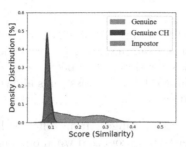 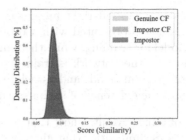

Fig. 1. Scores for the MC-based method. Left: genuine, impostor, and genuine CH distributions; Right: impostor, impostor CF, and genuine CF distributions.

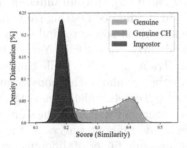 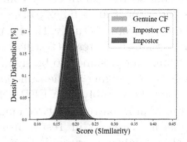

Fig. 2. Scores for the PC-based method. Left: genuine, impostor, and genuine CH distributions; Right: impostor, impostor CF, and genuine CF distributions.

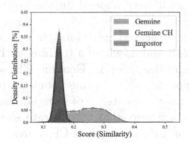 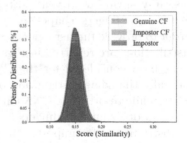

Fig. 3. Scores for the WLD-based method. Left: genuine, impostor, and genuine CH distributions; Right: impostor, impostor CF, and genuine CF distributions.

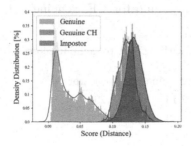 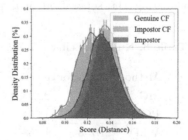

Fig. 4. Scores for the CNN-based method. Left: genuine, impostor, and genuine CH distributions; Right: impostor, impostor CF, and genuine CF distributions.

in this case. As left-right finger samples are put in the same category, each class is now represented with a total of 12 samples, 10 of which are fed into the model for training, while the remaining 2 samples are used for validation. Doing this, the network is trained to look for similarities between same fingers of different hands and associate them to the same class, thus allowing to evaluate the existence of such shared patterns.

The obtained results show that a pair of same fingers from different hands do not posses similarities that allow the user to be recognized when one finger is used for enrollment and the other one for recognition. This is evident by comparing the EERs achieved in Test-1 and Test-3, which are basically the same, meaning that scores generated by comparing same fingers from different hands of the same subject are similar to those obtained when comparing same fingers of different subjects. Actually, the former comparison seems to find some more similarities than the latter, as testified by the slightly worse EERs. Yet, such similarities cannot be assumed to be significant. Training a CNN while considering CH fingers as belonging to the same class further reinforce this considerations, as shown by the notably-high EER achieved in Test-4, which means the CNN cannot find shared patterns between pairs of fingers associated to the same class.

Interestingly, results in Test-5 also show that different fingers of the same subject share slightly more similarities than the same finger of different persons. Eventually, results in Test-2 suggest that the same fingers of different individuals are more similar than different fingers of different persons. Such resemblance may not necessarily spring from vein patterns, as it may depend on the geometric similarity of same fingers' shapes.

In order to provide further evidence of the observed behaviors, the computed score distributions are reported in Figs. 1, 2, 3 and 4, where a training with 318 classes has been considered for the CNN-based approach. Genuine CH scores show basically the same distribution of impostor scores using geometry-based approaches, while resorting to CNNs highlights the existence of some similarities between pairs of symmetric fingers. CNNs are also able to generate slightly-different distributions for impostor, impostor CF and genuine CF scores, while geometry-based approaches cannot.

The distribution separations are quantitatively evaluated through the Kullback-Leibler divergences reported in Table 3, where the values obtained when evaluating the separation of impostor, impostor CF, genuine CH, and

Table 3. Kullback-Leibler divergences with respect to genuine scores.

Method	impostor	genuine CH	genuine CF	impostor CF
MC	2.232	2.129	2.144	2.297
PC	1.877	1.761	1.747	1.956
WLD	1.718	1.658	1.633	1.790
CNN	0.237	0.106	0.058	0.281

genuine CF distributions from that of genuine scores are considered. As can be seen, for CNNs genuine CH and genuine CF scores are slightly closer to the genuine ones than the impostors, while impostor CF scores are even farther.

5   Conclusions

A study regarding the similarity of the vein structure of symmetrical fingers of the hands for the purpose of biometric recognition has been conducted. The obtained results show that, although symmetrical fingers of the same subject show more resemblance than same fingers from different persons, such similarities are not significant enough to be exploited for recognition purposes.

References

1. Choi, J.H., Song, W., Kim, T., Lee, S.R., Kim, H.C.: Finger vein extraction using gradient normalization and principal curvature. In: SPIE Electronic Imaging (2009)
2. Das, R., Piciucco, E., Maiorana, E., Campisi, P.: Convolutional neural network for finger-vein-based biometric identification. IEEE Trans. Inf. Forensics Secur. **14**(2), 360 373 (2018)
3. Fang, Y., Wu, Q., Kang, W.: A novel finger vein verification system based on two-stream convolutional network learning. Neurocomputing **290**, 100–107 (2018)
4. Huang, B., Dai, Y., Li, R., Tang, D., Li, W.: Finger-vein authentication based on wide line detector and pattern normalization. In: International Conference on Pattern Recognition (2010)
5. Huang, G., Liu, Z., Van Der Maaten, L., Weinberger, K.Q.: Densely connected convolutional networks. In: IEEE Conference on computer Vision and Pattern Recognition (2017)
6. Kumar, A., Wang, K.: Identifying humans by matching their left palmprint with right palmprint images using convolutional neural network. In: First International Workshop on Deep Learning and Pattern Recognition (2016)
7. Lee, E.C., Lee, H.C., Park, K.R.: Finger vein recognition using minutia-based alignment and local binary pattern-based feature extraction. Int. J. Imaging Syst. Technol. **19**(3), 179–186 (2009)
8. Lee, E.C., Park, K.R.: Image restoration of skin scattering and optical blurring for finger vein recognition. Opt. Lasers Eng. **49**(7), 816–828 (2011)
9. Miura, N., Nagasaka, A., Miyatake, T.: Feature extraction of finger vein patterns based on iterative line tracking and its application to personal identification. Syst. Comput. Jpn. **35**(7), 61–71 (2004)
10. Miura, N., Nagasaka, A., Miyatake, T.: Extraction of finger-vein patterns using maximum curvature points in image profiles. IEICE Trans. Inf. Syst. **E90–D**(8), 1185–1194 (2007)
11. Pascual, J.E.S., Uriarte-Antonio, J., Sanchez-Reillo, R., Lorenz, M.G.: Capturing hand or wrist vein images for biometric authentication using low-cost devices. In: International Conference on Intelligent Information Hiding and Multimedia Signal Processing (IIH-MSP) (2010)
12. Qin, H., Qin, L., Xue, L., He, X., Yu, C., Liang, X.: Finger-vein verification based on multi-features fusion. Sensors **13**(11), 15048–15067 (2013)

13. Rosdi, B.A., Shing, C.W., Suandi, S.A.: Finger vein recognition using local line binary pattern. Sensors **11**(12), 11357–11371 (2011)
14. Russakovsky, O., et al.: Imagenet large scale visual recognition challenge. Int. J. Comput. Vis. **115**(3), 211–252 (2015)
15. Shaheed, K., Liu, H., Yang, G., Qureshi, I., Gou, J., Yin, Y.: A systematic review of finger vein recognition techniques. Information **9**(9), 213 (2018)
16. Song, J.M., Kim, W., Park, K.R.: Finger-Vein Recognition based on deep DenseNet using composite image. IEEE Access (2019)
17. Wu, J.D., Liu, C.T.: Finger-vein pattern identification using principal component analysis and the neural network technique. Expert Syst. Appl. **38**(5), 5423–5427 (2011)
18. Xu, Y., Fei, L., Zhang, D.: Combining left and right palmprint images for more accurate personal identification. IEEE Trans. Image Process. **24**(2), 549–559 (2014)
19. Yang, G., Xi, X., Yin, Y.: Finger vein recognition based on (2d) 2 pca and metric learning. BioMed Res. Int. **2012** (2012)
20. Yang, W., Hui, C., Chen, Z., Xue, J.H., Liao, Q.: FV-GAN: finger vein representation using generative adversarial networks. IEEE Trans. Inf. Forensics Secur. **14**(9), 2512–2524 (2019)
21. Yin, Y., Liu, L., Sun, X.: SDUMLA-HMT: a multimodal biometric database. In: Sun, Z., Lai, J., Chen, X., Tan, T. (eds.) CCBR 2011. LNCS, vol. 7098, pp. 260–268. Springer, Heidelberg (2011). https://doi.org/10.1007/978-3-642-25449-9_33
22. Zhou, Y., Kumar, A.: Human identification using palm-vein images. IEEE Trans. Inf. Forensics Secur. **6**(4), 1259–1274 (2011)
23. Zuiderveld, K.: Contrast limited adaptive histogram equalization. In: Graphics Gems IV (1994)

Improving Multi-scale Face Recognition Using VGGFace2

Fabio Valerio Massoli[(✉)][iD], Giuseppe Amato[iD], Fabrizio Falchi[iD],
Claudio Gennaro[iD], and Claudio Vairo[iD]

ISTI-CNR, via G. Moruzzi 1, 56124 Pisa, Italy
{fabio.massoli,giuseppe.amato,fabrizio.falchi,claudio.gennaro,
claudio.vairo}@isti.cnr.it

Abstract. Convolutional neural networks have reached extremely high performances on the Face Recognition task. These models are commonly trained by using high-resolution images and for this reason, their discrimination ability is usually degraded when they are tested against low-resolution images. Thus, Low-Resolution Face Recognition remains an open challenge for deep learning models. Such a scenario is of particular interest for surveillance systems in which it usually happens that a low-resolution probe has to be matched with higher resolution galleries. This task can be especially hard to accomplish since the probe can have resolutions as low as 8, 16 and 24 pixels per side while the typical input of state-of-the-art neural network is 224. In this paper, we described the training campaign we used to fine-tune a ResNet-50 architecture, with Squeeze-and-Excitation blocks, on the tasks of very low and mixed resolutions face recognition. For the training process we used the VGGFace2 dataset and then we tested the performance of the final model on the IJB-B dataset; in particular, we tested the neural network on the 1:1 verification task. In our experiments we considered two different scenarios: (1) probe and gallery with same resolution; (2) probe and gallery with mixed resolutions.

Experimental results show that with our approach it is possible to improve upon state-of-the-art models performance on the low and mixed resolution face recognition tasks with a negligible loss at very high resolutions.

Keywords: Low-Resolution face recognition ·
Convolutional neural networks · Face verification

1 Introduction

Face Recognition (FR) is nowadays among the hottest topic in computer vision. Thanks to the extremely high computational power reached by the modern GPUs, the use of Deep Learning techniques [6,7] has become state-of-the-art to solve FR task. Even though such algorithms perform well when tested against images taken under controlled conditions, e.g. high-resolution and frontal pose, a

M. Cristani et al. (Eds.): ICIAP 2019 Workshops, LNCS 11808, pp. 21–29, 2019.
https://doi.org/10.1007/978-3-030-30754-7_3

sudden drop in their performance has been observed when they are tested against images taken under uncontrolled conditions, e.g. low-resolution. For example, this situation occurs in the context of surveillance systems [12] which typically rely on cameras with limited resolution. Thus, a probe with variable low resolution has to be matched against high-resolution galleries.

Two common techniques used to deal with low-resolution face recognition tasks are the Super Resolution [9,11] and the projection of the LR probe and the high-resolution (HR) gallery into a common space [4].

In our work we address the tasks of low and mixed resolutions face recognition by fine-tuning a Deep Convolutional Neural Network on very low-resolution images. In order to fine-tuned the original model, we used two random extractions to decide whether to down sample the image and at which resolution, comprised in the range of [8, 256] pixels. A schematic view of the procedure is shown in Fig. 1.

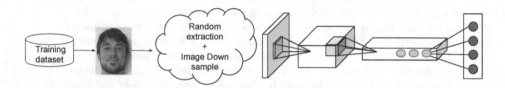

Fig. 1. Schematic view of the training procedure.

After the training phase, we tested the model on the 1:1 verification protocol on the IARPA Janus Benchmark-B (IJB-B) dataset [8]. In particular, we considered the case of probe and gallery with the same resolution and the even more challenging scenario of probe and gallery with mixed resolution.

2   Related Works

In this section, we briefly mentioned some related works.

Super Resolution [9] (SR, or Face Hallucination) is a procedure in which a deep model is used to synthesize a high-resolution image starting from a low-resolution probe. A frequent objection to this technique is that the synthesis process is not optimized for discrimination tasks. Thus, the information about the identity of the person might be lost. In [11], the attempt is to address this issue by introducing an identity loss in order to impose the identity information during the training process. Hence, the aim is to recover the initial low-resolution image identity in the high-resolution one.

In [10], a two-branches model which learns nonlinear transformations in order to map high and low-resolution images into a common space has been proposed. One branch accepts the HR images as inputs while the other one admits the LR images. Both branches produce features vectors that are then projected into a common space where their distance is evaluated. The error on the distance is then backprogated only through the bottom branch with the goal of minimizing the distance between features vectors of HR and LR images.

In [5], Shekhar et al. tackled the LR FR problem by means of a generative technique rather than a discriminative one, building their approach on learning class specific dictionaries that, moreover, resulted to be robust with respect to illumination variations.

3 Methodology

3.1 Datasets Description

We used two different datasets in order to train and test the performance of the model. Specifically, we used the VGGFace2 [1] dataset for training. It contains 3.31 million images from 9131 identities with a high variation in pose and ages of the subjects. Among all the identities, 500 of them were originally designed for test purposes. For this reason, we used only 8631 identities during our training.

Instead, for the test procedure, we used the IJB-B [8] dataset that has been designed for test purposes only. It contains more than 76 K images, 21K from still images and 55 K frames from 7 K videos, corresponding to 1845 different identities. We used it in order to measure the performance of our neural net on the 1:1 verification protocol. For this task, we needed to evaluate the similarity between face descriptors represented as L2-normalized 2048-d deep features vectors.

During the test phase, we used different down sampled versions of the IJB-B dataset in order to test the model on the 1:1 verification protocol with descriptors at the same and mixed resolutions.

3.2 Training Strategy

By using the VGGFace2 training dataset we fine-tuned the pre-trained model from [1]. It is a ResNet-50 [2] architecture equipped with Squeeze-and-Excitation blocks [3]. For the fine-tuning we made a first trial in which we kept the entire net frozen with the exception of the last fully connected layer. However, we obtained better results by fine-tuning the entire neural net. The intuition was that there were patterns in the new low-resolution images that the model needed to adjust for our goals. In the very first steps of our experiments, we tested various hyperparameters such as batch size, learning rate, momentum and weight decay for the optimizer. We obtained the best results setting the initial value for the learning rate at $5.e^{-4}$ and dropping its value by a factor of 5 every time the loss reached a plateau. We used a batch size of 256 and a weight decay of $1e^{-5}$.

During the fine-tuning of the model, for each input image, we used two random extractions. The two extracted numbers, a float and an integer, were uniformly distributed in the range [0, 1] and [3, 8], respectively. The first one was used in order to decide if to down sample an image or not. Each image was down sampled if the first extracted number was below a specific "down-sampling probability" that we fixed before training. Instead, the second one was used, as exponent of a power of two, in order to decide at which resolution to down sample the image. Specifically, the image was first down sampled so that the shortest side was equal to the extracted resolution, while keeping the original aspect ratio of the image, and then it was resized at the original dimensions. In both the down sampling and up sampling operations we used the bilinear interpolation algorithm from the PIL python library.

In Fig. 2 an example of down sampled images at various resolutions is shown.

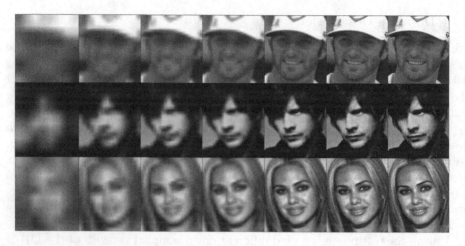

Fig. 2. From left to right: example of images down sampled at resolution of 8, 16, 24, 32, 64, 128 and 256 pixels.

After this first preprocessing phase, the images were resized so that the size of the shortest side was 256 pixels, then a random crop was applied in order to select a 224×224 pixels region which matched the input of the network.

We split the training dataset into training set and validation set. Specifically, during the training phase, we used two versions of the latter split in order to monitor the performance of the model on both low and high-resolution domains. On one version, we down sampled all the images to a reference resolution of 24 pixels and on the other one we used them at full resolution. In both cases the images were then resized at 256 pixels and a center crop was applied.

4　1:1 Face Verification Results

In this section we present our experimental results obtained by using the 1:1 verification protocol on the IJB-B dataset.

As a base line, we chose the state-of-the-art model showed in Table VII [1] (penultimate row) and we first tried to reproduce that result. As a reference, we considered the 1:1 verification True Acceptance Rate (TAR) value at a False

Acceptance Rate (FAR) equals to 1.e^{-3}. We obtained a value of 0.898 which is 0.01 below the quoted 0.908 value. A difference of 1% can be attributed to a possible difference in the image crop and preprocessing phases. This difference is not fundamental to our analysis since we considered the relative improvement.

As a first result, in Fig. 3 we show the Receiver Operating Characteristic (ROC) curves we obtained considering probe and gallery at the same resolution. Results at 128 pixels are not shown since they are similar to the ones at the original size.

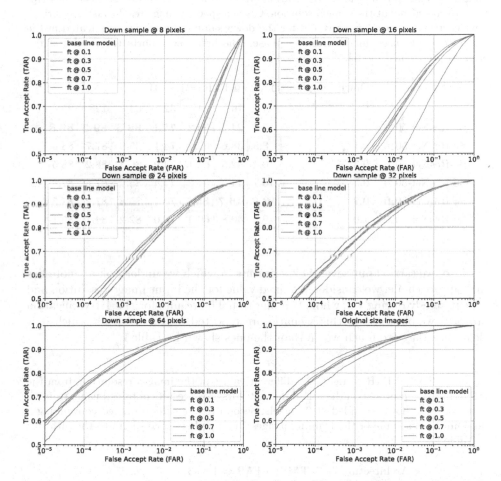

Fig. 3. ROC curves, for the 1:1 verification protocol on the IJB-B dataset, for different values of the image resolution. The pre-trained model has been reported as "base line model" while the "ft" models are the fine tuned ones. The value after the "@" symbol in the legend, represents the probability we used, while training the model, in order to decide whether to reduce the input resolution or not. Results at 128 pixels are not shown since they are similar to the ones at the original size.

As we can see from Fig. 3, the models display a notable improvement for resolution up to 24 pixels. In order to highlight these achievements with respect to the original model we considered a reference value for TAR at FAR = $1.e^{-3}$. The results are shown in Table 1. We especially acknowledged the largest margin of improvement at 16 pixels.

Table 1. True Acceptance Rate (TAR @ FAR = $1.e^{-3}$), for different values of the images resolution, from the 1:1 verification protocol on the IJB-B dataset. Face descriptors are considered at the same resolution. Given a specific image resolution, the various rows correspond to different values for the down sample probability (indicated in the second column) used in the training phase. The first row reports the results of the original pre-trained model.

Architecture	Down-sampling probability	TAR (@ FAR = 1.e−3)						
		8	16	24	32	64	128	256
Se-ResNet-50 [1]		4.8	24.4	60.2	**77.0**	**88.3**	**89.5**	**89.8**
Se-ResNet-50_ft	0.1	8.5	38.6	62.2	74.1	85.9	87.7	88.0
Se-ResNet-50_ft	0.3	10.4	42.5	64.1	74.9	86.3	88.2	88.5
Se-ResNet-50_ft	0.5	10.7	44.2	64.2	74.4	85.7	87.5	87.8
Se-ResNet-50_ft	0.7	**13.9**	**46.7**	**65.7**	74.7	85.3	87.2	87.5
Se-ResNet-50_ft	1.0	9.4	40.8	60.4	70.0	82.2	84.7	85.1

Also, we carried out several experiments in which we undertook a "more linear" approach, i.e. we considered a fixed value for the input image resolution and kept it steady during the whole training run. The results for the 1:1 verification protocol we obtained in this scenario are reported in Table 2 from which it is clear that they are much worse than the ones shown in Table 1.

Table 2. TAR @ FAR = $1.e^{-3}$, for different values of the images resolution, from the 1:1 verification protocol on the IJB-B dataset. First row: results obtained using training images always down sampled at 24 pixels. Second row: results obtained considering a random down sample of the training images (the numbers correspond to the fifth row in Table 1).

Architecture	TAR (@ FAR = 1.e−3)						
	8	16	24	32	64	128	256
Se-ResNet-50_ft[a]	3.9	9.7	32.5	52.2	68.1	73.2	75.0
Se-ResNet-50_ft[b]	13.9	46.7	65.7	74.7	85.3	87.2	87.5

[a]Fixed resolution
[b]Randomly selected resolution

A possible justification for such a drop in the performance is that low-resolution images do not carry valuable knowledge, as high-resolution ones do, thus the model is not able to learn enough discriminative features.

Up to now, we have contemplated the case in which we evaluated the similarity between face descriptors at the same resolution. Our study became even more challenging when we analyzed the mixed scenario in which descriptors had different resolutions. Perhaps, these are the most interesting results regarding surveillance systems application. Table 3 reports the results of this study considering the fine tuned model from Table 1 for which we set the down sampling threshold to 0.7. The numbers represent the value of the TAR at FAR $= 1.\mathrm{e}^{-3}$ while in between brackets we have reported, as a reference, the results from the original model. As it is clear from Table 3, even though our training causes a small decrease in the performance at resolution levels higher than or equal to 32 pixels, the improvements for lower resolutions completely outweigh the mentioned loss.

Table 3. True Acceptance Rate (TAR @ FAR $= 1.\mathrm{e}^{-3}$) for mix-resolution face verification with a model trained by using a down sample probability of 0.7. For comparison, between brackets we reported the value from the original model.

Resolution (pixel)	Resolution (pixel)						
	8	16	24	32	64	128	256
8	13.9 (4.8)						
16	11.1 (0.2)	46.7 (24.4)					
24	8.5 (0.2)	51.0 (18.3)	65.7 (60.2)				
32	7.2 (0.2)	50.0 (9.0)	69.1 (65.4)	74.7 (77.0)			
64	5.6 (0.2)	44.2 (2.9)	69.3 (60.4)	78.1 (80.5)	85.3 (88.3)		
128	5.3 (0.3)	41.9 (2.4)	68.2 (57.9)	78.1 (80.1)	86.2 (88.9)	87.2 (89.7)	
256	5.2 (0.3)	41.5 (2.3)	68.0 (57.5)	78.2 (80.1)	86.3 (89.0)	87.4 (89.7)	87.5 (89.8)

5   Conclusions

In this paper we proposed a training approach to fine-tune a CNN architecture on the task of low and mixed resolution Face Recognition. We tested two different training strategies. In the first case, we let the image resolution be randomly extracted while in the second one we kept it fixed. According to our measurements, the first strategy gave us the best results for both low resolution and mixed resolution tasks. In both cases we have observed a drop within 3% percent in the model performance at resolutions strictly higher than 24 pixels but the decrease has been outweighed by the improvement we obtained in the low resolution regime. In particular, regarding the face verification task with both templates at the same low resolution, we measured a TAR value (at a reference value of the FAR $= 1.e^{-3}$) of 65.7%, 46.7% and 13.9% considering resolutions of 24, 16 and 8 pixels respectively.

The improvements we reached on the mixed resolution face verification task, i.e. when probe and gallery have different resolutions, are even more interesting for surveillance system applications. To the best of our knowledge this is the first paper that investigate these topics.

As already said, in this case too we measured a drop of a few percent in the performance of the model for resolutions from 32 pixels and above, but the improvements at 24 pixels and below totally outweighed that decrease.

Specifically, we observed the higher improvements considering a down sample probability equal to 0.7.

To conclude, the measurements showed that our training campaign has been highly effective showing improvements in the low and mixed resolution face verification tasks up to a factor 30 w.t.r. to the base line model.

Acknowledgments. This publication is based upon work from COST Action 16101 "MULTI-modal Imaging of FOREnsic SciEnce Evidence" (MULTI-FORESEE), supported by COST (European Cooperation in Science and Technology).

References

1. Cao, Q., Shen, L., Xie, W., Parkhi, O.M., Zisserman, A.: Vggface2: a dataset for recognising faces across pose and age. In: 2018 13th IEEE International Conference on Automatic Face and Gesture Recognition (FG 2018), pp. 67–74. IEEE (2018)
2. He, K., Zhang, X., Ren, S., Sun, J.: Deep residual learning for image recognition. In: Proceedings of the IEEE Conference on Computer Vision and Pattern Recognition, pp. 770–778 (2016)
3. Hu, J., Shen, L., Sun, G.: Squeeze-and-excitation networks. In: Proceedings of the IEEE Conference on Computer Vision and Pattern Recognition, pp. 7132–7141 (2018)
4. Jian, M., Lam, K.M.: Simultaneous hallucination and recognition of low-resolution faces based on singular value decomposition. IEEE Trans. Circuits Syst. Video Technol. **25**(11), 1761–1772 (2015)
5. Shekhar, S., Patel, V.M., Chellappa, R.: Synthesis-based robust low resolution face recognition. arXiv preprint arXiv:1707.02733 (2017)
6. Wang, F., Cheng, J., Liu, W., Liu, H.: Additive margin softmax for face verification. IEEE Signal Proc. Lett. **25**(7), 926–930 (2018)
7. Wen, Y., Zhang, K., Li, Z., Qiao, Y.: A discriminative feature learning approach for deep face recognition. In: Leibe, B., Matas, J., Sebe, N., Welling, M. (eds.) ECCV 2016. LNCS, vol. 9911, pp. 499–515. Springer, Cham (2016). https://doi.org/10.1007/978-3-319-46478-7_31

8. Whitelam, C., et al.: Iarpa janus benchmark-b face dataset. In: Proceedings of the IEEE Conference on Computer Vision and Pattern Recognition Workshops, pp. 90–98 (2017)
9. Yu, X., Fernando, B., Ghanem, B., Porikli, F., Hartley, R.: Face super-resolution guided by facial component heatmaps. In: Proceedings of the European Conference on Computer Vision (ECCV), pp. 217–233 (2018)
10. Zangeneh, E., Rahmati, M., Mohsenzadeh, Y.: Low resolution face recognition using a two-branch deep convolutional neural network architecture. arXiv preprint arXiv:1706.06247 (2017)
11. Zhang, K., et al.: Super-identity convolutional neural network for face hallucination. In: Proceedings of the European Conference on Computer Vision (ECCV), pp. 183–198 (2018)
12. Zou, W.W., Yuen, P.C.: Very low resolution face recognition problem. IEEE Trans. Image Proc. **21**(1), 327–340 (2012)

Blind Print-Cam Data Hiding Exploiting Color Perception

Federico Baldessari, Giulia Boato[iD], and Federica Lago[(✉)][iD]

University of Trento, 38123 Trento, TN, Italy
federico.baldessari@alumni.unitn.it,
{giulia.boato,federica.lago-1}@unitn.it

Abstract. Augmented Reality is becoming a fundamental technique to provide an easy access to additional information directly from the surrounding environment. It is however crucial that the mean through which the information is accessed is as integrated in the environment as possible. To this end, several data hiding techniques have been devised in the years to encode information in images in an imperceptible way. However, these techniques are frequently strongly affected by printing and re-acquisition process. This work presents an application developing a data hiding technique robust to printing and camera acquisition (print-cam), thus allowing to recover inserted data (hundreds or thousands of information bits) from printed images in a robust way (e.g., for different size of printed cover image, in different illumination conditions, with various geometric distortions). Performance and robustness of the proposed solution are tested with respect to different metrics to prove the feasibility of the technique.

Keywords: Data hiding · Augmented Reality · Print-cam process

1 Introduction

The fusion between the digital world and the real world is becoming possible thanks to advances in Augmented Reality (AR), that allows digital information to be shown to a user in addition to the surrounding real-world environment. In this way, it is possible to alter the perception of the environment without leaving the physical world, giving the user a more realistic experience than in Virtual Reality where the environment is entirely replaced by a simulated one. To create an immersive experience, a clear understanding of the world is essential. Thus, several solutions based on image recognition were devised, thanks to the ability of this technique to identify different objects and scenarios. However, the insertion of new data can be challenging, and a server is required to store the information associated to objects. Thus, QR-Codes and other similar markers are frequently adopted thanks to their convenience and to the amount of data they are able to store, despite their lack of visual appeal.

© Springer Nature Switzerland AG 2019
M. Cristani et al. (Eds.): ICIAP 2019 Workshops, LNCS 11808, pp. 30–38, 2019.
https://doi.org/10.1007/978-3-030-30754-7_4

In order to develop our application, we decided to focus on data hiding techniques that grant an imperceptible and robust information embedding [2–4]. The most common techniques are those based on transform domain watermarking, that, however, also present some drawbacks: Discrete Cosine Transform (DCT) methods [2,14] are not able to work properly under strong geometric distortions, while Discrete Wavelet Transform (DWT) [1,11,15] methods might lead to low performances due to small shift that might occur when reading the print-cam version of an image. Furthermore, due to the lack of directional selectivity the watermarking capacity of DWT methods is small [8].

A work similar to the one we propose is the one in [1], where a watermarking method suitable for mobile applications is presented. However, this work does not take into account distortions or print-cam operations that are fundamental for real scenarios. Indeed, the process of printing an image and then taking a photo of the printed picture to get back to its digital representation, makes the final image different from the original one due to several random distortions, including global geometric distorts, local random nonlinear geometric distortions, and non linear pixel value distortion. This makes the context very different from classical watermarking techniques, which consider many different types of robustness attacks but rarely this specific print-cam process.

Different studies dealing with print-scan have been published, although there is no ideal method capable of resisting print-scan geometric problem (rotation, translation, and scaling) [5]. Print-cam is even more complicated since it introduces perspective distortion due to the position and angle of the camera with respect to the object, and illumination distortions. In 2006, Kim et al. [7] repeatedly embedded a 63-bit fingerprint in the spatial domain of color images printed re-captured images, so that the data could be extracted with auto-correlation. Unfortunately, this method required lots of manual work before being able to recover the hidden data. In 2008, Pramila et al. [15] proposed to apply conventional watermarking techniques in the print-cam process by introducing a frame around the image to remove geometrical distortion after extracting the corner points. However, the DWT based watermarking technique required to capture the image carefully since it was able to resist only light geometric distortions. In 2012, Thongkor and Amornraksa [16] proposed a print-cam watermarking scheme for photo authentication in Thai national ID card. The method was a spatial domain watermarking performed in the blue color channel of the picture. Although the method showed interesting results, the decoding was non-blind, requiring the original cover image. In 2017, Le [10] proposed spatial data hiding for screen monitor working on variations in the blue channel of the same image over time, that, however, allowed for the embedding of only 8-bit of information for each image. In 2018, Gourrame et al. [5] designed a zero-bit watermarking based on the Fourier transform and a specific correction pre-process. However, it was a zero-bit watermarking, meaning that the software was capable of detecting the presence or the absence of the watermark in the marked object but no information was extracted. Nguyen et al. [12] in 2017 presented another interesting approach where the image is divided into hundreds of small tiles and the gaps between the tiles are used to encode black or white regions of a given QR-Code. While the modification to the original image remains highly impacting and the decoding phase showed some problems, the idea to use QR-Code as a wrapper for the secret message remains interesting. To the best of our knowledge there are no methodologies allowing for high capacity, not strongly visible impact, blind and robust detection.

Here we devise a solution that combines all advantages mentioned above: it is a blind data hiding technique, imperceptibly encoding a large amount information (up to 4096 bits) inside an image in such a way that the receiver can retrieve the full information without prior knowledge on the original image. Our solution is also robust against printing and re-capturing, allowing anyone to use a standard printer for inserting new information in the digital world, which can simply be captured with a smartphone or a tablet to have access to advertisement or AR applications.

2   Methodology

In this paper, we devise a method to encode and decode hundreds or thousands of bits in or from an image in a blind and fully automatic way, requiring robustness to print-cam process. The various steps, discussed in the following sections, are combined into a real-time application[1] accessible from smartphones, tablets and computers with different operating systems, which allowed us to extensively test the feasibility of the devised solution for several devices and real scenarios.

Encoding. This procedure works block-wise to embed a message $\mathcal{M}$, constituted by an $M \times M$ matrix of zeros and ones, into an image $\mathcal{I}$ of size $N \times N$, with $N > M$. Thus, each bit in $\mathcal{M}$ is encoded in a square of size $K \times K$, with $K = N/M$. This is done by creating an *activation matrix* AM of size $N \times N$, composed by $M \times M$ squares of size $K \times K$ encoding a vertical line if the bit to encode is a 0, and a horizontal line otherwise. For the embedding, the blue channel was chosen as changes this channel affect less the image quality [2,9,13] and because human eyes are less sensitive to blue variations [6]. For each pixel in the blue channel ($c = 2$) of $\mathcal{I}$ in position (x, y), the embedding follows Eq. (1)

$$\mathcal{I}^*(x, y, c) = \mu_b + AM(x, y) \cdot AV \tag{1}$$

where $\mathcal{I}^*$ is the encoded image, and μ_b is the average in the blue channel of the $K \times K$ square in which the pixel (x, y) is contained. Bits in $AM(x, y)$ are scaled by an *activation value* AV that can either be a constant or work as dynamic masking following Eq. (2)

$$AV = 50 \cdot \left(\frac{\sigma_r^2 + \sigma_g^2}{2 \cdot 255} + 1 \right) \tag{2}$$

---

[1] https://wizardly-bardeen-e48e37.netlify.com/.

where σ_r^2 and σ_g^2 represent the variances of the red and green channels. As depicted in Fig. 1, using Eq. (2) allows to better exploit human color perception to achieve invisibility while making the encoded message robust. Given the advantages of the dynamic masking, experiments in Sect. 3 were performed using it. Finally, the image is normalized to fit the range [0–255] and a black border of fixed size is added to ease the detection.

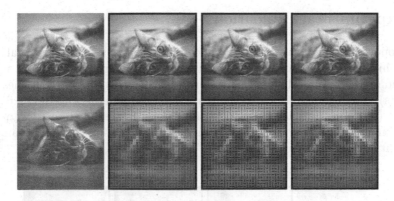

Fig. 1. From left to right the cover image and the images encoding the same message with $AV = 50$, $AV = 100$ and dynamic masking with AV $\in$ [50–100] respectively. The top row shows the color image, while the bottom row the blue-filtered images. (Color figure online)

Decoding. The decoding algorithm is able to retrieve the embedded message from a printed encoded image, robustly with respect to size, position and rotation. The algorithm has two phases: image identification and message decoding. The first phase consists in identifying with standard OpenCV functions the biggest square with a black border, which is removed. Then, some geometrical distortions are corrected using Four Point Perspective Transformation.

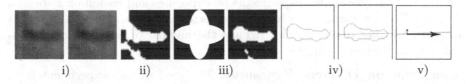

i)   ii)   iii)   iv)   v)

Fig. 2. Steps performed to identify and extract a line and determine its orientation. (Color figure online)

The decoding phase blurs the image identified and normalized in the previous phase to decrease noise. Then it divides the image into squares and the message is decoded following the steps depicted in Fig. 2: (i) identifying a safe region as an inner square of size 50% of the square size, (ii) detecting the contours inside the region that might identify a line, (iii) using a mask composed by two perpendicular ellipses to remove false-positives, (iv) fitting a line inside the contours, and (v) extracting the orientation of the line. The orientation is then used to decide whether the bit encoded was a zero (in case of a vertical line) or a one (in case of a horizontal line).

3   Experimental Evaluation

The proposed method was tested in real condition of natural and artificial light. To do this six images have been printed on paper using a laser printer with a resolution of 600 ppi in different sizes. Of these, five encoding 29×29 messages (841 bits), five encoding 49×49 messages (2401 bits) and one encoding a 64×64 message (4096 bits). Examples on how the different encoding affect the quality of the image, can be seen in Fig. 3, where it also possible to notice an high invisibility of the message.

Fig. 3. From left to right the cover image, and the images with a *Lorem Ipsum* message encoded with 29×29, 49×49 and 64×64 bits.

Then, for each experiment, different pictures were captured freehandly using either a reflex camera (Nikon D3100), a smartphone (Xiaomi Mi 8 Lite) or a tablet (iPad Mini 4). Since the reflex does not support the application directly, the images captured by this device have been decoded using an Asus Zenbook. The pictures analyzed in the experiments on exposures and resolution were shot using the Nikon camera, since it allows a better understanding of the results thanks to a higher resolution that reduces the number of mistakes, as demonstrated in the last experiment.

Experiment on Different Exposures. The goal of this experiment is to understand how random variations in pixels introduced by different light conditions affect the performances of the devised algorithm. Since digital cameras tend to mitigate the problem of low or high light by automatically adjusting the exposition time, we manually changed the exposition time while maintain the same light condition. Varying the exposition time, it was possible to shot 20 pictures (for a total of 140 images), using as target the 64×64 encoded image, capturing different levels of light as shown in Table 1. The darker the image the worst the results. In dark conditions, in fact, the errors are more than 8% on average with a peak at 9.32%. Another notable result is that overexposed images have better results than images with balanced light since the line seems to stand out with respect to the background. For −0.6 the average error was 0.02%, while for standard light condition it was 0.48%.

Table 1. Performance in terms of error rate for different exposures [−0.6–0.6]

	−0.6	−0.4	−0.2	0	0.2	0.4	0.6
Avg	0.02	0.04	0.17	0.48	1.34	3.52	8.11
Std	0.01	0.03	0.06	0.09	0.17	0.26	0.65

Experiment on Rotation. Perspective transformations lead to errors caused by the approximations performed by the algorithm to guess pixels that are not in the original data that might affect performances. A total of 320 shots of the 64 × 64 encoded image (40 for each degree of rotation) were taken at different angles, considering a rotation on the y-axis between 5 and 60°. The error rate reported in Table 2 starts to strongly increase from 15°, reaching a 27.31% for a rotation of 60°. Nevertheless, the accuracy for lower rotations is sufficiently high to allow robustness and let the method be suitable for many real scenarios.

Table 2. Performances in terms of error rate for different degrees of rotation

	5°	10°	15°	20°	30°	40°	50°	60°
Avg	0.41	0.48	0.71	1.39	2.08	2.86	7.86	27.31
Std	0.16	0.12	0.16	0.22	0.52	0.46	1.09	4.34

Experiment on Resolution. Another important aspect to take into consideration is the distance from the target, as it affects the final resolution of the target image and hence performances. To test this, 50 pictures were taken at three different distances from the 64 × 64 encoded image. This translates to three different resolutions: high (2818×2815 pixels - full resolution), medium (1584×1581 pixels - about 30% of the original resolution), and low (1099 × 1096 pixels - 15% of the original resolution). As can be seen in Table 3, the performance decreases the more remote the camera is from the code of interest. However, even for the smallest resolution tested, the error remains rather low.

Table 3. Performances in terms of error rate for different resolutions.

	High	Medium	Low
Avg	0.13	0.66	5.39
Std	0.69	0.14	0.77

Experiments on Device Performances. Different devices have been taken into account to prove that the results are not device-dependent. The performance of the devices was measured in terms of error rate and time to decode the message. For these tests 20 shots for each of the 5 sample images were taken for each tested device, for a total of 300 images. Results obtained for some sample images for the three different devices can be seen in Table 4, which proves that it is possible to encode 841 bits with error rate always below 1.3% even for the smallest images. The Nikon and the Xiaomi were capable of decoding also 2401 bits of information in different conditions. The iPad showed severe limits in decoding caused by a lower resolution compared to other devices under the same conditions (see Fig. 4).

Since we are targeting real-time applications, an important analysis concerns the time needed by the algorithm to decode the message. Table 5 shows the average response time for different cameras to decode 841 bits and 2401 bits information respectively. The time is reasonable for most scenarios, however, the Xiaomi appears to be the one with lower performances. This suggests that our method works better for high-end devices and that future work should focus on optimizing the algorithm to work also on lower-end devices.

Table 4. Error rate on several sample images with different encoded messages and print size in cm (reported in the first and second rows respectively) for different devices.

	29 × 29 (841 bits)						49 × 49 (2401 bits)			
	13 × 13		6.5 × 6.5		3.25 × 3.25		13 × 13		6.5 × 6.5	
	Avg	Std	Avg	Std	Avg	Std	Avg	Std	Avg	Std
Nikon	0.00	0.00	0.00	0.00	0.06	0.07	0.07	0.03	0.39	0.40
Xiaomi	0.00	0.00	0.01	0.03	1.00	1.27	0.18	0.07	5.19	3.93
iPad	0.39	0.15	0.30	0.27	1.32	1.40	15.10	2.00	28.07	3.89

Table 5. Average decoding time (in seconds) for 29 × 29 and 49 × 49 messages

	Nikon	Xiaomi	iPad
29 × 29	0.12	0.98	0.40
49 × 49	0.24	2.9	0.92

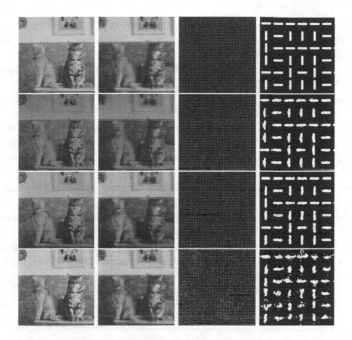

Fig. 4. From left to right the original image, the blue-filtered image, the decoded message and a 6 × 6 zoom into a portion of the message. From top to bottom the original image and the image captured with the Nikon, the Xiaomi and the iPad. (Color figure online)

4 Conclusions

This paper describes an application developing a blind print-cam data hiding that allows encoding of large amounts of information and fast and robust detection, making it suitable for user-driven real-time applications. Performances are good for high-end devices, allowing room for improvements on old devices, where a QR-Code is a lot faster. The results show that the method is robust to light, rotation and resolution changes in the print-cam scenario. Moreover, it is possible to correctly read thousand of bits in good light condition, in particular for high-resolution devices which effectively decode four thousand bits.

References

1. Al-Otum, H., Al-Shalabi, N.E.: Copyright protection of color images for android-based smartphones using watermarking with quick-response code. Multimedia Tools Appl. **77**(12), 15625–15655 (2018)
2. Barni, M., Bartolini, F., Piva, A.: Multichannel watermarking of color images. IEEE Trans. Circuits Syst. Video Technol. **12**(3), 142–156 (2002)
3. Boato, G., et al.: Watermarking robustness evaluation based on perceptual quality via genetic algorithms. IEEE Trans. Inf. Forensics Secur. **4**(2), 207–216 (2009)

4. Cancellaro, M., et al.: A commutative digital image watermarking and encryption method in the tree structured Haar transform domain. Signal Process. Image Commun. **26**(1), 1–12 (2011)
5. Gourrame, K., et al.: A zero-bit Fourier image watermarking for print-cam process. Multimedia Tools Appl. **78**(2), 2621–2638 (2019)
6. Hänninen, H., Nuutinen, M., Oittinen, P.: Visibility and annoyance of digital watermarks. Graph. Arts Finland **36**, 1 (2007)
7. Kim, W., Lee, S.H., Seo, Y.: Image fingerprinting scheme for print-and-capture model. In: Zhuang, Y., Yang, S.-Q., Rui, Y., He, Q. (eds.) PCM 2006. LNCS, vol. 4261, pp. 106–113. Springer, Heidelberg (2006). https://doi.org/10.1007/11922162_13
8. Kingsbury, N.: Complex wavelets for shift invariant analysis and filtering of signals. Appl. Comput. Harmonic Anal. **10**(3), 234–253 (2001)
9. Kutter, M., Jordan, F.D., Bossen, F.: Digital watermarking of color images using amplitude modulation. J. Electron. Imaging **7**(2), 326–333 (1998)
10. Le, N.T.: Invisible watermarking optical camera communication and compatibility issues of IEEE 802.15.7r1 specification. Opt. Commun. **390**, 144–155 (2017)
11. Najafi, E.: A robust embedding and blind extraction of image watermarking based on discrete wavelet transform. Math. Sci. **11**(4), 307–318 (2017)
12. Nguyen, M., et al.: A tile based colour picture with hidden QR code for augmented reality and beyond. In: Symposium on Virtual Reality Software and Technology. ACM (2017)
13. Parisis, A., Carré, P., Fernandez-Maloigne, C.: Colour watermarking: study of different representation spaces. In: Colour in Graphics, Imaging, and Vision (2002)
14. Poljicak, A., Mandic, L., Agic, D.: Discrete fourier transform-based watermarking method with an optimal implementation radius. J. Electron. Imaging **20**(3), 033008 (2011)
15. Pramila, A., Keskinarkaus, A., Seppänen, T.: Watermark robustness in the print-cam process. In: Signal processing, pattern recognition, and applications (2008)
16. Thongkor, K., Amornraksa, T.: Digital image watermarking for photo authentication in Thai national id card. In: IEEE Conference on Electrical Engineering/Electronics, Computer, Telecommunications and Information Technology (2012)

A Database for Face Presentation Attack Using Wax Figure Faces

Shan Jia[1,2], Chuanbo Hu[2], Guodong Guo[2], and Zhengquan Xu[1(✉)]

1 Wuhan University, Wuhan 430072, China
{jias,xuzq}@whu.edu.cn
2 West Virginia University, Morgantown 26505, USA
{chuanbo.hu,guodong.guo}@mail.wvu.edu

Abstract. Compared to 2D face presentation attacks (e.g. printed photos and video replays), 3D type attacks are more challenging to face recognition systems (FRS) by presenting 3D characteristics or materials similar to real faces. Existing 3D face spoofing databases, however, mostly based on 3D masks, are restricted to small data size or poor authenticity due to the production difficulty and high cost. In this work, we introduce the first wax figure face database, WFFD, as one type of super-realistic 3D presentation attacks to spoof the FRS. This database consists of 2200 images with both real and wax figure faces (totally 1400 faces) with a high diversity from online collections. Experiments on this database first investigate the vulnerability of three popular FRS to this kind of new attack. Further, we evaluate the performance of several face presentation attack detection methods to show the attack abilities of this super-realistic face spoofing database.

Keywords: Wax figure face · Face presentation attack · Face recognition

1 Introduction

With the widespread face recognition technologies, the security and privacy risks of face recognition systems (FRS) have been increasingly become as a critical issue in both academia and industry. Face presentation attacks are one of the most easily realized threats by presenting an artificial object or a copy or synthetic pattern of faces to the biometric data capture subsystem [8]. Based on the way to generate the face artifact, face presentation attacks can be classified into 2D modalities (which present printed/digital photographs or recorded videos on the mobile/tablet), and 3D type (by wearing a mask or presenting a synthetic model).

Because of the simplicity, efficiency, and low cost of making 2D type attacks, current systems and research pay more attentions to 2D face presentation

Supported by Wuhan University.

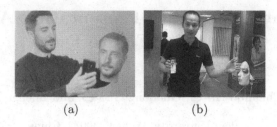

(a)   (b)

Fig. 1. Examples of 3D presentation attack cases. (a) Android phones fooled by a 3D-printed head, (b) iPhone X face ID unlocked by a 3D mask.

attacks. However, with similar 3D structures or materials to real faces, 3D face presentation attacks are more hyper-realistic, and therefore, more powerful to attack the FRS while more difficult to detect. For example, as shown in Fig. 1, even some systems, which have already taken presentation attack detection (PAD) into consideration, can be fooled by the 3D face presentation attacks.

Existing 3D presentation attacks are mostly based on wearable face masks. 3D facial mask spoofing was previously thought impossible to become a common practice in the literature [1], because compared to 2D type attacks, 3D masks are much more difficult and high-cost to manufacture, requiring special 3D devices and materials. In recent years, the rapid advancement of 3D printing technologies and services has made it easier and cheaper to make 3D masks. Several 3D mask attack databases have been created based on the third-party services [2,3], by self-manufacturing [4], or from online resources [5]. However, they are restricted to small data sizes (mostly less than 30 subjects) or low mask qualities. This will not only limit the attack abilities of these fake faces, but also limit research works in reporting robust detection performance against 3D presentation attacks.

To address this problem, we take advantage of the popularity and publicity of numerous celebrity wax figure museums in the world, and collect a large number of wax figure images to form the new Wax Figure Face Database (WFFD). These life-size wax figure faces are all carefully designed and made in clay with wax layers, silicone or resin materials, so that they are super-realistic and similar to real faces. With the development of wax figure manufacture technologies and services, we think the easily obtainable and super-realistic wax figure faces will pose threat to the face recognition systems. Therefore, we introduce these wax figure faces as a new challenging type of 3D face presentation attacks in this paper, and analyze their impact on face recognition.

To the best of our knowledge, this is the first wax figure face database, also with a large data size and high diversity. Altogether, the WFFD consists of 2200 images of 450 subjects (with both real and wax figure faces, totally 4400 faces), which are diversified in subject age, ethnicity, face pose, facial expression, recording environment, and cameras, and therefore closer to the practical situation. Based on the new database, we first investigate the vulnerability of three popular face recognition systems to these super-realistic presentation attacks, and further evaluate the performance of several popular face PAD methods to show the attack ability of this 3D face spoofing database.

2 Related Work

Most existing 3D face presentation attack databases create attacks by presenting wearable face masks, which are made of different materials with similar 3D face characteristics to the real faces. 3DMAD [2] is the first publicly available 3D mask database. It used the services of ThatsMyFace[1] to manufacture 17 masks of users, and recorded 255 video sequences with an RGB-D camera of Microsoft Kinect device for both real access and presentation attacks. This database is widely used by providing color images, depth images, and manually annotated eye positions of all face samples.

With the development of 3D modeling and printing technologies, from 2016, more mask databases were created. 3DFS-DB [4] is a self-manufactured and gender-balanced 3D face spoofing database. They made 26 printed models using two 3D printers: the ShareBot Pro and the CubeX[2], which are relatively low-cost and worth about 1000 and 2000 €, respectively. Acrylonitrile Butadiene Styrene (ABS) plastic material is used to generate the physical artifacts. HKBU-MARs [3] is another 3D mask spoofing database with more variations to simulate the real world scenarios. It generated 12 masks from two companies (ThatsMy-Face and REAL-F[3]) with different appearance qualities. 7 camera types and 6 typical lighting settings are also included to form totally 1008 videos. To include more subjects, the SMAD database [5] collected and compiled videos of people wearing silicone masks from online resources. It contains 65 genuine access videos of people auditioning, interviewing, or hosting shows, and 65 attacked videos of people wearing a complete 3D structure (but not customized) mask around the head which fits well with proper holes for the eyes and mouth.

Besides, there have been some 3D mask spoofing databases with special lighting information for more effective detection. The MLFP database [6] (Multispectral Latex Mask based Video Face Presentation Attack database) is a unique multispectral database for face presentation attacks using latex and paper masks. It contains 1350 videos of 10 subjects in visible, near infrared (NIR), and thermal spectrums, which are captured at different locations (indoor and outdoor) in an unconstrained environment. Similarly, the ERPA database [7] also provides the RGB and NIR images of both bona fide and 3D mask attack presentations captured using special cameras. This is a small dataset with frame images of 5 subjects stored. The depth information is also provided. Both rigid resin-coated masks and flexible silicone masks are considered.

These databases have played a significant role in designing multiple detection schemes against 3D face presentation attacks. However, they still face the problems of small database size, low diversity, or poor authenticity, which will certainly limit the development of effective and practical detection schemes.

---

[1] http://thatsmyface.com/.

[2] https://www.sharebot.it. and http://www.cubify.com.

[3] http://real-f.jp/en_the-realface.html.

(a)   (b)

Fig. 2. Examples of images of WFFD database. (a) Protocol I, (b) Protocol II.

3   The Wax Figure Face Database

To address the issues in existing 3D face presentation attack databases, we introduce the new WFFD database with a large size and high diversity as super-realistic 3D presentation attacks. The details of the data collection process, and the evaluation protocols are presented in this section.

This Wax Figure Face Database is based on numerous celebrity wax figure images from online resources. These user-customized and life-size wax figure faces are all carefully designed and made in clay with wax layers, silicone or resin materials, so that they are super-realistic. We first downloaded multiple celebrity wax figure faces as attacks with a high diversity in subject age, ethnicity, face pose, expression, recording environment, and cameras, and then collected the corresponding celebrity images as real access attempts. For each subject, the wax figure face and real face were finally grouped in one image to show the high authenticity, as the examples shown in Fig. 2(a).

Further, we introduce one more challenging scenario where the wax figure face and real face were originally recorded together, as shown in Fig. 2(b). With the same recording environment, and even the same face poses and facial expressions, these images are more difficult to distinguish.

Altogether, the WFFD consists of 2200 images with both real and wax figure faces of 740 subjects, totally 4400 faces. Table 1 compares the characteristics of WFFD with six existing 3D face presentation attack databases. To evaluate the performances of the face PAD methods on the WFFD database, we further designed three protocols. (1) Protocol I contains images grouped manually, which means the wax figure faces and real faces came from different recording devices and environment. (2) Protocol II contains the wax figure faces and real faces recorded in the same environment with the same cameras. (3) Protocol III combines previous two protocols to simulate the real-world operational conditions. More details about the images used in each protocol are shown in Table 2.

4   Experiments

In this section, we first investigate the vulnerability of three popular face recognition systems to these super-realistic 3D presentation attacks, and then evaluate the performance of several popular face PAD methods on the proposed database.

Table 1. Comparison of 3D face presentation attack databases

Database	Year	#Sub	#Sam	Format	Material	Image description
3DMAD [2]	2013	17	255	Video	Paper, resin	2D, 2.5D
3DFS-DB [4]	2016	26	520	Video	Plastic	2D, 2.5D, 3D
HKBU-MARs [3]	2016	12	1008	Video	/	2D
SMAD [5]	2017	/	130	Video	Silicone	2D
MLFP [6]	2017	10	1350	Video	Latex, paper	Multispectral
ERPA [7]	2017	5	86	Image	Resin, silicone	Multispectral, depth
WFFD (proposed)	2019	740	2200	Image	Wax figure	2D

Table 2. Number of images in each evaluation protocol

Protocol	#Training	#Development	#Testing	#Total
Protocol I	600	200	200	1000
Protocol II	720	240	240	1200
Protocol III	1320	440	440	2200

*Note that the three subsets have no overlap.

4.1   Performance Evaluation Metrics

Based on the ISO/IEC metrics, for the evaluation of the vulnerability of FRSs, the Impostor Attack Presentation Match Rate (IAPMR) metric was used to report the results, which can be considered as an indication of the attack success chances if the FRS is evaluated regarding its PAD capabilities. It is defined as the proportion of impostor attack presentations using the same Presentation Attack Instrument (PAI) species in which the target reference is matched in a full-system evaluation of a verification system. For the detection performance evaluation, we reported the results using the Attack Presentation Classification Error Rate (APCER), the Bona Fide Presentation Classification Error Rate (BPCER), and the Average Classification Error Rate (ACER).

4.2   Vulnerabilities of Face Recognition Systems

Three FARs were considered to show the vulnerability towards detecting fake faces using the proposed WFFD database, so that the attack abilities of the super-realistic database can be demonstrated. They are two publicly available FRSs: OpenFace [24] and Face++ [25], and a commercial system Neurotechnology VeriLook SDK [23]. Using the thresholds recommended by these FRSs, we calculated the IAPMR values on three protocols of the WFFD database, as presented in Table 2.

Table 2 shows that over 92% of the images in the three protocols of the WFFD were successfully compared using the Openface and Face+, which means the high attack success chances of the proposed WFFD database on these two face recognition systems. However, lower values of the IAPMR can be seen when the VeriLook SDK was employed on the three protocols. This is attributed to the fact that some faces with special poses or low qualities cannot be identified by the VeriLook SDK, therefore, leading to less successful matches.

Table 3. IAPMR of three face recognition systems

Protocol	Openface	Face++	VeriLook
Threshold	0.99*	1e-5†	36**
Protocol I	93.29%	92.60%	76.14%
Protocol II	96.73%	96.22%	88.12%
Protocol III	95.25%	94.72%	81.75%

*Using a squared L2 distance threshold;
†Using the confidence threshold at the 0.001% error rate; **Using the matching score when FAR = 0.1%.

In addition, by comparing the results for Protocol I and Protocol II, we can observe that higher IAPMR values were achieved for images in Protocol II, where the fake faces and real faces were recorded in the same scenarios with the same cameras. This leads to the higher attack abilities of images in Protocol II.

4.3   Detection Performance of Face PAD Algorithms

Several face PAD methods were evaluated on the WFFD database to show how they can work for the proposed super-realistic 3D presentation attacks. These PAD methods were based on different features, including the multi-scale LBP [2], the color LBP [26], the Haralick features [15], the reflectance properties [29], the multi-level Local Phase Quantization (LPQ) [27], deep features based on the ResNet-50 model [28] and VGG-16 model [19]. They all achieved high detection performance against 2D spoofing attacks or 3D mask attacks.

In this experiment, for each image in the WFFD database, the two face regions were first detected, cropped and normalized into 64*64 pixel images. Based on different PAD methods, features were extracted from the face images, and then fed into a Softmax classifier with a cross-entropy loss function.

The detection results on Protocol I and Protocol II of the proposed WFFD are shown in Table 3. For the Protocol I, we can see that existing seven face PAD methods achieved high detection error rates, ranging from 17% to 46%. We attribute the poor performances to the high diversity and super-realistic attacks in the WFFD database, therefore, making it difficult to detect real faces from wax figure faces recorded in different scenarios Table 4.

Table 4. Detection error rates (%) on Protocol I and Protocol II of the WFFD

Method	Protocol I				Protocol II			
	EER	APCER	BPCER	ACER	EER	APCER	BPCER	ACER
Multi-scale LBP [2]	33.17	31.22	31.22	31.22	36.62	37.32	33.45	35.39
Color LBP [26]	33.17	30.24	36.10	33.17	37.32	36.62	41.90	39.26
Haralick features [15]	32.19	25.85	37.07	31.46	38.38	41.55	24.65	33.10
Reflectance [29]	41.95	40.00	52.19	46.10	44.37	50.70	44.37	47.53
Multi-level LPQ [27]	24.88	24.88	25.36	25.12	33.10	35.56	22.89	29.22
ResNet-50 based [28]	**17.07**	**20.49**	**18.04**	**19.27**	**20.42**	19.37	**24.29**	**21.83**
VGG-16 based [19]	45.85	50.73	41.95	46.34	48.94	40.14	52.82	46.48

Comparing the two groups of results in Table 3, we can see that most error rates for Protocol II are higher than the values for Protocol I. Such results are reasonable since recording the real faces and wax figure faces in the same scenarios with the same cameras results in less differences of the faces. Therefore, it is more difficult to detect the presentation attacks in this protocol, also meaning the higher attack abilities, which reached a similar conclusion with the results in Table 2. Overall, due to the highly discriminative features learned by the ResNet-50 models, the method [28] achieved the best results for both the two protocols. The multi-level LPQ [27] based method also performed relatively well, with the ACER under 30%.

The overall results of the seven evaluated PAD methods on the WFFD database are shown in Table 5. The ACER values ranged from 20.04% to 47.24%, showing the poor detection performance of these methods against the proposed wax figure face presentation attacks, and therefore, the strong attack abilities of the WFFD database in face recognition.

Table 5. Detection error rates (%) on Protocol III of the WFFD

Methods	EER	APCER	BPCER	ACER
Multi-scale LBP [2]	34.56	33.33	32.92	33.13
Color LBP [26]	36.81	35.38	35.79	35.58
Haralick features [15]	36.81	36.40	32.92	34.66
Reflectance [29]	44.78	46.01	46.22	46.11
Multi-level LPQ [27]	28.63	29.45	25.15	27.30
ResNet-50 based [28]	**18.81**	**19.43**	**20.65**	**20.04**
VGG-16 based [19]	48.67	45.19	49.28	47.24

5   Conclusion

To address the limitations in existing 3D face presentation attack databases, we have proposed a new database, WFFD, composed of wax figure faces with high diversity and large data size as super-realistic face presentation attacks. The database will be made publicly available in order to help the development and fair evaluation of different PAD algorithms. Extensive experiments have demonstrated the vulnerability of popular face recognition systems to these attacks, and the performance degradation of several existing PAD methods in detecting real faces from wax figure faces, showing the challenges when wax figure face are used for 3D attacks.

Some motion based methods, such as head movement and blink detection based may seem quite effective in detecting wax figure fake faces if the faces are recorded in videos. However, nowadays the high-tech wax figure technologies have realized the intelligent wax figures, which can not only move but also sense people and change its behavior based on its surroundings. Therefore, it is demanding to investigate more discriminative and powerful methods to detect these new challenging 3D face presentation attacks in the future.

References

1. Zhang, Z., Yan, J., et al.: A face antispoofing database with diverse attacks. In: 2012 5th IAPR International Conference on Biometrics (ICB), pp. 26–31. IEEE (2012)
2. Erdogmus, N., Marcel, S.: Spoofing in 2D face recognition with 3D masks and anti-spoofing with kinect. In: 2013 IEEE Sixth International Conference on Biometrics: Theory, Applications and Systems (BTAS), pp. 1–6. IEEE (September 2013)
3. Liu, S., Yang, B., Yuen, P.C., Zhao, G.: A 3D mask face anti-spoofing database with real world variations. In: Proceedings of the IEEE Conference on Computer Vision and Pattern Recognition Workshops, pp. 100–106 (2016)
4. Galbally, J., Satta, R.: Three-dimensional and two-and-a-half-dimensional face recognition spoofing using three-dimensional printed models. IET Biometrics 5(2), 83–91 (2016)
5. Manjani, I., Tariyal, S., Vatsa, M., Singh, R., Majumdar, A.: Detecting silicone mask-based presentation attack via deep dictionary learning. IEEE Trans. Inf. Forensics Secur. 12(7), 1713–1723 (2017)
6. Agarwal, A., Yadav, D., Kohli, N., Singh, R., Vatsa, M., Noore, A.: Face presentation attack with latex masks in multispectral videos. In: Proceedings of the IEEE Conference on Computer Vision and Pattern Recognition Workshops, pp. 81–89 (2017)
7. Bhattacharjee, S., Marcel, S.: What you can't see can help you-extended-range imaging for 3D-mask presentation attack detection. In 2017 International Conference of the Biometrics Special Interest Group (BIOSIG), pp. 1–7. IEEE (September 2017)
8. ISO/IEC JTC 1/SC 37 Biometrics, Information Technology–Biometric presentation attack detection–Part 1: Framework. International Organization for Standardization (2016)
9. Kim, Y., Na, J., Yoon, S., Yi, J.: Masked fake face detection using radiance measurements. JOSA A 26(4), 760–766 (2009)
10. Zhang, Z., Yi, D., Lei, Z., Li, S.Z.: Face liveness detection by learning multispectral reflectance distributions. In: FG, pp. 436–441 (March 2011)
11. Steiner, H., Kolb, A., Jung, N.: Reliable face anti-spoofing using multispectral SWIR imaging. In: 2016 International Conference on Biometrics (ICB), pp. 1–8. IEEE (June 2016)

12. Kose, N., Dugelay, J.L.: Countermeasure for the protection of face recognition systems against mask attacks. In: 2013 10th IEEE International Conference and Workshops on Automatic Face and Gesture Recognition (FG), pp. 1–6. IEEE (April 2013)
13. Kose, N., Dugelay, J.L.: Shape and texture based countermeasure to protect face recognition systems against mask attacks. In: Proceedings of the IEEE Conference on Computer Vision and Pattern Recognition Workshops, pp. 111–116 (2013)
14. Naveen, S., Fathima, R.S., Moni, R.S.: Face recognition and authentication using LBP and BSIF mask detection and elimination. In: 2016 International Conference on Communication Systems and Networks (ComNet), pp. 99–102. IEEE (July 2016)
15. Agarwal, A., Singh, R., Vatsa, M.: Face anti-spoofing using Haralick features. In: 2016 IEEE 8th International Conference on Biometrics Theory, Applications and Systems (BTAS), pp. 1–6. IEEE (September 2016)
16. Hamdan, B., Mokhtar, K.: The detection of spoofing by 3D mask in a 2D identity recognition system. Egypt. Inform. J. **19**(2), 75–82 (2018)
17. Wang, Y., Chen, S., Li, W., Huang, D., Wang, Y.: Face anti-spoofing to 3D masks by combining texture and geometry features. In: Zhou, J., et al. (eds.) CCBR 2018. LNCS, vol. 10996, pp. 399–408. Springer, Cham (2018). https://doi.org/10.1007/978-3-319-97909-0_43
18. Menotti, D., et al.: Deep representations for iris, face, and fingerprint spoofing detection. IEEE Trans. Inf. Forensics Secur. **10**(4), 864–870 (2015)
19. Lucena, O., Junior, A., Moia, V., Souza, R., Valle, E., Lotufo, R.: Transfer learning using convolutional neural networks for face anti-spoofing. In: Karray, F., Campilho, A., Cheriet, F. (eds.) ICIAR 2017. LNCS, vol. 10317, pp. 27–34. Springer, Cham (2017). https://doi.org/10.1007/978-3-319-59876-5_4
20. Ali, A., Hoque, S., Deravi, F.: Gaze stability for liveness detection. Pattern Anal. Appl. **21**(2), 437–449 (2018)
21. Liu, S.Q., Lan, X., Yuen, P.C.: Remote photoplethysmography correspondence feature for 3D mask face presentation attack detection. In: Proceedings of the European Conference on Computer Vision (ECCV), pp. 558–573 (2018)
22. Hernandez-Ortega, J., Fierrez, J., Morales, A., Tome, P.: Time analysis of pulse-based face anti-spoofing in visible and NIR. In: Proceedings of the IEEE Conference on Computer Vision and Pattern Recognition Workshops, pp. 544–552 (2018)
23. http://www.neurotechnology.com/verilook.html
24. Amos, B., Ludwiczuk, B., Satyanarayanan, M.: Openface: a general-purpose face recognition library with mobile applications. CMU Sch. Comput. Sci. 6 (2016)
25. https://www.faceplusplus.com/face-compare-sdk/
26. Boulkenafet, Z., Komulainen, J., Hadid, A.: Face anti-spoofing based on color texture analysis. In: 2015 IEEE International Conference on Image Processing (ICIP), pp. 2636–2640. IEEE (September 2015)
27. Benlamoudi, A., Samai, D., Ouafi, A., Bekhouche, S.E., Taleb-Ahmed, A., Hadid, A.: Face spoofing detection using multi-level local phase quantization (ML-LPQ). In: Proceeding of the First International Conference on Automatic Control, Telecommunication and signals ICATS15 (November 2015)
28. Tu, X., Fang, Y.: Ultra-deep neural network for face anti-spoofing. In International Conference on Neural Information Processing, pp. 686–695. Springer, Cham (November 2017). https://doi.org/10.1007/978-3-319-70096-0_70
29. Kose, N., Dugelay, J.L.: Reflectance analysis based countermeasure technique to detect face mask attacks. In: 2013 18th International Conference on Digital Signal Processing (DSP), pp. 1–6. IEEE (July 2013)

Analysis of "User-Specific Effect" and Impact of Operator Skills on Fingerprint PAD Systems

Giulia Orrù[(✉)], Pierluigi Tuveri, Luca Ghiani, and Gian Luca Marcialis

Department of Electrical and Electronic Engineering, University of Cagliari,
Cagliari, Italy
{giulia.orru,pierluigi.tuveri,luca.ghiani,marcialis}@diee.unica.it

Abstract. Fingerprint Liveness detection, or presentation attacks detection (PAD), that is, the ability of detecting if a fingerprint submitted to an electronic capture device is authentic or made up of some artificial materials, boosted the attention of the scientific community and recently machine learning approaches based on deep networks opened novel scenarios. A significant step ahead was due thanks to the public availability of large sets of data; in particular, the ones released during the International Fingerprint Liveness Detection Competition (LivDet). Among others, the fifth edition carried on in 2017, challenged the participants in two more challenges which were not detailed in the official report. In this paper, we want to extend that report by focusing on them: the first one was aimed at exploring the case in which the PAD is integrated into a fingerprint verification systems, where templates of users are available too and the designer is not constrained to refer only to a generic users population for the PAD settings. The second one faces with the exploitation ability of attackers of the provided fakes, and how this ability impacts on the final performance. These two challenges together may set at which extent the fingerprint presentation attacks are an actual threat and how to exploit additional information to make the PAD more effective.

Keywords: Liveness detection · User-specific effect · Skilled operator

1 Introduction

In the development of biometric systems, the study of the techniques necessary to preserve the systems' integrity and thus to guarantee their security, is crucial. Fingerprint authentication systems are highly vulnerable to artificial reproductions of fingerprint made up of materials such as silicon, gelatine or latex, also called spoofs or fake fingerprints [1]. To counteract this possibility, Fingerprint Liveness Detection (FLD), also known as Fingerprint Presentation Attacks Detection (FPAD), is a discipline aimed to design pattern recognition-based algorithms for distinguishing between live and fake fingerprints. Detecting

© Springer Nature Switzerland AG 2019
M. Cristani et al. (Eds.): ICIAP 2019 Workshops, LNCS 11808, pp. 48–56, 2019.
https://doi.org/10.1007/978-3-030-30754-7_6

presentation attacks is not trivial because we have an arms-race problem, where we potentially are unaware of the materials and methods adopted to attack the system [2].

In the last decade, most of the previously proposed PAD methods have focused on using handcrafted image features, for example LBP, BSIF [7], WLD [8] or HIG [9]. Over the years, PAD methods have been refined and recently CNN-based methods are outnumbering local image descriptors methods [12,13].

In order to assess the performance of FPAD algorithms by using a common experimental protocol and data sets, the international fingerprint liveness detection competition (LivDet) is organized since 2009 [3]. Each edition is characterized by a different set of challenges that must be dealt with by the competitors. Working on the LivDet competitions since its birth, that is, developing a wide experience in providing large sets of data for assessing the state of the art on this topic, we realized that some data acquisition methods influence the FPAD systems performance. For this reason, the 2017 edition of the LivDet was focused on assessing how much the composition and the data acquisition methods influence the PAD systems. In particular, we faced here with the followings points:

- the presence of different operators for creating and submitting spoofs, that is, two levels of operators which provided spoofs and attacked the submitted algorithms - can spoofing be an actual threat independently of the ability of attackers, or an expert is necessary to break a fingerprint PAD?;
- when a PAD must be integrated into a fingerprint verification system, the templates of genuine users are available, and there is no good reason to neglect them even during the PAD design. We referred to the additional information coming from the enrolled user as "user-specific effect" [5].

These aspects have been analyzed only marginally in the LivDet 2017 report [4] for sake of space. Moreover, the above points were not addressed by the previous editions of LivDet, whose history and results over the years are reported in [3].

With regard to the "user-specific effect", we reported in [5] that some specific components or minute details are dependent on the user's skin characteristic. Ref. [5] reports a statistical study on the relationships of textural features coming from the same fingerprints of the same user and even from his/her different fingerprints. The correlation we measured suggests that the consequent "bias" introduced into a PAD can be beneficial if the PAD must be integrated into a fingerprint verification system. Moreover, it does not affect the overall PAD performance when it is used for the generic user of detecting a presentation attack. What we called "user-specific effect" helps in improving the correct classification of an alive fingerprint of a genuine user, and this is crucial into a fingerprint verification system where the rate of rejected genuine users must be kept as low as possible. From this point of view, the fusion with a non-zero error system, namely, the PAD, may put that rate in danger, as noticed in other publications as [15].

The paper is organized as follows: Sect. 2 describes the purpose of the experimentation. The experimental methodology is presented in Sect. 3. Experiments are shown in Sect. 4. Conclusions are drawn in Sect. 5.

Table 1. Types and accuracy of the algorithms participating in LivDet 2017. The accuracy of the three sensors used (**1** = Green bit, **2** = Digital persona, **3** = Orcanthus) and the overall have been reported.

Algorithm	Type	Accuracy [%]			
		1	2	3	Overall
SSLFD	N.A	93.58	94.33	93.14	93.68
JLW_A	Deep learning	95.08	94.09	**93.52**	94.23
JLW_B	Deep learning	**96.44**	**95.59**	93.71	95.25
OKIBrB20	Hand-crafted	84.97	83.31	84.00	84.09
OKIBrB30	Hand-crafted	92.49	89.33	90.64	90.82
ZYL_1	Deep learning	95.91	**95.13**	91.66	94.23
ZYL_2	Deep learning	**96.26**	**94.73**	93.17	94.72
SNOTA2017_1	N.A	95.03	91.26	91.58	92.62
SNOTA2017_2	N.A	94.04	86.72	86.74	89.17
ModuLAB	Deep learning	94.25	90.40	90.21	91.62
ganfp	Deep learning	95.67	93.66	**94.16**	94.50
PB_LivDet_1	Hand-crafted	93.85	89.97	91.85	91.89
PB_LivDet_2	Hand-crafted	92.86	90.43	92.60	91.96
hanulj	Deep learning	**97.06**	92.34	92.04	93.81
SpoofWit	Hand-crafted	93.66	88.82	89.97	90.82
LCPD	Hand-crafted	89.87	88.84	86.87	88.52
PDfV	Hand-crafted	92.86	93.31	N.A	N.A

2   Proposed Analysis

In real applications, the FPAD system works together with a recognition system in order to protect it from spoofing attacks. The integration of the PAD to the authentication system may reduce the recognition performance due to some live genuine sample's rejection [15]. In last years it was noticed that the presence of the same users both in the train set and in the test set, increased the PAD accuracy of the system. In fact, the existence of artifacts due to the human skin (person-specific) and to the particular curvature of ridges and valleys (finger-specific) can impact in PAD systems' performance [5,6] and can be exploit to improve the integrated system. In particular, the data acquired during the recognition system's initial enrollment phase can be used to lower the PAD error rate and consequently, to improve the integrated system performance. This approach may be referred to as "user-specific", whilst the other one may be referred to as "generic user". It is important to emphasize that stand-alone PAD systems are usually considered based on "generic user" approaches. Usually, a generic user approach is claimed to avoid biased results. This was evident in some early works [10,14] where an unexpected and unexplained drop of error rates occurred

Table 2. Number of samples for each scanner and each part of the dataset.

Dataset	Train				Test			
	Live	Wood glue	Ecoflex	Body double	Live	Gelatine	Latex	Liquid ecoflex
Green bit	1000	400	400	400	1700	680	680	680
Orcanthus	1000	400	400	400	1700	680	658	680
Digital persona	999	400	400	399	1700	679	670	679

when some users were present both in the train and in the test set, because the user-specific effect was not yet clear in the mind of the scholars.

However, this biasing may be desired under certain circumstances. In fact, as already mentioned, the positive influence of the user-specific effect on the live/fake classification can be exploited in real applications, where the enrolment phase allows to record the user fingerprint image previously. It is therefore possible to state that the "generic-user" approach is the main resource when the final user population is unknown (for example in forensic applications or border checks); the "user-specific" approach can be used to improve security of an integrated fingerprint verification system (for example authentication on mobile or bank account), in which the attacks are finalize to break the verification step and not to simply being disguised for another person.

On the other hand, common sense tells us that the system's performance is influenced by the attacker's ability to replicate the fingerprint. Although it is known that fakes can be produced with commonly used materials, even if these are of excellent quality, the attacker must know how to use them to spoof the system. In fact, we believe that an average skilled attacker may have the technique needed to circumvent the matcher, but more skills are needed to spoof an integrated system (both matcher and liveness detector). Although the impact of image quality has been used to classify fingerprints [10,11], to the best of our knowledge, no one has ever analyzed the impact of the operator's skill level.

3   Dataset and Experimental Protocol

LivDet 2017 [4] consisted of data from three fingerprint sensors: Green Bit DactyScan84C, Orcanthus Certis2 Image and Digital Persona U.are.U 5160. It is composed of almost 6000 images for each scanner. Live images came from multiple acquisitions of all fingers of different subjects.

The LivDet 2017 fake images were collected using the cooperative method. Each dataset consists of two parts, the train set, used to configure the algorithms, and the test set, used to evaluate the algorithms performance. Moreover, the materials used in the training set are different with respect to the test set as we can see in Table 2.

The test set can be partitioned into three parts, a user-specific (US) portion, composed by fingerprint belonging to users already present in the train set, and

Table 3. Average accuracy and EERs [%] comparison between deep learning and hand-crafted methods. The distinction between User-Specific and Generic User experiments and between high skilled operator and a low skilled operator is reported. The average accuracy refers to the entire test set.

	Average accuracy [%]	Average EER [%]			
		High skilled	Low skilled	User-specific	Generic user
Deep learning	94.0(±1.9)	8.1(±2.9)	6.5(±2.4)	2.6(±1.4)	8.1(±2.9)
Hand-crafted	90.0(±3.1)	12.5(±4.6)	10.8(±3.7)	5.7(±3.4)	12.5(±4.6)

the other two partitions are generic user (GU), meaning they are composed by fingerprint belonging to user not present in the train set, in which the fakes are made by two different operators HS (High Skilled) and LS (Low Skilled), described in more detail below. The false samples of the US partition were made by the operator HS. On the basis of this subdivision we therefore had:

$$TestSet = \{US(HS), GU(HS), GU(LS)\}$$

Using the two partitions, $US(HS)$ and $GU(HS)$, separately to test the algorithms, we can compare the user-specific effects with the generic-user case. In this experiment we left out the $GU(LS)$ partition to avoid an operator bias.

The second evaluation concerned the comparison between operators with different degrees of skill in replicating fingerprints. In particular, operator HS has a high experience in creating fakes because he has participated in multiple LivDet editions, while for operator LS this was the first edition in which he participated. Fingerprint replication requires a lot of experience, as the accuracy of the fakes heavily affects system performance. For this evaluation, partitions $GU(HS)$ and $GU(LS)$ were used separately as test set. The two operators used the same acquisition protocol using the same materials.

The Table 1 shows the results of LivDet 2017 for the three sensors, the total accuracy and the type of algorithm presented, making a distinction between deep learning based or hand-crafted features based. The table shows that in 2017 in FPAD the solutions adopted are equally distributed between deep learning and hand-crafted algorithms. Furthermore, we see that the performance of the algorithms that use deep learning techniques are better than the classic ones of about 10% points.

4   Results

In this session the comparisons between User-Specific (US) and Generic User (GU) experiments and between highly skilled operator (HS) and a lowly skilled operator (LS) experiments were reported.

In the previous papers the user-specific effect was highlighted only for PAD systems based on hand-crafted features. The high number of algorithms participating in LivDet 2017 based on deep learning methods allow us to have a

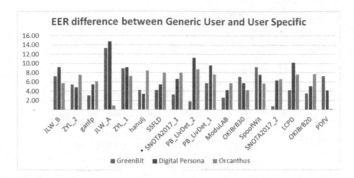

Fig. 1. Comparison between User Specific and Generic User experiments. Each bar is the result of the EER difference between US and GU.

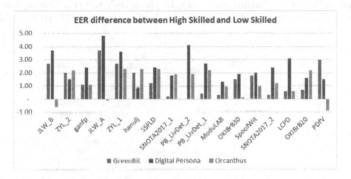

Fig. 2. Comparison between high skilled operator and low skilled operator. Each bar is the result of the EER difference between HS and LS.

clearer view on this effect. Table 3 shows a comparison between deep-learning based methods and handcrafted features based methods, obtained by comparing the average accuracy and the EERs related to the analyzed case studies. This table shows that deep learning appears to be more competitive than handcrafted techniques, as anticipated in Table 1. Furthermore it is clear that even the standard deviation is more limited and therefore it is an index of how the deep learning performances have more or less the same performance and with smaller fluctuations with respect to the others. The table clearly confirms the existence of the user-specific effects for all the algorithms presented: on average the error for the generic user system is more than double the user-specific one. This result is confirmed by Fig. 1, in which the EER difference between GU and US systems has been reported for each algorithm presented.

To get a graphical view of these results, the ROCs related to the comparisons between user-specific and generic user for the average of the three best algorithms are reported in Fig. 3. These results demonstrate that the user-specific effect influences liveness detection methods regardless of their characteristics. To assess whether a person-specific or finger-specific effect is more influential, a more in-

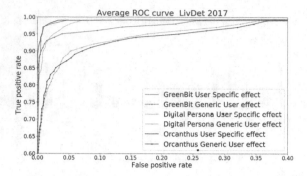

Fig. 3. Average ROC of the three best LivDet2017 algorithms, calculated for the three scanners. In the ROC the blue, green and black line respectively indicates the green bit, digital persona and orcanthus data sets. In the graph the continuous line indicates the US effect, instead the dotted line indicates the trend of the GU ROC. (Color figure online)

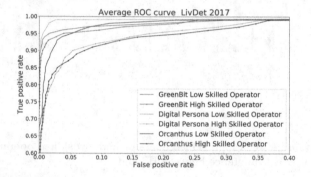

Fig. 4. Average ROC of the three best LivDet2017 algorithms, calculated for the three scanners. In the ROC the blue, green and black line respectively indicates the Green Bit, Digital Persona and Orcanthus data sets. In the graph the continuous line indicates the Low skilled operator in the spoof fabrication fingerprint, instead the dotted line indicates the trend of High skilled operator making fake samples in the ROC curve. (Color figure online)

depth analysis is required. This evidence supports the possible exploitation of user-specific effects to improve the performance of FPAD when integrated with personal identity verification systems, especially when these are used by one or a few users, as in the case of mobile authentication systems.

The other analysis carried out concerns the influence of the operator's ability to spoof PAD systems. The results, shown in Table 3 and Figs. 2, 3 and 4, confirm the intuitive hypothesis that the attacker's skills profoundly influence the performance of these systems for both hand-crafted and deep learning methods. In particular, from Fig. 4, which shows the comparisons between a low skilled and high skilled operator for the average of the three best algorithms, it is possible to deduce that this difference is not only due to the ability to create fakes, but also to the ability to use fakes to "cheat" the system. In fact, a skilled operator produces excellent fakes and knows how to use them to spoof the FPAD system, thus induces a higher EER. Depending on the sensor, the difference between the continuous curve (LS) and the dotted curve (HS) is more pronounced. Above all, the curves regarding the Green Bit sensor, which is the simplest to use as it has a scanner area almost double compared to the other sensors, have a similar trend. Conversely, the other two sensors, in addition to a smallest area, are much more difficult to use and a correct acquisition require a remarkable experience.

5 Conclusions

In this paper, we extended the report on the LivDet 2017 competition edition, in order to point out the main results about two more challenges proposed which were not detailed in the official report for sake of space.

The obtained results can be viewed as a demonstration on what the state of the art on fingerprint PAD can reach on both challenges. Participants used deep learning and hand-crafted features based methods for the task, also the number of competitors was the biggest with respect to other editions.

Reported results allowed us to confirm that the positive influence of the user-specific effect on the liveness classification can be exploited in integrated systems where the enrolment phase is necessary, thus making available samples of the specific user for the PAD design.

Furthermore, it has been shown that the operator's ability to create and use fake replicas heavily affects performance. This pointed out that, to being a serious threat for fingerprint verification system a minimum level of skill is required beside the ability to provide reliable replicas of the targeted user.

References

1. Matsumoto, T., Matsumoto, H., Yamada, K., Hoshino, S.: Impact of artificial "gummy" fingers on fingerprint systems. Datenschutz und Datensicherheit (2002). https://doi.org/10.1117/12.462719
2. Marasco, E., Ross, A.: A survey on antispoofing schemes for fingerprint recognition systems. ACM Comput. Surv. **47**(2), 28 (2014). https://doi.org/10.1145/2617756. 36 p
3. Ghiani, L., Yambay, D.A., Mura, V., Marcialis, G.L., Roli, F., Schuckers, S.A.: Review of the fingerprint liveness detection (LivDet) competition series: 2009 to 2015. IMAVIS **58**, 110–128 (2017)
4. Mura, V., et al.: LivDet fingerprint liveness detection competition 2017. In: 2018 ICB, Gold Coast, QLD, pp. 297–302 (2017). https://doi.org/10.1109/ICB2018. 2018.00052
5. Ghiani, L., Marcialis, G.L., Roli, F., Tuveri, P.: User-specific effects in fingerprint presentation attacks detection: insights for future research. In: 2016 ICB, Halmstad, pp. 1–6 (2016). https://doi.org/10.1109/ICB.2016.7550081

6. Ghiani, L., Marcialis, G.L., Roli, F.: Fingerprint presentation attacks detection based on the user-specific effect. In: IEEE IJCB, Denver, CO, pp. 352–358 (2017). https://doi.org/10.1109/BTAS.2017.8272717
7. Ghiani, L., Hadid, A., Marcialis, G.L., Roli, F.: Fingerprint liveness detection using local texture features. IET Biometrics **6**(3), 224–231 (2017). https://doi.org/10.1049/iet-bmt.2016.0007
8. Gragnaniello, D., Poggi, G., Sansone, C., Verdoliva, L.: Fingerprint liveness detection based on weber local image descriptor. In: IEEE BioMS, Naples, pp. 46–50 (2013). https://doi.org/10.1109/BIOMS.2013.6656148
9. Gottschlich, C., Marasco, E., Yang, A.Y., Cukic, B.: Fingerprint liveness detection based on histograms of invariant gradients. In: IEEE IJCB, Clearwater, FL, pp. 1–7 (2014). https://doi.org/10.1109/BTAS.2014.6996224
10. Galbally, J., Alonso-Fernandez, F., Fierrez, J., Ortega-Garcia, J.: A high performance fingerprint liveness detection method based on quality related features. FGCS **28**(1), 311–321 (2012). https://doi.org/10.1016/j.future.2010.11.024
11. Bhogal, A.P.S., Söllinger, D., Trung, P., Uhl, A.: Non-reference image quality assessment for biometric presentation attack detection. In: 5th IWBF, Coventry, pp. 1–6 (2017). https://doi.org/10.1109/IWBF.2017.7935080
12. Nogueira, R.F., de Alencar Lotufo, R., Campos Machado, R.: Fingerprint liveness detection using convolutional neural networks. IEEE TIFS **11**(6), 1206–1213 (2016). https://doi.org/10.1109/TIFS.2016.2520880
13. Kim, H., Cui, X., Kim, M., Nguyen, T.H.B.: Fingerprint generation and presentation attack detection using deep neural networks. In: IEEE MIPR, San Jose, CA, USA, pp. 375–378 (2019). https://doi.org/10.1109/MIPR.2019.00074
14. Jia, X., et al.: Multi-scale local binary pattern with filters for spoof fingerprint detection. Inf. Sci. **268**, 91–102 (2014). https://doi.org/10.1016/j.ins.2013.06.041
15. Chingovska, I., Anjos, A., Marcel, S.: Anti-spoofing in action: joint operation with a verification system. In: IEEE CVPR Workshops, Portland, OR, pp. 98–104 (2013). https://doi.org/10.1109/CVPRW.2013.22

PatReCH: International Workshop on Pattern Recognition for Cultural Heritage

Enriching Character-Based Neural Machine Translation with Modern Documents for Achieving an Orthography Consistency in Historical Documents

Miguel Domingo[(✉)] and Francisco Casacuberta

PRHLT Research Center, Universitat Politècnica de València, Valencia, Spain
{midobal,fcn}@prhlt.upv.es

Abstract. The nature of human language and the lack of a spelling convention make historical documents hard to handle for natural language processing. Spelling normalization tackles this problem by adapting their spelling to modern standards in order to get an orthography consistency. In this work, we compare several character-based machine translation approaches, and propose a method to profit from modern documents to enrich neural machine translation models. We tested our proposal with four different data sets, and observed that the enriched models successfully improved the normalization quality of the neural models. Statistical models, however, yielded a better result.

1 Introduction

The linguistic variation in historical documents has always been a concern for scholars in humanities [3]. On the one hand, human language evolves over time. On the other hand, spelling conventions were not created until recently. Therefore, orthography changes depending on the author and time period. Sometimes, this variety is astonishing. Laing [21] pointed out that, for instance, the data in *LALME* (Linguistic Atlas of Late Medieval English) indicate 45 different forms recorded for the pronoun *it*, 64 for the pronoun *she* and more than 500 for the preposition *through*.

Historical documents are an important part of our cultural heritage. Thus, interest in effective natural language processing for these documents is on the rise [3]. However, the aforementioned linguistic problems suppose an additional challenge. Spelling normalization aims to solve these problems. Its goal is to achieve an orthography consistency by adapting the document's spelling to modern standards. Figure 1 shows an example.

In this work, we compare several normalization approaches that rely on character-based machine translation (MT), and propose a method for enriching neural machine translation (NMT) systems by profiting from modern documents. Our main contributions are as follow:

© Springer Nature Switzerland AG 2019
M. Cristani et al. (Eds.): ICIAP 2019 Workshops, LNCS 11808, pp. 59–69, 2019.
https://doi.org/10.1007/978-3-030-30754-7_7

> Bien responde la esperança
> en que engañado he viuido
> al cuydado que he tenido
> de tu estudio y tu criança!
>
> Bien responde la esperanza
> en que engañado he vivido
> al cuidado que he tenido
> de tu estudio y tu crianza!

Fig. 1. Example of adapting a document's spelling to modern standards. Characters that need to be adapted are denoted in red. Its modern versions are denoted in teal. Example extracted from [11]. (Color figure online)

- Comparison of several character-based MT normalization approaches.
- New character-based NMT approach enriched with modern documents.

The rest of this document is structured as follows: Sect. 2 introduces the related work. Then, in Sect. 3 we present the different normalization approaches. Section 4 describes the experiments conducted in order to assess our proposal. The results of those experiments are presented and discussed in Sect. 5. Finally, in Sect. 6, conclusions are drawn.

2 Related Work

Some approaches to spelling normalization include creating an interactive tool that includes spell checking techniques to assist the user in detecting spelling variations [2]. Porta et al. [32] made use of a weighted finite-state transducer, combined with a modern lexicon, a phonological transcriber and a set of rules. Scherrer and Erjavec [37] combined a list of historical words, a list of modern words and character-based statistical machine translation (SMT). Bollman and Søgaard [4] took a multi-task learning approach using a deep bi-LSTM applied at a character level. Ljubevsic et al. [25] applied a token/segment-level character-based SMT approach to normalize historical and user-created words. Korchagina [20] made use of rule-based MT, character-based SMT (CBSMT) and character-based NMT (CBNMT). Domingo and Casacuberta [10] evaluated word-based and character-based MT approaches, finding character-based to be more suitable for this task and that SMT systems outperformed NMT systems. Tang et al. [43], however, compared many different neural architectures and reported that the NMT models are much better than SMT models in terms of CER. Finally, Hämäläinen et al. [15] evaluated SMT, NMT, an edit-distance approach, and a rule-based finite state transducer, and advocated for a combination of these approaches to make use of their individual strengths.

Character-based MT strikes to be a solution in MT to reduce the training vocabulary by dividing words into a sequence of characters, and treating each character as if it were a basic unit. Although it was already being researched in SMT [26,44], its interest has increased with NMT. Some approaches to CBNMT consist in using hierarchical NMT [22], a character level decoder [7], a character level encoder [9] or, for alphabets in which words are composed by fewer characters, by constructing an NMT system that takes advantage of that alphabet [8].

Backtranslation [38] is a useful technique to increase the training data by creating synthetic text from monolingual data. It has become the norm in MT when building state-of-the-art NMT systems, especially in resource-poor scenarios [31]. Given a monolingual corpus in the target language, and an MT system trained to translate from target to source, the synthetic data is generated by translating the monolingual corpus with the MT system. After that, the synthetic data is used as the source part of the corpus, and the monolingual data as the target part. Finally, this new corpus is mixed with the available training data in order to train a new MT system.

3 Normalization Approaches

In this section, we review different approaches to tackle the orthography problem inherent in historical documents and achieve a spelling consistency, and propose a new method which profits from modern documents to enrich its system.

These approaches rely on MT, which aims at finding the most likely translation $\hat{y}$ [5] for a given source sentence $\mathbf{x}$:

$$\hat{y} = \arg\max_{y} Pr(\mathbf{y} \mid \mathbf{x}) \qquad (1)$$

3.1 Existing Approaches

Character-Based SMT. CBSMT focuses to compute Eq. (1) at a character level, using models that rely on a log-linear combination of different models [28]: namely, phrase-based alignment models, reordering models and language models; among others [19,47].

Considering the document's language as the source language and its normalized version as the target language, this approach follows a CBSMT strategy. In order to have the same conditions in both SMT and NMT approaches, the character-based strategy that is usually followed is the simplest approach: to split words into characters and, then, apply conventional SMT.

Character-Based NMT. Like CBSMT, CBNMT focuses to compute Eq. (1) at a character level, but modeling this expression with a neural network. This neural network usually follows an encoder-decoder architecture, featuring recurrent networks [1,41], convolutional networks [13] or attention mechanisms [45]. Model parameters are jointly estimated on large parallel corpora, using stochastic gradient descent [35,36]. At decoding time, the system obtains the most likely translation using a beam search method.

Like with the CBSMT approach, this normalization approach considers the original language as the source and its normalized version as the target, and focuses on a character-based strategy. The difference is that this approach follows an NMT strategy in stead of a SMT one.

3.2   Character-Based NMT Enriched with Modern Documents

Our normalization proposal is an extension of the CBNMT approach (see Sect. 3.1). The scarce availability of parallel training data is a frequent problem when working with historical documents [4]. This problem is specially troublesome for NMT approaches, which need an abundant quantity of parallel training data. To tackle this problem, we propose to use modern documents to enrich the NMT systems.

Following a backtranslation strategy [38], we propose to enrich the NMT models using modern documents to create synthetic data. With this aim, we follow these steps:

1. We train a CBSMT system—since SMT is less affected by the problem of scarce availability of training data—using the normalized version of the training dataset as source, and the original version as target.
2. We use this system to translate the modern documents, obtaining a new version of the documents which, hopefully, is able to capture the same orthography inconsistencies that the original documents have. This new version, together with the original modern document, conform a synthetic parallel data which can be used as additional training data.
3. We combine the synthetic data with the training dataset, replicating several times the training dataset in order to match the size of the synthetic data and avoid overfitting [6].
4. We use the resulting dataset to train the enriched CBNMT normalization system.

4   Experiments

In this section, we describe the experimental conditions arranged in order to assess our proposal: MT systems, corpora and evaluation metrics.

4.1   MT Systems

We trained our SMT systems with Moses [18], following the standard procedure: we estimated a 5-gram language model—smoothing it with the improved Kneser-Ney method—using SRILM [40], and optimized the weights of the log-lineal model with MERT [27].

NMT systems were built using OpenNMT-py [17]. We used long short-term memory units [14], with all model dimensions set to 512. We trained the system using Adam [16] with a fixed learning rate of 0.0002 [46] and a batch size of 60. We applied label smoothing of 0.1 [42]. At the inference time, we used a beam search with a beam size of 6.

Finally, we considered as baseline the quality of the original document with respect to its ground truth version, in which the spelling has already been normalized. Nonetheless, as a second baseline, we implemented a statistical dictionary. Using mgiza [12], we computed *IBM's model 1* [29] to obtain word alignments from source and target of the training set. Then, for each source word, we selected as its translation the target word which had the highest alignment probability with that source word. Finally, at translation time, we translated each source word with the translation that appeared in the dictionary. If a given word did not appear in the dictionary, then we left it untranslated.

4.2 Corpora

In order to asses our proposal, we made use of the following corpora:

Entremeses y Comedias [11]: A 17th century Spanish collection of comedies by Miguel de Cervantes. It is composed of 16 plays, 8 of which have a very short length.

Quijote [11]: The 17th century Spanish two-volumes novel by Miguel de Cervantes.

Bohorič [24]: A collection of 18th century Slovene texts written in the old Bohorič alphabet.

Gaj [24]: A collection of 19th century Slovene texts written in the Gaj alphabet.

As reflected in Table 1, the size of the corpora is small. Thus, the use of backtranslation to increase the training data. As *modern documents*, we selected half a million sentences from OpenSubtitles [23], a collection of movie subtitles in different languages. We selected the same Spanish sentences for *Entremeses y Comedias* and *Quijote*, and the same Slovene sentences for *Bohoric* and *Gaj*.

Table 1. Corpora statistics. $|S|$ stands for number of sentences, $|T|$ for number of tokens, $|V|$ for size of the vocabulary and $|W|$ for the number of words whose spelling does not match modern standards. M denotes millions and K thousand.

		Entremeses y Comedias	Quijote	Bohorič	Gaj
Train	$|S|$	35.6K	48.0K	3.6K	13.0K
	$|T|$	250.0/244.0K	436.0/428.0K	61.2/61.0K	198.2/197.6K
	$|V|$	19.0/18.0K	24.4/23.3K	14.3/10.9K	34.5/30.7K
	$|W|$	52.4K	97.5K	33.0K	32.7K
Development	$|S|$	2.0K	2.0K	447	1.6K
	$|T|$	13.7/13.6K	19.0/18.0K	7.1/7.1K	25.7/25.6K
	$|V|$	3.0/3.0K	3.2/3.2K	2.9/2.5K	8.2/7.7K
	$|W|$	1.9K	4.5K	3.8K	4.5K
Test	$|S|$	2.0K	2.0K	448	1.6K
	$|T|$	15.0/13.3K	18.0/18.0K	7.3/7.3K	26.3/26.2K
	$|V|$	2.7/2.6K	3.2/3.2K	3.0/2.6K	8.4/8.0K
	$|W|$	3.3K	3.8K	3.8K	4.8K
Modern documents	$|S|$	500.0K	500.0K	500.0K	500.0K
	$|T|$	3.5M	3.5M	3.0M	3.0M
	$|V|$	67.3K	67.3K	84.7K	84.7K

4.3   Metrics

We made use of the following well-known metrics in order to assess our proposal:

Character Error Rate (CER): number of character edit operations (insertion, substitution and deletion), normalized by the number of characters in the final translation.

Translation Error Rate (TER) [39]: number of word edit operations (insertion, substitution, deletion and swapping), normalized by the number of words in the final translation.

BiLingual Evaluation Understudy (BLEU) [30]: geometric average of the modified n-gram precision, multiplied by a brevity factor.

In order to ensure consistent BLEU scores, we used `sacreBLEU` [33]. Additionally, we applied approximate randomization tests [34]—with 10,000 repetitions and using a p-value of 0.05—to determine whether two systems presented statistically significant differences.

5   Results

Table 2 presents the results of our experimental session. As baseline, we assessed the spelling differences of the original documents with respect to their normalized version. Additionally, as a second baseline, we made use of a statistical dictionary for normalizing the spelling. With one exception in which CER yielded worse results, the statistically dictionary presented significant gains for all data sets according to all the metrics (up to 5 points according to CER, 28 points according to TER and 38 points according to BLEU).

Table 2. Experimental results. Baseline system corresponds to considering the original document as the document to which the spelling has been normalized to match modern standards. SD is the statistical dictionary. All results are significantly different between all systems. Best results are denoted in **bold**.

System	Entremeses y Comedias			Quijote			Bohorič			Gaj		
	CER	TER	BLEU	CER	TER	BLEU	CER	TER	BLEU	CER	TER	BLEU
Baseline	8.1	28.0	47.0	7.9	19.5	59.4	21.7	49.0	18.0	3.5	12.3	72.6
SD	7.8	18.9	66.8	3.9	5.5	89.3	16.2	20.7	56.1	7.6	8.8	79.8
CBSMT	**1.3**	**4.4**	**91.7**	**2.5**	**3.0**	**94.4**	**2.4**	**8.7**	**80.4**	**1.4**	**5.1**	**88.3**
CBNMT	2.4	8.0	84.8	4.2	7.6	85.1	37.0	45.1	40.1	39.0	42.5	45.4
Enriched CBNMT	1.9	7.2	85.9	3.3	4.5	91.9	28.7	37.3	49.0	36.4	40.7	47.3

The CBSMT approach yielded the most significant improvements for all data sets and according to all the metrics, with gains of up to 19 points according to CER, 40 points according to TER and 62 points according to BLEU.

With two exception, the CBNMT approach yielded better results than both baselines, but worse than the CBSMT approach. Those exceptions were with

Bohorič and *Gaj*, for which it yielded worse results than both baselines according to all the metrics. This behavior was already noticed by Domingo and Casacuberta [10]. Most likely, it is related with the small size of the corpora, and the nature of the Slovene language—specially in the case of *Bohorič*, whose documents were written while the Slovene language was having a big restructuring.

Following a backtranslation approach to enrich the neural systems using modern documents significantly improved the results, yielding gains of up to 8 points according to CER and TER, and 9 points according to BLEU. However, in the case of *Bohorič* and *Gaj*, these results are still worse than both baselines according to all the metrics. Nonetheless, these results are encouraging, since they show that we can profit from modern documents to improve neural systems. We shall further investigate this approach in a future work.

5.1   Analysis

Figure 2 shows an example of normalizing the spelling of a sentence from *Bohorič*.

Original: dobro manengo, de otshe kerstiti, koker je kristus goripostavel, inu koker ima katholshka zir kuv navado kerstiti.
Normalized: dobro manengo, da hoče krstiti, kakor je kristus goripostavil, in kakor ima katoliška cerkev n avado krstiti.

SD: dobro manengo, da meni drugi, kakor je kristus cerkvena, in kakor ima katholshka cerkev navado drugi.
CBSMT: dobro manengo, da hoče krstiti, kakor je kristus goripostavil, in kakor ima katoliška cerkev n avado krstiti.
CBNMT: dobro manengo, da otže krztiti, kokor ju krotiti.
Enriched CBNMT: dobro manengo, da otže krstiti, kakor je kriztus goripostavil, in koker ima katoliška cerkev nava

Fig. 2. Example of modernizing a sentence from *Bohorič* with all the different approaches. Unnormalized characters that should have been normalized are denoted in red. Characters which were successfully normalized are denoted in teal. (Color figure online)

From all the corpora, *Bohorič* has the biggest differences in its orthography due to the Slovene language having a big restructuring in the period in which their documents were written. Therefore, 23 changes are needed in order to update its spelling to match modern Slovene standards.

The statistical dictionary was able to correct 11 of these errors. However, since it is a word-based approach, it introduced more mistakes than it was able to correct: while only a few characters of some words needed a change in their spelling, the statistical dictionary suggested new words.

For this example, the CBSMT approach was able to achieve a perfect normalization.

The CBNMT approach was able to correct 2 characters, and successfully determined that the combination *sh* should be normalized as a single character. However, it made a wrong correction. Furthermore, half of the sentence is gone. This is a known miss-behavior of neural systems in MT.

Finally, the enriched CBNMT approach was able to handle the neural miss-behavior. Although the last few characters are still missing. Moreover, most of the unnormalized characters have been successfully corrected. A behavior worth noting, however, is how the system was able to successfully normalized the first appearance of the word *koker*, but not its second appearance.

6   Conclusions and Future Work

In this work, we proposed a normalization method based on backtranslation, to enrich CBNMT systems using modern documents. We tested our proposal in different data sets, observing significant gains for all metrics.

Additionally, we compared several normalization approaches, reaching the conclusion than CBSMT systems are more suitable for this task. We believe that this is specially true due to the scarce availability of parallel training data when working with historical documents [4].

As a future work, we would like to further research the use of modern documents to enrich the neural systems. In this work, we randomly selected 500 thousand lines from modern documents, in order to balance the quantity between synthetic and real data, and use the same data for corpora who belonged to the same language. We should further investigate about how to balance synthetic and real data. Additionally, instead of randomly selecting the data, we would like to use a data selection approach to find the most suitable data for each corpus.

Acknowledgments. The research leading to these results has received funding from the European Union through *Programa Operativo del Fondo Europeo de Desarrollo Regional (FEDER)* from Comunitat Valencia (2014–2020) under project *Sistemas de frabricación inteligentes para la indústria 4.0* (grant agreement IDIFEDER/2018/025); and from Ministerio de Economía y Competitividad (MINECO) under project *MISMIS-FAKEnHATE* (grant agreement PGC2018-096212-B-C31). We gratefully acknowledge the support of NVIDIA Corporation with the donation of a GPU used for part of this research.

References

1. Bahdanau, D., Cho, K., Bengio, Y.: Neural machine translation by jointly learning to align and translate (2015). arXiv:1409.0473
2. Baron, A., Rayson, P.: VARD2: a tool for dealing with spelling variation in historical corpora. In: Postgraduate Conference in Corpus Linguistics (2008)
3. Bollmann, M.: Normalization of historical texts with neural network models. Ph.D. thesis, Sprachwissenschaftliches Institut, Ruhr-Universität (2018)
4. Bollmann, M., Søgaard, A.: Improving historical spelling normalization with bi-directional LSTMs and multi-task learning. In: Proceedings of the International Conference on the Computational Linguistics, pp. 131–139 (2016)
5. Brown, P.F., Pietra, V.J.D., Pietra, S.A.D., Mercer, R.L.: The mathematics of statistical machine translation: parameter estimation. Comput. Linguist. **19**(2), 263–311 (1993)
6. Chatterjee, R., Farajian, M.A., Negri, M., Turchi, M., Srivastava, A., Pal, S.: Multi-source neural automatic post-editing: FBK's participation in the WMT 2017 ape shared task. In: Proceedings of the Second Conference on Machine Translation, pp. 630–638 (2017)

7. Chung, J., Cho, K., Bengio, Y.: A character-level decoder without explicit segmentation for neural machine translation. In: Proceedings of the Annual Meeting of the Association for Computational Linguistics, pp. 1693–1703 (2016)
8. Costa-Jussà, M.R., Aldón, D., Fonollosa, J.A.: Chinese-Spanish neural machine translation enhanced with character and word bitmap fonts. Mach. Transl. **31**, 35–47 (2017)
9. Costa-Jussà, M.R., Fonollosa, J.A.: Character-based neural machine translation. In: Proceedings of the Annual Meeting of the Association for Computational Linguistics, pp. 357–361 (2016)
10. Domingo, M., Casacuberta, F.: Spelling normalization of historical documents by using a machine translation approach. In: Proceedings of the Annual Conference of the European Association for Machine Translation, pp. 129–137 (2018)
11. Jehle, F.: Works of Miguel de Cervantes in Old- and Modern-Spelling. Indiana University Purdue University Fort Wayne (2001)
12. Gao, Q., Vogel, S.: Parallel implementations of word alignment tool. In: Proceedings of the Association for Computational Linguistics Software Engineering, Testing, and Quality Assurance Workshop, pp. 49–57 (2008)
13. Gehring, J., Auli, M., Grangier, D., Yarats, D., Dauphin, Y.N.: Convolutional sequence to sequence learning (2017). arXiv:1705.03122
14. Gers, F.A., Schmidhuber, J., Cummins, F.: Learning to forget: continual prediction with LSTM. Neural Comput. **12**(10), 2451–2471 (2000)
15. Hämäläinen, M., Säily, T., Rueter, J., Tiedemann, J., Mäkelä, E.: Normalizing early English letters to present-day English spelling. In: Proceedings of the Workshop on Computational Linguistics for Cultural Heritage, Social Sciences, Humanities and Literature, pp. 87–96 (2018)
16. Kingma, D.P., Ba, J.: Adam: a method for stochastic optimization. arXiv preprint arXiv:1412.6980 (2014)
17. Klein, G., Kim, Y., Deng, Y., Senellart, J., Rush, A.M.: OpenNMT: open-source toolkit for neural machine translation. In: Proceedings of the Association for Computational Linguistics: System Demonstration, pp. 67–72 (2017)
18. Koehn, P., et al.: Moses: open source toolkit for statistical machine translation. In: Proceedings of the Annual Meeting of the Association for Computational Linguistics, pp. 177–180 (2007)
19. Koehn, P., Och, F.J., Marcu, D.: Statistical phrase-based translation. In: Proceedings of the Conference of the North American Chapter of the Association for Computational Linguistics on Human Language Technology, pp. 48–54 (2003)
20. Korchagina, N.: Normalizing medieval German texts: from rules to deep learning. In: Proceedings of the Nordic Conference on Computational Linguistics Workshop on Processing Historical Language, pp. 12–17 (2017)
21. Laing, M.: The linguistic analysis of medieval vernacular texts: Two projects at Edinburgh'. In: Rissanen, M., Kytd, M., Wright, S. (eds.) Corpora across the Centuries: Proceedings of the First International Colloquium on English Diachronic Corpora, vol. 25427, pp. 121–141. St Catharine's College Cambridge (1993)
22. Ling, W., Trancoso, I., Dyer, C., Black, A.W.: Character-based neural machine translation. arXiv preprint arXiv:1511.04586 (2015)
23. Lison, P., Tiedemann, J.: OpenSubtitles 2016: extracting large parallel corpora from movie and TV subtitles. In: Proceedings of the International Conference on Language Resources Association (2016)
24. Ljubešić, N., Zupan, K., Fišer, D., Erjavec, T.: Dataset of normalised Slovene text KonvNormSl 1.0. Slovenian language resource repository CLARIN.SI (2016). http://hdl.handle.net/11356/1068

25. Ljubešic, N., Zupan, K., Fišer, D., Erjavec, T.: Normalising slovene data: historical texts vs. user-generated content. In: Proceedings of the Conference on Natural Language Processing, pp. 146–155 (2016)
26. Nakov, P., Tiedemann, J.: Combining word-level and character-level models for machine translation between closely-related languages. In: Proceedings of the Annual Meeting of the Association for Computational Linguistics, pp. 301–305 (2012)
27. Och, F.J.: Minimum error rate training in statistical machine translation. In: Proceedings of the Annual Meeting of the Association for Computational Linguistics, pp. 160–167 (2003)
28. Och, F.J., Ney, H.: Discriminative training and maximum entropy models for statistical machine translation. In: Proceedings of the Annual Meeting of the Association for Computational Linguistics, pp. 295–302 (2002)
29. Och, F.J., Ney, H.: A systematic comparison of various statistical alignment models. Comput. Linguist. **29**(1), 19–51 (2003)
30. Papineni, K., Roukos, S., Ward, T., Zhu, W.J.: BLEU: a method for automatic evaluation of machine translation. In: Proceedings of the Annual Meeting of the Association for Computational Linguistics, pp. 311–318 (2002)
31. Poncelas, A., Shterionov, D., Way, A., Maillette de Buy Wenniger, G., Passban, P.: Investigation backtranslation in neural machine translation. In: Proceedings of the Annual Conference of the European Association for Machine Translation, pp. 249–258 (2018)
32. Porta, J., Sancho, J.L., Gómez, J.: Edit transducers for spelling variation in old Spanish. In: Proceedings of the Workshop on Computational Historical Linguistics, pp. 70–79 (2013)
33. Post, M.: A call for clarity in reporting BLEU scores. In: Proceedings of the Third Conference on Machine Translation, pp. 186–191 (2018)
34. Riezler, S., Maxwell, J.T.: On some pitfalls in automatic evaluation and significance testing for MT. In: Proceedings of the Workshop on Intrinsic and Extrinsic Evaluation Measures for Machine Translation and/or Summarization, pp. 57–64 (2005)
35. Robbins, H., Monro, S.: A stochastic approximation method. Ann. Math. Stat. **22**, 400–407 (1951)
36. Rumelhart, D.E., Hinton, G.E., Williams, R.J.: Learning representations by back-propagating errors. Nature **323**(6088), 533 (1986)
37. Scherrer, Y., Erjavec, T.: Modernizing historical Slovene words with character-based SMT. In: Proceedings of the Biennial International Workshop on Balto-Slavic Natural Language Processing, pp. 58–62 (2013)
38. Sennrich, R., Haddow, B., Birch, A.: Improving neural machine translation models with monolingual data. arXiv preprint arXiv:1511.06709 (2015)
39. Snover, M., Dorr, B., Schwartz, R., Micciulla, L., Makhoul, J.: A study of translation edit rate with targeted human annotation. In: Proceedings of the Association for Machine Translation in the Americas, pp. 223–231 (2006)
40. Stolcke, A.: SRILM - an extensible language modeling toolkit. In: Proceedings of the International Conference on Spoken Language Processing, pp. 257–286 (2002)
41. Sutskever, I., Vinyals, O., Le, Q.V.: Sequence to sequence learning with neural networks. Proc. Adv. Neural Inf. Process. Syst. **27**, 3104–3112 (2014)
42. Szegedy, C., et al.: Going deeper with convolutions. In: Proceedings of the IEEE Conference on Computer Vision and Pattern Recognition, pp. 1–9 (2015)

43. Tang, G., Cap, F., Pettersson, E., Nivre, J.: An evaluation of neural machine translation models on historical spelling normalization. In: Proceedings of the International Conference on Computational Linguistics, pp. 1320–1331 (2018)
44. Tiedemann, J.: Character-based PSMT for closely related languages. In: Proceedings of the Annual Conference of the European Association for Machine Translation, pp. 12–19 (2009)
45. Vaswani, A., et al.: Attention is all you need. In: Advances in Neural Information Processing Systems, pp. 5998–6008 (2017)
46. Wu, Y., et al.: Google's neural machine translation system: bridging the gap between human and machine translation (2016). arXiv:1609.08144
47. Zens, R., Och, F.J., Ney, H.: Phrase-based statistical machine translation. In: Jarke, M., Lakemeyer, G., Koehler, J. (eds.) KI 2002. LNCS (LNAI), vol. 2479, pp. 18–32. Springer, Heidelberg (2002). https://doi.org/10.1007/3-540-45751-8_2

A Comparative Analysis of Two Commercial Digital Photogrammetry Software for Cultural Heritage Applications

Kaitlyn Kingsland(✉) iD

Institute for Digital Exploration, University of South Florida,
Tampa, FL 33620, USA
kkingsland@usf.edu

Abstract. The paper seeks to evaluate the literature on digital photogrammetry processing software, comparing Agisoft Photoscan (now known as Agisoft Metashape, beginning with version 1.5) RealityCapture and to test the two programs in a real-world situation to further examine the difference in the software and resulting model. Tests were carried out for the evaluation of Photoscan, and RealityCapure—two European based digital photogrammetry programs—using the same artifact and data in all three tests. The artifact is part of the Farid Karam Collection of Antiquities, housed at the University of South Florida (USF) Libraries Tampa Special Collections. The chosen artifact for study, the aryballos inv. no. 68, was captured in ideal conditions to better evaluate multiple programs with the same data. The digital artifact was examined based upon knowledge and photographs of the physical artifact and evaluated relatively and comparatively between the programs.

Keywords: Digital heritage · Software · Photogrammetry

1 Introduction

Cultural heritage is increasingly incorporating digital technologies into their techniques and methods. New 3D digital tools provide unique advantages for outreach, education, and preservation of artifacts and sites. Using these tools, museums and historic sites are able to not only provide greater accessibility to the general public but also accessibility for researchers who may otherwise be unable to find these artifacts and sites [1]. Digital tools allow the global academic community to view these artifacts and sites from anywhere without risk and can provide the researcher with tools that may be more accurate than analogue methods [2, 3].

Digitization methods in cultural heritage applications have included laser scanning and structured light scanning for a few decades, but still remain expensive—in terms of equipment and expertise necessary for the documentation and processing [3–6]. Digital photogrammetry, however, is relatively inexpensive—both monetarily and experientially—making it the most accessible digitization option when compared to the other techniques, though the quality of results depends largely on the equipment. Digital photogrammetry programs have been evaluated for accuracy in the digitization of

M. Cristani et al. (Eds.): ICIAP 2019 Workshops, LNCS 11808, pp. 70–80, 2019.
https://doi.org/10.1007/978-3-030-30754-7_8

large-scale sites, but the evaluation of the software for the purpose of small-scale digital photogrammetry has been largely unexplored. Software reviews using drone photogrammetric surveys address several advantages and issues with the photogrammetric software. Agisoft Photoscan (now Agisoft Metashape in version 1.5) is the most commonly discussed licensed software for digital cultural heritage. Evaluations assert the software's reliability and reproducibility in digital reconstructions [1–14]. Digital cultural heritage institutions and companies often discuss the use of RealityCapture by CapturingReality. It is the software of choice for digital reconstruction of heritage sites for CyArk. Unfortunately, RealityCapture has yet to be critically evaluated in any academic publication.

1.1 Case Study: The Farid Karam M.D. Lebanon Antiquities Collection at the USF Libraries Special Collections

The Farid Karam M.D. Lebanon Antiquities Collection consists of 149 artifacts of various material types from Lebanon donated to the University of South Florida Tampa Library Special Collections in 1998 by Dr. Farid Karam, M.D. for exhibition to the student body. In August of 2018, the Institute for Digital Exploration (IDEx) digitized many of the artifacts using digital photogrammetry to increase accessibility, with the results available as a virtual collection of the IDEx website (www.usfidex.com) and the IDEx Sketchfab (https://skfb.ly/6KKGp), [15]. One of these artifacts was chosen for comparative tests.

Fig. 1. Photograph of the aryballos inv. no. 68.

The specific artifact which will be used in this paper was the aryballos inv. no. 68 (Fig. 1). This artifact was chosen due the nature of the material and its simple, yet unique shape. Made out of ceramic, this artifact lacks reflective and translucent surfaces which tend to be problematic in the processing of digital photogrammetric models. It has several unique textural and geometric features for different processing software to analyze and recognize for reconstruction in the virtual space. This experiment seeks to evaluate the differences between the Agisoft Photoscan and RealityCapture, using the case study of the aryballos inv. no. 68 from this collection of ancient artifacts with data captured in optimal conditions.

2   Methods

The programs were tested using images captured in an ideal light environment and using a stable set of conditions and settings in order to determine more specifically what types of differences the programs would produce in the resulting digital model. Using a light box, tripod, and the same camera settings, the differences in the textures and meshes of the digital models and the user experience could be more accurately determined without having the experience differ based upon the specific model.

2.1   Data Acquisition

The images were captured using a Nikon D3400 camera with a focal length of 50 mm lens which sat atop a tripod for each set of images at three specific heights. Each image was taken at 6000 pixels by 4000 pixels with a dpi of 300 as a JPEG. The F-stop of f/7.1, 1/60 s exposure time, and an ISO speed of 200. The contrast settings were normal, as well as the saturation and sharpness. The exposure and white balance were set to manual. The colors were calibrated using an auto grey-balance card and color checker card was placed on the turn table near the object so that it was present in most of the images. This color-checker card also contains a scale bar which was used for scaling later in order to provide an accurately sized model. Since the images were taken in a light box, no flash was necessary.

The light box that was an AmazonBasics Portable Photos Studio which is 25 in. by 30 in. by 25 in. and lights the object inside on all sides. A flap closes in the front with a camera-sized opening at three different heights for better lighting control and was used during data capture. Each position was captured at the three heights, using a tripod for the camera to produce stable, consistent images, the turntable was set to stop 24 times for each rotation at each height and at each of two artifact orientations in order to capture all sides of the artifact, including the underside.

Inside the light box, there is a Bluetooth enabled turn table that can be controlled by a smartphone. IDEx used the foldio360 app which connected not only to the turn table but also to the camera using this same software. The app allows individuals to control the number of stops during the rotation which subsequently determines the number of images. Manual control of the turn table is also possible via this app. However, this manual functionality was not used during data acquisition in order to create a standardized and controlled set of images.

2.2 Data Processing

After data capture was completed, the images were brought into Agisoft Photoscan Professional (version 1.4.4) and RealityCapture (version CLI 2018). The processing occurred at separate times on the same machine. There were no other programs running during the processing. Each step in the processing was run three separate times for each program to determine consistency and accuracy in results and processing times. Prior to each run a different save file was used to process the images to minimize risk of the algorithm remembering or reprocessing completed steps. It is of importance to note that the author has the same level of experience using each program.

The data in Photoscan was run in two separate chunks for each object orientation. The standard Photoscan workflow was run using default settings on all processed unless otherwise stated. Photo alignment quality was set to high due to the small nature of the object. The dense cloud was also set to high with aggressive depth filtering. The two chunks were then manually cleaned of the support material before attempting automatic alignment. After alignment, the chunks were merged and meshed at high quality. The mesh was inspected for holes and quality prior to texturing. Upon texturing, the model was checked for accuracy, with images being manually selected or unselected where texture was inaccurate. Upon completion of processing, the model was scaled using the scale bars which were present during data capture and then exported as an OBJ with a 4k texture output (Fig. 2).

Fig. 2. Screenshots of the various processing steps of the aryballos inv. no. 68 in Photoscan. (1a, 1b) Sparse cloud resulting from the align images function, with two different chunks processed for the two artifact positions. (2a) Dense cloud of the chunk featured in 1b. (2b) Aligned dense clouds from the two chunks featured in 1a and 1b with support material manually removed. (3) Untextured mesh from the build mesh process. (4) Final textured mesh after fixing the bad textures.

For RealityCapture, images were imported into the same block as separate blocks are not possible. Align images was run on default settings. Manual selection of control points was required to accurately align the images from both artifact orientations. Upon successful alignment, calculate model was run, which functions as the dense cloud and meshing functions of Photoscan. The resulting model was then manually cleaned in the RealityCapture software using the selection tools. Since the model initially contained more than five million triangles, the model was simplified to allow for a model small enough in file size to be easily disseminated on Sketchfab. This choice of five million triangles was decided upon since quality of the mesh does not visibly change after the decimation process and since this usually results in an exported model at a manageable file size. Upon simplification, the model was colorized and texturized. The resulting model was then exported as an OBJ using the mesh function for dissemination and study in other platforms (Fig. 3).

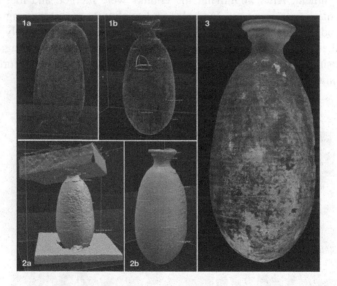

Fig. 3. Screenshots of the various processing steps of The aryballos inv. no. 68 in RealityCapture. (1a) Sparse cloud resulting from the align images function, showing initial misalignment from the automatic align images. (1b) Sparse cloud resulting from the align images function after manual selection of points to align images correctly. (2a) Initial mesh resulting from the calculate model function with support material prior to manual cleaning. (2b) Mesh resulting from the calculate model function with support material removed manually. (3) Final textured mesh after the colorize and texturize functions were completed.

3 Results

For The aryballos inv. no. 68, 169 images were captured in two artifact positions at three camera angles. The images were brought into the three different processing programs. Overall, RealityCapture was the faster than Photoscan (Fig. 4).

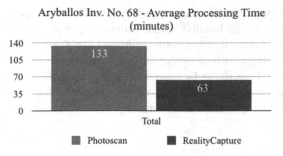

Fig. 4. Bar graph showing the total average processing time in Photoscan and RealityCapture.

Photoscan took an average total processing time of 133 min. The data processing time was inconsistent in the for the same steps of reconstruction of building a dense cloud, building the mesh, and building the texture (Table 1, Fig. 5). Manual processing took about 22 min, with the separate Photoscan chunks having to be manually aligned as automatic alignment failed. For the most part, the processing time for each step remained fairly consistent, with the exception of the build dense cloud function during which the first run yielded significantly shorter processing time than runs two and three. Eighty-three percent of that time was spent on automatic processes and 17 percent of that time—23 min —was from manual processes (Fig. 7, Table 3).

Table 1. Time and total average time for each step in all three runs completed in Photoscan.

Photoscan processing times (minutes)

	Run 1	Run 2	Run 3	Average
Image input	1	1	1	1
Image alignment	8	8	8	8
Build dense cloud	32	150	110	97
Align and merge chunks	20	20	20	20
Build mesh	2	2	2	2
Build texture	1	1	1	1
Manually fix texture and re-texture	3	3	3	3
Total	68	186	146	133

For RealityCapture, the total processing time took an average of 63 min (Table 2, Fig. 6). Reconstruction took an average of six minutes which consists of the build dense cloud and build mesh processes in Photoscan. Around 40 min were spent manually aligning the images using control points since the processes failed at automatic alignment, focusing on the support material alignment rather than the artifact itself. Manual cleaning of the model took less time than for the Photoscan process since many of the outlier points were removed from the model automatically and the cleaning was able to be completed in RealityCapture without exporting and manually editing in a different software. Again, RealityCapture remained fairly consistent in the processing times of each of the steps with an outlier in the reconstruction during the first run. The longer reconstruction time in the first run seems to be an outlier in the RealityCapture results. Manual processing took 53 min, or 79 percent of the total processing time while the remaining 21 percent was automatic processing (Fig. 7, Table 3).

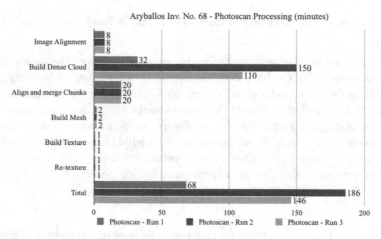

Fig. 5. Bar graph showing the results for each run and step in Photoscan.

Table 2. Time and total average time for each step in all three runs completed in RealityCapture.

RealityCapture processing times (minutes)				
	Run 1	Run 2	Run 3	Average
Image input	1	1	1	1
Image alignment	1	1	1	1
Manual image alignment	40	40	40	40
Reconstruction (build dense cloud, mesh)	13	3	3	6
Manual cleaning	10	10	10	10
Colorize and texturize (build texture)	4	5	5	5
Total	69	60	60	63

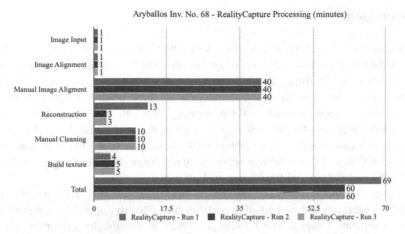

Fig. 6. Bar graph showing the results for each run and step in RealityCapture.

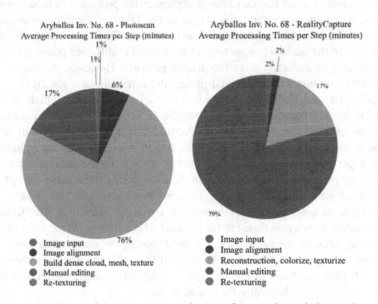

Fig. 7. Average amount of time spent on each step of processing relative to the other steps. Average tota processing time for Photoscan - 132 min; RealityCapture - 63 min.

Table 3. Average processing time for each step in Photoscan and RealityCapture.

	Photoscan	RealityCapture
Image input	1	1
Image alignment	8	1
Build dense cloud, mesh, texture	100	11
Manual editing	22	50
Re-texturing	1	0
Total	132	63

4   Discussion

While these results suggest, at a surface level, that RealityCapture is the most successful software of the two software, other factors must be considered and weighed in this evaluation. Aside from the obvious factor of cost, there are a few qualitative differences in the resulting models and functions of these programs which need to be discussed in this case of small-scale processing. Though Photoscan has the most reliable photo alignment for small-scale digitization, it does take the longest to process the data. In this case study, RealityCapture took the shortest time to process this model, though the majority of that time was spent manually connecting the images—triple that of the time spent on manual processing in Photoscan.

Photoscan provides a greater amount of control to the user and, in this study, yielded the lowest amount of manual processing time. RealityCapture lack the ability to process in separate chunks, like Photoscan, which is specifically important for capturing the underside of artifacts. As per the results of this specific case study, and in looking at the larger Virtual Karam Collection project, the problems in misalignment of images arise when the algorithm tries to align the table or surface underneath the artifact. This means that if the photos are not automatically aligned properly the first time, especially in the cases when an artifact is covered in different positions, a person must take the time to manually align the images properly. However, depending on the application and data quality, the manual processing time can vary greatly.

RealityCapture and Photoscan both offer manual editing tools which allows for researchers to simply purchase a single program in order to be able to provide the greatest quality results for dissemination. Additionally, the ability to edit both the texture and meshes within the RealityCapture and Photoscan programs is helpful for digitization experts and researchers in both saving time during the automatic processing and when using poor quality data or legacy data, suggesting that these two programs provide a greater versatility in producing models of any size with any data.

On the topic of cost, all of these programs require a license to use, though the license for Photoscan is a one-time fee for the user who will also, at the time of writing this, receive updates for newer versions without having to purchase a new license. RealityCapture is expensive for longer licenses of the software, but for a three-month license (which provides most of the features that digital heritage researchers require) this software creates a high-quality mesh and texture.

5   Conclusion

Photogrammetry is valuable for uses in cultural heritage applications, not only for accessibility via 3D modeling but also in creating archaeological documentation which would otherwise take significantly longer using analogue methods. Since a large amount of software have been created for the purposes of digital photogrammetric processing, the need to critically evaluate the strengths and weaknesses of each software is necessary.

Photoscan's ability to include all types of data as well as its versatility, reliability, and repeatability of its process has been proven many times in the literature. Its pervasiveness in cultural heritage digitization is not to be ignored. Photoscan provides a large amount of control during the processing of digital models and, with ideal data, has the shortest amount of manual processing time as presented in this case study.

As for RealityCapture, there is a distinct lack of literature about the program. Future research regarding RealityCapture is required. As for this case study, the automatic alignment algorithm did not successfully align the images in any of the three runs. In other projects on which the author has worked, RealityCapture has successfully aligned individual artifacts which were captured in different orientations, though the images used for these successful models were not taken in a lightbox or using a turn-table. In regard to this case study, the manual alignment of images was time consuming and ultimately resulted in almost the entirety of the processing being manual.

To conclude, in choosing a commercially available software, purpose is key. For the most part, the data suggests that the fastest and easiest—so long as it works the first time—is RealityCapture. For those instances where only a short term license is necessary and a simple interface is preferred, RealityCapture presents itself to be a valuable option, especially in cases where there is only one position of an artifact or site being captured, like in landscapes. Photoscan provides a greater amount of control especially in small scale practice. For long term users of digital photogrammetry, Photoscan is a relatively inexpensive option. The control over each step and its outcome before moving on allows users to engage in examination of the model without spending significant processing and time resources.

The creation of new software and iterations of software for digital photogrammetry is constant, with changes, improvements, and new uses. Constant evaluation and re-evaluation of these programs is required to keep up with the best and most current digital photogrammetry practices. Additionally, this case study focuses on only two of the most prominent digital photogrammetric desktop processing applications which are both European. Future research will evaluate these programs in comparison to American software solutions in digital photogrammetry.

Acknowledgements. The author would like to thank Davide Tanasi and Stephan Hassam for his help in editing and polishing this paper and appreciates the reviewers and many individuals who provided valuable comments, edits, and discussions that made this possible.

References

1. Zarnowski, A., Banaszek, A., Banaszek, S.: Application of technical measures and software in constructing photorealistic 3D models of historical building using ground-based and aerial (UAV) digital images. Rep. Geod. Geoinformatics **99**, 54 (2015). https://doi.org/10.2478/rgg-2015-0012
2. Barbasiewicz, A., Widerski, T., Karol, D.: The analysis of the accuracy of spatial models using photogrammetric software: Agisoft Photoscan and Pix4D. In: E3S Web Conferences, vol. 26, p. 00012 (2018). https://doi.org/10.1051/e3sconf/20182600012
3. Vacca, G., Furfaro, G., Dessì, A.: The use of the UAS images for building 3D model generation. Int. Arch. Photogramm. Remote Sens. Spatial Inf. Sci. **XLII-4/W8**, 217–223 (2018). https://doi.org/10.5194/isprs-archives-xlii-4-w8-217-2018

4. Dostal, C., Yamafune, K.: Photogrammetric texture mapping: a method for increasing the fidelity of 3D models of cultural heritage materials. J. Archaeol. Sci.: Rep. **18**, 430–436 (2018). https://doi.org/10.1016/j.jasrep.2018.01.024

5. Li, X., Chen, Z., Zhang, L., Jia, D.: Construction and accuracy test of a 3D model of non-metric camera images using Agisoft PhotoScan. Procedia Environ. Sci. **36**, 184–190 (2016). https://doi.org/10.1016/j.proenv.2016.09.031

6. Smith, M.W., Carrivick, J.L., Quincey, D.J.: Structure from motion photogrammetry in physical geography. Prog. Phys. Geogr. **40**(2), 247–275 (2016). https://doi.org/10.1177/0309133315615805

7. Jaud, M., Passot, S., Le Bivic, R., Delacourt, C., Grandjean, P., Le Dantec, N.: Assessing the accuracy of high resolution digital surface models computed by PhotoScan® and MicMac® in sub-optimal survey conditions. Remote Sens. **8**(6), 465 (2016). https://doi.org/10.3390/rs8060465

8. Pyka, K.: Comparison of quality of metric photos relative orientation in Micmac and PhotoScan. In: 2017 Baltic Geodetic Congress, BGC Geomatics. IEEE (2017)

9. Verhoeven, G.: Taking computer vision aloft – archaeological three-dimensional reconstructions from aerial photographs with photoscan. Archaeol. Prospect. **18**(1), 67–73 (2011). https://doi.org/10.1002/arp.399

10. Colomina, I., Molina, P.: Unmanned aerial systems for photogrammetry and remote sensing: a review. ISPRS J. Photogramm. Remote Sens. **92**, 79–97 (2014). https://doi.org/10.1016/j.isprsjprs.2014.02.013

11. Thomas, H., Kennedy, M.A.: A new methodology for accurate digital planning of archaeological sites without the aid of surveying equipment. J. Archaeol. Sci.: Rep. **10**, 887–892 (2016). https://doi.org/10.1016/j.jasrep.2016.06.006

12. Alidoost, F., Arefi, H.: Comparison of UAS-based photogrammetry software for 3D point cloud generation: a survey over a historical site. ISPRS Ann. Photogramm. Remote Sens. Spatial Inf. Sci. **IV-4/W4**, 55–61 (2017). https://doi.org/10.5194/isprs-annals-iv-4-w4-55-2017

13. Georgopoulos, A., Oikonomou, Ch., Adamopoulos, E., Stathopoulou, E. K.: Evaluating unmanned aerial platfroms for cultural heritage large scale mapping. Int. Arch. Photogramm. Remote Sens. Spatial Inf. Sci. **XLI-B5**, 355–362 (2016). https://doi.org/10.5194/isprsarchives-xli-b5-355-2016

14. Hendrickx, H., et al.: The reproducibility of SfM algorithms to produce detailed digital surface models: the example of PhotoScan applied to a high-alpine rock glacier. Remote Sens. Lett. **10**(1), 11–20 (2019). https://doi.org/10.1080/2150704X.2018.1519641

15. Tanasi, D., Hassam, S.N., Kingsland, K.: Learning through objects: 3D digital imaging and 3D printing for public outreach in archaeology. In: Proceedings of Visual Heritage 2018, Conference on Cultural Heritage and New Technologies (CHNT), 23. IEEE (2018)

Segmentation of Multi-temporal UV-Induced Fluorescence Images of Historical Violins

Piercarlo Dondi[1,2](✉) (iD), Luca Lombardi[3] (iD), Marco Malagodi[1,4] (iD),
and Maurizio Licchelli[1,5] (iD)

[1] CISRiC - Arvedi Laboratory of Non-Invasive Diagnostics, University of Pavia,
Via Bell'Aspa 3, 26100 Cremona, Italy
{piercarlo.dondi,marco.malagodi,maurizio.licchelli}@unipv.it
[2] Department of Civil Engineering and Architecture, University of Pavia,
Via Ferrata 3, 27100 Pavia, Italy
[3] Department of Electrical, Computer and Biomedical Engineering,
University of Pavia, via Ferrata 5, 27100 Pavia, Italy
luca.lombardi@unipv.it
[4] Department of Musicology and Cultural Heritage, University of Pavia,
Corso Garibaldi 178, 26100 Cremona, Italy
[5] Department of Chemistry, University of Pavia, via Taramelli 12, 27100 Pavia, Italy

Abstract. Monitoring the state of conservation of a historical violin is a difficult task. Multiple restorations during centuries have created a very complex and stratified surface, hard to correctly interpret. Moreover, the reflectance of the varnishes and the rounded morphology of the violins can easily produce noise, that can be confused for a real alteration. To properly compare multi-temporal images of the same instrument a robust segmentation is needed. To reach this goal we adopted a genetic algorithm to evolve in this direction our previous segmentation method based on HSV histogram quantization. As test set we used images of two important violins held in "Museo del Violino" in Cremona (Italy), periodically acquired during a six-month period, and images of a sample violin altered in laboratory to reproduce a long-term evolution.

Keywords: Segmentation · Genetic algorithm ·
UV induced fluorescence · Cultural Heritage · Historical violins

1 Introduction

Scientific analysis of artworks is a complex task that involves knowledge of different fields, such as materials science, chemistry or physics [12]. Computer science has an active role too, in particular image processing proved to be very helpful for researchers and restorers [20]. Notable examples involve the identification of

This work was partially granted by "Fondazione Arvedi-Buschini" of Cremona, Italy.

cracks in paintings [6,15], damage detection [4], image enhancement [13], authentication [16] and even artwork synthesis by deep learning [22].

In this paper we focus on a unique kind of artworks: historical violins. Their main difference respect to other more "traditional" pieces of art, such as painting or statues, is that historical musical instruments are both preserved in museums and played (even today), leading to a greater risk of damages and mechanical wear. Moreover, the multiple restorations occurred during centuries to maintain the instruments in use have created a very complex and stratified surface, hard to interpret. Several analytical techniques are commonly employed for analyzing these musical instruments such as stereomicroscopy, colorimetry, X-ray fluorescence (XRF) or Fourier transform infrared (FTIR) spectroscopy [3,11,18]. Among them, UV-induced fluoresce (UVF or UVIFL) photography is particularly effective for a preliminary examination, since it can highlight details of a violin surface not perceivable with visible light [2].

We previously analyzed UVIFL images of seven important violins made by Antonio Stradivari between 17th and 18th century, to point out the distribution of varnishes and materials on their entire surface [7]. Now we are interested in a more specific task, namely a multi-temporal study of the areas that are more subject to wear. Our goal is to provide researchers and restorers with a tool useful for the so-called preventive conservation, i.e. the constant monitoring of the state of conservation of an artwork to minimize the interventions on it [1].

This kind of monitoring on a historical violin presents various complexities. First of all, unlike searching areas with an established wear, that have precise chromatic characteristics [8], in this case we want to identify as fast as possible the beginning of a new alteration that can occur on any part of the surface both intact and ruined. Thus, we have no previous knowledge about the type of variation or a reference ground truth. Secondly, the acquisition is affected by various kinds of noise that cannot be completely avoided, such as wrong reflections due to the rounded morphology of the instrument and the high reflectance of the varnishes, or slightly variations in the positions of the object or of the lamps between different sessions (violins cannot be rigidly fixed to avoid damages). These systematic errors do not affect too much a global analysis of the entire surface, but they become critical when we focus only on specific areas to detect very small variations. The ideal solution would be a constant monitoring with various analytical and spectroscopic techniques to have an accurate mapping of the regions on interest. Unfortunately, this approach is very time consuming, limiting the number of instruments that can be checked at the same time. A complete verification with multiple techniques, to confirm the presence of an alteration, should be done only on the most likely altered areas.

Our idea is to exploit UVIFL images to identify meaningful regions of interest and then decide where and when apply further analyses. For this purpose, we need a segmentation very robust to environmental noise. Thus, comparing "stable" segmented images of the same instrument taken at distance of time only meaningful differences remain (minimization of the false positives). To reach this goal, we apply a genetic algorithm approach to evolve in this direction our previous method based on HSV histogram quantization [7].

The obtained method was tested on UVIFL images of two important violins, "Vesuvio" (1727) made by Antonio Stradivari and "Carlo IX" (c. 1566) made by Andrea Amati (previously analyzed during a six-month period using multiple non-invasive analytical techniques [10]) and images of a sample instrument artificially altered in laboratory. We created a publicly available dataset with the collected data[1].

The paper is structured as follow: Sect. 2 describes the basic principles of UVIFL photography and our dataset; Sect. 3 summarizes the main characteristics of the previous segmentation method and then describes the proposed evolution; Sect. 4 shows the achieved results; finally, Sect. 5 draws the conclusions and proposes the next steps.

2   UVIFL Photography and Dataset Specification

UVIFL photography is a non-invasive analytical technique based on the properties of some materials which, when excited by ultraviolet lights, emit radiations with longer wavelengths than those of the exciting source. Basically, when these materials are illuminated with a light in the UV-A range (315 400 nm), like a Wood's Lamp, they "produce" characteristic fluorescence colors in the visible light range (400–700 nm) [21]. Varnishes and substances used for restorations are generally sensible to UV-A light, thus UVIFL photography is very effective in Cultural Heritage studies to highlight meaningful features of the surface of an artwork [12]. In particular, in the case of historical musical instrument, UVIFL images are used to decide where to apply more precise but slower diagnostic techniques, like XRF or FTIR [19].

As said in the introduction, we used as test set images of a previous study [10]. This monitoring program investigated the back plates of the two violins (Fig. 1), focusing on the top (treble side, C1 and V1) and on the bottom (bass side, C2 and V2) areas. These two regions are more subject to alterations due to sweat and mechanical wear since always in direct contact with the musician when s/he plays the instrument. The two violins were selected based on their availability and frequency of use during the monitored period: one rarely played ("Carlo IX") and the other frequently played ("Vesuvio"). The acquisition protocol followed the specification defined in our previous works [7,9]. More precisely UVIFL photos were taken with a Nikon D4 full-frame digital camera with a 50 mm f/1.4 Nikkor objective, 30 s exposure time, aperture f/8, ISO 400. Two wood lamp tubes (Philips TL-D 36 W BBL IPP low-pressure Hg tubes, 40 W, emission peak ∼365 nm) provided a uniform UV-A lighting. Images were acquired at regular intervals for six months for a total of three sessions. We took both pictures of the entire back plates and macros of the two areas of interest (three for each area in each session) to be able to detect small alterations on the surface. To increase the dataset, we also took pictures of a sample violin (SV01)

---

[1] https://vision.unipv.it/research/UVIFL-Dataset/.

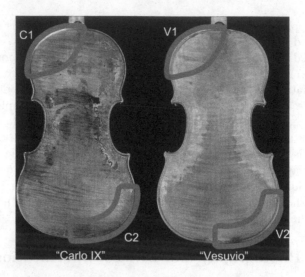

Fig. 1. Monitored areas [10] of back plates of Andrea Amati "Carlo IX" (c. 1566) and Antonio Stradivari "Vesuvio" (1727).

artificially altered in laboratory. We focused on the bottom part of the back plate, starting from a region already ruined and we slowly increased the wear moving toward the intact varnish. To simulate the effect of sweat and mechanical wear produced by a musician, we scrubbed the surface with a cloth wet with alcohol. The process was repeated 20 times to reproduce a long-term evolution. We slightly moved violin and lamps between the various sessions to simulate random environmental variations.

3   Segmentation Algorithm

3.1   Original Implementation

Our previous classification approaches [7,9] focused on highlighting the distribution of the main fluorescence colors of the entire surface of an instrument, with the goal to speed-up and make more efficient the standard examination of UVIFL imagery. Since the surface of each violin can be considered unique, due to the combination of different varnishes and different restorations, we cannot have a reference ground truth for every possible condition. For this reason, to group together similar fluorescence colors in a way that can be coherent for each instrument, we based our classification method on the physical principles of UV fluorescence. We designed a histogram quantization method that operates in HSV color space, where each channel has a different weight in function of its behavior tested experimentally. More precisely, Hue channel was divided in 12 bins, both Saturation and Value channels in 3 bins, with all ranges equally spaced, for a total of 108 possible classes. This configuration was chosen as a compromise between the need to discriminate different fluorescence colors and the need to group together similar regions. A pixel p belongs to a class C if its hue (H_p), saturation (S_p) and value (V_p) are inside the correspondent ranges of C (Eq. 1).

$$\{H_p \in C_H, S_p \in C_S, V_p \in C_V\} \rightarrow \{p \in C\} \tag{1}$$

The algorithm proved to be robust to environmental changes such as small variations in the lamps' angle of incidence or in the violin positions between different acquisition sessions. However, this property is valid only if we consider the entire surface of the violin. High resolution images of details, fundamental to detect small initial alterations, are inevitably more sensible to environmental errors.

3.2 Genetic Algorithm Implementation

Our main problem in finding an optimal solution is the limited amount of data: the acquisition of multi-temporal images of historical violins required several months to be significant and a continuous access for tests is granted only for few instruments. We have the artificially created sequence, but we want to verify if it is possible to train our method only with the "real" data. Since we have too few images to properly apply a deep-learning approach we chose genetic algorithms (GA), that can work efficiently even with a limited amount of data and are widely used in literature for image classification and segmentation [5,14]. The main steps of a GA are summarized in Algorithm 1.

Algorithm 1. Genetic Algorithm

1: Generate the initial population (P_0)
2: **while** stop condition is false **do**
    a) compute the fitness function (f) for the current population
    b) select the fittest individuals (P_f) as parents
    c) create new offspring (O_n) trough crossover of P_f
    d) apply mutation to O_n
    e) generate the new population P_n ($P_n = best(P_f) + O_n$)
3: Choose the fittest solution among the last P_n

We extracted from our previous method the parameters that we want to evolve to produce a more robust segmentation, and those that we want to maintain because more strictly related to the properties of UVIFL photography:

- Hue ranges are still equally spaced, but the number of bins (H_{range}) can change;
- Saturation bins are still 3, but they are no more equally spaced (S_{low} and S_{high} are respectively the upper and lower thresholds between bins);
- Value bins are still 3, but they are no more equally spaced (V_{low} and V_{high} are respectively the upper and lower thresholds between bins).

The five parameters (H_{range}, S_{low}, S_{high}, V_{low} and V_{high}) became the genes of our GA. As usual, in the initial population (P_0) genes values were randomly chosen, but we set the following constraints to avoid degenerated cases (such as a large unique range): $4 \leq H_{ranges} \leq 30$; $S_{low} < S_{high}$; $V_{low} < V_{high}$.

Choosing a good fitness function (f) is the most critical part in a GA. In our case we want to check if the current set of parameters produces a similar segmentation for all the images in the training data set (i.e. minimize the environmental noise). Thus, we performed a histogram comparison among the obtained segmentations using as index of similarity the alternative formulation of Pearson's χ^2 test (Eq. 2) put forward by Puzicha et al. [17]. The closer the value of the distance d is to zero, the greater the similarity between two histograms (H_1 and H_2). As a consequence, for each individual in the population, lower the d, higher the f.

$$d(H_1, H_2) = 2 \sum_i \frac{(H_1(i) - H_2(i))^2}{H_1(i) + H_2(i)} \tag{2}$$

During the selection phase, the fittest individuals (P_f) are identified (half of the population in this case) as parent for breading. Couple of chosen parents generate a new individual mixing their genes with crossover. Since in our case the genes are not all independent from each other, the crossover point/s cannot be chosen randomly as usually happens in GA. We fixed two crossover points one after H_{ranges} and one after S_{high}. In this way the new offspring always receive from the parents reasonable couples of genes.

Finally, mutation is applied to the offspring (O_n) to guarantee the diversity in the population. Since we have only 5 genes we changed at most one (randomly chosen) in each new individual applying a random variation in the range $[-3, +3]$. The new generation (P_n) is then created merging the fittest individuals of the previous generation (we applied elitism, thus only the best 20% passed) with the generated offspring.

For training we used the multi-temporal images of "Carlo IX". We know from the previous monitoring [10] that this violin had no alterations during the six-month period, thus variations in UVIFL images are only due to changes in environmental conditions that we want to manage. Training images were divided in three groups accordingly with the regions framed: the entire back plate, the top left (C1) and the bottom right (C2) areas. We excluded from training one image for each session of area C2 to be used later during tests. We run the procedure separately on the three subsets for 10 generations with a population large 20. Since we had no reference ground truth towards which to converge, the stop conditions were (i) reaching the maximum number of generations or (ii) the absence of changes in population for more than two iterations. At the end of the process we found three different solutions that were slightly different among each other, optimal only for the specific case. This result was expected because the input data were few. Thus, we took as a valid global solution the "intersection" among them, namely not the solution with the best fitness but a valid solution that appeared in all three cases with minimum difference in parameters:

$$H_{ranges} = 14; S_{low} = 45; S_{high} = 55; V_{low} = 16; V_{high} = 91.$$

It can be noticed that value H_{ranges} is closed to the original one (12), instead thresholds for Saturation and Value changed much more and with an opposite behavior: Saturation works better with a narrow central bin while the contrary for Value.

4 Results

We compared the previous and current segmentation on all the remaining multi-temporal image sequences.

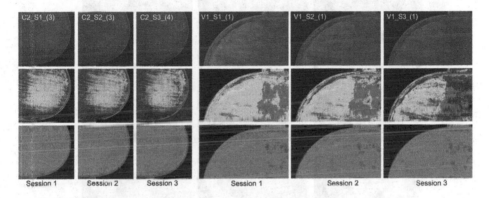

Fig. 2. Segmentation of areas with no alteration (C2 on the left and V1 on the right): original images with correspondent dataset IDs (first row); previous segmentation [7] (second row); current one (third row).

Firstly, we analyzed areas C2 and V1 where no meaningful alteration occurred during the sixth-month monitoring period [10] and thus eventual variations in the images are only due to environmental noise. In both cases the new approach outperforms the previous one producing a nearly identical segmentation for all three sessions (Fig. 2). This is particularly evident by comparing previous and current outcome in session 3 for area V1. The new method was also able to partially handle a large wrong reflection in area C2 session 3. Generally, images with so large reflections are discarded during the acquisition step, since the noise is evident even by naked eye, we used it in this case only for test purposes.

As similarity metric we chose the χ^2 test (Eq. 2) comparing the segmentation for session 1 (our reference initial state) with those for session 2 and 3 respectively (Table 1). As expected χ^2 values slow down with the new approach and remain stable between sessions, while with the old one change significantly. The slight increase in session 3 for area C2 is only due to the presence of the large reflection.

More interesting is the case of area V2 (Fig. 3) that suffered slight alterations between the three sessions (focused in the region inside the red rectangle). Comparing the two segmentations we can notice that alterations are more visible with

88   P. Dondi et al.

Table 1. Similarity measure (χ^2) among sessions for "Carlo IX" and "Vesuvio"

Area	S1–S2		S1–S3	
	Old	New	Old	New
C2	0.29	0.14	4.71	0.32
V1	0.26	0.01	1.59	0.01
V2	0.97	0.23	0.43	0.21

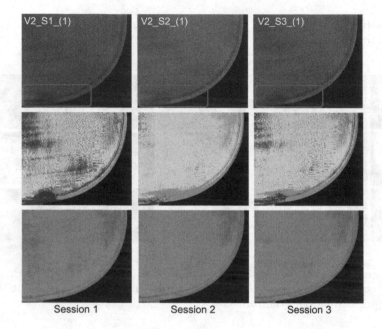

Fig. 3. Segmentation of area V2: sample images of the three sessions (first row), red circles highlight regions with slight alterations between sessions; previous segmentation [7] (second row); current one (third row). (Color figure online)

the previous method (second row) respect to the new one (third row). However, wrong and right variations have the same "weight" with the old method, while with the new one we achieved a more uniform segmentation less prone to errors. The quality of the result can be appreciated performing the weighted difference (Eq. 3) between the first and the third session in the two cases.

$$diff(s1, s3) = \begin{cases} 255 & if\ |s1 - s3| \geq th \\ 0 & if\ |s1 - s3| < th \end{cases} \tag{3}$$

We considered only the greatest differences ($th = 240$) for a better visualization and for excluding the effect of small misalignments among pictures. True Positives (TP) are highlighted in green and False Positives (FP) in red (Fig. 4). The outcomes clearly show that old approach is very sensitive producing a large

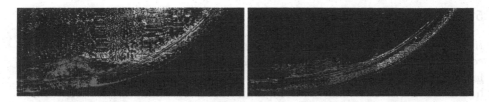

Fig. 4. Weighted difference between segmentations of Sessions 1 and 3 for V2: previous segmentation [7] (left); current one (right). True Positives (real alterations) in green and False Positives (noise) in red. (Color figure online)

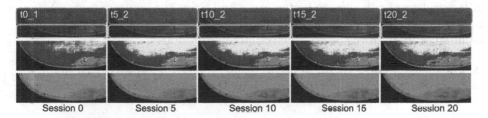

Fig. 5. Segmentation of SV01: sample images of the various sessions (first row), not altered areas highlighted in green, altered areas in red; previous segmentation [7] (second row); current one (third row) (Color figure online)

number of FP randomly diffused on the surface, while the new one is more focus with a significant reduction in the number of FP. This is coherent with our design principles. We want a segmentation able to highlight reasonable regions of interest on which perform further analyses, thus, we are not interested in a perfect detection of all TP pixels (it is enough to roughly highlight the correct areas), but it is crucial to minimize the FP to avoid unnecessary examinations. It also worth notice that the value of χ^2 is low also for V2 (Table 1) since the altered area is very small compared with the remaining of the surface that did not change among sessions.

Finally, we compared the two methods with the artificially created sequence SV01 (Fig. 5) to test the performances on a long time period. In this case we had a full control on the setup: we gradually worn out only the bottom part of the violin (first row, red rectangle), maintaining unaltered the upper region (green rectangle). Violin and lamps were slightly moved among sessions thus there are various kinds of noise in all images. Also in this case the current segmentation prove to be more robust than the previous one: variations are present only in the red region while the green one is stable among sessions (third row). On the contrary, the presence of environmental noise in the green region have a high impact in the older segmentation (second row). In this case the similarity check is not meaningful, since images significantly change among sessions.

90 P. Dondi et al.

5 Conclusions

In this paper we presented a robust segmentation method useful to perform comparison among multi-temporal UVIFL images of historical violins. Tests performed showed promising results: the proposed approach was able to efficiently handle environmental noise without losing meaningful alterations. The multi-temporal UVIFL images used for the experiments were collected in a public available dataset, the first of this kind to the best of the authors' knowledge.

As next step, we plan to increase our dataset with new sample images created in laboratory to simulate, as faithful as possible, various alteration conditions. A larger dataset will allow to better assess and refine the proposed segmentation method. We are also considering the integration with other image processing techniques to improve the early detection of alterations.

Acknowledgements. We would like to thank "Fondazione Museo del Violino Antonio Stradivari", "Friends of Stradivari" and "Cultural District of Violin Making of Cremona" for their collaboration.

References

1. Bradley, S.: Preventive conservation research and practice at the British museum. J. Am. Inst. Conserv. **44**(3), 159–173 (2005). https://doi.org/10.1179/019713605806082248
2. Brandmair, B., Greiner, P.S.: Stradivari varnish: scientific analysis of his finishing technique on selected instruments. Serving Audio (2010)
3. Bruni, S., Guglielmi, V.: Identification of archaeological triterpenic resins by the non-separative techniques FTIR and 13C NMR: the case of Pistacia resin (mastic) in comparison with frankincense. Spectrochim. Acta Part A Mol. Biomol. Spectrosc. **121**, 613–622 (2014). https://doi.org/10.1016/j.saa.2013.10.098
4. Cerra, D., Plank, S., Lysandrou, V., Tian, J.: Cultural heritage sites in danger—towards automatic damage detection from space. Remote Sens. **8**(9), 781 (2016). https://doi.org/10.3390/rs8090781
5. Chouhan, S.S., Kaul, A., Singh, U.P.: Soft computing approaches for image segmentation: a survey. Multimedia Tools Appl. **77**(21), 28483–28537 (2018). https://doi.org/10.1007/s11042-018-6005-6
6. Deborah, H., Richard, N., Hardeberg, J.Y.: Hyperspectral crack detection in paintings. In: 2015 Colour and Visual Computing Symposium (CVCS), pp. 1–6, August 2015. https://doi.org/10.1109/CVCS.2015.7274902
7. Dondi, P., Lombardi, L., Invernizzi, C., Rovetta, T., Malagodi, M., Licchelli, M.: Automatic analysis of UV-induced fluorescence imagery of historical violins. J. Comput. Cult. Herit. **10**(2), 12:1–12:13 (2017). https://doi.org/10.1145/3051472
8. Dondi, P., Lombardi, L., Malagodi, M., Licchelli, M.: Automatic identification of varnish wear on historical instruments: the case of Antonio Stradivari violins. J. Cult. Herit. **22**, 968–973 (2016). https://doi.org/10.1016/j.culher.2016.05.010
9. Dondi, P., Lombardi, L., Malagodi, M., Licchelli, M., Rovetta, T., Invernizzi, C.: An interactive tool for speed up the analysis of UV images of Stradivari violins. In: Murino, V., Puppo, E., Sona, D., Cristani, M., Sansone, C. (eds.) ICIAP 2015. LNCS, vol. 9281, pp. 103–110. Springer, Cham (2015). https://doi.org/10.1007/978-3-319-23222-5_13

10. Fichera, G.V., et al.: Innovative monitoring plan for the preventive conservation of historical musical instruments. Stud. Conserv. **63**(Suppl. 1), 351–354 (2018). https://doi.org/10.1080/00393630.2018.1499853

11. Fiocco, G., et al.: Approaches for detecting madder lake in multi-layered coating systems of historical bowed string instruments. Coatings **8**(5) (2018). https://doi.org/10.3390/coatings8050171

12. Janssens, K., Van Grieken, R.: Non-Destructive Micro Analysis of Cultural Heritage Materials, vol. 42. Elsevier, Amsterdam (2004)

13. Jmal, M., Souidene, W., Attia, R.: Efficient cultural heritage image restoration with nonuniform illumination enhancement. J. Electron. Imaging **26**(1), 1–15 (2017). https://doi.org/10.1117/1.JEI.26.1.011020

14. Paulinas, M., Ušinskas, A.: A survey of genetic algorithms applications for image enhancement and segmentation. Inf. Technol. Control **36**(3), 278–284 (2007)

15. Pizurica, A., et al.: Digital image processing of the Ghent Altarpiece: supporting the painting's study and conservation treatment. IEEE Signal Process. Mag. **32**(4), 112–122 (2015). https://doi.org/10.1109/MSP.2015.2411753

16. Polak, A., et al.: Hyperspectral imaging combined with data classification techniques as an aid for artwork authentication. J. Cultural Herit. **26**, 1–11 (2017). https://doi.org/10.1016/j.culher.2017.01.013

17. Puzicha, J., Hofmann, T., Buhmann, J.M.: Non-parametric similarity measures for unsupervised texture segmentation and image retrieval. In: Proceedings of 1997 IEEE Computer Society Conference on Computer Vision and Pattern Recognition, pp. 267–272, June 1997. https://doi.org/10.1109/CVPR.1997.609331

18. Rovetta, T., et al.: The case of Antonio Stradivari 1718 ex-San Lorenzo violin: history, restorations and conservation perspectives. J. Archaeol. Sci. Rep. **23**, 443–450 (2019). https://doi.org/10.1016/j.jasrep.2018.11.010

19. Rovetta, T., Invernizzi, C., Licchelli, M., Cacciatori, F., Malagodi, M.: The elemental composition of Stradivari's musical instruments: new results through non-invasive EDXRF analysis. X-Ray Spectrom. **47**(2), 159–170 (2018). https://doi.org/10.1002/xrs.2825

20. Stanco, F., Battiato, S., Gallo, G.: Digital Imaging for Cultural Heritage Preservation: Analysis, Restoration, and Reconstruction of Ancient Artworks. CRC Press, Boca Raton (2011)

21. Stuart, B.H.: Analytical Techniques in Materials Conservation. Wiley, Hoboken (2007)

22. Tan, W.R., Chan, C.S., Aguirre, H.E., Tanaka, K.: ArtGAN: artwork synthesis with conditional categorical GANs. In: 2017 IEEE International Conference on Image Processing (ICIP), pp. 3760–3764, September 2017. https://doi.org/10.1109/ICIP.2017.8296985

A Study of English Neologisms Through Large-Scale Probabilistic Indexing of Bentham's Manuscripts

Alejandro H. Toselli[1], Verónica Romero[1], Enrique Vidal[1],
Joan Andreu Sánchez[1(✉)], Louise Seaward[2], and Philip Schofield[2]

[1] PRHLT, Universitat Politècnica de València,
Camí de Vera s/n, 46022 València, Spain
{ahector,vromero,evidal,jandreu}@prhlt.upv.es
[2] Bentham Project, UCL Laws,
4-8 Endsleigh Gardens, London WC1H 0EG, UK
{louise.seaward,p.schofield}@ucl.ac.uk

Abstract. Probabilistic indexes (PI) are obtained from untranscribed handwritten text images by means of recently introduced lexicon-free, query-by-string, probabilistic keyword spotting techniques. PIs have proven to be a powerful tool that allow efficient, free textual searching in very large collections of handwritten historical documents. PIs convey uncertain information about the textual contents of the document images. However, text uncertainty is accurately modeled by the associated lexical probability distributions, which can be conveniently exploited in many applications. As an example of these applications, here we study the dating of a number of English neologisms in the large collection of Bentham's manuscripts, which encompass 90 000 images. The statistical techniques used for neologism dating are theoretically motivated and experiments on this collection are reported. Among other interesting contributions of this study, it provides sound evidence that some commonly assumed neologism introduction dates need to be revised.

Keywords: Handwritten text recognition ·
Historical document collections · Probabilistic indexing and search

1 Introduction

Probabilistic indexes (PIs) are obtained from untranscribed handwritten text images by means of recently introduced lexicon-free, query-by-string, probabilistic keyword spotting techniques [1,5,8,10,14,16]. PIs convey uncertain information about the textual contents of the handwritten document images. However,

Work partially supported by the BBVA Foundation through the 2017–2018 Digital Humanities research grant "Carabela", by Ministerio de Ciencia/AEI/FEDER/EU through the MIRANDA-DocTIUM project (RTI2018-095645-B-C22), and by EU JPICH project "HOME - History Of Medieval Europe" (Spanish PEICTI Ref. PCI2018-093122).

© Springer Nature Switzerland AG 2019
M. Cristani et al. (Eds.): ICIAP 2019 Workshops, LNCS 11808, pp. 92–102, 2019.
https://doi.org/10.1007/978-3-030-30754-7_10

text uncertainty is accurately modeled by the associated lexical probability distributions, which can be conveniently exploited in many applications. It is worth mentioning that probabilistic indexing is different from handwritten text recognition (HTR); while HTR aims at providing adequate transcripts of text images into (single) *sequences* of characters and words, probabilistic indexing do not explicitly care about word order and provides a map of (several) hypotheses of words that are likely written in each geometric position of the text image.

Analysis of historical texts is usually performed with transcripts produced by human experts. Unfortunately this is not feasible for large collections of untranscribed historical documents, and consequently automatic methods have to be designed for tackling this type of analysis. This problem has been researched for printed text [7]. Thus for example, Google Ngram viewer[1] is an important and useful tool for the type of analysis we have mentioned [6]. Figure 1 shows the result of searching the phrase "Queen Elizabeth II". It can be seen that this phrase becomes prominent when Queen Elizabeth became queen in 1952.

Analysis of large collections of historical manuscripts composed of hundreds of thousands of document images can be considered a big-data problem that has just recently started to be explored [1,5]. There have been some attempts

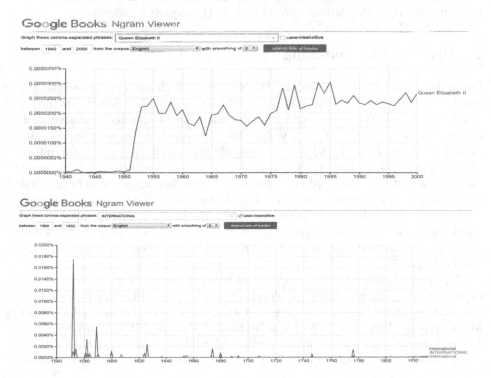

Fig. 1. Plot of the use of strings "Queen Elizabeth II" and "INTERNATIONAL" in the Google Ngram viewer.

---

[1] https://books.google.com/ngrams/info.

to undertake research on handwritten historical manuscripts, but this requires a lot of human effort and is prone to errors. Some effort has been carried out in the Bentham Project in this direction where many neologisms were supposed to have been coined by J. Bentham[2], but tools and techniques like the ones that we introduce in this paper are necessary to help scholars in these tasks.

This paper introduces new techniques to perform linguistic research on large collections of untranscribed historical manuscripts. Concretely, English neologisms that are supposed to have been coined by J. Bentham are researched on the Bentham's manuscripts. Neologisms are words introduced in a language at a given time, like the expression "Queen Elizabeth II" that we mentioned above. Figure 1 also shows the results of the word "INTERNATIONAL" in Google Ngram viewer, a word that was considered to be a J. Bentham's neologism. The techniques used in this paper are based on PIs and probabilistic techniques developed for neologisms dating. These techniques are theoretically motivated and experiments on this collection are reported. Note that the detection of neologisms is a use-case of PIs, but many other linguistic-oriented and information-extraction problems can be similarly considered.

Section 2 summarizes the PIs technology used in this paper, and the formal framework for detecting neologisms from these PIs is described in Sect. 3. Section 4 describes the dataset that is used in the experimental Sect. 5.

2   Probabilistic Indexing

Let x be an image region and c_v the sequence of characters representing a word v. Let R be a binary random variable which models whether (or not) a word v is written in the image x. A probabilistic index is a pruned representation of the distribution $P(R \mid c_v, x)$, where, for each page image, only those pairs (x, c_v) for which $P(R \mid c_v, x)$ is not negligible are stored. In general, the image regions (x) are arbitrary small zones of the images considered, but in most cases of interest they are word-sized zones or "bounding-boxes". A very detailed dissertation on PI concepts and efficient and effective machine learning methods to obtain accurate PIs is compiled in [10]. These methods relay on training optical and language models from a certain amount of transcribed images. Aspects and techniques leading to these concepts and methods can be seen in these papers: [2–5,9,11,12,14,15].

The performance of a PI can be evaluated in terms of its textual search capabilities; i.e., its capability to accurately honor (single) keyword queries. To this end, standard assessment measures such as Average Precision (AP) and Mean Average Precision (mAP) can be used. Values of AP and mAP near to 1.0 indicate very good performances while AP and/or mAP lower than 0.5 are often considered not good enough for practical search and retrieval applications.

---

[2] http://www.ucl.ac.uk/bentham-project/research-tools/neologisms-jeremy-bentham.

3   Neologism Detection Through PI

We define the following stochastic variables for this purpose:

$$X_{i,j} = \{\text{the word } i \text{ appears in year } j\}, \tag{1}$$

$$Y_i = \{\text{number of years before the word } i \text{ appears the first time from a given year}\}. \tag{2}$$

Note that $X_{i,j}$ is a boolean (True, T, or False, F) random variable which can be considered as a boolean OR combination over all events such as: {the word i appears in an image region $\mathbf{x}_j$}, where $\mathbf{x}_j$ is an image region of a document dated in year j. Therefore, following the discussion in [13] $p(X_{i,j} = T)$ can be approximated from the PIs defined in the previous section as follows [10]:

$$p(X_{i,j} = T) \approx \max_{\mathbf{x}_j} P(R \mid \mathbf{c}_i, \mathbf{x}_j) \, .$$

We are considering in expression (2) that the computation is restricted to a given and known period starting in year I and ending in year F. In this way the distribution $p(Y_i)$ is the distribution we are interested in. Note that $Y_i = y$ represents the event in which the word i appears in year $I + y$ and the complementary of $Y_i = y$, which is noted as $\overline{Y}_i = y$, represents the event in which the word i does not appear in year $I + y$. Then $p(Y_i)$ is approximated as:

$$p(Y_i = y) \approx \prod_{k=0}^{y-1} p(\overline{Y}_i = k) p(X_{i,I+y} = T)$$

$$= \prod_{k=0}^{y-1} (1 - p(X_{i,I+k} = T)) p(X_{i,I+y} = T) \tag{3}$$

for $y > 1$ and with $p(Y_i = 0) = p(X_{i,I} = T)$.

The expected behavior of expression (3) is that once the word is spotted with high confidence in one year, the probability of the following years becomes 0.

4   Bentham Papers

The collection used in this paper is based on parts of the so called Bentham Papers, handwritten in English by several writers. The whole digitized collection encompasses 100 000 page images of text authored by the renowned English philosopher and reformer Jeremy Bentham (1748–1832)[3]. It mainly contains writings in English, but also some pages are in French and Latin. Documents handwritten by J. Bentham himself over a period of sixty years, as well as fair copies handwritten by Bentham's secretarial staff, are included.

---

[3] http://www.ucl.ac.uk/Bentham-Project/.

These documents contains many words that are neologisms that have been coined by J. Bentham, but it is difficult to confirm this supposition without analyzing the transcripts. Analyzing the transcripts could, in turn, require a gigantic effort, and therefore we propose to use PIs for making possible this analysis. Among the interesting neologisms we can cite[4]:

- *INTERNATIONAL*: cited in 1780, in "An Introduction to the Principles of Morals and Legislation",
- *MAXIMIZE*: written in 1780–1782 and published in 1945 in "Of the Limits of the Penal Branch of Jurisprudence",
- *MINIMIZE*: cited in 1802, in "Principles of Judicial Procedure, The Works of Jeremy Bentham".

5 Experiments

5.1 Training Dataset

A subset of the Bentham's manuscripts was used to train and evaluate a system based on convolutional and recurrent neural networks (CRNN) for optical and language modeling, which was used to obtain the PI. Table 1 shows the main characteristics of this dataset.

Table 1. Main statistics of the dataset that was used to train the statistical models used to obtain PIs.

Manuscripts:	Train-Val	Test
Pages	846	367
Lines	23 942	12 363
Running words	177 692	89 450
Lexicon	11 510	7 294
Character set size	67	65

5.2 Obtaining Probabilistic Indexes (PI)

Convolutional and recurrent neural networks (CRNN) were used in this paper for optical character modeling. After training, the CRNN computes sequences of character posterior probabilities from a text line image, normalized to 64-pixel height maintaining the aspect ratio. Lexical and linguistic context is explicitly modeled by means of statistical character N-grams, estimated using the training image transcripts and represented as a weighted finite-state transducer. The CRNN output character probabilities are then incorporated to the transducer

---

[4] All possible neologisms is this paper are written in capital letters.

Table 2. Main statistics of Bentham PI used in this paper.

Computed	#Page images/*Indexed*	95 247/*89,911*
	#Spots	197 651 336
	Average #Spots/Page	2 198
Estimated	Running words	25 487 932
	Running words/Page	283
	Average #Spots/Running word	7.8

edges. See [16] for more information about the models, methods and workflow used to obtain the PI for the Bentham dataset.

The performance of the obtained PI was evaluated with the test set images according to the usual metrics generally adopted in the field of keyword spotting. More specifically, all the words in the test-set transcripts were used as query words to compute the retrieval average precision (AP) and mean AP (mAP). The results were $AP = 0.87$ and $mAP = 0.76$ [16]. Table 2 shows final indexing statistics for the Bentham collection. It is important to remark that about 49 000 page images were dated manually and these dated documents were used in the experiments that we describe below. Given the large amount of dated images, we are very confident about the results that are described below.

5.3 Detecting Neologisms

We used the technique described in Sect. 3 for detecting possible neologisms in the Bentham's collection in two steps. The whole list of neologisms is mentioned in the Introduction section (See footnote 2) and is composed of about 250 words. This list is referred as *UCL list* from now on.

Table 3. Some words that were removed from the UCL list according to Google Ngram statistics. Spots is the number of spots according to Google Ngram with a year before the year that is registered in UCL list.

Neologism	Year UCL list	Year Google	Spots
SUMMARINESS	1802	1791	4
SUPPLETIVE	1816	1682	4
CHARACTERIZABLE	1818	1696	6
REPEATABLE	1802	1505	7
FISCALITY	1825	1783	7
MINIMIZATION	1802	1767	9
CODIFY	1800	1631	12
PLURALISM	1818	1515	29

First, Google Ngram was used to remove possible words not coined by J. Bentham as follows. The possible neologisms that appear in the Google Ngram unigrams with a year before the year registered in the UCL list more than k times were considered not neologisms coined by J. Bentham. For example, the word "INTERNATIONAL" was attributed to J. Bentham in year 1780 according to Bentham Project, but Google Ngram shows many results for this word before this year. Inspecting the results provided by Google Ngram Viewer, it was confirmed that there is a text from 1621 with this word. Google Ngram may produce errors. Thus, the first spots for "INTERNATIONAL" were incorrect in Google Ngram. The less spots Google Ngram provides, the higher the possibility of there being incorrect spots. Therefore, all possible neologisms for which the number of spots provided by Google Ngram was above a threshold were discarded as a possible antecedent to J. Bentham's neologisms. The threshold was fixed to 4. In this way the number of potential number of neologisms attributed to J. Bentham decreased to about 150. Table 3 shows some words that were removed from the UCL list. Note that these words may be J. Bentham's neologisms but it would require a large human effort to check them in Google Ngram.

Second, we focused on those words for which the number of spots in Google Ngram was below 4. We applied the technique that is described in Sect. 3 for looking for possible neologisms. Figure 2 plots expression (1) for several words, although the potential neologisms was about 150. These spots were visually checked in the Bentham indexed collection. Note that our main goal was to check if PIs together with expression (1) was useful in analyzing possible J. Bentham's neologisms, not to confirm if a word is or is not a neologism, which would require the checking of other sources.

From the manual inspection we classified the potential neologisms into 5 classes:

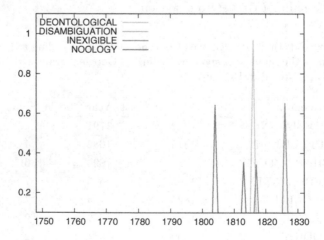

Fig. 2. Probability of several words from the UCL list of appearing the first time in a given year.

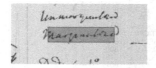

Fig. 3. The word "MARGINALIZED" that was spotted instead of "MARGINALIZE".

1. the words that do not appear in the PIs,
2. the words that appear in the PIs, but were incorrect spots,
3. the words which the PIs predicted some years before than the year in the UCL list,
4. the words which the PIs predicted the same year as the year in the UCL list,
5. the words which the PIs predicted some years later than the year in the UCL list.

Note that the words included in 1 might or might not be J. Bentham's neologisms or not, since they were not located in the PI. The number of these words was 95 word (Appendix A includes these words). We can not say if the PIs made mistakes or not, but given the AP and mAP that we got, we suspect with high confidence that these words were not in the J. Bentham's manuscripts.

The words that can provide more information about the technique described in Sect. 3 are the words from point 2 to 5, since they can inform us if the PI was correct or not in computing the year of words.

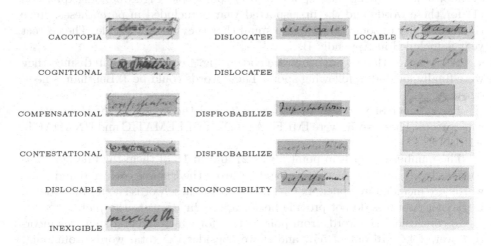

Fig. 4. Words which firsts spots were incorrect.

The words included in point 2 were incorrect spots and the total number was 1. The word was "MARGINALIZE" and the spotted word was "MARGINAL-IZED". Figure 3 shows this spotted word. Note that the word is located in an isolated line and there was not enough context for the language model to amend the error.

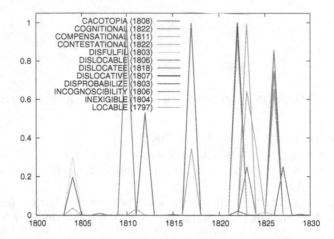

Fig. 5. Expression (1) for the words which the PIs predicted some years before than the year in the UCL list.

The number of words in point 3 was 30 (see these words in Appendix B), and the first spots for **12** of them were incorrect. These words and the incorrect spots are shown in Fig. 4 for illustrating the type of errors that we got with the PI. Checking these spots was feasible since the PIs are accompanied with the image file identifier and it took just a moment to check them. We can see that even for a human being these spots are very confusable. Figure 5 plots expression (1) for these words and the first spotted year is included in parentheses, since the probability of some spots was so small that they are not visible. The correct year is included in Appendix B.

The year for these words that are shown Fig. 4 could be updated since they were finally located in following spots. These words could be J. Bentham's neologisms.

The number of words in point 4 was **3**, and the first spot for these words was correct. These words were IMPERATION, THELEMATIC and UNADAPT-ABILITY.

The number of words in point 5 was 21 and in **18** of them the first spot was correct. In all cases the new year estimated from the PIs was corrected and these words are included in Appendix C. The dates for these words should be updated if the other sources do not provide better approximations to the year.

In conclusion, the words from point 2 to 5 for which the first spot was incorrect were 29% (16 out of 55), and if we consider the total words from point 1 to 5, the total number of words for which the first spot was incorrect were 11% (16 out of 150). So, note that checking 55 words is an affordable work to confirm/update the date for several potential neologisms.

6   Conclusion

This paper introduces Probabilistic Indexing as an effective technique for tackling problems with the analysis of huge volumes of historical handwritten documents. This type of analysis was not conceivable until recent years, but now this is feasible with the technique (or similar) introduced here. Note that with this big data problem, exact solutions are not expected, given the complexity of the historical handwritten documents, and only probabilistic solutions are possible. The high performance results that are obtained with Probabilistic Indexing allow us to be very confident with the obtained results. The technique introduced in this paper opens many other researching possibilities by using Probabilistic Indexing, like, dating documents, classifying documents according to their contents, extracting relevant information, etc. which we expect to explore in the near future.

Appendix A

ABSTRACTIVENESS ADVENTUREFUL ANTEMBLETIC ASSUMINGNESS BICAMERAL BURTHENMENT CONJECTURIST CRYPTODYNAMIC DECKLESS DEONTOLOGIST DISBURDENMENT DISCEPTATORIAL DISINTEGRITY DISMURDERED DISPENSATORIAL DISPROBATIVE EDUCLORATE ETYMOLOGIZATION EUDAIMONOLOGY EUDEMONIC EXALTATIVE EXEMPLIFICATIVE EXEMPTIVE GAEOSITY HERMITISH HOLOGRAPHY HYGIANTIC INCULPATIVE INDEPENDABLE INDISPELLABLE INFIRMATION INFLICTABLE IMPROBABILIZE INSPECTADLE INSTITUTIONALIST INTERPOLATIVE INVALIDSHIP LACONICALNESS MANAGEABILITY MARGINALIZER MARTYRIZER MATHETIC MATHETICO MELIORABILITY METAMOR-PHOTIC MESOLOGY MINUTATION MISAPPELLATION MISAPPREHENSIBLE MISLOCATE MISDECIDE MONEPIC MORPHOSCOPIC MURDERIZED NOOSCOPIC ORISTIC ORNAMENTABILITY PARADOXICALITY PATHEMATIC PAULISM PERJURIOUSNESS PHILOSOPHIZATION PHTHISOZOICS PHYSIURGIC PLAGUE-SOME POIOLOGY POPULICIDE PREDESIGNATE RATIOCINATORY REAUTHENTICATION RECIPROCAL-IZE RECTILINEARITY RIVALIZE SAGESHIP SANCTIONMENT SCRIBBLATORY SOMATALOGICAL STEADI-MENT SUBINTELLECT SUBORNATIVE SUPPLETIVE SWALLOWABLE THERAPEUTIST TRANSCRIPTURAL TRANSLOCATIVE UNAFFORDABLE UNBASTILLED UNBRIDG(E)ABLE UNDESPOTIC UNBURDENSOME-NESS UNCIRCUMLOCUTORY UNCLERGIABLE UNCOGNOSCIBLE UNCOUNTERBALANCED UNDISFUL-FILLED.

Appendix B

ACCUSATORIAL (1823 → 1803), AMBILATERAL (1832 → 1806), CACOTOPIA (1818 → 1816), CODIFIER (1830 → 1805), COGNITIONAL (1827 → 1825), COMPENSATIONAL (1824 → 1821), CONSIGNABLE (1808 → 1798), CONTESTATIONAL (1826 → 1823), DENEGATORY (1823 → 1822), DEONTOLOGICAL (1832 → 1815), DISAF-FIRMATIVE (1832 → 1811), DISAMBIGUATION (1827 → 1810), DISFULFIL (1818 → 1804), DISLOCABLE (1827 → 1821), DISLOCATEE (1827 → 1821), DISLOCATIVE (1827 → 1821), DISPROBABILIZE (1827 → 1811), INEXI-GIBLE (1818 → 1816), INCOGNOSCIBILITY (1824 → 1809), LOCABLE (1827 → 1823), LOCATEE (1827 → 1821), MODIFICAND (1832 → 1813), OMNICOMPETENT (1827 → 1822), PERUSABLE (1829 → 1797), PREHENSOR (1829 → 1824), RESWALLOW (1818 → 1811), RETROACTIVITY (1829 → 1827), SEDUCTIONIST (1817 → 1816), SUBSTANTIVAL (1832 → 1821), UNAVOWABLE (1802 → 1801).

Appendix C

ALLEVIATING (1789 → 1793), CONTRECTATIVE (1786 → 1827), DEMANDATIVE (1820 → 1826), DETERIORA-TIVE (1800 → 1825), DIVESTITIVE (1802 → 1803), HUMILIATIVE (1810 → 1828), IMPERATION (1786 → 1786),

INEXCLUDIBLE (1816 → 1822), INEXCLUSIVELY (1789 → 1827), INTERROGABLE (1802 → 1810), LOCUPLE-
TATIVE (- → 1805), MISEXPRESSIVE (1816 → 1826), NOOLOGY (1811 → 1812), ONERATIVE (1802 → 1824),
ORNABILITY (1811 → 1813), PLACEABLE (1802 → 1806), QUISQUILIOUS (1802 → 1828), SCRIPTITIOUS (1802
→ 1811), SUMMARINESS (1802 → 1828), UNDETECTIBLE (1802 → 1823), UNDILATORY (1802 → 1806).

References

1. Bluche, T., et al.: Preparatory KWS experiments for large-scale indexing of a vast medieval manuscript collection in the HIMANIS project. In: Proceedings of ICDAR, vol. 01, pp. 311–316 (2017)
2. Fischer, A., Frinken, V., Bunke, H., Suen, C.: Improving HMM-based keyword spotting with character language models. In: Proceedings of ICDAR, pp. 506–510, August 2013
3. Fischer, A., Keller, A., Frinken, V., Bunke, H.: Lexicon-free handwritten word spotting using character HMMs. Pattern Recogn. Lett. **33**(7), 934–942 (2012)
4. Frinken, V., Fischer, A., Manmatha, R., Bunke, H.: A novel word spotting method based on recurrent neural networks. IEEE Trans. Pattern Anal. Mach. Intel. **34**(2), 211–224 (2012)
5. Lang, E., Puigcerver, J., Toselli, A.H., Vidal, E.: Probabilistic indexing and search for information extraction on handwritten German Parish records. In: Proceedings of ICFHR, pp. 44–49, August 2018
6. Lin, Y., Michel, J., Lieberman, E., Orwant, J., Brockman, W., Petrov, S.: Syntactic annotations for the Google books NGram corpus. In: Proceedings of ACL, vol. 2, pp. 169–174 (2012)
7. Michel, J., et al.: Quantitative analysis of culture using millions of digitized books. Science **331**(6014), 176–182 (2011)
8. Puigcerver, J., Toselli, A., Vidal, E.: Word-graph and character-lattice combination for KWS in handwritten documents. In: Proceedings of ICFHR, pp. 181–186 (2014)
9. Puigcerver, J., Vidal, E., Toselli, A.H.: Probabilistic interpretation and improvements to the HMM-filler for handwritten keyword spotting. In: Proceedings of ICDAR, pp. 731–735 (2015)
10. Puigcerver, J.: A probabilistic formulation of keyword spotting. Ph.D. thesis, Universitat Politècnica de València (2018)
11. Toselli, A., Puigcerver, J., Vidal, E.: Two methods to improve confidence scores for Lexicon-free word spotting in handwritten text. In: Proceedings of ICFHR, pp. 349–354 (2016)
12. Toselli, A.H., Puigcerver, J., Vidal, E.: Context-aware lattice based filler approach for key word spotting in handwritten documents. In: Proceedings of ICDAR, pp. 736–740, August 2015
13. Toselli, A.H., Vidal, E., Puigcerver, J., Noya-García, E.: Probabilistic multi-word spotting in handwritten text images. Pattern Anal. Appl. **22**(1), 23–32 (2019)
14. Toselli, A.H., Vidal, E., Romero, V., Frinken, V.: HMM word graph based keyword spotting in handwritten document images. Inf. Sci. **370–371**, 497–518 (2016)
15. Toselli, A.H., Vidal, E.: Fast HMM-filler approach for key word spotting in handwritten documents. In: Proceedings of ICDAR (2013)
16. Toselli, A.H., Romero, V., Vidal, E., Sánchez, J.A.: Making two vast historical manuscript collections searchable and extracting meaningful textual features through large-scale probabilistic indexing. In: Proceedings of ICDAR (2019)

Modern vs Diplomatic Transcripts for Historical Handwritten Text Recognition

Verónica Romero[1]([✉]), Alejandro H. Toselli[1], Enrique Vidal[1],
Joan Andreu Sánchez[1], Carlos Alonso[2], and Lourdes Marqués[2]

[1] PRHLT, Universitat Politècnica de València,
Camí de Vera s/n, 46022 València, Spain
{vromero,ahector,evidal,jandreu}@prhlt.upv.es
[2] Instituto Andaluz de Patrimonio Histórico, Centro de Arqueología Subacuática,
Consejería de Cultura, Junta de Andalucía,
Avda. Duque de Nájera, 3, 11002 Cádiz, Spain
{carlos.alonso.v,lourdes.marquez.carmona}@juntadeandalucia.es
http://www.prhlt.upv.es

Abstract. The transcription of handwritten documents is useful to make their contents accessible to the general public. However, so far automatic transcription of historical documents has mostly focused on producing diplomatic transcripts, even if such transcripts are often only understandable by experts. Main difficulties come from the heavy use of extremely abridged and tangled abbreviations and archaic or outdated word forms. Here we study different approaches to train optical models which allow to recognize historic document images containing archaic and abbreviated handwritten text and produce modernized transcripts with expanded abbreviations. Experiments comparing the performance of the different approaches proposed are carried out on a document collection related with Spanish naval commerce during the XV–XIX centuries, which includes extremely difficult handwritten text images.

Keywords: Handwritten text recognition · Historical documents · Modern transcripts

1 Introduction

In the last years, there is an increasing interest to digitally preserve and provide access to handwritten historical documents residing in libraries, museums, and archives. Such documents are a unique public asset, forming the collective and evolving memory of our societies. Many of these historical documents have an

Work partially supported by the BBVA Foundation through the 2017–2018 Digital Humanities research grant "Carabela", by Miniterio de Ciencia/AEI/FEDER/EU through the MIRANDA-DocTIUM project (RTI2018-095645-B-C22), and by EU JPICH project "HOME – History Of Medieval Europe" (Spanish PEICTI Ref. PCI2018-093122).

M. Cristani et al. (Eds.): ICIAP 2019 Workshops, LNCS 11808, pp. 103–114, 2019.
https://doi.org/10.1007/978-3-030-30754-7_11

outstanding cultural value in subjects as diverse as literature, botanic, mathematics, medicine or religion, to name a few.

Unless the information retained in these documents is converted to a digital form, searching for information and accessibility in general is limited if not impossible. A large number of institutions have already undertaken mass digitization of paper documents, and the storage in digital libraries. However, to make these document collections really useful, they need to be transcribed.

So far automatic transcription of historical documents has mostly focused on producing diplomatic transcripts. This kind of transcription records only the characters as they appear on the image, without change or interpretation. With regard to producing automated transcripts, this is a very convenient setting, since this enforces a one-to-one mapping from glyphs depicted in the images to corresponding characters in the transcripts. Clearly, this allows to train optical character models in a rather straightforward way. However, many historical documents are typically replete of extremely abridged and tangled abbreviations and archaic or outdated word forms. Therefore, diplomatic transcripts are often only understandable by experts. In order to make the documents more accessible and their contents more generally usable, they should be transcribed with modern word spelling, expanded abbreviations, amended writing mistakes and modifications and/or additions of punctuation marks.

In this paper, we study several approaches to train optical models which allow to recognize historic document images containing archaic and abbreviated handwritten text and produce modernized transcripts with expanded abbreviations. As mentioned above, the commonly accepted rational so far is that, for adequate optical models training, the transcripts should ideally correspond exactly to the actual characters as observed in the image, even though this would makes it difficult or impossible to obtain modernized transcript. However, in [27] and [2] it has been shown that using modernized transcripts to train the models can lead to achieve useful results. Here, we study this and other approaches that do not use the diplomatic accurate correspondence to generate modernized transcripts.

The rest of the paper is structured as follows. Section 2 describes the main features of the modernized transcripts. Section 3 describes the "Carabela" collection, related with travels and Spanish naval commerce during the XV-XIX centuries, which is used in the study. Then, the handwritten text recognition (HTR) technology, based on *Convolutional-Recurrent Neural Networks* (CRNN) is explained in Sect. 4. The experimental framework and the obtained results are presented in Sects. 5 and 6. The final section concludes the paper, outlining the future directions of research that should be developed.

2   Modernized Transcripts

Main features of modernized transcripts generally include:

- Archaic words forms are replaced with modern spellings,
- Abbreviated words are expanded,
- Writing mistakes are fixed,

Fig. 1. Page examples of the Carabela collection.

– Punctuation marks are modified or added according to present rules.

In many (or most) historical documents, these transformations are typically needed for large percentages of words. In the Carabela collection, considered in this work (see Sect. 3), more than the 25% of the words exhibit (often major) differences between their diplomatic versions and the modernized ones. A similar trend can be observed in other collections, such as the Alcaraz dataset [27], that presents a 26% of discrepancies; the Wiensankturlrich [19] dataset, with a 22%, and the HATEM dataset [21], with a 28%. A particularly notable collection where this problem is specially relevant is the medieval French-Latin "Chancery" collection [2], where it is estimated that about 60% of the Latin words and 20% of the French words are abbreviated.

3   The Carabela Collection

The Carabela collection is composed of manuscripts related with Spanish travels and naval commerce during the XV–XIX centuries. Specifically it encompasses about 150.000 page images of specific interest for underwater archeology, belonging to the *Archivo General de Indias* and the *Archivo Histórico Provincial de Cádiz*. These documents contain essential information to locate and identify remains of thousands of shipwrecks occurred during the considered historical period.

The transcription of these images is generally very difficult. On the one hand, the physical documents do not follow any arrangement standard and they typically have a very variable layouts and writing styles with different degrees of difficulty. On the other hand, the images suffer the typical paper degradation problems encountered in handwritten historical documents, such as presence of smear, significant background variation, uneven illumination, and dark spots. In addition, show-through and bleed-through problems often make it difficult or impossible to distinguish between background and foreground. The combination of these problems makes the automatic recognition of these documents a extremely difficult process.

In this paper we have used a small subset from the Carabela collection composed of 341 pages from different periods and writing styles in old Spanish. For this subset a careful ground truth transcripts have been produced. Some example images of this subset are shown in Fig. 1.

This set was endowed with two different types of annotations: the line position information and the transcripts. In order to produce the ground-truth as much automatically as possible, first text lines were automatically detected using a system presented in [7] and detection errors were manually corrected, resulting in a set of 10 528 text line images.

On the other hand, a transcript of each line image was semi-automatically carried out using CATTI [20], an interactive assistive approach where system and user expert work together in order to obtain the correct transcripts. Both character-level diplomatic transcripts and the corresponding modernized versions were simultaneously produced (also predicted by CATTI). To this end, we have adapted to the Carabela needs the word tagging mechanism proposed in [11], where tags were annotated using the standard XML TEI format.[1] For most of these tags, adequate shortcuts were defined based on a special escape character ("$"). These shortcuts can be easily converted into TEI and have proved very convenient to avoid handling otherwise cumbersome fully expanded TEI transcripts, both for the HTR/CATTI systems and for the human transcribers. The main tags adopted in this work are listed in Table 1.

Table 1. Transcription word tags.

Description	Tagged transcript
Modernization	arcaicWord$:modernizedWord
Abbreviation Expansion	abbreviation$.expandedWord
Hyphenated word prefix	prefix$>fullWord
Hyphenated word suffix	suffix$<fullWord
Superscript	$^character(s)
Crossed out word	$#word
Signature	$r
Illegible word	$i
Stamp	$s

These tags can be used to add text features to transcribed words. For instance: Arcaic word forms are written diplomatically and tagged with the corresponding modernized forms; abbreviations are transcribed as such and tagged with the corresponding full-form expansion; in a hyphenated word, both its initial part and its continuation are marked and tagged with the complete word; crossed-out words are tagged and transcribed if they are readable, otherwise they are labeled as illegible. In Fig. 2 we can see a transcription example using the defined tags.

---

[1] http://www.tei-c.org/index.xml.

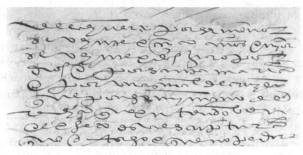

de la Guerta$:Huerta por ser menor
de veinte e$:y çinco$:cinco años, e$:y maior$:mayor
de veinte e$:y dos juro por
Dios e$:y por Santa María
e$:y por vna$:una señal de cruz en
que puse mi mano de$>derecha
recha$<derecha que entiendo bien
el efeto$:efecto desta$:de@esta escriptura$:escritura
que olorgo, e$:y que no pediré

Fig. 2. Examples of the Carabela transcripts.

A partition of the 341 pages into four blocks was defined for cross-validation evaluation. The average values of the statistics of the different partitions are shown in Table 2. The number of running words that have associated a tag is shown in the *Tagged words* row. It is important to remark that the percentage of tagged words is more than the 25%.

Table 2. Basic statistics of the Carabela database and average values for the 4 blocks of the cross-validation partition.

Number of:	Total	Average
Pages	341	85.25
Lines	10,528	2,632
Running words	82,590	20,648
Tagged words	21,160	5,290
Character set size	88	88

4   Handwritten Text Recognition Technology

Given a handwritten line image represented by a feature vector sequence, $\mathbf{x} = x_1 x_2 \ldots x_m$, the Handwritten Text Recognition problem can be formulated as the problem of finding a most likely word sequence, $\hat{\mathbf{w}} = \hat{w}_1 \hat{w}_2 \ldots \hat{w}_l$, i.e., $\hat{\mathbf{w}} = \arg\max_{\mathbf{w}} \Pr(\mathbf{w} \mid \mathbf{x})$. The most traditional approaches to solve this problem were based on N-gram language models and HMMs with Gaussian mixture emission distributions (HMM-GMM) for optical modeling [29]. However, significant improvements in optical modeling were demonstrated by approaching emission probabilities with multilayer perceptrons (HMM-MLP) [3,6] and also by training the HMM-GMMs with discriminative training techniques [25].

In the last decade, notable improvements in HTR accuracy have been achieved by using Recurrent Neural Networks (RNNs) for optical modeling. As of now, the state-of-the-art optical modeling HTR technology is based on deeply layered neural network models which consist of a stack of several *convolutional* layers followed by one or more RNN composed of special "neurons" called *Bidirectional Long Short Term Memory* (BLSTM) units [3,4,9,13]. Finally, a softmax output layer computes an estimate of the probabilities of each character in the training alphabet plus a special "non-character" symbol. The overall architecture is often referred to as *Convolutional-Recurrent Neural Networks* (CRNN) [22].

The experiments reported in this paper were obtained using this kind of CRNNs for character optical modeling. The detailed structure of the implemented CRNN is given in Subsect. 5.2. A CRNN is trained by stochastic gradient descend with the RMSProp method [24] on minibatches to minimize the so called *Connectionist Temporal Classification* (CTC) cost function [8]. Dropout techniques [14] are also used to reduce training overfitting, which has been proved to effectively improve recognition accuracy [3,13]. In order to decide when to stop the training iterations, a *development set* (which may be a excerpt of the training set proper) is used. It is worth noting that all the techniques, associated and software tools required for this approach are now implemented and readily available in the HTR *Laia Toolkit* [16], based on the Torch machine learning platform.

As previously discussed, for a given text line image, a trained CRNN estimates a sequence of character posterior probability vectors. While raw images can be directly accepted as input, results can often be improved if images are previously deskewed, deslanted, cleaned, contrast-enhanced, and/or size-normalized [1,5,18,28].

CRNNs have proved able to capture by themselves lexical and linguistic context to some extent. However, classical language model methods, which explicitly aim at modeling contextual regularities and constraints, can often help CRNNs to further improve HTR results. The most traditional approach consist on using statistical character N-grams.

Trained N-gram contextual constraints can be applied to the CRNN output character probabilities in several ways [4]. Here N-grams are represented as a stochastic finite-state transducer. The edge probabilities of this transducer are then obtained by adequately combining the estimated N-gram probabilities with CRNN output character posteriors, suitably scaled with character priors [4]. The resulting stochastic transducer, along with the classical Viterbi decoding algorithm (also known as "token- or message-passing"), are used to obtain an optimal transcription hypothesis of the original input line image.

5   Experimental Framework

5.1   Optical Modeling

Three different ways to train the optical models to obtain modernized transcripts has been studied in this paper. The first one just consists on using totally mod ernized transcripts. In this case, every CRNN output unit represents one of the characters in the modernized training transcripts plus a special "non-character" symbol, making a total of 89 output units. We will refer to this approach as "*plain modern*". Clearly, this approach is the least demanding one in terms of ground truth production, since diplomatic transcription is often much more time consuming and require more specialized experts.

The second approach was introduced in [11] and more recently adopted in [17]. In this approach, both diplomatic and modernized transcripts are used for training and the resulting HTR system is expected to produce the same kind of dual transcripts for the test images. As in [17], here the tagging process was directly modeled at the optical level; that is, the CRNN was trained with line images and the corresponding raw tagged transcripts, where each tag is just considered as one more symbol in the transcript. In this way, the number of optical units of the CRNN grows to 98. That is, the previous 89 plus an extra symbol for every tag ("\$:", "\$.", "\$>", "\$<", "\$^", "\$#", "\$r", "\$i", "\$s"). This approach will be called "*word tagged*". Note that this approach may extremely stress the capabilities of the CRNN, since in many cases (particularly in some modern-izations, as well as in most abbreviation and hyphenation expansions) it has to learn to predict many more characters as they are written in the image.

Finally, the third approach aims at avoiding the just mentioned prediction stress as much as possible. To this end, rather than training the CRNN with the tagged transcripts, it is trained with the shortest sequence of edit operations at character level that are required to transform the diplomatic transcript in the corresponding modernized and/or expanded form. That is, for every word whose modernized version differs from the diplomatic one, the Levenshtein distance is computed and, the sequence with minimum number of single-character edit operations (i.e. insertions, deletions or substitutions) is used. This approach will be referred to as "*char tagged*".

In the following example we can see the sequence used to train the CRNN according the *char tagged* approach for the text in Fig. 2. The substitution edit operation is coded as "a/b", meaning that the character "a" in the diplomatic transcript is substituted by the character "b" in the modernized one. The inser-tions are coded as "$\_/a$" and the deletions as "$a/\_$". In the case of hyphenations, the characters that are not in the image, but are included in the tagged tran-script, are coded as "$>/a$" and "$</d$" for prefix and suffix, respectively. Finally, the blank space is coded as "$@$", and therefore the symbol "$\_/@$" means that an space has been included in the modernized transcript.

de @ l a G/H u e r t a @ p o r @ s e r @ m e n o r
de @ v e i n t e @ e/y ç/c i n c o @ a ñ o s , @ e/y m a i/y o r
de @ v e i n t e @ e/y @ d o s @ j u r o @ p o r
D i o s @ e/y @ p o r @ p o r @ S a n t a @ M a r í a
e/y @ p o r @ v/u n a @ s e ñ a l @ d e @ c r u z @ e n
q u e @ p u s e @ m i @ m a n o @ d e >/r >/e >/c >/h >/a
</d </e r e c h a @ q u e @ e n t i e n d o @ b i e n
e l @ e f e _/c t o @ d e _/@ _/e s t a @ e s c r i p/_ t u r a
q u e @ o t o r g o , @ e/y @ q u e @ n o @ p e d i r é

Note that, although *char tagged* provides additional valuable information, the number of CRNN output units becomes much larger. Including only the edit operations seen in training, the number of final output units is 877.

Finally, it is interesting to remark that with *char tagged* or *word tagged* training, the HTR result for each text line image is a diplomatic-modernized pair, which may be a highly desirable outcome in some applications. However, this is at the expense of investing extra labeling effort to produce more detailed training transcripts. In contrast, training data labeling is much less demanding for *plain modern* training, but it can only provide modernized output.

5.2   System Setup

Experiments were carried out to test the different optical modeling options described previously.

The four different partitions previously defined were used in the experiments for cross-validation. That is, we carried out four rounds, with each of the partitions used once as test and the remaining 3 partitions used as training. For each round 3 different models were trained, one for every optical modelling option studied. Experiments were carried out using the CRNN technology described in the previous section. All the line images were scaled to a height of 64 pixels and contrast enhancement and noise removal as in [26] were applied. Then, the line images of the training partitions were used to train the corresponding CRNN. The CRNN topology consists of 4 CNN layers of 16, 32, 64 and 96 maps, with kernels sizes of 3×3 pixels and horizontal and vertical strides of 1 pixel. Leaky Rectifier Linear Units (LeakyReLU) [12] are used as the activation function, and their outputs are then fed to a maximum pooling layer. After the convolutional block, three BLSTM-RNN layers of 256 units are appended, with dropout applied at the input of each of them to reduce overfitting. Finally, a linear fully-connected layer with dropout is used after the recurrent block. The training of the optical models was carried out with the HTR *Laia Toolkit*[2].

The transcripts of the training were used to train three different character-based 8-gram models depending of the characters defined in the optical models. The Kneser-Ney back-off smoothing [10] was used in these language models. The training of the language models was carried out using the SRILM toolkit [23].

---

[2] https://github.com/jpuigcerver/Laia.

Every language model, along with the trained CRNN, was subsequently used with the Kaldi [15] (Viterbi) decoder to produce the recognition hypotheses for all the test-set image lines.

5.3   Assessment Measures

The quality of the automatic transcripts obtained with the different optical modeling approaches is measured by means of the well known character and word error rates (CER and WER). They are defined as the minimum number of character/words that need to be substituted, deleted, or inserted to match the recognition output with the corresponding reference transcripts, divided by the total number of words in the reference. In order to make all the proposed approaches fully comparable, in the present work, only the modernized output of each approach is evaluated.

6   Experimental Results

The experiments presented here aim at comparing the accuracy of the different training approaches discussed in Sect. 5.1, namely: *plain modern, word tagged* and *char tagged*. As discussed above, the last two approaches provide diplomatic-modernized pairs, but only the modernized part is used for evaluation, so that the three methods are exactly comparable. Four-blocks cross-validation was used in these experiments. Table 3 shows the WER and the CER obtained for the different approaches.

Table 3. Test set CER and WER (in %) for each training approach.

Training approach	CER	WER
Plain modern	17.8	34.6
Word tagged	24.3	41.5
Char tagged	18.2	34.6

From the results we can seen that *plain modern* training yields the best results (34.6% of WER and 17.8% of CER). However, the *char tagged* approach, in spite of using a very large number of output units ("characters"), achieves almost the same accuracy (only 0.4 points worse in CER). In both cases the vast majority of errors are related with hyphenated words. In addition, this approach allows HTR systems to recognize characters as diplomatic-modernized pairs, thereby allowing to simultaneously produce both diplomatic and modernized transcripts. Depending on the application, this additional information can be very valuable. The WER obtained for the diplomatic transcription is 37.6%.

With respect to *word tagged* training, although it provides good results in [17], the results for the Carabela collection are worse than those obtained with the other two approaches. This can be explained by the differences in the two tagged corpora. Whereas the corpus used in [17] have a small number of labeled running words and the variability for each class label is quite low, in the Carabela's manuscripts the number of archaic and abbreviated words is very higher. In this case, the WER obtained for the diplomatic transcription is 44.7%.

7   Conclusion

This paper has dealt with the problem of obtaining modernized transcripts from historical manuscripts. The behavior of three different approaches have been tested. The less demanding approach, called *plain modern*, is the one that have obtained the best results. However, the *char tagged* approach, that requires a large number of output units, has obtained a very similar result. Moreover, this last approach not only returns the modernized transcript, but the diplomatic version, which may be very desirable in some applications, is also obtained. Taking into account the many difficulties exhibited by these handwritten documents, the preliminary results obtained are quite encouraging.

Future work will be related to a more in-depth study of the *char tagged* approach. In the obtained results, a large quantity of the obtained errors were related with the hyphenated words. In future works we will study new codifications to overcome this problem.

References

1. Bloomberg, D.S., Kopec, G.E., Dasari, L.: Measuring document image skew and orientation. In: SPIE, vol. 2422, pp. 302–316 (1995)
2. Bluche, T., et al.: Preparatory KWS experiments for large-scale indexing of a vast medieval manuscript collection in the HIMANIS project. In: 2017 14th ICDAR, vol. 01, pp. 311–316 (2017)
3. Bluche, T., Ney, H., Kermorvant, C.: The LIMSI/A2iA handwriting recognition systems for the HTRtS contest. In: ICDAR, pp. 448–452 (2015)
4. Bluche, T.: Deep neural networks for large vocabulary handwritten text recognition. Ph.D. thesis, Ecole Doctorale Informatique de Paris-Sud, May 2015
5. Buse, R., Liu, Z., Caelli, T.: A structural and relational approach to handwritten word recognition. IEEE Trans. SMCS, Part B **27**(5), 847–861 (1997)
6. España-Boquera, S., Castro-Bleda, M., Gorbe-Moya, J., Zamora-Martínez, F.: Improving offline handwriting text recognition with hybrid HMM/ANN models. IEEE Trans. PAMI **33**(4), 767–779 (2011)
7. Fawzi, A., Gadea, M.P., Martínez-Hinarejos, C.D.: Baseline detection on Arabic handwritten documents. In: Proceedings of the 2017 ACM Symposium on Document Engineering, DocEng 2017, pp. 193–196. ACM (2017)
8. Graves, A., Fernández, S., Gomez, F., Schmidhuber, J.: Connectionist temporal classification: labelling unsegmented sequence data with recurrent neural networks. In: ICML, pp. 369–376 (2006)

9. Graves, A., Liwicki, M., Fernández, S., Bertolami, R., Bunke, H., Schmidhuber, J.: A novel connectionist system for unconstrained handwriting recognition. IEEE Trans. PAMI **31**(5), 855–868 (2009)
10. Kneser, R., Ney, H.: Improved backing-off for N-gram language modeling. In: ICASSP 1995, vol. 1, pp. 181–184. IEEE Computer Society (1995)
11. Leiva, L.A., Toselli, A.H., Bordes-Cabrera, I., Hernández-Tornero, C., Vidal, E., Bosch, V.: Transcribing a 17th-century botanical manuscript: longitudinal evaluation of document layout detection and interactive transcription. Digit. Scholarsh. Humanit. **33**(1), 173–202 (2017)
12. Maas, A.L., Hannun, A.Y., Ng, A.Y.: Rectifier nonlinearities improve neural network acoustic models. In: International Conference on Machine Learning, vol. 30 (2013)
13. Moysset, B., et al.: The A2iA multi-lingual text recognition system at the second Maurdor evaluation. In: ICFHR, pp. 297–302 (2014)
14. Pham, V., Kermorvant, C., Louradour, J.: Dropout improves recurrent neural networks for handwriting recognition. CoRR abs/1312.4569 (2013)
15. Povey, D., et al.: The Kaldi speech recognition toolkit. In: ASRU, December 2011
16. Puigcerver, J.: Are multidimensional recurrent layers really necessary for handwritten text recognition? In: ICDAR, vol. 01, pp. 67–72 (2017)
17. Quirós, L., Bosch, V., Serrano, L., Toselli, A.H., Vidal, E.: From HMMs to RNNs: computer-assisted transcription of a handwritten notarial records collection. In: 2018 16th International Conference on Frontiers in Handwriting Recognition, pp. 116–121 (2018)
18. Roeder, P.: Adapting the RWTH-OCR handwriting recognition system to French handwriting. Ph.D. thesis, RWTH Aachen University, Aachen, Germany (2009)
19. Romero, V., Toselli, A.H., Sánchez, J.A., Vidal, E.: Handwriting transcription and keyword spotting in historical daily records documents. In: 2016 12th IAPR Workshop on Document Analysis Systems (DAS), pp. 275–280, April 2016
20. Romero, V., Toselli, A.H., Vidal, E.: Multimodal Interactive Handwritten Text Transcription. Series in MPAI. World Scientific Publishing, Singapore (2012)
21. Sánchez, J.A., Bosch, V., Romero, V., Depuydt, K., de Does, J.: Handwritten text recognition for historical documents in the transcriptorium project. In: Proceedings of the DATeCH 2014, pp. 111–117, New York, NY, USA (2014)
22. Shi, B., Bai, X., Yao, C.: An end-to-end trainable neural network for image-based sequence recognition and its application to scene text recognition. CoRR abs/1507.05717 (2015)
23. Stolcke, A.: SRILM—an extensible language modeling toolkit. In: The 7th International Conference on Spoken Language Processing (ICSLP 2002), vol. 2, July 2004
24. Tieleman, T., Hinton, G.: Lecture 6.5-RMSProp: divide the gradient by a running average of its recent magnitude. COURSERA Neural Netw. Mach. Learn. **4**(2), 26–30 (2012)
25. Toselli, A.H., Vidal, E.: Handwritten text recognition results on the Bentham collection with improved classical n-gram-HMM methods. In: International Workshop on Historical Document Imaging and Processing, pp. 15–22 (2015)
26. Villegas, M., Romero, V., Sánchez, J.A.: On the modification of binarization algorithms to retain grayscale information for handwritten text recognition. In: Paredes, R., Cardoso, J.S., Pardo, X.M. (eds.) IbPRIA 2015. LNCS, vol. 9117, pp. 208–215. Springer, Cham (2015). https://doi.org/10.1007/978-3-319-19390-8_24

27. Villegas, M., Toselli, A.H., Romero, V., Vidal, E.: Exploiting existing modern transcripts for historical handwritten text recognition. In: 2016 ICFHR, pp. 66–71, October 2016
28. Vinciarelli, A., Luettin, J.: A new normalization technique for cursive handwritten words. Pattern Recogn. Lett. **22**(9), 1043–1050 (2001)
29. Vinciarelli, A., Bengio, S., Bunke, H.: Off-line recognition of unconstrained handwritten texts using HMMs and statistical language models. IEEE Trans. PAMI **26**(6), 709–720 (2004)

Improving Ancient Cham Glyph Recognition from Cham Inscription Images Using Data Augmentation and Transfer Learning

Minh-Thang Nguyen[1]($\boxtimes$) (iD), Anne-Valérie Schweyer[2] (iD), Thi-Lan Le[1] (iD),
Thanh-Hai Tran[1] (iD), and Hai Vu[1] (iD)

[1] Computer Vision Department, MICA International Research Institute, Hanoi
University of Science and Technology, Hanoi, Vietnam
thang.nm153518@sis.hust.edu.vn
[2] French National Center for Scientific Research, Paris, France

Abstract. Ancient Cham glyphs have mostly appeared in inscriptions on stones at some museums in Vietnam. Unfortunately, these inscriptions are being abrasive by the time. To conserve Cham heritage as well as to make them widely accessible and readable by users, digitization and recognition of ancient Cham glyphs become necessary. In our previous work, we have built the first dataset of champ inscription images, manually segmented them in glyphs and annotated by an ancient Cham expert. We adapted some automatic recognition methods and conducted experiments on the manually denoised dataset. The aim of this paper is to extend that earlier research to work on noising data. To this end, we face two main issues. Firstly, the current pre-built dataset is still small which is usually a main drawback for deep learning based methods. Therefore, some data augmentation techniques will be evaluated and investigated to increase the number and variation of samples in the dataset. Second, even with the augmented dataset, the fact of training a deep model from scratch could be very long and sometimes cannot meet a good local minimum. Therefore, we use a simple transfer learning procedure which inherits knowledge from similar or of the same family language. Experiments on both the raw test set and its denoised version show very promising results (64.4% and 88.5% of F1-score on two test sets respectively).

Keywords: Ancient document analysis · Data augmentation · Transfer learning · Image classification

1 Introduction

Inscription is one of the most precious resources and surviving evidences in terms of historical significance of a certain ancient kingdom. The inscriptions

© Springer Nature Switzerland AG 2019
M. Cristani et al. (Eds.): ICIAP 2019 Workshops, LNCS 11808, pp. 115–125, 2019.
https://doi.org/10.1007/978-3-030-30754-7_12

could be words or letters written, engraved, painted, or traced on stone, brick or even on ritual objects in gold, silver or bronze. This was done to transmit a political and religious message to everyone, as well as visibly designate and claim a territory. In addition, they can reveal lifestyle, financial condition, culture, and additionally executive laws followed by numerous rulers and dynasties specific to those regions.

The ancient Cham inscriptions considered in our work are taken from the coastal provinces at North Central and South Central Coast of Vietnam. These inscriptions have a composite of characters that evolved during the reign of several dynasties and kingdoms. To ensure that people don't lose their connect with the past as recorded in stones, the existence of ancient Cham inscriptions is very important both in term of quantity and variety of historical contents. It is the shame that, with elapsed time, these engravings which are as easily altered as chronicles have gradually deteriorated to an undecipherable state. Although **estampages** that are inked replicas of an inscription surface are taken for many of them, it is very difficult to preserve these estampages.

Therefore, a document image analysis (DIA) system for the end-to-end semi-automated or automated processing of inscriptions is essential. Besides aiming to preserve, recover, study and make accessible the corpus of inscriptions of ancient Cham, the DIA system plays the important role in identifying, analyzing, extracting, structuring, and transferring document contents to obtain computer-readable description from document images. In addition, every year, anthropology discoveries bright to light-weight new inscriptions, one also desires a tool for the longer term generation. In other words, the hidden benefit behind a DIA system is that we might remain adapted to new patterns of the corpus.

In our previous study, we has contributed to classify Cham glyphs in ideal conditions (glyphs have been manually denoised) [12]. However, it is unclear whether these findings can be generalized to noisy visual inputs. In this study, evaluations of the impact of noise on different classifiers will be performed. Apart from the reliability of models, the small amount of available data in our case study is also one of the most concerns. To overcome this challenge, data augmentation and transfer learning will be investigated for ancient Cham glyph recognition problem.

The remaining of this paper is organized as follows: Sect. 2 summarizes the related works. Section 3 presents ancient Cham scripts. Section 4 introduces the dataset. Sections 5 and 6 describe the proposed methods and the experimental results. Finally, we conclude this work in Sect. 7.

2 Related Works

Access to documents is a major problem in historical research on Cham, and the few document digitization programs have not provided any classification, transliteration, or translation, making their exploitation practically impossible. The catalogs of epigraphic collections are available [10], but accessibility to the texts remains restricted [9]. Moreover, diachronic linguistics on the ancient Cham languages are non-existent because of the lack of accessibility to written sources.

The Cham inscriptions program at New York University[1] proposed methodologies for digital epigraphy but worked only 2 years and it only provided classical works that disconnect texts from their context.

To the best of our recollection, no program has attempted to extract and index the content of ancient Cham scripts to facilitate the work of the researchers (historians, archaeologists, etc.). The only work that we have identified on the extraction, recognition, transliteration and indexing of ancient manuscripts from Southeast Asia was done by a group of researchers led by the L3i in the AMADI project [11]. The aim of this was to develop methods of analyzing ancient documents written on palm leaf manuscripts. The scripts studied come from Indonesia (in Balinese and Sundanese) and Cambodia (in Khmer). This project made it possible to develop annotated databases, algorithms of segmentation and analysis of the structure of documents, methods of character recognition and transliteration.

3 Characteristics of Ancient Cham Script

Champa is the name given to a confederation of kingdoms that formed the origin of the Cham civilization between the beginning of the 1st millennium AD and the end of the 15th century.

The Structure of Ancient Cham Script. The writing of the inscriptions is alphasyllabic, i. e. a syllable - and not a letter - is a basic element, formed by one or more consonants associated with a vowel or diphthong. Each character - or combination of characters - thus represented forms a glyph that must be treated as a whole when read.

The alphabet was used to write texts in Sanskrit and ancient Cham. The reason for this bilingualism seems to be that the texts are not intended for the same readers: the Sanskrit texts were intended for the Indian gods who read and understand this language, while the Cham texts were intended for human beings to respect the donations made.

The Gradual Disappearance of Ancient Cham. If Sanskrit is still a living language in India today, it must be said that only a few specialists in the world are able to decipher and understand the ancient Cham today. A Cham today can neither read nor understand the texts in the ancient Cham, as the language and writing have evolved so much. Thus, when the few epigraphists in the world, specialists in reading and analysing ancient inscriptions, have disappeared, we will no longer be able to access the invaluable historical documents that are the inscriptions of Champa.

4 Cham Glyphs Dataset

Overall, there are 4 stages in the process, starting with establishing the inventory of inscriptions, to annotation (shown in Fig. 1). The first thing we need to do is

---

[1] http://isaw.nyu.edu/publications/inscriptions/campa/.

to establish the inventory of inscriptions and their precise location (in situ or in a museum). After that, we obtain well estampages of these inscriptions. Then, we separate each line from the inscription. After removing noise and separating each character from each line, we check each character by following the transcription of the text. Lastly, we distribute each character in a database according to ancient Cham alphabet.

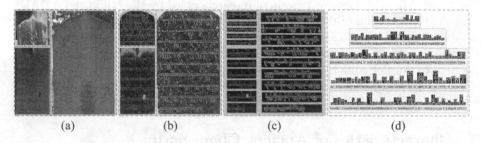

(a)   (b)   (c)   (d)

Fig. 1. Ground-truth construction process (l.t.r: inventory inscriptions in (a), generating estampages of the inscription surface in (b), separating each line from each estampages in (c) and then annotation each glyphs in (d)).

The dataset establishment encountered several difficulties at the beginning. This is because the writing system, which gives priority to characters or combinations of characters rather than words, therefore produces a discontinuous sequence of letters or groups of letters, which results in deciphering the inscriptions made more difficult, since it is never easy to break down the words. In addition, the use of character combinations breaks the linear unity of the lines. Thus, the ancient Cham is written in an apparent disorder, with glyphs that extend beyond lines upwards and downwards. It is therefore difficult to standardize the presentation of documents and the separation of lines is never easy. In addition, there is the irregularity of the very support of the texts (stone, bricks or even metal), which, when copied onto the estampages, produces a visual noise that complicates deciphering. *For all these reasons, the cutting of lines and words still has to be done manually at this stage*. Consequently, the dataset contains 37 classes with 1607 glyphs corresponding two kinds of test set, *the raw test set* and *the denoised test set* (see Fig. 2).

5   Methodology

Figure 3 illustrates the proposed framework for ancient Cham glyph recognition including 3 main steps: data augmentation, feature extraction and classification. In our previous study [12], we have investigated three features (HOG, NPW and CNN-based features) and two classification techniques (k-nearest neighbor classifier and the support vector machine (SVM) with a linear kernel). We have also pointed out that the proposed method in [12] obtained quite good results

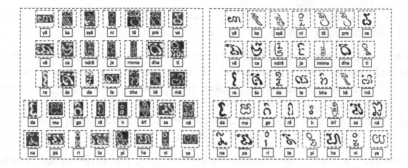

Fig. 2. Two kinds of test set. The left hand is the raw test set, whereas the other hand is the denoised test set.

on *the denoised glyph images*. However, the performance of the method decreases dramatically while working with the raw glyph images due to the present of noise and the low number of images for each glyph class. To extend our work, novel data augmentation methods and transferring knowledge from an existing network through fine-tuning are investigated in this paper. In Fig. 3, these techniques are marked in blue-blocks.

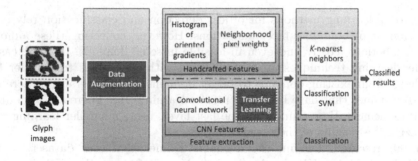

Fig. 3. The proposed framework for ancient Cham glyph recognition.

5.1 Data Augmentation

In our case, we regularly encounter the lack of sufficient amounts of the training data. To deal with this problem, data augmentation has been proposed and proved to be efficient and effective for automatically collecting a large number of training data. Our process consist of three parts. The first stage randomly transforms an raw pattern, comprising rotation and shear. The second stage randomly distorts some corners of the transformed pattern to form a new pattern based on Leung's method [4] and Xu's method [3]. The last stage implemented another distortion method which is called the elastic transform augmentation method. The augmentation methods are divided into two main groups: conventional transformations and distortions. Each is briefly described below.

Conventional Transformations. These consist of using a combination of affine transformations to manipulate the training data. The most popular methods are: rotation, refection, scaling (zoom in/out) and shearing [2]. Meanwhile, for each input image, we generate a "duplicated" image that is rotated, sheared. Both the raw image and generated images are fed into classifiers. For a dataset of size N, we generate a dataset of $10 \times N$ size.

Distortions. Moreover, to produce more variable, three distortion methods related to the surface are applied. These operations aim to eliminate distortions caused by the surface after inscriptions has already been engraved, and also include possible noise caused by the method of acquiring the image (for example, scanning). The first is Leung's off-line sample generation method, which distorts a pattern on a given binary image [4]. The second is Xu's on-line sample generation [3], which maps each sampling point to its new position in the distorted pattern. The third is elastic deformation [5] where image deformations were created by first generating random displacement fields followed by multiplied by a scaling factor α that controls the intensity of the deformation.

5.2   Transfer Learning

Recent deep learning methods for object detection and classification rely on a large amount of bounding box annotations. However, collecting these annotations is laborious, costly and even in-feasible in some domains. In these cases, transfer learning techniques are usually used with the aim is to transfer the knowledge from existing domains to target domains. In the literature, there are many techniques that have been for transfer learning [16]. There are some fine-tuning implementation: truncating the last layer, using a smaller learning rate or freezing the weights of the first few layers.

In our research domain, the available Khmer character dataset named SleukRith containing Khmer characters extracted from ancient Khmer palm leaf scripts [1] shares certain common characteristics with our ancient Cham. Therefore, in this paper, we propose to apply the transfer learning technique by fine-tuning the GoogleNet [15] on SleukRith dataset [1]. For this, after freezing the weights in the original network up to the last block, we train the whole "stitched" model altogether with the ancient Cham glyph images (see Fig. 4).

6   Experimental Results

To evaluate the performance of the proposed framework, we use two test sets named **_the raw test set_** and **_the denoised test set_** described in Sect. 4. For each class, 70% of samples are used for training and the remaining are used for testing.

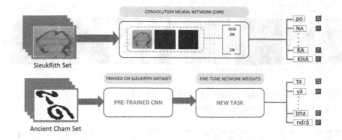

Fig. 4. Fine-tuning the GoogleNet on SleukRith dataset.

As in our previous work, we reported only the results for *the denoised test set*. In order to understand the performance of the proposed method in [12] on the test set containing noisy images, we performed the experiments on both *the raw test set* and *the denoised test set*. Table 1 shows the results obtained for both kinds of test set. It is immediately apparent from the data that the classification rate of the method based on HOG features witnessed a stable stage, whereas the other performances corresponding to and NPW features and learned features from CNNs experienced a significant drop in comparison with the those obtained for *the denoised test set* [12].

The phenomena is caused by several reasons. It is fact that the majority of images in the raw dataset contains salt and pepper noise, which can be eliminated by Gaussian filters in the pre-processing step of HOG method. By contrast, for computing NPW features, the values of each block in rectangle images will change significantly when they contains one part of other glyphs in neighbor areas shown in Fig. 5, which results in a considerable amount of inaccuracy in weight vectors. Likewise, the other performance on features learned from CNNs was downward. In order to clarify why the performance of this is sensitive to noise, we examine the filter outputs from the network under noise. In Fig. 6 we examine the response for two kinds of inputs respectively. It is noticeable that the effect of noise gives rise to many activation layers in the first layer "conv1/7 × 7_s2", which also propagate to the responses in the last layer "inception_5b/output".

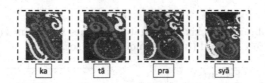

Fig. 5. The presence of surrounding information besides the interested glyphs (in red) in the raw dataset. (Color figure online)

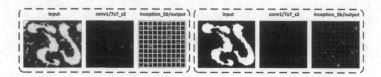

Fig. 6. Visualization of feature maps of two layers of the GoogleNet obtained for glyphs in the raw dataset and the denoised dataset.

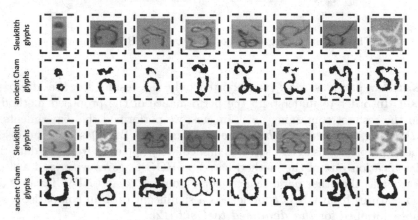

Fig. 7. Appearance similarities between SleukRith's glyphs and ancient Cham's glyphs.

To evaluate the influence of data augmentation in the recognition accuracy, we performance different experiments by applying and combining data augmentation methods as described in Sect. 5. The experimental results in comparison with the baseline [12] are summarized in Table 2. As a whole, the results are lower degrees in comparison with the baseline [12] in terms of the best performances of both situations. This is because, in linear transformations, they only lead to an image-level transformation through depth and scale and actually not helpful for dividing a clear boundary between data manifolds. Such data augmentation does not improve data distribution which is determined by higher-level features [14]. However, in details, what a surprise is that it approximately two-fold improves the performances of some classifiers on **the raw test set** on average in Fig. 8a.

Table 1. F1-score obtained on six investigated schemes for Cham glyph classification with (a) in the raw test set and (b) the denoised test set.

(a)

Classification	Features		
	CNN	HOG	NPW
K-NN	0.283	**0.601**	0.006
SVM	0.333	**0.610**	0.038

(b)

Classification	Features		
	CNN	HOG	NPW
K-NN [12]	**0.863**	0.684	0.414
SVM [12]	**0.781**	0.717	0.383

Table 2. The F1-score obtained by using data augmentation methods for (a) the raw test set and (b) the denoised test set.

(a)

	KNN classifier			SVM classifier		
	CNN features	HOG	NPW	CNN features	HOG	NPW
No data augmentation	0.28	0.60	0.01	0.33	**0.61**	0.04
Augmentation method						
rotation	0.33	**0.61**	0.13	**0.40**	0.54	0.09
rotation + online	**0.61**	0.68	0.01	0.37	0.55	0.002
rotation + offline	0.21	0.27	0.01	0.07	0.12	0.01
shear	0.35	0.57	0.13	0.35	0.47	0.09
shear + online	0.27	0.59	0.02	0.35	0.48	0.02
shear + offline	0.12	0.23	0.03	0.06	0.12	0.02
elastic deformation	0.003	0.58	**0.18**	0.001	0.56	**0.14**

(b)

	KNN classifier			SVM classifier		
	CNN features	HOG	NPW	CNN features	HOG	NPW
No data augmentation [12]	**0.86**	**0.68**	**0.41**	0.78	**0.72**	**0.38**
Augmentation method						
rotation	0.78	0.68	0.35	0.81	0.72	0.27
rotation + online	0.78	0.68	0.31	0.82	0.21	0.23
rotation + offline	0.15	0.27	0.02	0.12	0.17	0.01
shear	0.35	0.64	0.27	0.80	0.68	0.28
shear + online	0.78	0.66	0.35	**0.85**	0.68	0.35
shear + offline	0.12	0.28	0.01	0.24	0.21	0.01
elastic deformation	0.80	0.66	0.24	0.83	0.72	0.23

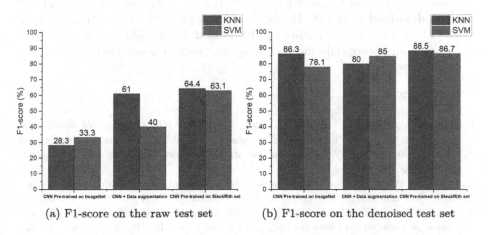

(a) F1-score on the raw test set   (b) F1-score on the denoised test set

Fig. 8. The performances of classifiers based on CNN features evaluate on two kinds of test set.

Finally, for transfer learning, the performances recorded during the preliminary investigation [12] seems be a spectacular surge when adapting features learned by a deep CNN (see Table 1(b)), the results illustrated in Fig. 8 indicates the best performance was achieved by freezing weights, especially in *the raw test set*. In a detailed manner, our method increases over the existing best results by 31.1% on *the raw test set* (64.4 *vs.* 33.3) and 3.4% on the denoised test set (88.4 *vs.* 86.3). In particular, F1-scores for "*la*" class (see Fig. 2 and 4th glyph from right to left at 4th line in Fig. 7) is the most remarkable increase by 45% for KNN and 22% for SVM following confusion matrices. It is obvious that the transfer learning method works well when the source set and the target set are same characteristics. We argued that the SleukRith set [1] contains noisy images which is similarity with respect to *our raw test*. Furthermore, both SleukRith's glyphs and ancient Cham's glyphs similar appearance in several cases (shown in Fig. 7).

7   Conclusion

In this paper, we extended our preceding work with investigating performances on two kinds of test set, one is *the raw set* and the other is *the denoised set*. The results on *the raw test set* significantly reduced compared with the results on *the denoised test set*, which led us to experiment with some well-known methods for small data problems. We demonstrated that the traditional data augmentation techniques could not allow to achieve a significant improvement on the challenging dataset as our ancient Cham glyph dataset as the ancient Cham language has its own characteristics. Nevertheless, we have shown how a simple transfer learning procedure yields promising results on our own dataset, especially an approximately twofold increase on *the raw test set*. However, there are disparities in terms of F1-score metric between *the orignal test set* and *the denoised test set*. In the future, we proceed to investigate proper methods to achieve better results on *the raw data*. In addition, we will take into account an appropriate method for synthetic data generation.

References

1. Valy, D., Verleysen, M., Chhun, S., Burie, J.C.: A new Khmer Palm leaf manuscript dataset for document analysis and recognition: SleukRith set. In: Proceedings of the 4th International Workshop on Historical Document Imaging and Processing, pp. 1–6. ACM (2017)
2. Perez, L., Wang, J.: The effectiveness of data augmentation in image classification using deep learning. arXiv preprint arXiv:1712.04621 (2017)
3. Xu, N., Wang, W., Qu, X.: On-line sample generation for in-air written Chinese character recognition based on leap motion controller. In: Ho, Y.-S., Sang, J., Ro, Y.M., Kim, J., Wu, F. (eds.) PCM 2015. LNCS, vol. 9314, pp. 171–180. Springer, Cham (2015). https://doi.org/10.1007/978-3-319-24075-6_17

4. Leung, K.C., Leung, C.H.: Recognition of handwritten Chinese characters by combining regularization, fisher's discriminant and distorted sample generation. In: Proceedings of the 10th International Conference on Document Analysis and Recognition, pp. 1026–1030 (2009)
5. Simard, P.Y., Steinkraus, D., Platt, J.C.: Best practices for convolutional neural networks applied to visual document analysis. In: ICDAR, vol. 3, no. 2003 (2003)
6. Dalal, N., Triggs, B.: Histograms of oriented gradients for human detection. In: IEEE Computer Society Conference on Computer Vision and Pattern Recognition (CVPR), vol. 1, pp. 886–893 (2005)
7. Junior, O.L., Delgado, D., Gonçalves, V., Nun, U.: Trainable classifier-fusion schemes: an application to pedestrian detection. In: Intelligent Transportation Systems, vol. 2 (2009)
8. Takahashi, K., Takahashi, S., Cui, Y., Hashimoto, M.: Remarks on computational facial expression recognition from HOG features using quaternion multi-layer neural network. In: Mladenov, V., Jayne, C., Iliadis, L. (eds.) EANN 2014. CCIS, vol. 459, pp. 15–24. Springer, Cham (2014). https://doi.org/10.1007/978-3-319-11071-4_2
9. Griffith, A., Lepoutre, A., Southworth, W.A., Thanh, P.: The Inscriptions of Campa at the Museum of Cham Sculpture in Da Nang. VNU-HCM Publishing House (2012)
10. Schweyer, A.-V.: Chronologie des inscriptions publiées du Campā. In: Bulletin de l'Ecole française d'Extrême-Orient, vol. 86, pp. 321–344 (1999)
11. Kesiman, M., et al.: Benchmarking of document image analysis tasks for palm leaf manuscripts from Southeast Asia. J. Imaging 4(2), 43 (2018)
12. Nguyen, M.-T., Schweyer, A.-V., Le, T.-L., Tran, T.-H., Vu, H.: Preliminary results on ancient cham character recognition from cham inscription images. In: 2nd International Conference on Multimedia Analysis and Pattern Recognition (2019)
13. Nordlöf, J.: Comparative Analysis of Models for Real-Time Pattern Recognition (2014)
14. Zhu, X., Liu, Y., Li, J., Wan, T., Qin, Z.: Emotion classification with data augmentation using generative adversarial networks. In: Phung, D., Tseng, V.S., Webb, G.I., Ho, B., Ganji, M., Rashidi, L. (eds.) PAKDD 2018. LNCS (LNAI), vol. 10939, pp. 349–360. Springer, Cham (2018). https://doi.org/10.1007/978-3-319-93040-4_28
15. Szegedy, C., et al.: Going deeper with convolutions. In: Proceedings of the IEEE Conference on Computer Vision and Pattern Recognition, pp. 1–9 (2015)
16. Pan, S.J., Yang, Q.: A survey on transfer learning. IEEE Trans. Knowl. Data Eng. 22(10), 1345–1359 (2009)
17. Fei-Fei, L.: ImageNet: crowdsourcing, benchmarking and other cool things. In: CMU VASC Seminar, vol. 16, pp. 18–25 (2010)
18. Goodfellow, I., et al.: Generative adversarial nets. In: Advances in Neural Information Processing Systems, pp. 2672–2680 (2014)
19. Lake, B.M., Salakhutdinov, R., Tenenbaum, J.B.: Human-level concept learning through probabilistic program induction. Science 350(6266), 1332–1338 (2015)
20. Dalal, N., Triggs, B.: Histograms of oriented gradients for human detection. In: 2005 IEEE Computer Society Conference on Computer Vision and Pattern Recognition, CVPR 2005, vol. 1, pp. 886–893. IEEE (2005)
21. Kumar, S.: Neighborhood pixels weights-a new feature extractor. Int. J. Comput. Theory Eng. 2(1), 69 (2010)

Oracle Bone Inscription Detector Based on SSD

Lin Meng[1]([✉])(iD), Bing Lyu[1], Zhiyu Zhang[1], C. V. Aravinda[2](iD),
Naoto Kamitoku[1], and Katsuhiro Yamazaki[1]

[1] Department of Electronic and Computer Engineering, Ritsumeikan University,
Kusatsu, Shiga 525-8577, Japan
menglin@fc.ritsumei.ac.jp
[2] Department of Computer Science and Engineering,
NMAM Institute of Technology, Nitte, Karkala Taluk, Karnataka, India
aravinda.cv@nitte.edu.in

Abstract. This paper introduces Oracle Bone Inscription Detector
which based on Single Shot Multibox Detector, for segmenting and recognizing Oracle Bone Inscriptions from rubbing images. Oracle Bone
Inscription which is the one of the oldest and most mysterious ancient
characters, used about 3000 years ago in china, and lots of these literature are stored by rubbing images. Because that only few of specialists
understand the Oracle Bone Inscriptions, lots of Oracle Bone Inscriptions are waiting for be understood for helping researchers know the
history, culture, economy etc. Currently, deep learning method of single
shot multibox detector achieves a good performance for segmentation
and recognition, and may achieve a good performance for Oracle Bone
Inscription detection. However, we fond the Single Shot Multibox Detector is weak at small object detection. This research equips and extends
Single Shot Multibox Detector for Oracle Bone Inscription detection, and
analyzes the mis-detection for achieving a better accuracy. The experimental results shows that Precision, Recall and F value achieve 0.95,
0.83 and 0.88 respectively, and proves the effectiveness of extended Single Shot Multibox Detector in Oracle Bone Inscription detection.

Keywords: Oracle Bone Inscriptions Detector ·
Single Shot Multibox Detector · Deep learning ·
Culture heritage protection

1 Introduction

Currently, for understanding the politics, economy, culture of the history, unlocking the ancient literature become an huge needs. However, for some reasons lots
of these ancient literature can only be read by few specialists based on their experience, such as Oracle Bones Inscriptions (OBIs), Kuzushi characters [1]. Oracle

Supported by Japan Society for the Promotion of Science (JSPS) (18K18337).

bone inscriptions are the oldest kind of characters, were inscribed on cattle bone or turtle shells about 3000 years ago. OBIs are important ancient literature in Asia, for the reason is that Chinese characters was evaluated from OBIs in several thousand years, which are wildly used in Asia. Hence, understanding the OBIs is important for researching world history, character evaluations, etc. This paper focuses on the OBIs detection and recognition form rubbing images for protecting the culture heritage.

For some political and historic reasons, the OBIs are buried in ruins about 3000 years, still which were found about 120 years ago. Hence, few literature describes the OBIs, and only few specialists can read the OBIs. The most common OBI storage method involves rubbing, where the OBI surface is reproduced by placing a piece of paper over the subject and then rubbing the paper with rolled ink. Researchers are trying to recognize OBIs with the assistant of computer. Unfortunately, some characters are broken, some of them are unclear, and some of them are have bigger and smaller noises because of the aging. These problems increase the difficult of OBIs recognition with the assistant of computer. Furthermore, the character are described here and there un-uniformly in the Oracle Bone, it let the characters should be detected at first. However, the aging processing and un-uniformed placement let the character detection becomes difficult [2].

Currently, deep learning methods become a hottest topic on the research field of pattern recognition, object detection etc. This paper aims to detect and recognize the OBIs from rubbing images by single shot multibox detector (SSD) [3], which is an state-of-the-art model for object detection and recognition. In this paper, we aim to detect and recognize OBIs by SSD, and extend the SSD for overcoming the weak points of SSD.

The contributions of this research are shown as follows: In the authors' opinion, no paper introduces deep learning method for detecting and recognizing OBIs in the same time. Hence, it is the first challenge for using deep learning base method for detecting and recognizing the OBIs. Of course, the first dataset of OBIs was built for training and testing the SSD.

Section 2 describes the current research related to OBIs recognition methods, including image processing and deep learning. Section 3 goes over the research flow of our SSD based OBIs detector. Section 4 shows the recognition and experimental results and discussion. Section 5 concludes the paper with a brief summary and mention of future work.

2   Related Work

Various researchers have attempted to recognize OBIs by image processing. Currently, with the technologies evolve, especially in the are of deep learning, research are also trying to understand OBIs by deep learning.

2.1 Conventional Image Processing

Hung-Hsiang Chou is the first researcher who tried to recognize OBIs by computers about 50 years ago. However, for the limited computation power, Chou did not achieve an existing accuracy. Late, Li et al. [4,5] use non-directed graph for recording the features of end-points, three-cross-points, five-cross-points, blocks, net-holes, etc. Li et al. [6] proposed a DNA method for recognizing OBIs. However, due to the age of OBIs, these methods did not achieve good results too.

We have previously proposed several methods for recognizing OBIs by template matching. However, the template matching is very weak when the original character was tilted. For overcoming the problem of template matching, we have designed a two-stage recognition system that consists of line features and checkpoint recognition for recognizing OBIs. This method extracts line points using Hough transform and a proposed clustering method and then calculates the distance between the line points of the target OBI image and those of the templates, using the shortest distance for searching a similar template in Hough space [2,12]. The experimental results show that almost 90% of the inscriptions on the third-most similar templates were recognized, and only 70% of the inscriptions on the first-most similar templates were recognized.

2.2 Deep Learning

Currently, Deep learning are widely used in the field of object detection and classification with exciting accuracy. Hence, Researchers are try to recognize the OBIs by deep learning. Guo et al. aimed to represent OBIs using convolutional neural network based models of deep learning [7]. They generated a dataset named Oracle-20K and achieved a good recognition rate by proposed CNN for training and testing it. However, the character images of Oracle-20K were collected from a website, comprising images that were drawn by Uncle Hanzi who is a Chinese character research specialist named Richard Sears, in the present day. It means that the paper does not discuss the real image of OBIs and does not consider the numerous characteristics of OBIs such as non-uniformity, inclinations, noises and breaks.

Due to the unavailability of public OBIs data, we generated an OBI dataset composed of real rubbing images (the first dataset of its kind) and used it for recognizing by deep learning. To ensure sufficient training before recognition, we proposed several data augmentation methods and tuning the parameter such as dropout, filter numbers etc. AlexNet model [8] is used for the OBIs recognition. The experimental results show that 184 difference characters OBIs recognition rate achieves 92.3%, and the data set consists of 2,000 images including 538 test images and the training data was augmented into 9.69 million items [9]. Also, LeNet [13] and GoogLeNet [10] are tested too, however AlexNet achieved a better accuracy.

However, the characters should be cut from literature at first, which takes a long time, makes the method is not effectiveness and can not be used for reading the literature directly. This paper is the first research, which uses SSD (Single

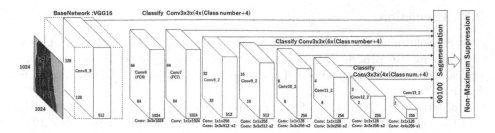

Fig. 1. SSD based OBIs detector.

Shot Multi detector, a state-of-the-art object detection method) for detecting and recognizing the OBIs in the same time.

3 SSD Based OBIs Detector

3.1 SSD: Single Shot Detector

SSD was designed for detecting and recognizing the objects with a high-speed and good-accuracy, which is proved by the testing of PascalVOC dataset [3]. PascalVOC is a large dataset, which have 20 classes, including dogs, trains, etc, which are the bigger and clearer objects in the images.

Figure 1 shows the model of SSD, every boxes means a conventional layer. For example in $Conv8\_2$, 512 means channel number and 32 means the scalar of 32. $Conv : 3 \times 3 \times 512, s2$ means the parameter to the next layer, 3×3 is size of filter, 2 the stride.

Current SSD only fit for the image of 300×300 and 512×512 which are called $SSD300$, $SSD512$. And it is weak in detecting the smaller objects. Hence, we extend the $SSD512$ to $SSD1024$, which can test 1024×1024 sized image. The red box of $Conv8\_2$ is added for $SSD1024$.

In the processing, SSD uses the VGG16 as a basenetwork for generating feature map. Then, the feature maps are revised smaller by the conventional layer ($Conv6to16$). All of the feature maps stored in the default size, which are convented by a filter which size is 3×3.

3.2 BaseNetwork for Feature Map Generation

VGG16 is applied as the base network of SSD, which is AlexNet liked model and developed in 2015 [14]. It used for generating the feature maps. It consists of 16 layers and 3 connected layers. $FC6$, $FC7$ of VGG are revised into $Conv6$ and $Conv7$ in SSD, and pooing size is revised from 2×2 to 3×3 and stride is revised from 2 to 1.

3.3 Prediction

The convolutional feature layers are add to the end VGG, and these layers decrease in size progressively and allow predicting of detections at multiple scales. The convolutional model for predicting detections is different for each feature layer.

In detail of $SSD1024$, the feature map (128×128) are generated by VGG. and the images are divided into 128×128 by using the feature map (128×128) for prediction. In the next layer, the feature map (64×64) are generated. And the images are dived into 64×64 by using the feature map (64×64) for prediction. In SSD1024, the $Conv5\_3$, $Conv7$ is defined as 4, and the left are defined as 6,6,6,4,4, Hence, the default box number is $128 \times 128 \times 4 + 64 \times 64 \times 4 + 32 \times 32 \times 6 + 16 \times 16 \times 6 + 8 \times 8 \times 6 + 4 \times 4 \times 6 + 2 \times 2 \times 4 + 1 \times 1 \times 4 = 90100$. Default boxes and aspect ratios are used for prediction, base on the current SSD.

4 Experimentation

This section introduces the experimental results of $SSD1024$, and comparing with $SSD300$ and $SSD512$. 330 rubbing images are used for testing the accuracy of proposal SSD, consisting 240 training images and 190 testing images. The rubbing images are scaned form BOOK [11]. In the dataset, 40 kinds character and the other characters are defined as "others" are used for testing the recognition accuracy. Figure 2 shows the 40 kinds testing characters, () recodes the pronunciation of the characters.

4.1 Experimental Condition

The deep learning framework is Caffe. The CPU is Intel Xeon E5–1620v3 3.5 GHz, GPU is Nvidia CeForce GTX1080ti ×3, and memory is 64 GB.

Learning rate is set at 0.001, threshold of confidence is 0.5, optimization algorithm is SGD, and the epoch is 1,200 thousand.

The *Recall*, *Precision* and *Harmonic Means(Fvalue)* are calculated for measuring the accuracy of proposal, by formula (1) (2) and (3). CRC is the

Fig. 2. Testing characters.

corrected recognized character number; MRC is the mis-recognized character number; TC is the total character number.

$$Recall = \frac{CRC}{TC} \tag{1}$$

$$Precision = \frac{CRC}{CRC + MRC} \tag{2}$$

$$Harmonic\ Mean = 2 \times \frac{Recall \times Precision}{Recall + Precision} \tag{3}$$

4.2 Recognition Results

Figures 3, 4 and 5 list three recognition results of $SSD300$, $SSD512$, $SSD1024$. the recognized characters are sounding by white bounding box.

In Fig. 3, there are 30 characters exist in the rubbing image. $SSD300$ only recognized two characters correctly, otherwise, $SSD512$ and $SSD1024$ achieved at 12 and 26 characters correct recognition, respectively. In Fig. 4, there are 24 characters exist in the rubbing image. $SSD300$ does not recognize any characters, otherwise, $SSD512$ and $SSD1024$ achieved at 10 and 20 characters correct recognition, respectively. In Fig. 5, there are 40 characters exist in the rubbing image. $SSD300$ only recognized 12 characters correctly, otherwise, $SSD512$ and $SSD1024$ achieved at 24 and 34 characters correct recognition, respectively.

The experimental results show that the $SSD1024$ achieves better accuracy than $SSD300$, $SSD512$. We also find that the accuracy are become better with increasing the size of input images. However, the bigger noise in the center of Fig. 3, is mis-detected as a character. It means, the bigger noise may mis-detected as a character in the $SSD1024$ wit the size increased.

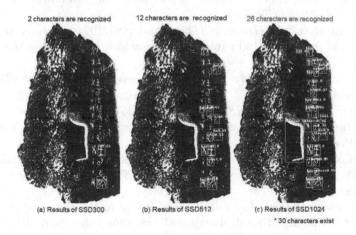

2 characters are recognized   12 characters are recognized   26 characters are recognized

(a) Results of SSD300   (b) Results of SSD512   (c) Results of SSD1024

* 30 characters exist

Fig. 3. Recognition results 1.

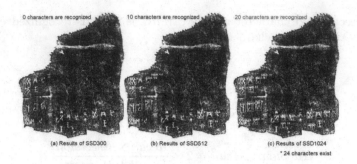

Fig. 4. Recognition results 2.

Fig. 5. Recognition results 3.

4.3 Accuracy Analysis

Table 1 shows the *Recall*, *Precision*, *Harmonic Means* and *Training time* of $SSD300$, $SSD512$, $SSD1024$. As the table shown, it takes a long time for training the three models. Layers are added in the $SSD1024$, causing that the $SSD1024$ takes two days for training, twice than the $SSD300$ and $SSD512$. However, the testing time are almost same, hence the training time does not influence of $SSD1024$ utilization.

In term of *Recall*, $SSD300$, $SSD512$ and $SSD1024$ correctly recognized 1599, 1996 and 2018 from 190 rubbing images which have 2658 characters and achieved at 0.61, 0.759, 0.82, respectively.

In term of *Precision*, only 1% difference between $SSD300$, $SSD512$ and $SSD1024$ which are near 95%. The correct recognized characters have a large increase in $SSD1024$ than $SSD300$ and $SSD512$, however there are little increase in the mis-recognition of $SSD1024$, causing the $SSD1024$ do not achieve a toppest *Precision*.

In term of *Harmonic Means*, $SSD1024$ achieves a best performance than the $SSD300$ and $SSD512$. It means that the $SSD1024$ is the best method in the these models.

Figure 6 shows the detail distribution of Recall in the three model. Vertical axis shows the ranging of recall, horizontal axis shows the distribution of every ranges. For example, the vertical axis of [0, 0.1] shows that about 3.6%, 1.0%, 1.0% of 190 testing images only achieve very low *Recall* which is between [0, 0.1] by $SSD300$, $SSD512$ and $SSD1024$,respectively; the vertical axis of (0.9,

Table 1. Experimental results of SSD300, SSD512 and SSD1024.

Model	Recall	Precision	Harmonic mean	Training time
SSD300	0.61	0.935	0.738	20 h 20 s
	1599/2658	1599/1709		
SSD512	0.759	0.956	0.846	30 h 40 s
	1996/2658	1996/2087		
SSD1024	0.82	0.946	0.884	48 h 20s
	2180/2658	2180/2303		

1.0] shows that about 21.2%, 33.5%, 40.7% of 190 testing images only achieve high *Recall* which is between (0.9, 1.0] by *SSD*300, *SSD*512 and *SSD*1024, respectively. Figure 6 also shows that the *SSD*1024 achieves reducing the low *Recall* testing images and give a excited increasing in the case of high *recall*.

4.4 Mis-recognition Analysis

The experimental results show that *Harmonic Mean* of *SSD*1024 achieve at 0.884, However the *Precision* is lower than *SSD*512 about 1%. The reason is that *SSD*1024 recognized some noises as characters. This subsection analyze the mis-recognition. Table 2 shows the mis-recognition of three models in detail. The mis-recognition is classified as three cases. Mis-case 1 is the character which belongs to 40 test characters is recognized as other character. Mis-case 2 is the character which belongs to 40 test characters is not recognized as themself. Mis-case 3 is the noise is recognized as characters. Mis-case 4 is the character which are not detected.

Comparing with the *SSD*300, *SSD*1024 recuded the Mis-case 1 and Mis-case 2. In term of Mis-case 4, a large number characters which are not detected in SSD300 and SSD512, are detected successfully by *SSD*1024. In means the *SSD*1024 achieves at characters detection than *SSD*300 and *SSD*512 for the reason of enlarge the image into 1024 × 1024.

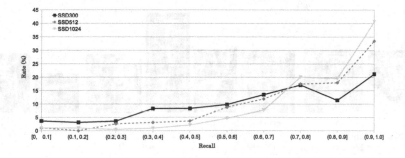

Fig. 6. Recall results of SSD300, SSD512 and SSD1024.

Table 2. Mis-recognition analysis.

Model	Mis-recognized characters			Without detected characters (mis-case 4)	Total mis-recognition characters
	Mis-case 1	Mis-case 2	Mis-case3		
SSD300	39	46	25	947	1084
SSD512	44	23	24	597	688
SSD1024	31	38	54	411	534

However, in term of the Mis-case 2 and Mis-case3, about more 15 characters do not recognized as themself, and about more 30 noises are detected as characters. The reasons is the images are enlarge, and nosises are enlarge too, and recognized as characters. It proved that increasing the image size more than 1024 is not easy to achieve more accuracy.

Figure 7 shows the mis-recognition examples of four cases about SSD2014. (a) and (b) are examples of mis-case 1, tow characters are recognized as others, we found the two rubbing images are broken and the (a) are very blurred. (c) and (d) are examples of mis-case 2, the characters are not recognized as themselves. Rubbing image of Fig. 7(c) is very blur, and a part of Fig. 7 is recognized as the different character. (e) and (f) is recognized as characters, even if there are not characters. For the reason of the rubbing images are broken like a characters. (g) and (h) are not detected as characters for the reason of the characters are too small to be detected in the images.

4.5   Discussion

The experimental results shows the following problems still exist. One is the characters are tilt, which is shown in Fig. 8(a). Because of the characters are tile, only 9 characters are recognized in the $SSD1024$. When we rotated the Fig. 8(a), the 12 characters are recognized which is shown in Fig. 8(b). Furthermore, in the case of the rubbing image is very blur, the OBIs can not achieve a better accuracy too.

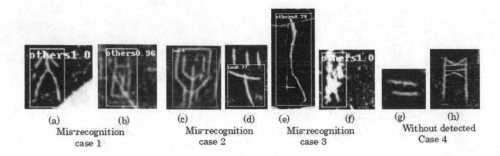

(a)   (b)   (c)   (d)   (e)   (f)   (g)   (h)
Mis-recognition   Mis-recognition   Mis-recognition   Without detected
case 1   case 2   case 3   Case 4

Fig. 7. Mis-recognition.

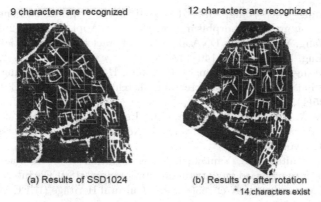

9 characters are recognized   12 characters are recognized

(a) Results of SSD1024   (b) Results of after rotation
* 14 characters exist

Fig. 8. Rotation results.

5   Conclusion

This paper extends the SSD to SSD1024 and achieves a good accuracy of OBIs detection and recognizing. Also, it first generate a training and testing database for OBIs detecting. The most contribution is that the $SSD1024$ achieves detecting smaller OBIs from rubbing images correctly. Also, we analyze the mis detection and list mis-type. The experimental results show that the bigger noise are detected as characters should be overcome in the future. Additional experiments such as adding testing data is necessary for proving the effectiveness of $SSD1024$ in the future work. Currently, state-of-the-art models of object detection are designed such as YOLO v3 [15]. Using these for OBIs detection and comparing the performance may be a challenge.

Acknowledgments. This work was supported by a Grant-in-Aid for Scientists (18K18337) from JSPS. Also, we are thank you for the supporting from Art research center of Ritsumeikan University.

References

1. Meng, L., Aravinda, C.V., Uday Kumar Reddy, K.R., Izumi, T., Yamazaki, K.: Ancient asian character recognition for literature preservation and understanding. In: Ioannides, M., et al. (eds.) EuroMed 2018. LNCS, vol. 11196, pp. 741–751. Springer, Cham (2018). https://doi.org/10.1007/978-3-030-01762-0_66
2. Meng, L.: Two-stage recognition for oracle bone inscriptions. In: Battiato, S., Gallo, G., Schettini, R., Stanco, F. (eds.) ICIAP 2017. LNCS, vol. 10485, pp. 672–682. Springer, Cham (2017). https://doi.org/10.1007/978-3-319-68548-9_61
3. Liu, W., et al.: SSD: single shot multibox detector. In: Leibe, B., Matas, J., Sebe, N., Welling, M. (eds.) ECCV 2016. LNCS, vol. 9905, pp. 21–37. Springer, Cham (2016). https://doi.org/10.1007/978-3-319-46448-0_2
4. Li, F., Woo, P.Y.: The coding principle and method for automatic recognition of Jia Gu Wen characters. Int. J. Hum.-Comput. Stud. **53**(2), 289–299 (2000)

5. Li, Q.S., Yang, Y.X., Wang, A.M.: Recognition of inscriptions on bones or tortoise shells based on graph isomorphism. Comput. Eng. Appl. **47**(8), 112–114 (2008)
6. Li, Q.S., Yang, Y.X.: Sticker DNA algorithm of oracle-bone inscriptions retrieving. Comput. Eng. Appl. **44**(28), 140–142 (2008)
7. Guo, J., Wang, C., Roman-Rangel, E., Chao, H., Rui, Y.: Building hierarchical representations for oracle character and sketch recognition. IEEE Trans. Image Process. **25**(1), 104–118 (2016)
8. Krizhevsky, A., Sutskever, I., Hinton, G.E.: ImageNet classification with deep convolutional neural networks. In: Advances in Neural Information Processing Systems (NIPS 2012), vol. 25 (2012)
9. Meng, L., Kamitoku, N., Yamazaki, K.: Recognition of oracle bone inscriptions using deep learning based on data augmentation. In: 2018 IEEE International Conference on Metrology for Archaeology and Cultural Heritage (IEEE MetroArchaeo 2018), October 2018
10. Szegedy, C., et al.: Going deeper with convolutions. In: 2015 IEEE Conference on Computer Vision and Pattern Recognition (CVPR 2015) (2015)
11. Zuo, P.M: Shanghai Bo Wu Guan Cang Jia Gu Wen Zi. Shanghai Bo Wu Guan (2009)
12. Meng, L., Tsuji, T., Izumi, T., Ochiai, A., Yamazaki, K.: Recognition of oracle bone inscriptions by extracting principal lines using dependency matrix on hough transform. J. Inst. Image Electron. Eng. Jpn. **47**(4) (2018). (In Japanese)
13. Yann, L., Bottou, L., Bengio, Y., Haffner, P.: Gradient-based learning applied to document recognition. In: Proceeding of the IEEE (1998)
14. Simonyan, K., Zisserman, A.: Very deep convolutional networks for large-scale image recognition. In: NIPS (2015)
15. Redmon, J., Farhadi A.: YOLOv3: an incremental improvement. In: Computer Vision and Pattern Recognition (2018)

Shot Boundary Detection for Automatic Video Analysis of Historical Films

Daniel Helm$^{(\boxtimes)}$ ⓘ and Martin Kampel ⓘ

Institute of Visual Computing and Human-Centered Technology, TU Wien,
Vienna, Austria
{daniel.helm,martin.kampel}@tuwien.ac.at

Abstract. In automatic video content analysis and film preservation, Shot Boundary Detection (SBD) is a fundamental pre-processing step. While previous research focuses on detecting Abrupt Transitions (AT) as well as Gradual Transitions (GT) in different video genres such as sports movies or news clips only few studies investigate in the detection of shot transitions in historical footage. The main aim of this paper is to create an SBD mechanism inspired by state-of-the-art algorithms which is applied and evaluated on a self-generated historical dataset as well as a publicly available dataset called Clipshots. Therefore, a three-stage pipeline is introduced consisting of a Candidate Frame Range Selection based on the network DeepSBD, Extraction of Convolutional Neural Network (CNN) Features and Similarity Calculation. A combination of pre-trained backbone CNNs such as ResNet, VGG19 and SqueezeNet with different similarity metrics like Cosine Similarity and Euclidean Distance are used and evaluated. The outcome of this paper displays that the proposed algorithm reaches promising results on detecting ATs in historical videos without the need of complex optimization and re-training processes. Furthermore, it points out the main challenges concerning historical footage such as damaged film reels, scratches or splices. The results of this paper contribute a significant base for future research on automatic video analysis of historical videos.

Keywords: Shot Boundary Detection · Video content analysis ·
Deep learning · Convolutional neural networks · Historical footage

1 Introduction

In the last decade the amount of available multimedia data has increased exponentially, which results in the need for automatic video analysis systems [8].

In domains such as video archival or historical film preservation, automated video analysis techniques are needed to find and annotate specific content in multimedia data [16]. Furthermore, these methods accomplish efficient and innovative ways to create new visual representations of specific historical domains such as the Holocaust[1].

---

[1] https://www.vhh-project.eu/en/summary/ - last visit: 2019/05/29.

© Springer Nature Switzerland AG 2019
M. Cristani et al. (Eds.): ICIAP 2019 Workshops, LNCS 11808, pp. 137–147, 2019.
https://doi.org/10.1007/978-3-030-30754-7_14

A fundamental and first step for automatic video analysis and annotation systems is *Shot Boundary Detection (SBD)* [8,15] which is the scope of this paper. A literature review shows that SBD has been an active research field for decades [7,14,17]. Studies have focused on traditional computer vision techniques such as histogram-based [9,17], motion-based [4,10] or edge-based [1] approaches. However, recent research indicates that the most promising methods for SBD are implemented by using deep learning techniques [6,8,14]. While the detection of shots in video genres such as sports movies or news clips has been the main focus of past research, fewer studies have investigated on historical footage which displays specific challenges such as splices, damaged film reels or scratches which occur during the digitization process of analog films [12,16]. In order to counteract these challenges and find efficient SBD approaches applied to historical video data, this paper focuses on the two following questions:

1. Question 1 (Q1): *Can state-of-the-art-based SBD approaches be used for detecting shot boundaries in historical videos without optimization and retraining of these algorithms?*
2. Question 2 (Q2): *What are the main challenges on detecting shot boundaries in historical videos compared to publicly available video datasets?*

A shot is defined as a number of consecutive frames related to the same content and is triggered by starting as well as ending a recording with one camera. A further structural level in film-making is the so-called scene. A scene is built by connecting one to several recorded shots with specific boundaries. A professionally or semi-professionally created movie or video clip consists of a varying number of combined scenes which together form the final movie. Figure 1 visualizes the basic components of a film or video clip [7,17].

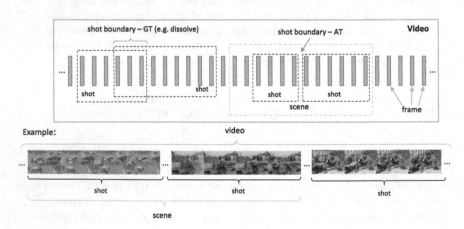

Fig. 1. Basic components of a semi-professional or professional video (inspired by [12]).

There are two main types of shot boundaries which are used to connect single shots: Abrupt Transition (AT) and Gradual Transition (GT). ATs are defined by a significant semantic change between two consecutive frames. That means that the next shot appears directly after the last frame of the previous shot. A GT is described as a smoother change of two adjacent shots and includes several frames of both shots. This is achieved by transition techniques such as fades, wipes or dissolves [8,12]. This paper proposes a SBD algorithm inspired by [6,7,14] in order to detect ATs in a self-generated historical video dataset. The core idea is to use a combination of pre-trained methods out-of-the-box which forms together a new SBD algorithm. Furthermore, this algorithm is evaluated on historical videos as well as the publicly available dataset [14]. The outcome of this paper shows promising results without the need of optimization and re-training processes of the proposed algorithms. Finally, it demonstrates the main challenges related to historical footage which raises the number of false detections of ATs.

The structure of this paper is organized as follows: Sect. 2 gives an overview of state-of-the-art technologies used for SBD. In Sect. 3 the proposed SBD algorithm as well as the datasets are presented. The results are reported in Sect. 4. Finally, the paper closes with a conclusion in Sect. 5.

2 State-of-the-Art

A literature review indicates that SBD tends to provide more promising results using deep learning approaches [6,8,14] instead of traditional computer vision algorithms such as histogram-based [9,17], motion-based [4,10] or edge-based [1] approaches.

Li et al. [17] have published a technique to find ATs as well as GTs by using a traditional histogram-based method. The core idea of that approach is to handle ATs like GTs based on the calculation of the Multilevel Difference of Color Histograms (MDCH). This algorithm has been evaluated with the TRECVID2001 dataset [13].

Tong et al. [15] have published one approach of SBD method based on a state-of-the-art Convolutional Neural Network and focus on detecting ATs and GTs. The network is trained with the ImageNet [11] data set with 50000 training iterations and can predict a probability among 1000 classes. In a further step, the five classes with the highest probability predicted on a given input image/frame are selected as high-level features and describe the frame content. These high-level features can be used for a more robust shot detection because frames corresponding to the same shot share similar TAGs whereas frames of different shots do not. Finally, the proposed algorithm is evaluated by using the TRECVID [13] data set and shows promising results compared to other state-of-the-art approaches.

Similar to the approach of Tong et al. [15], Xu et al. [8] have explored a further CNN-based SBD technique. Their network is trained with the ImageNet dataset [11] and forms the core of the SBD framework. The extracted feature vectors of each frame are evaluated by calculating the cosine similarity metric. As a pre-processing step, they have built a candidate segment selection based on an adaptive thresholding mechanism.

Jiang et al. [5] present a SBD mechanism based on the Place-centric deep network (PlaceNet) [3]. The approach consists of three main stages: candidate segment selection, shot detection network and shot boundary verification. This approach is based on the CNN models GoogleLeNet and ResNet50 and is trained on place categories instead of object categories.

Gygli [6] presents a different approach. The algorithm focuses on detecting shot transitions such as ATs and GTs by using a 3D Convolutional Neural Network. Therefore, a large-scale data set is generated and labeled automatically. Each video is split into snippets of 10 frames. Some of these snippets are combined with different types of shot transitions such as wipes or fades. Finally, the automatically generated dataset consists of transition snippets as well as of non-transition snippets and can be used to train the proposed 3D-CNN end-to-end. The algorithm is evaluated by using the data set RAI [2].

Hassanien et al. [7] have published a shot boundary detection mechanism based on a 3D Convolutional Neural Network (3D-CNN), called DeepSBD, to detect abrupt as well as gradual transitions in videos. Therefore, a dataset of over 3.5 million frames containing non- transitions, abrupt-transitions as well as gradual transitions such as fades, wipes and dissolves is generated and published. This dataset is used to train the proposed DeepSBD network. Finally, the approach is evaluated on different published benchmark datasets such as TRECVID 2001 test set by calculating Precision, Recall and $F_{1,Score}$ metrics.

The approach published by Tang et al. [14] is inspired by [7] and contributes a further fast and accurate SBD method. In a first step the whole video is filtered in order to select candidate segments including shot transitions. The ATs are detected by using a 2D ConvNet which is trained on a similarity function between two images and is able to locate the position of ATs. In order to locate GTs a 3D CNN network based on the idea of DeepSBD [7] is used. Whereas most studies are focused on developing models to detect shots in professionally or semi-professionally recorded videos, the authors of this paper have published a self-generated dataset called ClipShots [14], which contains more challenging videos including hand-held vibrations or large occlusions.

Table 1 visualizes a comparison of the results of Precision, Recall as well as $F_{1,Score}$ of the proposed state-of-the-art algorithms.

Table 1. Comparison of Precision, Recall and $F_{1,Score}$ between state-of-the-art Shot Boundary Detection mechanisms.

Method	Precision	Recall	$F_{1,Score}$	Evaluated on
Zongjie Li et al. [17]	0.89	0.84	0.87	partly TRECVID [13]
Hassanien et al. [7]	0.933	0.897	0.914	TRECVID [13]
Tang et al. [14]	0.909	0.921	0.915	TRECVID [13]
Jingwei et al. [8]	0.968	0.989	0.978	TRECVID [13]
Gygli [6]	0.86	0.906	0.876	RAI [2]
Tong et al. [15]	0.926	0.847	0.895	TRECVID [13]
Jiang et al. [5]	0.885	0.885	0.88	TRECVID [13]

3   Methodology

In order to answer Q1, an SBD method inspired by the state-of-the-art methods [6,7,14] is implemented and evaluated. Therefore, two datasets are used to assess the proposed algorithm.

3.1   Datasets

A literature review demonstrates that there exist a various number of publicly available datasets used to evaluate SBD mechanisms such as the TRECVID series [13], RAI [2], Clipshots [14] or DeebSBD [7]. There is no dataset available which can be used to evaluate SBD algorithms on historical footage. In this paper the proposed algorithm is evaluated using the published dataset Clipshots [14] as well as a self-generated dataset including historical videos related to the National-socialism and to the Holocaust and is called Efilms_DB.

The dataset Clipshots has been created to promote research on automatic SBD. This set contains 500 test videos of different genres such as news clips, sports movies, documentaries or daily life and is a collection of publicly available benchmark datasets such as the TRECVID series [13] or DeepSBD [7]. Furthermore, this dataset includes challenging videos related to camera motion as well. The annotations of that videos include the labeling of the shot boundaries such as ATs and GTs for each video. Figure 2a demonstrates frames of randomly selected example videos with the corresponding groundtruth annotations. The annotations display an AT between the mentioned frame numbers.

The Efilms_DB dataset includes videos related to the Holocaust and the National-socialism published during the project Ephemeral Films[2]. The self-generated dataset used in this paper consists of 66 videos with varying numbers of frames. Moreover, the shot boundaries in these videos are annotated by experts of the consortium of the new Horizon 2020 project Visual History of the Holocaust. All videos are digitized with a framerate of 24 fps and have a resolution of 960×720. Due to 63 gray scale and only 3 color videos included in the dataset, all movies are converted into the gray scale color space. Figure 2b visualizes frames of randomly selected example videos of this collection. The annotations demonstrate occurring ATs in the example videos. The dataset includes an overall number of 7214 annotated shot transitions. A first evaluation of the generated dataset and the corresponding annotations shows that there is a significant imbalance between the available number of ATs (7145) and GTs (69) in the videos.

Historical videos display different challenges such as video quality scratches or damaged film reels compared to the Clipshots dataset. These challenges raise the number of false detections and occur during the digitization process of related videos. Figure 3a shows a so-called Kadersprung between consecutive video frames. This phenomenon is related to the adjustment of the exposure time after changing a film reel. Figure 3b demonstrates a damaged film reel in

---

[2] http://efilms.ushmm.org/ - last visited: 2019/05/30.

a)   b)

Fig. 2. Example frames of randomly selected videos of the Clipshots dataset (a) and Efilms dataset (b) with the corresponding groundtruth annotations. (Color figure online)

consecutive recorded frames. While example frames (see Fig. 3c) display challenges concerning video quality, Fig. 3d visualizes occurred scratches as well as press cuts in film reels. All these types of challenges raise the number of false detections of ATs due to the significant change of the pixel values between two consecutive frames [12,16].

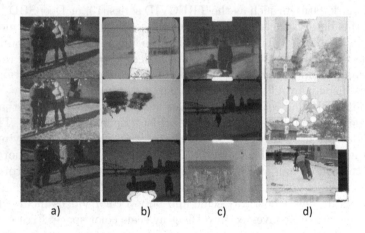

a)   b)   c)   d)

Fig. 3. Challenges for automatic SBD algorithms related to historical videos. (a) Exposure (Kadersprung) (b) Damaged film reel (c) Video quality (d) Scratches and press cuts

3.2   Evaluation of the Proposed Algorithm

In order to get comparable results, the proposed algorithm as well as the assessed state-of-the-art approaches are evaluated on the previous mentioned datasets, Clipshots and Efilms_DB. The results are analyzed by calculating and comparing the metrics, Precision (1), Recall (2) and $F_{1,Score}$ (3).

$$P = \frac{TP}{TP + FP} \tag{1}$$

$$R = \frac{TP}{TP + FN} \tag{2}$$

$$F_{1,Score} = 2 * \frac{P * R}{P + R} \tag{3}$$

where TP (True Positives) represent the correctly detected shot transitions, FP (False Positives) is the number of truly false detections and FN (False Negatives) corresponds to the relevant shot transitions which are not detected. The combination of *Precision* and *Recall* is represented as the harmonic mean called $F_{1,Score}$.

3.3 Proposed Shot Boundary Detection Method

In this paper a deep learning-based approach is used to explore the performance on the Efilms_DB as well as the Clipshots dataset. The pipeline of the method consists of three stages and is inspired by [6,7,14]: the Candidate Selection, CNN Feature Extraction and Similarity Comparison. Figure 4 illustrates the whole pipeline of the proposed approach.

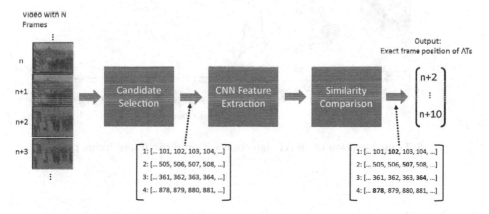

Fig. 4. Overview of the three-stage pipeline of the proposed SBD algorithm (inspired by [6,7,14]).

In the first stage a basic implementation of the DeepSBD[3] method is used to detect a range of frames which includes an AT or GT. As the focus in this paper is on ATs, the GTs are discarded. Therefore, a given input video is split in segments of 16 frames with an overlap of 8 frames. The core of the DeepSBD implementation is a 3D-CNN model which is able to assign each given segment in one out of three classes: Non-Transition (NT), AT as well as GT. The network is trained on the DeepSBD dataset. The output of the Candidate Selection stage is a range of frames corresponding to the given segment and includes an AT whereas the exact frame position of the transition is not detected. However, this

---

[3] https://github.com/Tangshitao/ClipShots_basline - last visit: 2019/06/09.

stage is used to perform a pre-selection in order to reduce computational costs. Moreover, the frame resolution is reduced by a factor 2.

After pre-selection of frame range candidates, including an AT, backbone CNN networks are used to extract representative features for each frame in the candidates list. In this investigation the CNN models ResNet, SqueezeNet as well as VGG19 are explored. All models are used by loading the pre-trained ImageNet weights.

Finally, in the last stage all extracted features are compared by calculating similarities between two frames. Therefore, the Euclidean Distance and the Cosine Similarity metric are used. After applying the last stage of the pipeline, the maximum of the calculated similarity distances corresponding to one candidate frame range is extracted and represents the exact frame position of an AT. Figure 5 displays the calculated Cosine Similarities of one selected example.

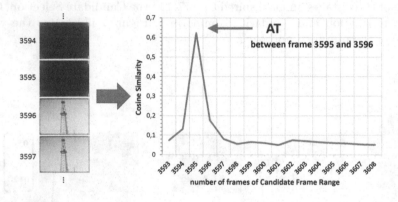

Fig. 5. Demonstration of an AT detection within a candidate frame range.

4 Results

The proposed algorithm is evaluated on the Efilms_DB and the Clipshots dataset in order to get comparable results. Table 2 displays an overview of the results on both datasets by using the backbone CNNs SqueezeNet, VGG19, ResNet as well as AlexNet. Furthermore, the Cosine Similarity and the Euclidean Distance measures are assessed by calculating Precision, Recall and $F_{1,Score}$. For the pre-selection of transition candidates, the pre-trained network DeepSBD is applied. The results in the table show that the best scores are reached with the DeepSBD. The reason for that is that this network is only able to predict frame ranges which are compared with the groundtruth ranges. A positive detection is triggered if there is at least one frame overlap between the groundtruth range and the predicted range. Further experiments show significant lower scores for the Precision. The final evaluation is done by comparing the exact frame position of an AT with the groundtruth position. The comparison between the experiments shows that there is no significant difference between all evaluated experiments. A further experiment evaluates the SBD method based on a pre-trained $AlexNet+Cosine$[4] without using the Candidate Selection stage, DeepSBD. The results in Table 2 point out that all experiments using DeepSBD show significant higher scores. The results of the proposed algorithm show no significant difference between the evaluated Efilms_DB and the Clipshots dataset (see Table 2). The most promising results on the Clipshots dataset are reached by using $DeepSBD+SqueezeNet+Cosine$.

Table 2. Results of proposed SBD algorithm on Efilms_DB including 66 historical videos and Clipshots dataset including 500 videos of different genres such as sports movies, news clips or daily life.

Method	Efilms			Clipshots		
	Precision	Recall	$F_{1,Score}$	Precision	Recall	$F_{1,Score}$
DeepSBD	0.944	0.818	0.877	0.895	0.694	0.773
DeepSBD+SqueezeNet+Cosine	0.892	0.839	0.865	**0.895**	**0.898**	**0.897**
DeepSBD+SqueezeNet+Euclidean	0.888	0.836	0.861	0.893	0.900	0.89
DeepSBD+VGG19+Cosine	**0.893**	**0.841**	**0.866**	0.894	0.899	0.896
DeepSBD+VGG19+Euclidean	0.887	0.835	0.860	0.894	0.898	0.896
DeepSBD+ResNet+Cosine	0.892	0.840	0.865	0.893	0.899	0.896
DeepSBD+ResNet+Euclidean	0.891	0.830	0.864	0.892	0.900	0.890
AlexNet+Cosine	0.737	0.649	0.69	0.738	0.546	0.628

However, for Efilms_DB, the analysis of the number of TP, FN, FP displays that the experiment $DeepSBD+VGG19+Cosine$ indicates the most promising results due to the highest number of TPs and lowest number of FPs as well as FNs compared to the other ones (Table 3).

Table 3. Overview of the number of TP, FP, FN of proposed SBD algorithm on Efilms_DB.

Experiments	TP	FP	FN	All (Pred)	All (GroundTruth)
DeepSBD+SqueezeNet+Cosine	5998	726	1147	6724	7145
DeepSBD+SqueezeNet+Euclidean	5972	752	1173	6724	7145
DeepSBD+VGG19+Cosine	**6006**	**718**	**1139**	**6724**	**7145**
DeepSBD+VGG19+Euclidean	5966	758	1179	6724	7145
DeepSBD+ResNet+Cosine	6000	724	1145	6724	7145
DeepSBD+ResNet+Euclidean	5994	730	1151	6724	7145

---

[4] https://github.com/owenzlz/Shot_Boundary_Detection_Using_CNN_features.git- last visit: 2019/06/11.

5 Conclusion

This paper focuses on the evaluation of a new proposed SBD approach inspired by state-of-the-art solutions. It is evaluated on a self-generated historical dataset, called Efilms_DB as well as on the publicly available Clipshots dataset. One main objective of this paper is to answer the research question Q1: Can state-of-the-art SBD approaches be used for detecting shot boundaries in historical videos without optimization and retraining of these algorithms? The analysis of the historical dataset displays an imbalance between ATs and GTs. The dataset includes about 99% ATs. Therefore, the focus in this paper is on detecting ATs in a first step. The evaluation demonstrates that the proposed algorithm shows promising results detecting ATs in historical videos. Without the need of further optimization and re-training of the networks, it reaches a $F_{1,Score}$ of 0.866. Due to different challenges in historical footage such as damaged film reels, splices, scratches, video quality or noise, the expectation has been an increase in false detections which results in a decrease of the $F_{1,Score}$. However, the comparison of the calculated scores between the Clipshots dataset and the Efilms_DB indicates no significant performance differences.

The analysis of the number of TP, FP and FN displays that the method combining $DeepSBD + VGG19 + CosineSimilarity$ reaches the most promising results compared to the other experiments. However, there is room for improvements of the proposed algorithm on detecting ATs. Furthermore, the detection of GTs is much harder due to the smoother change between two consecutive shots and varying length of one GT. Future research focuses on reducing FP detections triggered by scratches, splices or different exposures as well as FN detections which occur due to semantic similar recorded situations.

Acknowledgement. This project has received funding from the European Union's Horizon 2020 research and innovation programme under the Grant Agreement No. 822670.

References

1. Adjeroh, D., Lee, M.C., Banda, N., Kandaswamy, U.: Adaptive edge-oriented shot boundary detection. EURASIP J. Image Video Process. **2009**(1), 859371 (2009). https://doi.org/10.1155/2009/859371
2. Baraldi, L., Grana, C., Cucchiara, R.: Shot and scene detection via hierarchical clustering for re-using broadcast video. In: Azzopardi, G., Petkov, N. (eds.) CAIP 2015. LNCS, vol. 9256, pp. 801–811. Springer, Cham (2015). https://doi.org/10.1007/978-3-319-23192-1_67. https://www.ebook.de/de/product/25073344/computer_analysis_of_images_and_patterns.html
3. Bolei, Z., Agata, L., Aditya, K., Aude, O., Antonio, T.: Places: a 10 million image database for scene recognition. IEEE Trans. Pattern Anal. Mach. Intell. **40**(6), 1452–1464 (2018). https://doi.org/10.1109/TPAMI.2017.2723009
4. Bouthemy, P., Gelgon, M., Ganansia, F.: A unified approach to shot change detection and camera motion characterization. IEEE Trans. Circ. Syst. Video Technol. **9**(7), 1030–1044 (1999). https://doi.org/10.1109/76.795057

5. Jiang, D., Kim, J.: Video searching and fingerprint detection by using the image query and PlaceNet-based shot boundary detection method. Appl. Sci. **8**(10), 1735 (2018). https://doi.org/10.3390/app8101735
6. Gygli, M.: Ridiculously fast shot boundary detection with fully convolutional neural networks. Biochimica et Biophysica Acta **89**, 95–108 (2018). https://doi.org/10.1109/RoEduNet.2013.6511763
7. Hassanien, A., Elgharib, M.A., Selim, A., Hefeeda, M., Matusik, W.: Large-scale, fast and accurate shot boundary detection through spatio-temporal convolutional neural networks. CoRR abs/1705.03281 (2017). http://arxiv.org/abs/1705.03281
8. Xu, J., Song, L., Xie, R.: Shot boundary detection using convolutional neural networks. In: VCIP 2016–30th Anniversary of Visual Communication and Image Processing, pp. 1–4 (2017)
9. Küçüktunç, O., Gudukbay, U., Ulusoy, Ö.: Fuzzy color histogram-based video segmentation. Comput. Vis. Image Underst. **114**, 125–134 (2010). https://doi.org/10.1016/j.cviu.2009.09.008
10. Porter, S., Mirmehdi, M., Thomas, B.: Temporal video segmentation and classification of edit effects. Image Vis. Comput. **21**(13–14), 1097–1106 (2003). https://doi.org/10.1016/j.imavis.2003.08.014
11. Russakovsky, O., et al.: ImageNet large scale visual recognition challenge. Int. J. Comput. Vis. **115**(3), 211–252 (2015). https://doi.org/10.1007/s11263-015-0816-y
12. Seidl, M., Zeppelzauer, M., Mitrović, D., Breiteneder, C.: Gradual transition detection in historic film material - a systematic study. J. Comput. Cult. Herit. **4**(3), 10:1–10:18 (2011). https://doi.org/10.1145/2069276.2069279
13. Smeaton, A.F., Over, P., Doherty, A.R.: Video shot boundary detection: seven years of TRECVid activity. Comput. Vis. Image Underst. **114**(4), 411–418 (2010). https://doi.org/10.1016/j.cviu.2009.03.011
14. Tang, S., Feng, L., Kuang, Z., Chen, Y., Zhang, W.: Fast video shot transition localization with deep structured models. CoRR abs/1808.04234 (2018). http://arxiv.org/abs/1808.04234
15. Tong, W., Song, L., Yang, X., Qu, H., Xie, R.: CNN-based shot boundary detection and video annotation. In: 2015 IEEE International Symposium on Broadband Multimedia Systems and Broadcasting, pp. 1–5 (2015). https://doi.org/10.1109/BMSB.2015.7177222
16. Zeppelzauer, M., Mitrović, D., Breiteneder, C.: Archive film material - a novel challenge for automated film analysis. Frames Cin. J. **1**(1) (2012). http://publik.tuwien.ac.at/files/PubDat_216640.pdf
17. Li, Z., Liu, X., Zhang, S.: Shot boundary detection based on multilevel difference of colour histograms. In: Proceedings - 2016 1st International Conference on Multimedia and Image Processing, ICMIP 2016, pp. 15–22 (2016). https://doi.org/10.1109/ICMIP.2016.24

The *Epistle to Cangrande* Through the Lens of Computational Authorship Verification

Silvia Corbara[1]([✉]), Alejandro Moreo[1], Fabrizio Sebastiani[1], and Mirko Tavoni[2]

[1] Istituto di Scienza e Tecnologie dell'Informazione Consiglio Nazionale delle Ricerche, 56124 Pisa, Italy
{silvia.corbara,alejandro.moreo,fabrizio.sebastiani}@isti.cnr.it
[2] Dipartimento di Filologia, Letteratura e Linguistica Università di Pisa, 56126 Pisa, Italy
mirko.tavoni@unipi.it

Abstract. The *Epistle to Cangrande* is one of the most controversial among the works of Italian poet Dante Alighieri. For more than a hundred years now, scholars have been debating over its real paternity, i.e., whether it should be considered a true work by Dante or a forgery by an unnamed author. In this work we address this philological problem through the methodologies of (supervised) *Computational Authorship Verification*, by training a classifier that predicts whether a given work is by Dante Alighieri or not. We discuss the system we have set up for this endeavour, the training set we have assembled, the experimental results we have obtained, and some issues that this work leaves open.

Keywords: Machine learning · Authorship Verification · Digital humanities · Dante Alighieri · Medieval Latin

1 Introduction

The *Epistle to Cangrande*, from now on "EpXIII", is the thirteenth of the letters from Dante Alighieri's epistolary corpus that have survived until our times. Written in Latin, it is addressed to Can Francesco della Scala, known as Cangrande I, the ruler of the Italian cities of Verona and Vicenza at the beginning of the 14th century. Scholars traditionally divide it into 90 paragraphs and into 2 thematic portions: the first portion (paragraphs 1–13 – hereafter EpXIII(I)) is the dedicatory section, with proper epistolary characteristics, while the second portion (paragraphs 14–90 – hereafter EpXIII(II)) contains an exegesis of Alighieri's *Divine Comedy*, and in particular a commentary of the first few lines of its third part, the *Paradiso*. EpXIII became renowned over the centuries, especially because it would be the only analysis we have received from Dante Alighieri of his own masterpiece. However, since the start of the 19th century the authenticity of EpXIII has been questioned, and the issue has remained

M. Cristani et al. (Eds.): ICIAP 2019 Workshops, LNCS 11808, pp. 148–158, 2019.
https://doi.org/10.1007/978-3-030-30754-7_15

unsolved. The academic community is split between those who consider EpXIII authentic, those who consider it a forgery, and those who consider authentic the first portion but not the second.

To support the forgery thesis, scholars (e.g., [5]) point out numerous passages in the composition where the logical sequence of discourse is cumbersome, or even incoherent, with itself or with other writings by Alighieri. Moreover, many have noticed that there is a profound dissimilarity between EpXIII(I) and EpXIII(II), in their themes, style, and rhythm [10]. Even figuring out a timeframe when the letter could have been written is not a trivial problem.

Among those who believe EpXIII to be authentic, some (e.g., [2, pp. 280–1]) claim that there is a lexical coherence that cuts through the entire EpXIII, and an inner cohesive logic. Additionally, [1] observes that a forger would have followed more closely Alighieri's prose, and thus, paradoxically, the style dissimilar from Alighieri's should be seen as a further proof of authenticity. Many also note that the author of EpXIII offers some non-traditional and potentially controversial explanations for some exegetical and linguistic aspects of the *Divina Commedia*, and this could indicate a prominent author, since a lesser personality would have probably trodden on more ordinary, "safer" grounds. For a more comprehensive discussion of this controversy, see the analysis in [2,17].

Given this debated and yet unsolved problem, and in order to gain a fresh perspective over it and thus offer scholars yet another useful tool for investigation, in this work we have applied to the "whodunnit" of EpXIII the methodologies of (supervised) *Computational Authorship Verification* (AV), a task concerned with using training data to generate a binary classifier that predicts whether a given text of unknown or disputed paternity was written by a given candidate author or not.

This article is structured as follows. In Sect. 2 we give a brief introduction to AV, also hinting at related works that have applied AV to Latin texts. In Sect. 3 we discuss the methods we have employed to tackle the EpXIII mystery, and the features we have used for generating the vectorial representations of texts that will be fed to the learning algorithm (and to the classifier, once trained). In Sect. 4 we present the results of our experiments, in which we also assess the accuracy of our classifier over the entire dataset we have used, and establish the relative contribution of the various features. Finally, Sect. 5 discusses issues that this work leaves open, and possible avenues towards their solution.

2   Computational Authorship Verification

Authorship Analysis (AA) can be defined broadly as "any attempt to infer the characteristics of the creator of a piece of linguistic data" [11, p. 238], which includes the author's biographical information (age, gender, mother tongue, etc.), as well as their identity. The core of this practice, also known as "stylometry", relies on the idea to identify the author not from the artistic value of the text, or from the meaning of the concepts proposed within it, but from a quantitative analysis of the document's style. Here, "style" is intended as a summary statistics emerging from one or more numerical features that describe linguistic traits present in written texts, which are believed to remain more or less constant in an author's production and, conversely, to vary in noticeable fashion across different authors [11, p. 241]. These unique stylistic features are also known as "style markers".

This definition allows for every kind of textual trait, as long as it can be counted (hopefully: easily counted). It is the researcher's task to identify and extract the features that they deem most discriminative, i.e., most helpful for determining authorship. In particular, scholars started experimenting with this practice (well before the age of computers) by employing a single set of features comparable to the linguistic elements studied in classical philology, such as the frequencies of word lengths, sentence lengths, *hapax legomena*, and other specific terms. However, in the late 20th century, starting from the work of Mosteller and Wallace [16] on the *Federalist Papers*, the practice veered towards employing several sets of high-frequency features in parallel. Even though this approach captures textual traits of apparently minimal significance, this practice has proven effective in a variety of authorship analysis tasks, since the phenomena involved tend to be out of the conscious control of the author, and hence hard to modify or imitate. The noted historian Carlo Ginzburg describes this approach (as applied not only to text authorship issues, but to many other types of investigation as well) in his essay *Clues*, calling it the *Evidential Paradigm* [8].

The values of these stylistic features are collectively used as a simplified representation of the text, and employed for analyzing its authorship. This may be done via various methods, which are usually classified into similarity-based or machine learning -based. In the former class, specific algorithms are implemented to compute the similarity between different texts based upon a chosen similarity measure. In the latter class, a classifier is trained from a number of labelled training examples, using vectors of the chosen features (the style markers) as representations of the texts of interest; this enables the machine to leverage the values of the features in the training examples in order to classify new unlabelled documents. In the machine learning approach, AA is seen as an instance of (supervised) text classification, a task which generically deals with learning to classify text into a set of predefined classes, where the classes may represent topics, sentiments, literary genres, languages, and so on, depending on the application requirements.

In machine learning -based AA, the most popular methods still make use of "classical" machine learning algorithms, such as support vector machines (SVMs) or logistic regression (LR), even if deep learning algorithms have sometimes proved more accurate. This trend has also been confirmed in the PAN 2018 Author Identification shared task [13], where most of the systems presented were based on SVMs. This is due to two different reasons. On the one hand, in some application domains there is a systematic scarcity of annotated data, which clashes with the fact that deep learning methods typically require very large training sets. On the other hand, deep learning methodologies notoriously lack on the explainability side, which is undesirable when the investigation concerns a case of genuine controversy and it is indeed advisable that the factors supporting the conclusion drawn by the system can be properly exhibited [11, p. 307]. Both issues are especially relevant in the humanities, where the documents available are usually rather limited in number (as in the case of medieval Latin) and the main objective of computational studies is certainly not to replace the philologist, but to support their research with supplementary evidence and tools, which then need to be as explicit as possible.

The problem of EpXIII is an instance of *Authorship Verification* (AV), a subtask of ΛΛ that consists in determining whether a document of unknown or disputed paternity has been written by a given candidate author or by someone else. It is thus different from *Closed-set Authorship Attribution*, where the goal is to infer, for a document of unknown or disputed paternity, the most likely author among a finite set of candidate authors [14]. AV is thus a binary classification task, where the positive training examples are texts known to be by the candidate author, and the negative training examples are texts known to be by other "similar" authors writing in the same language.

In the humanities, AV is not a frequently tackled task: usually, scholars have more than one possible candidate author for a given document, and thus approach their research in a closed set authorship attribution setting. Some examples of such works are [3] for the 15th Book of Oz, [12] on the works by Monk of Lido and Gallus Anonymous, and the many works presented at a recent workshop about the true identity of pseudonymous novelist Elena Ferrante [19]. An exception to this pattern is [18] on Pliny the Younger's "Letter on the Christians" to Trajan, which is indeed framed as an AV problem.

3   AV Methods Applied to EpXIII

We have approached the problem of the authorship of EpXIII as a supervised binary classification task implemented via a linear classifier. After a few initial test with Logistic Regression (LR) and SVMs, we finally decided to stay with the former, since (a) preliminary experiments on our data had indicated that the two had a similar level of accuracy, and (b) unlike for SVMs, the output of LR admits a probabilistic interpretation, i.e., it can be interpreted as the ("posterior") probability that the document belongs to the class. See [4, pp. 205-6] for a more complete description of LR.

As discussed in Sect. 2, computational methods for AV map a textual document into a vector of features, each representing some linguistic phenomenon that is deemed related to authorship. To this aim, we have selected a combination of different feature types, since this approach usually yields better performance than just using a single type of features [9]. Each feature type we have used has been shown effective to some extent in other authorship-related tasks. The set of features we ended up using is the following:

– Character n-grams ($n \in \{3, 4, 5\}$);
– Word n-grams ($n \in \{1, 2\}$);

- Function words (from a list of 74 Latin function words);
- Verbal endings (from a list of 245 regular Latin verbal endings);
- Word lengths (from 1 to 23 characters);
- Sentence lengths (from 3 to 70 words).

Note that we ignore punctuation marks, since they were not inserted by the authors (punctuation was not used in medieval Latin, and such marks have been introduced into texts for editorial purposes).

In order to deal with the high dimensionality of the feature space we subject the feature types resulting in a sparse distribution (character n-grams and word n-grams) to a process of dimensionality reduction. First, we perform feature selection via the Chi-square function, i.e.,

$$\chi^2(t_k, d_j) = \frac{[\Pr(t_k, c_i) \Pr(\bar{t_k}, \bar{c_i}) - \Pr(t_k, \bar{c_i}) \Pr(\bar{t_k}, c_i)]^2}{\Pr(t_k) \Pr(\bar{t_k}) \Pr(c_i) \Pr(\bar{c_i})} \tag{1}$$

where probabilities are interpreted on the event space of documents; in other words, $\Pr(t_k, c_i)$ represents the probability that, for a random document that belongs to class c_i, feature t_k appears in the document. In our experiments we have selected the best 10% character n-grams and the best 10% word n-grams.

We have then performed feature weighting via the tfidf function in its standard "ltc" variant, i.e.,

$$\text{tfidf}(t_k, d_j) = \text{tf}(t_k, d_j) \cdot \log \frac{|D|}{\#D(t_k)} \tag{2}$$

where $\text{tfidf}(t_k, d_j)$ is the weight of feature t_k for document d_j, D is the collection of documents, $\#D(t_k)$ is the *document frequency* of feature t_k (i.e., the number of documents in which the feature appears at least once), and

$$\text{tf}(t_k, d_j) = \begin{cases} 1 + \log \#(t_k, d_j) & \text{if } \#(t_k, d_j) > 0 \\ 0 & \text{otherwise} \end{cases} \tag{3}$$

where $\#(t_k, d_j)$ is the number of occurrences of feature t_k in document d_j.

3.1   The Training Set

As already explained in Sect. 1, EpXIII consists of two sections, EpXIII(I) and EpXIII(II), distinct from each other for purpose and style. More importantly, not all scholars agree that the two sections are from the same author. We have thus decided to split the AV problem into two different AV sub-problems, and thus to train two different classifiers, one for EpXIII(I) and another for EpXIII(II). In order to train and evaluate these classifiers, we have created two datasets of medieval Latin texts, by including in each such dataset documents which can be considered, linguistically and stylistically speaking, similar to the document (EpXIII(I) or EpXIII(II)) we are dealing with. The positive class (Dante) is represented by all known works in Latin that are unquestionably by Alighieri: his other

12 epistles for the EpXIII(I) dataset, and *De Vulgari Eloquentia* and *Monarchia* for the EpXIII(II) dataset.[1] Conversely, for the negative class (NotDante) we have assembled two sets of Latin texts by coeval authors: a set of 282 epistles from more than 20 different authors (for the EpXIII(I) dataset) and a set of 28 miscellaneous texts, mostly literary commentaries and treatises, from 19 different authors (for the EpXIII(II) dataset); all the documents date between the 13th and the 15th century (see [6] for more details on these two datasets). In the end, as described in Column 1 of Table 1, the EpXIII(I) and EpXIII(II) datasets consist of 294 and 30 texts, respectively.

Table 1. The two datasets and the results obtained on them.

	1	2	3	4	5	6	7
	# full docs	# training docs	Prediction	Pr(Dante)	F_1(Dante)	Macro-F_1	Micro-F_1
EpXIII(I)	294	1310	NotDante	0.24	0.957	0.886	0.981
EpXIII(II)	30	12312	NotDante	0.39	0.400	0.688	0.775

We have preprocessed all the documents by

- Lower-casing the entire text.
- Removing any symbol that has been inserted by the curator of the edition, such as titles, page numbers, quotation marks, square brackets, etc; this cleans the documents from obvious editorial intervention.
- Marking the citations in Latin with asterisks, and the citations in languages different from Latin (mostly Florentine vernacular) with curly brackets; this is both to ignore them in the computation (since they are the production of someone different than the author of the text) and to mark a potential authorial-related feature for future development, i.e., the usage of citations in different languages.
- Replacing every occurrence of character "v" with character "u"; the reason for this lies in the different approaches followed by the various editors of the texts included, regarding whether to consider "u" and "v" as the same character or not.[2]

Additionally, in order to increase the number of training samples, we subject all documents in both datasets to a segmentation policy, i.e., we split each document into segments and consider each resulting segment as a separate, additional training document. This approach is a common practice in ML-based AA when only few labelled texts are available [15, p. 514]. More in detail, by employing

---

[1] Other works by Alighieri, including the *Divine Comedy*, are not included in these two datasets since Alighieri wrote them not in Latin but in the Florentine vernacular (*volgare*), which was to form the basis of what is nowadays the Italian language.

[2] In the medieval writing there was only one grapheme, represented as a lowercase "u" and a capital "V", instead of the two modern graphemes "u-U" and "v-V".

the Natural Language Toolkit (NLTK) sentence tokenizer module[3], we split each document into sentences; if a sentence is too short (fewer than 8 words) we join it with the subsequent one, unless it is the last sentence in the text, in which case we join it with the previous one. We then join the sentences thus derived into segments of n consecutive sentences each, without overlapping, and we consider each segment as a single labelled example; the current value of n we use is 3. The final result of this procedure is shown in the first 2 columns of Table 1.

4   Experiments

We train our two "Dante vs. NotDante" classifiers by optimizing hyperparameter C (the inverse of the regularization strength) via stratified 10-fold cross-validation, using a grid search on the set {0.0001, 0.001, 0.01, 0.1, 1, 10, 100, 1000}.

The predictions by the optimized classifiers are shown in Column 3 of Table 1, which shows that the classifiers consider both EpXIII(I) and EpXIII(II) the production of someone else than Alighieri. Column 4 lists the posterior probabilities returned by the LR classifier, and indicate that the classifier attributes a probability of 0.24 (resp., 0.39) to the fact that EpXIII(I) (resp., EpXIII(II)) was written by Alighieri; in other words, the hypothesis that Alighieri might be the true author is rejected with more strength for EpXIII(I) than for EpXIII(II).

In order to determine the degree of reliability of our two classifiers, and hence establish how trustworthy the above predictions about EpXIII(I) and EpXIII(II) are, we subject the algorithm to a "leave-one-out" validation test, which consists in predicting, for each dataset D, for each author a represented in the dataset, and for each document d in the dataset, whether a is the author of d or not, where the prediction is issued by a "a vs. (NOT a)" binary classifier trained on all documents in D/d. We exclude from this analysis authors which have only 1 text in the dataset, which means that we train binary classifiers for 5 authors for EpXIII(I) and 6 authors for EpXIII(II); this leads to $5 \times 294 = 1470$ predictions for EpXIII(I) and $6 \times 30 = 180$ predictions for EpXIII(I). Note that, in order to recreate the conditions of the actual classification of EpXIII(I) and EpXIII(II), and in order to avoid any overlap between test and training samples, (i) we test only on the original entire documents (thus ignoring the segments), and, (ii) when document d is used as a test document, we exclude from the training set all the segments derived from d. As evaluation measures we use the well-known *macroaveraged* F_1 and *microaveraged* F_1.

The results of these experiments are shown in Columns 6 and 7 of Table 1. As it can be seen, the classifiers, and especially the one for EpXIII(I), obtain a good level of accuracy (notwithstanding the small size of many training sets), in line with other state-of-the-art methods.

Column 5 of the same table reports the F_1 results for the two "Dante vs. NotDante" classifiers. In this case the F_1 values for EpXIII(II) are much lower

---

[3] https://www.nltk.org/api/nltk.tokenize.html.

Table 2. Results of the feature ablation study; (-) indicates the feature type omitted.

		All features	(-) char n-grams	(-) word n-grams	(-) function words	(-) verbal endings	(-) word lengths	(-) sentence lengths
EpXIII(I)	Macro-F_1	0.886	0.727 (-17.95%)	0.784 (-11.51%)	0.795 (-10.27%)	0.908 (+2.48%)	0.886 (0.00%)	0.886 (0.00%)
	Micro-F_1	0.981	0.947 (-3.47%)	0.979 (-0.20%)	0.985 (+0.41%)	0.983 (+0.20%)	0.981 (0.00%)	0.981 (0.00%)
EpXIII(II)	Macro-F_1	0.688	0.486 (-29.33%)	0.463 (-32.66%)	0.671 (-2.44%)	0.690 (+0.29%)	0.688 (0.00%)	0.679 (-1.29%)
	Micro-F_1	0.775	0.590 (-23.88%)	0.528 (-31.88%)	0.750 (-3.25%)	0.775 (0.00%)	0.775 (0.00%)	0.741 (-4.38%)

than for EpXIII(I); here, the classifier is penalized for not attributing *Monarchia* to Alighieri (since *Monarchia* is one of the two texts by him in the dataset, this mistake alone makes recall equal 0.50, and prevents the value of F_1 – which is the harmonic mean of precision and recall – to be high enough), while it correctly classifies 26 out of the 28 negative examples.

4.1   Feature Ablation and Feature addition

In order to further analyze the behaviour of our classifiers, we have conducted a study of individual feature types via either feature ablation or feature addition. In the feature ablation study the single feature type t is omitted, and the resulting Macro-F_1 and Micro-F_1 values are compared with the analogous values resulting from the "all features" study reported in Columns 6 and 7 of Table 1. In the feature addition study only the single feature type t is used, and the resulting Macro-F_1 and Micro-F_1 values are compared with the analogous values obtained by a hypothetical classifier that uses the empty set of features, i.e., by the random classifier.[4]. The results of the feature ablation study are shown in Table 2, while the results of the feature addition study are shown in Table 3.

The feature addition study indicates that all feature types used are in principle informative, as shown by the (often dramatic) improvements in accuracy that each feature type brings about with respect to the random classifier. However, the feature ablation study shows that the very same feature types, when removed from an "all features" classifier, bring about a much less dramatic deterioration (if any deterioration at all – see e.g., word lengths). We think this has two possible explanations. First, some feature types are, when other feature types are already present, redundant; this may be the case, e.g., for verbal endings, since the same character string that forms a verbal ending may already be present

---

[4] "The" random classifier is indeed an abstraction; by the accuracy of the random classifier we mean the average accuracy of all possible classifiers, i.e., of all possible ways the test set might be classified. It is easy to show that this is equivalent to the accuracy of a classifier for which half of the positives are true positives while the other half are false negatives, and half of the negatives are true negatives while the other half are false positives.

Table 3. Results of the feature addition study; (+) indicates the feature type inserted.

		Random classifier	(+) char n-grams	(+) word n-grams	(+) function words	(+) verbal endings	(+) word lengths	(+) sentence lengths
EpXIII(I)	Macro-F_1	0.217	0.818 (+276.96%)	0.630 (+190.32%)	0.559 (+157.60%)	0.523 (+141.01%)	0.429 (+97.70%)	0.368 (+69.59%)
	Micro-F_1	0.264	0.958 (+262.88%)	0.907 (+243.56%)	0.799 (+202.65%)	0.732 (+177.27%)	0.558 (+111.36%)	0.527 (+99.62%)
EpXIII(II)	Macro-F_1	0.149	0.390 (+161.74%)	0.367 (+146.31%)	0.532 (+257.05%)	0.449 (+201.34%)	0.363 (+143.62%)	0.230 (+54.36%)
	Micro-F_1	0.151	0.426 (+182.12%)	0.476 (+215.23%)	0.625 (+313.91%)	0.462 (+205.96%)	0.310 (+105.30%)	0.204 (+35.10%)

in the feature set as a character n-gram. Second, when the dimensionality of the vector space is already high, adding other dimensions may bring about (or increase) overfitting; this is especially true in our case, in which the amount of training data is small.

Aside from these considerations, both experiments seem to show that the feature types that contribute most to AV accuracy are word n-grams and character n-grams, followed by function words and verbal endings; conversely, the contribution of word lengths and sentence lengths seems to be comparatively smaller.

5 Conclusion and Future developments

The predictions output by our classifier seem to align with the theory that the entire EpXIII was the work of a malicious forger. Nevertheless, the conclusions presented here should not be considered definitive. As stated before, the methods displayed here are only the current stage of a project which we consider to be far from completion. The ideas we want to pursue in the near future in order to improve the system can be divided into 3 areas: (a) the datasets, (b) genre and topic bias, and (c) the feature set.

First of all, we intend to expand the datasets with additional documents. Working with medieval Latin makes this task more difficult than when working with modern languages. One possibility we are exploring is the addition of the texts made available by Kabala in [12] to our datasets; since these are one to two centuries older than the ones in our datasets, it remains to be seen whether this addition would be beneficial or detrimental.

As already mentioned in Sect. 1, EpXIII, if proved authentic, would be the only commentary that we have received by Alighieri on his own *Divine Comedy*. Unfortunately, this also means that, while one of the documents we want to classify (i.e., EpXIII(II)) is a commentary on the *Divine Comedy*, no other training document from class Dante is. On the contrary, some documents that are contained in the corpus of EpXIII(II) are, since at the time the *Divine Comedy* had attracted the attention of learned people. It is thus possible that the EpXIII(II) classifier is (at least partially) recognizing the topic of a document, and not its author[5]. This suspicion is reinforced by the fact that, as feature types, we use both character and word n-grams, which are effective features in classification by topic.

In order to understand whether the dataset is biased by topic and/or by genre, we have run two additional experiments. The first one consisted in labelling each EpXIII(II) text according to whether it consists or not of a commentary on a literary work, and running a leave-one-out validation test obtained by repeatedly training "Commentary vs. NotCommentary" classifiers *on the very same feature set* used for the "Dante vs. NotDante" experiment. The second experiment was analogous, aside from the fact that the EpXIII(II) texts were now labelled according to whether they discussed Alighieri's *Divine Comedy* or not, thus implementing a "Comedy vs. NotComedy" distinction. Note that the former experiment is about *classification by genre*, while the second is about *classification by topic*, which are two dimensions conceptually orthogonal to the one we are interested in, i.e., *classification by author* (or: authorship verification). Both experiments returned F_1 values of 1.00. This suggests that the results presented in Sect. 4 are likely influenced by both genre bias and topic bias present in the dataset, i.e., that those results are not entirely due to the classifier's ability to recognize authorship, as instead one would hope; on the other hand, refraining from inserting commentaries on literary works, and even on the *Divine Comedy* itself, in the NotDante dataset, would prevent us from comparing EpXIII with all the writers who might conceivably be its authors. This is an important open issue, that we plan to address by using methods devised in the field of "fair machine learning" (see, e.g., [7]).

Finally, we intend to further improve the feature set by experimenting with different feature types: for example, employing a POS-tagger for Latin could result in the detection of authorial traits related to the syntactic habits of the author.

References

1. Ascoli, A.R.: Access to authority: dante in the epistle to cangrande. In: Baranski, Z.G. (ed.) Seminario Dantesco Internazionale/International Dante Seminar 1, pp. 309–352. Le Lettere, Firenze (1997)
2. Azzetta, L.: Epistola XIII. In: Baglio, M., Azzetta, L., Petoletti, M., Rinaldi, M. (eds.) Nuova edizione commentata delle opere di Dante, Epistole. Egloge. Questio de aqua et terra, vol. 5, pp. 271–487. Salerno Editrice, Roma (2016)
3. Binongo, J.N.G.: Who wrote the 15th Book of Oz? An application of multivariate analysis to authorship attribution. Chance **16**(2), 9–17 (2003)
4. Bishop, C.M.: Pattern Recognition and Machine Learning. Springer, New York (2006)
5. Casadei, A.: Sempre contro l'autenticità dell'Epistola a Cangrande. Studi Danteschi **LXXXI**, 215–246 (2016)

---

[5] Note that this specific problem is, as stated, confined to the classifier of EpXIII(II), and does not affect the one for EpXIII(I). Still, in the EpXIII(I) dataset there might be other types of topic bias that we have not detected yet.

6. Corbara, S., Moreo, A., Sebastiani, F., Tavoni, M.: L'Epistola a Cangrande al vaglio della computational authorship verification: Risultati preliminari (con una postilla sulla cosiddetta "XIV Epistola di Dante Alighieri"). In: Casadei, A. (ed.) Atti del Seminario "Nuove Inchieste sull'Epistola a Cangrande". Pisa University Press, Pisa (2019, forthcoming)
7. Dwork, C., Immorlica, N., Kalai, A.T., Leiserson, M.D.: Decoupled classifiers for group-fair and efficient machine learning. In: Proceedings of the 1st ACM Conference on Fairness, Accountability and Transparency (FAT 2018), pp. 119–133, New York(2018)
8. Ginzburg, C.: Clues, myths and the historical method. In: Clues: Roots of an Evidential Paradigm, pp. 96–125. Johns Hopkins University Press, Baltimore (1989)
9. Grieve, J.: Quantitative authorship attribution: an evaluation of techniques. Lit. Linguist. Comput. **22**(3), 251–270 (2007)
10. Hall, R.G., Sowell, M.U.: Cursus in the can grande epistle: a forger shows his hand? Lectura Dantis **5**, 89–104 (1989)
11. Juola, P.: Authorship attribution. Found. Trends Inf. Retrieval **1**(3), 233–334 (2006)
12. Kabala, J.: Computational authorship attribution in medieval Latin corpora: the case of the Monk of Lido (ca. 1101–08) and Gallus Anonymous (ca. 1113–17). Language Resources and Evaluation, pp. 1–32 (2019). https://doi.org/10.1007/s10579-018-9424-0
13. Kestemont, M., et al.: Overview of the author identification task at PAN-2018: cross-domain authorship attribution and style change detection. In: Working Notes of the Conference and Labs of the Evaluation Forum (CLEF 2018), pp. 1–25. Avignon (2018)
14. Koppel, M., Schler, J., Argamon, S.: Computational methods in authorship attribution. J. Am. Soc. Inform. Sci. Technol. **60**(1), 9–26 (2009)
15. Luyckx, K., Daelemans, W.: Authorship attribution and verification with many authors and limited data. In: Proceedings of the 22nd International Conference on Computational Linguistics (COLING 2008), pp. 513–520. Manchester (2008)
16. Mosteller, F., Wallace, D.L.: Inference and Disputed Authorship: The Federalist. Addison-Wesley, Reading (1964)
17. Sasso, G.: Sull'Epistola a Cangrande. La Cultura **3**, 359–446 (2013). https://doi.org/10.1403/75324
18. Tuccinardi, E.: An application of a profile-based method for authorship verification: investigating the authenticity of Pliny the Younger's letter to Trajan concerning the Christians. Digit. Scholarsh. Humanit. **32**(2), 435–447 (2016)
19. Tuzzi, A., Cortelazzo, M.A. (eds.): Drawing Elena Ferrante's profile. Workshop Proceedings. Padova University Press, Padova (2017)

A Cockpit of Measures for Image Quality Assessment in Digital Film Restoration

Alice Plutino[1]([⊠]) [iD], Michela Lecca[2] [iD], and Alessandro Rizzi[1] [iD]

[1] Dip. di Informatica Milano, Università degli Studi di Milano, Milan, Italy
{alice.plutino,alessandro.rizzi}@unimi.it
[2] Fondazione Bruno Kessler, ICT Center, Trento, Italy
lecca@fbk.eu

Abstract. We present an alternative approach for the quality assessment of the digital restoration of a degraded film. Instead of summarizing the film quality by an unique value, here we propose a set of basic measures that account for different film visual features. These measures describe over time global and local properties of the film, like brightness, contrast, color distribution entropy, color variations and perceptual intra-frame color changes. They are relevant to estimate the level of *readability* of the visual content of the film and to quantify the perceptual differences between the original and restored film. The measures proposed here are viewed as the parameters showed in a car or airplane cockpit and necessary to control the machine status and performance. The idea of cockpit would like to contribute to the automation of the digital restoration process and of its evaluation that are currently still performed for the most part manually by video editors and curators and thus often biased by subjective issues.

Keywords: Image quality · Film restoration · Image enhancement.

1 Introduction

The expression *film restoration* denotes a complex process devoted to rescue and preserve the content of decaying films. Film restoration is today a territory with uncertain boundaries, still without codified rules and shared methodologies [2]. The restoration must take into account a plethora of different aspects, from the physical and chemical features of the film to the cultural context in which the film has been produced and should be restored. For this reason, the restoration involves several fields of study like philology, history, chemistry, physics, optics and computer science, and this makes its automation a challenging issue [5,6,19]. In the last decades, many techniques for the Digital Restoration (DR) have been proposed [1,4,14,16]. In DR the film to be restored is first digitized, i.e. it is transferred from analog to digital support. Then it undergoes to a series of unsupervised image processing algorithms, which lower or even remove artifacts like flickering, scratches, color fading due to the aging or to the presence of

© Springer Nature Switzerland AG 2019
M. Cristani et al. (Eds.): ICIAP 2019 Workshops, LNCS 11808, pp. 159–169, 2019.
https://doi.org/10.1007/978-3-030-30754-7_16

dust [8]. One advantage of DR with respect to the analog restoration is the possibility in DR to study and test the effects of restoration algorithms without directly intervening on the analog support and thus without risking to damage irreparably the original data. Moreover, the DR provides better results on color correction thanks to the use of image enhancers and color grading algorithms that independently analyze and process the color components, differently from the analog counterpart, where the color is treated as a single entity and usually corrected by simulating a printing process [3,7]. In particular, the independent analysis of the color components is fundamental to study degrading effects in films with color subtractive format, like for instance color fading that usually affects only one of the emulsion layers of the film and thus only one of the corresponding digitized image channel.

One of the main problem to be addressed in digital and in analog restoration regards the evaluation of the quality of the results. This task is generally left to the film curator or the film owner and is completely subjective, thus often biased by personal aesthetic cues. In the best case, there are references to make comparisons or the colourist is an expert in the restoration of the specific support, but in the worst case the references are missing, and the assessment is left to the personal preferences of the curator or to the assumption of how a scene should have looked like. Providing an objective judgment is an open problem due to the lack of agreed measures for evaluating the image quality and due to the difficulty of modeling all the features that concur to the image quality assessment and that are still today poorly understood [11]. Many subjective and objective measures for capturing the complex nature of the image quality have been proposed in the literature, e.g. [11]. Nevertheless, we argue that a single measure difficulty suffice to this purpose.

In this work we thus propose a novel toolkit for the unsupervised computation of more no-reference image quality measures relevant to the evaluation of the film restoration quality and able to support the activity of domain experts in choosing the restoring algorithms more suitable for the film at the hand.

We call our tool *the cockpit* since the measures it computes (here the brightness and its local changes, the contrast, the entropy of the color distribution of each film frame and the intra-frame perceptual color variation) can be viewed as the parameters controlling the status and the performance of a machine, like a car or an airplane. We tested the cockpit on different scenes of films whose colors are restored through one or more image enhancement methods, to demonstrate the importance of the use of many measures for quality assessment, the reliability of our method and to lay the foundations for a future more complete cockpits for film restoration.

2   The Cockpit

As mentioned in Sect. 1, the quality assessment is a complex mechanism that is hard to be described by a single feature. To provide a more comprehensive image quality assessment, many features must be taken into account. In particular, these features must capture visual properties revealing the level of *readability* of the visual content. Specifically, we say that an image is *readable* if an human observer can clearly understand and describe its content punctually and globally.

The cockpit we propose takes as input a film sequence, and estimates five no-reference objective measures frame by frame. We have chosen these features among many others since they are very popular and intuitive and they have been already employed to assess the performance of algorithms of image enhancement that may be relevant for film restoration, see for instance [10].

Let I, $|I|$ and x be respectively a frame of a film F, the number of pixels in I and a pixel of I. The measures provided by the cockpit are:

1. Mean Brightness B: the mean brightness B of a gray level image I is the average of the intensity values of I over $|I|$. For any color image I, the cockpit computes the value B for each channel of I and for the image L^*. The image L^* is computed by converting the RGB values to $L^*a^*b^*$ color space using a value of gamma of 2.2 and the D65 as reference illuminant.

2. Multi-Resolution contrast C [13]: the cockpit computes this measure on the image L^*. The local contrast of L^* at x is the mean value of the L^1 distances between $L^*(x)$ and the intensities of the eight pixels surrounding x in the 3×3 window centered at x. The mean local contrast of L^* is the average of the values d over $|I|$. The multi-resolution contrast C of L^* is the average of the mean local contrasts of a set of images $L_1^*, \ldots, L_K^*$ $K(>1)$ obtained by sequentially half-scaling L^*, with $L_1^* := L^*$.

3. Deviance from Histogram Flatness F: this is a measure of the entropy of the distribution of L^*. Let $H(L^*)$ be the histogram of L^*, normalized to sum up to 1. The deviance of $H(L^*)$ from the histogram flatness is the L^1 distance between $H(L^*)$ and the uniform probability density function over the range of I (typically $[0, 255]$).

4. Coefficient of Local Variation V: this is the mean value of the relative standard deviations $\sigma(x)$ computed at each pixel x of L^*. The value $\sigma(x)$ is the ratio between the standard deviation and the mean of L^* in a 9×9 window (where the mean differs from zero). The value of V quantifies the local dispersion of the probability distribution of L^* and relates information of brightness and contrast.

5. Color Difference ΔE: the cockpit provides the intra-frame normalized sum of color differences CIE ΔE which is the L^2 distance between two consecutive frames in the perceptual color space CIEL^*a*b*, for each x.

We notify that we do not want to promote these features as the best ones for assessing image quality, conversely other features can be employed and/or added. Nevertheless, these features are of interest, since they provide fundamental information about visual features strongly related to the readability of an image and at the same time they offer an important example about the need to analyze jointly different aspects to obtain a reliable quality evaluation. The image enhancers usually increase the values of B, C and V, while decrease the value of F. Considering only one of these measures may lead to wrong conclusions. In fact, for instance, an exaggerate increment of B does not imply necessarily a good restoration result, indeed it may even correspond to an over-enhancement that made the frame homogeneous removing important details. In this case, the values of C, F and V are very important to have a more reliable analysis of the enhancement performance. Analogously, a remarkable increase of C might highlight also noisy pixels, making the frame unpleasant and poorly understandable. In this case, checking V may help. Robustness to flickering (i.e. frequent changes of brightness across frames of the same shot) is monitored by observing the measures described above over time: the more slowly they change the lower the flickering. In particular, ΔE provides an information about the perceptual changes of colors over time. Moreover, these cockpit measures may underline changes in digital frame content and/or restoration effects that could be in some cases not clearly visible by a quick inspection by human observers.

3   Experiments

To measure the reliability of the evaluation provided by the cockpit, we considered some sequences of different films restored through different manual or automatic techniques and we compare the cockpit measures on the input and output sequences.

Table 1. Main features of the films used in our experiments,

Film	N. of frames	Main features	Applied enhancers
Fiat 508 (1931)	888	Black & White movie Flickering Dust and Scratches Silver Fading	DR + ACE
La lunga calza verde (1961)	265	Animation Movie Colour Fading	STRESS
La Ciudad en la Playa (1961)	222	Super 8 movie Strong colour fading Dust and Scratches	RSR
I funerali delle vittime della strage di Piazza della Loggia (1974)	131	Super 8 movie Color fading Dust and Scratches Instability	Manual Restoration ACE CLAHE

3.1   Datasets

The films considered here come from restorations performed at the MIPS Lab of the Computer Science Department at the University of Milano. For each film we analyzed through the image quality cockpit a selection of frames. The main features of these films and the sequences extracted from them in our tests are reported in Table 1 along with the list of enhancers applied (see Figs. 1 and 2 for some examples).

3.2 Image Enhancers

The algorithms we used to improve the readability of our test sequences include three spatial color algorithms [12], [9,17] belonging to the Milano Retinex family [15], and the popular technique Contrast-limited adaptive histogram equalization [20]. We chose the algorithms [12], [9,17] among many others since they have been already used for film restoration, e.g. [16,18], while the method [20] for its popularity. Here we shortly describe these approaches, applied frame by frame as image enhancers:

1. Random Spray Retinex [12] (RSR): RSR processes independently the channels of any input image and rescales the channel intensity $I(x)$ of each pixel x by a strictly positive value $w(x)$. This latter is computed by sampling the neighborhood of x by N random sprays, i.e. N sets of m pixels randomly sampled around x with radial density, and averaging the reciprocals of the maximum intensities of the sprays

2. Spatio-Temporal Retinex-Inspired Envelope with Stochastic Sampling [9] (STRESS): STRESS basically implements the pipeline of RSR, but stretches the intensity $I(x)$ between two values $w_-(x)$ and $w_+(x)$ computed by reworking respectively the minimum and maximum intensities of the random sprays sampled around x;

3. Automatic Color Equalization [17] (ACE): As RSR and STRESS, ACE reworks the color channels of the input image separately. It maps the channel intensity of any pixel x on to a new value, that is a weighted average of the differences $f(I(x) - I(y))$ over the number of pixels $y \neq x$ of I, where f is a real-valued positive function. There are different expressions for f. In our experiments, f is the L^1 norm. The weight of the term $f(I(x) - I(y))$ is a value inversely proportional to the distance of x from y.

4. Contrast Limited Adaptive Histogram Equalization [20] (CLAHE): CLAHE stretches locally the distribution of one or more color components as done by the histogram equalization. A clip limit on the contrast is introduced to avoid over-enhancement and to reduce the amplification of noise. CLAHE operates separately on image patches and then interpolates bilinearly the intensities of close enhanced patches to remove possible artifacts. The implementation of CLAHE used here works on L^*. In our experiments we consider squared patches with size 8×8 and we set the clip limit to 0.01.

3.3 Results

The results we report here show how some restoration techniques are evaluated by the cockpit. We do not want to promote any of these techniques, but only

Fig. 1. Comparison between the original and the restored frames of the film: (a) Fiat 508, (b) La lunga calza verde and (c) La Ciudad en la playa. (Color figure online)

Fig. 2. I funerali delle vittime della strage di Piazza della Loggia, in clockwise order: the original frame, its manual restoration and the enhancement by CLAHE and ACE. (Color figure online)

illustrate how the cockpit measures describe the restoration quality, allowing also the comparison of different aspects of the restoration process.

The film Fiat 508 (see Fig. 1(a)), an old advertisement of this car. It has been digitized in a DVD video copy that converted its frame from black & white to color, saving in this way also the yellowish alteration due to the aging and to the decaying of the film support. The frames we analyzed here were processed by video editors that removed the effects of dust, scratches and flickering by specific software. Here we further applied ACE to improve the colors and the details of the frames. Figure 1(a) shows an example of frame restoration by ACE while Fig. 3 reports the cockpit results over the chosen sequence. We observe that ACE smoothed over time the values of B and V with respect to the original version, meaning that ACE further attenuated the flickering. ACE also increased C and V, thus it improves the detail visibility, while flattened the color distribution, i.e. it widened the dynamic range of the scene by lowering F. The peak located around the 435th frame visible in the plots of the measures B, C, F, V and

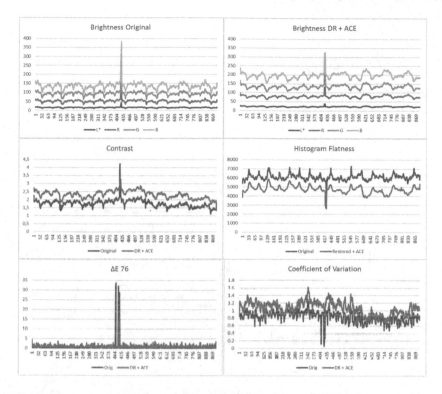

Fig. 3. The cockpit results on the sequence from Fiat 508. (Color figure online)

ΔE of both the input and output films was due to a completely burnt and white frame caused by the decay of the original film. Here we note that the peak was significantly lowered by the use of DR and ACE, that therefore attenuated the discontinuity of the film around the damaged frame, where the content was completely lost.

La Lunga Calza Verde is an animation by Roberto Gavioli (see Fig. 1(b)): its features differ completely from those of natural images, on which the majority of image quality metrics are set. For this reason it is really hard to find no-reference quality metrics that provides trustworthy results for the evaluation of this kind of films. Nevertheless, our cockpit provides interesting information. The frames we analyzed come from the digitization of the original film made in a private laboratory. They are in good conservation conditions but present a soft color fading due to the aging. To remove this effect, we applied the algorithm STRESS. The cockpit results are displayed in Fig. 4. We first observe that STRESS determined a variation of the color of the original sequence from reddish to greenish. This effect was caused by the enhancement of the channels green and blue that in the original version were degraded. Nevertheless, the trend of ΔE over time remains more or less unchanged, although the slight variations of V on the plot plateaus observable on the enhanced version reveal that STRESS introduces some noise in

166   A. Plutino et al.

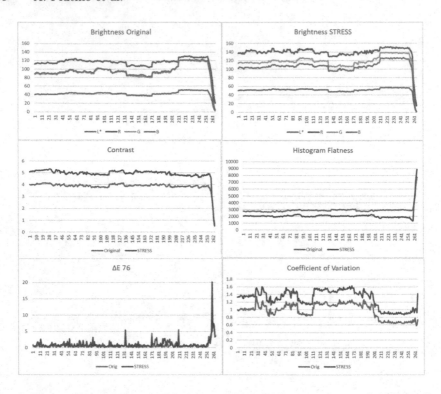

Fig. 4. The cockpit results on the sequence from La lunga calza verde. (Color figure online)

the output sequences. In general, the values of B, C, V increase and F decreases by using STRESS. The strong growth or decrease of the cockpit measures at the end of the scene is due to the a fade-out effect.

La Ciudad en la Playa (see Fig. 1(c)), a documentary about tourism in Uruguay, by Ferruccio Musitelli, offers a significant case of study.

The sequence we analyze comes from the digitization of the original 16 mm film. This presents strong color fading due to wrong storing conditions and aging, that determined a strong loss in contrast and details. The cockpit measures for this sequence enhanced by RSR (see Fig. 1(c) for an example) is shown in Fig. 5. The brightnesses of the color channels and of L^* of the output images are very similar to those of the original ones, apart from the last frames where the value B of the blue channel of the enhanced version are lower than those of the original one. The values of C, V and F are increased by RSR. On the restored sequence, the cockpit measures over time are more noisy than those of the original version. This effect is due to the big increase of color saturation and brightness induced by RSR, that also enhanced irrelevant details corresponding to noise and remarkably modifies the intra-frame color perceptual distances ΔE.

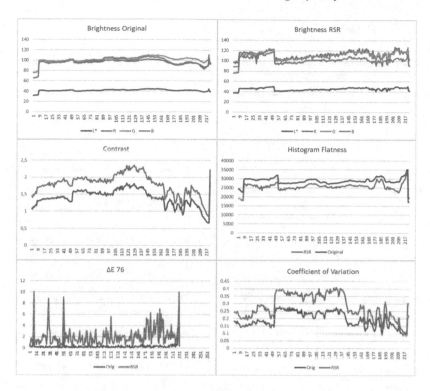

Fig. 5. The cockpit results on the sequence from La Ciudad en la Playa (Color figure online)

The sequence from I funerali delle vittime di Piazza della Loggia (see Fig. 2) come from the digitization of a Super8 documentary in good conservation conditions, but subject to decay and color fading. The film has been manually restored by cleaning dust and scratch, enhancing the colors and reducing the blurring effects due to the motion of the camera. To illustrate the advantage of the use of the cockpit in the comparison of different enhancement methods, we restored this sequence also by ACE and CLAHE. The results obtained by ACE, CLAHE and by the manual operations are reported in Fig. 6. The brightness of the frames restored by ACE and CLAHE over time is smoother than that restored manually. Regarding B, the highest value is achieved by CLAHE, while the manual restoration and ACE perform similarly. The manual restoration does not change very much the contrast, that is remarkably increased by ACE while decreased by CLAHE. All the restoration methods increase V, whose greatest value is reached by ACE. The histogram flatness is increased by CLAHE while remains unchanged for the other restoration methods.

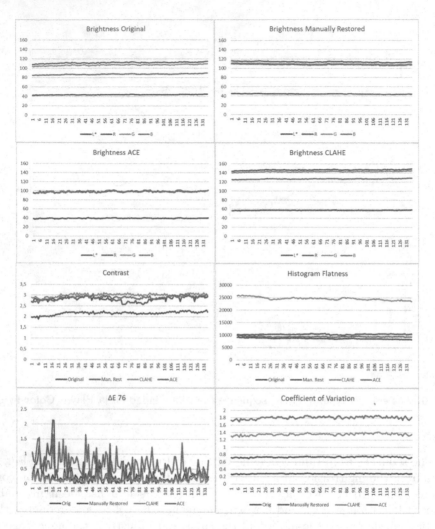

Fig. 6. The cockpit results on the sequence from I funerali delle vittime di Piazza della Loggia. (Color figure online)

4   Conclusions

In order to support film restoration attempts with objective measures preserving as much as possible the main characteristics of the restoration pipeline, we have proposed a cockpit of basic measures instead of an unique overall image quality index. Our cockpit is a valuable tool to estimate the enhancement in readability that different methods made on sequences of decaying digitized film. This quality assessment support is useful not only to compare the original frames with the restored ones, but also to evaluate which is the best restoration and to provide to the user a quality control during the process. Future work will be devoted to extend the measures of the cockpit in order to provide a more comprehensive description of the restoring results and to publish the cockpit on a website to make its use open source.

References

1. Farup, I., Islam, A.T.: Spatio-temporal colour correction of strongly degraded movies. In: Proceedings of SPIE, Color Imaging XVI: Displaying, Processing, Hardcopy, and Applications, vol. 7866 (2011)
2. Boarini, V., Opela, V.: Charter of film restoration. J. Film Preserv. **83**, 37–39 (2010)
3. Catanese, R.: Lacune Binarie. Il restauro dei film e le tecnologie digitali, Bulzoni (2013)
4. Chambah, M., Besserer, B., Courtelleont, P.: Recent progress in automatic digital restoration of color motion pictures. In: Proceedings of SPIE - The International Society for Optical Engineering, vol. 4663, pp. 98–109 (2002). cited By 18
5. Cornwell-Clyne, A.: Colour Cinematography. Chapman and Hall (1936)
6. Enticknap, L.: The Culture and Science of Audiovisual Heritage. Palgrave MacMillan, Basingstoke (2013)
7. Fossati, G.: From Grain to Pixel. Amsterdam University Press, Amsterdam (2009)
8. Kokaram, A.C.: Motion Picture Restoration - Digital Algorithms for Artefact Suppression in Degraded Motion Picture Film and Video. Springer, London (1998)
9. Kolas, O., Farup, I., Rizzi, A.: Spatio-temporal retinex inspired envelope with stochastic sampling: a framework for spatial color algorithms. J. Imaging Sci. Technol. **55**, 07 (2011)
10. Lecca, M., Simone, G., Bonanomi, C., Rizzi, A.: Point-based spatial colour sampling in milano-retinex: a survey. IET Image Process. **12**(16), 833–849 (2018)
11. Pedersen, M., Hardeberg, J.Y.: Full-reference image quality metrics: classification and evaluation. Found. Trends® Comput. Graph. Vis. **7**(1), 1–80 (2012)
12. Provenzi, E., Fierro, M., Rizzi, A., De Carli, L., Gadia, D., Marini, D.: Random spray retinex: a new retinex implementation to investigate the local properties of the model. IEEE Trans. Image Process. **16**(1), 162–171 (2007)
13. Rizzi, A., Algeri, T., Medeghini, G., Marini, D.: A proposal for contrast measure in digital images. In: Conference on Colour in Graphics, Imaging, and Vision, vol. 2004, no. 1, pp. 187–192 (2004)
14. Rizzi, A., Berolo, J.A., Bonanomi, C., Gadia, D.: Unsupervised digital movie restoration with spatial models of color. Multimedia Tools Appl. **75**(7), 3747–3765 (2016)
15. Rizzi, A., Bonanomi, C.: Milano Retinex family. J. Electron. Imaging **26**(3), 031207 (2017)
16. Rizzi, A., Chambah, M.: Perceptual color film restoration. SMPTE Motion Imaging J. **119**(8), 33–41 (2010)
17. Rizzi, A., Gatta, C., Marini, D.: A new algorithm for unsupervised global and local color correction. Pattern Recogn. Lett. **24**(11), 1663–1677 (2003)
18. Rizzi, A., Berolo, A.J., Bonanomi, C., Gadia, D.: Unsupervised digital movie restoration with spatial models of color. Multimedia Tools Appl. **75**(7), 3747–3765 (2016)
19. Uccello, P.: Cinema. tecnica e Linguaggio, San Paolo (1997)
20. Zuiderveld, K.: Contrast limited adaptive histogram equalization. In: Graphics Gems IV, pp. 474–485. Academic Press Professional Inc. (1994)

Augmented Reality for the Valorization and Communication of Ruined Architecture

Raissa Garozzo[1], Giovanni Pasqualino[2], Dario Allegra[2(✉)], Cettina Santagati[1], and Filippo Stanco[2]

[1] Department of Civil Engineering and Architecture, University of Catania,
Catania, Italy
raissa.garozzo@unict.it, cettina.santagati@dau.unict.it
[2] Department of Mathematics and Computer Science, University of Catania,
Catania, Italy
{allegra,fstanco}@dmi.unict.it

Abstract. This paper is focused on the valorization and the communication about the Mother church of Santa Maria delle Grazie in the Ancient Misterbianco (Catania), one of the rare surviving vestiges of the eruption of Mount Etna in 1669 and the earthquake in Val di Noto in 1693. The project, starting from a 3D digital surveys carried out through reality-based techniques, uses an Augmented Reality approach to propose a virtual re-positioning of some significant elements of the church, removed during the eruption. This study required a deep architectural study and an archival documents research to exactly identify the original location of the re-positioned artworks. Then, a 3D reconstruction carried out to get accurate 3D models of them and Augmented Reality application allows the visitors to experience the current church environment enriched with these original artefacts, in order to achieve a more powerful learning/visiting experience.

Keywords: Augmented Reality · Cultural Heritage ·
3D reconstruction · Photogrammetry

1 Introduction

Preservation and accessibility of ancient artefacts are among the most challenging problems in the field of Cultural Heritage. In this context, the transmission of information becomes highly significant to allow a deeper knowledge of the architectural asset to all type of users (e.g., students, researchers). The use of the most innovative communication systems to explore and understand the architectural heritage allows to expand the way in which information is spread and the number of people reached. This is possible by employing more attractive and involving communication tools.

M. Cristani et al. (Eds.): ICIAP 2019 Workshops, LNCS 11808, pp. 170–178, 2019.
https://doi.org/10.1007/978-3-030-30754-7_17

Among these technologies, 3D reconstruction has played a key-role in the last decade. The opportunity to get a 3D digital version of an artefacts allows to conduct multiple studies on its geometry and make it available for different aims. On the other hand, 3D reconstruction is also employed in other industrial and research field, like medicine, engineering, biology and so on [1,3,7,12,13,18]. A popular technology which takes the advantage of 3D digital is Augmented Reality (AR). It allows an interactive experience in real-world environment which is enhanced by generated perceptual information. Although such experiences may involve multiple senses, 3D models led an enhanced vision experience. In a nutshell, through the screen of a proper devices (e.g., smartphones, tablets, smartglasses, etc.) the user is able to see 3D mesh superimposed to the real world. This is different by other similar technology like Virtual Reality (VR) where the world the user perceive is totally computer-generated.

In this paper we aim to improve the knowledge of the visitors in order to achieve a more powerful learning experience, through the virtual re-positioning of elements in their original location, by implementing a proper AR-based application. This required an architectural study of the Mother church Santa Maria delle Grazie of the ancient Misterbianco, to identify the original location of the case-study artworks. The locations we identified have been confirmed by archival sources. Subsequently, the case-study artworks, namely a baptismal font and a statue of Holy Mary, have been reconstructed by using photogrammetric approaches. Finally, a proper Augmented Reality application have been developed to allow the visitors to experience the current church environment enhanced with the original artefacts.

The rest of the paper is organised as follows: in Sect. 2 several related works are discussed, the Sect. 3 describes the case study, in Sect. 4 the 3D data acquisition and processing methodology is illustrated. Finally, in Sect. 5 is describing the augmented reality application, with a focus on the application design.

2   Related Works

Augmented reality is a technology that enhances the perception of the physical world by overlaying digital contents - in addition or subtraction - to the real environment. It is a field with a versatile range of applications, used in many fields including Cultural Heritage, recreation and education. In literature we find several applications that exploit the potentialities of AR in Cultural Heritage domain, as it allows to observe with new eyes monuments or ruins. The "augmentation" of the real-world environment can lead towards an intuitive access to museum information and enhance the impact in the museum exhibition [6] or help in better understanding and closely viewing fragile artefacts [11]. Other potentialities can be found in history education and heritage visualisation, such as Holocaust education [5] or app aimed to understand the history of the city [8,10]. Other studies are addressed to simulate on site the virtual reconstruction of a building or the virtual recontextualisation of findings especially in presence of archaeological and/or ruined sites, buildings and wandering findings [4]. The

AR potentialities can also be exploited according a playful aspect such as the Pilot project developed for the archaeological site and the exhibition area at Sutton Hoo via an engaging game that connects the site with the British Museum where the objects that have been excavated from the site are exhibited [2] or exploiting Artificial Intelligence to recognise monuments via a Deep Learning approach [20]. Our research is aimed to exploit mobile AR potentialities for the virtual recontextualization of findings and artworks, now kept in a museum, that were part of the decorative apparatus of a church buried under a destructive lava flow in 1669, in order to recuperate the lost identity of a place by means of an enriched narrative process.

3   Case Study

The case study is the church of Santa Maria delle Grazie in the ancient Misterbianco (Catania, Italy), buried by lava during the destructive volcanic eruption of 1669. The church was recently brought to light by excavations carried out by the Superintendence of Cultural Heritage of Catania. Fleeing from lava, the villagers have rescued several furnishings of the church, in the extreme attempt to preserve something of the ancient place of worship. The rescued objects (e.g, paintings, statues and other furnishings) were placed in the newly built churches of Misterbianco [16]. Some of them are actually held in the Museum of Sacred Art of Misterbianco, as well as other findings discovered during the excavations. Particularly, the experimentation was carried out on the marble statue of Our Lady, attributed to the Gagini's school [17] and the baptismal font. The Madonna with the infant, currently kept in a chapel of the Mother church of Misterbianco, was originally located in a monumental purpose-built niche on the northern wall of the ancient church (Fig. 1). Differently, the pedestal and the basin of the baptismal font were located next to the main entrance of the old church, on the octagonal base where it can be noticed the traces of the removed parts (Fig. 2).

4   3D Data Acquisition and Processing of Artefacts

The methodological process followed for the acquisition and the creation of the models consists of several phases. We used Structure from Motion (SfM) approach that allows to obtain 3D textured models of real objects from a dataset of images [9,14,15]. After a first on-site inspection at the church of Madonna delle Grazie and the Museum of Sacred Art in Misterbianco, we designed a shooting project taking into account the need of good lighting conditions and the possibility that objects could not be moved from the exhibition (most of them are walled or too heavy). Natural enlightenment has been chosen whenever possible, while a photographic set has been arranged for the museum rooms. Another problem caused by the walled pieces was due to the fact that each item was too close to the others, so during the images acquisition step there was few space to move around the objects and not always a 360° turn around the object was granted. We used a Nikon D5300 with a focal length of 25 mm. The resolution was

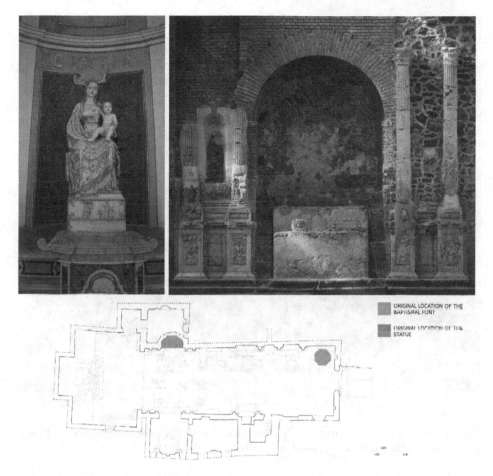

Fig. 1. The statue of the Holy Mary in its current location; the orthoimage of the monumental niche that previously housed the statue and the plan of the Mother church of the Ancient Misterbianco, including the former location of the objects.

24 megapixels (Holy Mary statue model) and 17.9 megapixels (Baptismal font model). The photographic datasets were automatically processed with Agisoft Metashape. After the first step of the alignment, we got a sparse reconstruction, then a dense reconstruction has been created (Fig. 3). The workflow has been completed with the creation of a triangulated mesh and the texture mapping. The 3D textured models have been saved in obj format and processed in Autodesk RecapPhoto for improving and optimizing the mesh quality (filling hole, decimation, etc.) for a better use in real-time visualization.

Fig. 2. The original configuration of the baptismal font: the pedestal and the basin are located above the original base through a photo-montage

5   Augmented Reality Application

To make 3D models effectively available and user friendly, an application based on augmented reality has been developed. Its main features is the possibility to look at and interact with a revival 3-D digital model of a work of art. In this work, the intent is to take advantage of the works of art even if they are not physically available to the user. To this aim, we have developed a software for iOS and Android. The app has been developed using Unity [19] engine, version 2019.1.5. It is an environment with an integrated game engine, provided by Unity Technologies, that is typically employed to produce digital games for different platform, such as PC, consoles, mobile devices, and websites. Unity encodes the algorithms in two different program languages: C# and JavaScript (it will be deprecated in the next release). In this work, we employed C# to develop the entire software. The main advantage of Unity is the simplicity in managing multimedia resources and the user-friendly development GUI, as well as the multiplatform builder. To implement the augmented reality features has

OBJECT	Holy Mary statue	Baptismal font
Number of images	195	43
Image resolution (pixels)	4000x6000	5184x3456
Number of mesh polygon	539.651	59.054

Fig. 3. The textured polygonal meshes of the baptismal font and the statue of Holy Mary. The blue boxes stand for the camera views within the images acquisition process. The table shows some characteristics of the photos acquired and the generated models (Color figure online)

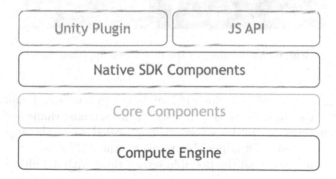

Fig. 4. The proposed framework.

been used Wikitude [21]. It is a software library and framework for mobile apps used to create augmented reality experiences.

Wikitude offers several possible approach to create application based on augmented reality depending on the development environment and platform you decide to use. Figure 4 shows architecture of Wikitude SDK. Core Components includes three major parts that are used by every Wikitude SDK: SLAM Engine, Image Recognition Engine ad Object Recognition. These engine are wrapped either by the Native API or JavaScript API and Unity Plugin uses them.

5.1 Application Design

In Unity, each application consists of scenes that represent the levels and/or the various screens of the app. Within the scenes are the Gameobjects that

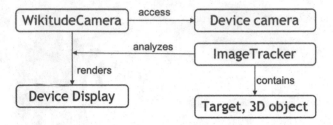

Fig. 5. The pipeline of the propose AR system.

Fig. 6. An example of the developed application.

represent "containers" within which it is possible to add functionality through special scripts. The application is composed of two screens; Home and ARScene.

Home: represents the initial screen that is loaded when the app is opened. Through a special button it is possible to access the ARScene.

ARScene: implements all the possible interactions with 3D object offered by augmented reality.

ARScene. This scene is mainly composed of two Gameobjects; WikitudeCamera and ImageTracker:

- WikitudeCamera: accesses to the smartphone camera and renders 3D objects on the screen whose targets have been recognized. Camera resolution and framerate are automatically set by the SDk based on the capabilities of the device.
- ImageTracker: contains one or more targets (in this case QR Code) to which one or more 3d objects are associated; it analyzes the frames captured by the camera and detects any stored targets. Implement extended tracking which makes the SDK continue to scan the environment even if the target image is no longer visible; this allows you to continue to see the 3D object on the screen even if its target is no longer present on the scene (Fig. 5).

6   Conclusions

This work highlighted the potentialities of mobile AR app for the enhancement and understanding a ruined site with missing artworks onsite (Fig. 6). The recontextualisation of the artworks has a double value: one strictly linked with a proper fruition of the site, virtually putting in place the missing findings, the other one is mainly linked with the lost identity of the site, for centuries buried under the lava flow. However several questions remain open: the issue related with the poor internet coverage of the site, still under 12 m below street level; the possibility to use a different tracking way allowing the user to recognise the scene via an image rather than a QRcode. Future works will be focused on experimenting on the latter issue.

Acknowledgment. The authors thank Father Giovanni Condorelli (president) and the members of the Monasterium Album Foundation for having given access to the site; proff. Giuseppe D'Angelo and Stella Paternò of the Istituto Industriale Archimede in Catania within the educational project "3D Digital Invasions - Low cost digital technologies for the fruition and enhancement of the historical-artistic heritage"; Dr Grazia Pennisi coordinator of the project "L'abbraccio di ETNA (rigenerati dalla lava)".

References

1. Allegra, D., et al.: Low cost handheld 3D scanning for architectural elements acquisition. In: Smart Tools and Apps for Graphics - Eurographics Italian Chapter Conference, pp. 127–131 (2016). https://doi.org/10.2312/stag.20161372
2. Angelopoulou, A., et al.: Mobile augmented reality for cultural heritage. In: Venkatasubramanian, N., Getov, V., Steglich, S. (eds.) MOBILWARE 2011. LNICST, vol. 93, pp. 15–22. Springer, Heidelberg (2012). https://doi.org/10.1007/978-3-642-30607-5_2
3. Bottino, A., De Simone, M., Laurentini, A., Sforza, C.: A new 3-D tool for planning plastic surgery. IEEE Trans. Biomed. Eng. **59**(12), 3439–3449 (2012). https://doi.org/10.1109/TBME.2012.2217496
4. Campi, M., di Luggo, A., Palomba, D., Rosaria, P.: Digital survey and 3D reconstructions for augmented accessibility of archeological heritage, February 2019. https://doi.org/10.5194/isprs-archives-XLII-2-W9-205-2019
5. Challenor, J., Ma, M.: A review of augmented reality applications for history education and heritage visualisation Jennifer. Multimodal Technol. Interact. **39**, 1–20 (2019). https://doi.org/10.3390/mti3020039
6. Clini, P., Quattrini, R., Frontoni, E., Pierdicca, E., Nespeca, R.: Real/not real: pseudo-holography and augmented reality applications for cultural heritage. In: Handbook of Research on Emerging Technologies for Digital Preservation and Information Modeling, pp. 201–227 (2016). https://doi.org/10.4018/978-1-5225-0680-5.ch009
7. Dai, Y., Tian, J., Dong, D., Yan, G., Zheng, H.: Real-time visualized freehand 3D ultrasound reconstruction based on GPU. IEEE Trans. Inf Technol. Biomed. **14**(6), 1338–1345 (2010). https://doi.org/10.1109/TITB.2010.2072993
8. Harrach, M., Devaux, A., Mathieu, B.: Interactive image geolocalization in an immersive web application, February 2019. https://doi.org/10.5194/isprs-archives-XLII-2-W9-377-2019

9. Kersten, T., Lindstaedt, M.: Potential of automatic 3D object reconstruction from multiple images for applications in architecture, cultural heritage and archaeology. Int. J. Herit. Digit. Era **1**(3), 399–420 (2012). https://doi.org/10.1260/2047-4970.1.3.399

10. Krogstie, J., Haugstvedt, A.C.: Use of mobile augmented reality for cultural heritage. In: Fundamentals of Wearable Computers and Augmented Reality, pp. 411–432, August 2015. https://doi.org/10.1201/b18703-20

11. Kyriakou, P., Hermon, S.: Can I touch this? Using natural interaction in a museum augmented reality system. Digit. Appl. Archaeol. Cult. Herit. **12**, e00088 (2019). https://doi.org/10.1016/j.daach.2018.e00088

12. Laing, R., Leon, M., Isaacs, J.: Monuments visualization: from 3D scanned data to a holistic approach, an application to the city of Aberdeen. In: International Conference on Information Visualisation, pp. 512–517, July 2015. https://doi.org/10.1109/iV.2015.91

13. Nguyen, C.V., et al.: 3D scanning system for automatic high-resolution plant phenotyping. In: International Conference on Digital Image Computing: Techniques and Applications (DICTA), pp. 1–8, November 2016. https://doi.org/10.1109/DICTA.2016.7796984

14. Remondino, F., Spera, M.G., Nocerino, E., Menna, F., Nex, F.: State of the art in high density image matching. Photogram. Rec. **29**(146), 144–166 (2014). https://doi.org/10.1111/phor.12063

15. Russo, M., Manferdini, A.M.: Integrated multi-scalar approach for 3D cultural heritage acquisitions, pp. 337–360, January 2015. https://doi.org/10.4018/978-1-4666-8379-2.ch011

16. Santonocito, M.: Misterbianco Ieri. Grafiche Artigianelli - Trento (1988)

17. Scuderi, S.: Perché è S. Antonio Abate il patrono? In: Calabró, J. (ed.) Le Case dei Gelsi - Misterbianco, una storia di donne e di uomini lungo un millennio, pp. 126–130. Giuseppe Maimone Editore (2016)

18. Stanco, F., Tanasi, D., Allegra, D., Milotta, F.L.M., Lamagna, G., Monterosso, G.: Virtual anastylosis of Greek sculpture as museum policy for public outreach and cognitive accessibility. J. Electron. Imaging **26**(1) (2017). https://doi.org/10.1117/1.JEI.26.1.011025

19. Unity: https://docs.unity3d.com/Manual

20. Palma, V.: Towards deep learning for architecture: a monument recognition mobile app, February 2019. https://doi.org/10.5194/isprs-archives-XLII-2-W9-551-2019

21. Wikitude: https://www.wikitude.com/documentation

Classification of Arabic Poems:
from the 5th to the 15th Century

Mourad Abbas[1]([✉])[iD], Mohamed Lichouri[1][iD], and Ahmed Zeggada[2]

[1] Computational Linguistics Department, CRSTDLA,
16000 Algiers, Algeria
{m.abbas,m.lichouri}@crstdla.dz
[2] Saad Dahleb University, 09000 Blida, Algeria
ahmed_zeggada@hotmail.fr
https://sites.google.com/site/mouradabbas9

Abstract. This paper describes a system for classification of Arabic poems according to the eras in which they were written. We used machine learning techniques where we applied a bunch of filters and classifiers. The best results were achieved by using the Multinomial Naïve Bayes (MNB) algorithm, with an accuracy equal to 70.21%, an F1-Score of 68.8% and a Kappa equal to 0.398, without filtering stop words. We observed that the stop words can have a positive impact on the accuracy but also a negative impact if it is used with word tokenizer preprocessing.

Keywords: Text classification · Arabic Language · Poems ·
Eras identification · Stop words · Word tokenizer · Ngram tokenizer

1 Introduction

Text classification is the task of assigning predefined categories to free-text documents according to their content. Arabic text classification and especially Arabic poetry classification has its own difficulties and limits resulting from the nature of Arabic language which is a rich language in varieties with very complex inflections that make an ordinary analysis a very complicated task. With the advent of the Internet and Worldwide web, we can easily find a big number of texts including Arabic poetry. With such ready corpora of poems available, interesting experiments can be devised to classify them.

The aim of this paper is to highlight the most efficient algorithms that are applied to Arabic poetry classification, in order to predict the category of those poems regarding their eras among the following ones: Pre-Islamic era, Umayyad era, Andalusian era and Abbasid era. Note that the pre-Islamic era extends from 478 AD to 624 AD. The Umayyad era from 625 AD to 750 AD. The Abassid era from 750 AD until 1258 AD. The Andalusian era is the longest one, almost 8 centuries. It started from 750 AD and ended in 1492 AD. Furthermore, we want to show the impact of both stop words and tokenizers on categorization system's performance. Several experiments using different classifiers were applied

© Springer Nature Switzerland AG 2019
M. Cristani et al. (Eds.): ICIAP 2019 Workshops, LNCS 11808, pp. 179–186, 2019.
https://doi.org/10.1007/978-3-030-30754-7_18

such as K-Nearest Neighbors, Decision trees algorithm J48, Bagging classifier (Bag), Naïve Bayes (NB), Multinomial Naïve Bayes (MNB), Multi Class Classifier (MCC), Random Forest (RF). Note that this study is about classification of Arabic poems according to their era within the Weka environment [6]. To our knowledge, this is the first study dealing with Arabic poems era classification according to the mentioned eras. The rest of the paper is organized as follows: we present in the Related Work section most of the known work related to the application of text classification techniques on Poetry datasets. Then we describe in the Data section, the dataset we used in our study. In Preprocessing and Features section, we give an overview on the steps that we followed for representing data in a suitable form necessary for machine learning techniques performance. Then we discuss the findings and we conclude our paper and shed light on some of our perspective work.

2   Related Work

Computational studies on Poems have been carried out for many languages. Indeed, poem recognition has been done for English in [1], poet detection in [2] and poem subjects detection [3]. For Punjabi language, poem subjects detection has been shown in [4]. Another work dealing with Chinese Language, has been conducted on Classical Poetry Artistic Conception [5]. For Arabic Language, most of the works have been achieved to solve the problem of Arabic Poets Identification, Poems Identification and Recognition. Al-Harbi et al. [7], tried to identify Arabic poems according to the following classes of Arabic poetry: Hekmah (Wisdom), Retha (Elegiac), Ghazal (Love), Madeh (Praise), Heja (Satire), Wasf (Description). They applied a set of classifiers using a dataset composed of 1,949 poems. They obtained an accuracy of 49.15%. With a similar purpose, Alsharif et al. [8] used a dataset including 1231 poems, in order to classify poems within a less number of poetry classes which are: Retha (Elegiac), Ghazal (Love), Fakhr (Pride) and Heja (Satire). Four main machine learning algorithms were compared: Naïve Bayes, SVMs, VFI and Hyperpipes. The best precision achieved was 79% using Hyperpipes with non-stemmed, non-rooted, mutually deducted feature vectors containing 2000 features. In [11], the authors have performed a study on a set of text documents to be classified into two classes: poem and prose. They have explored a set of features, namely: Shape, Rhyme, Meter and Word Frequency. They used Naive Bayes Classifier while applying a rooting process, which yielded an accuracy of 66%. In [9], a research work was conducted to build a prototype search engine for classical Arabic poems. The dataset used in this work is made of 161 poems. The authors applied a set of features such as structure, rhyme, writing style, and word usage which achieved a precision of 96.94% and a recall of 92.24%. Another work done by the same authors [10] yielded an accuracy of 99.81% on a set of 513 poems, using the Naïve Bayes Classifier and the Visual Features. In [12], authors have investigated the categorization of Ottoman poems according to their poets (authorship attribution) and time periods. They used 2955 poems of 10 poets for the period ranging from the 15th to 19th century. They achieved an accuracy of 95.53% by using SVM. In [13] and [14], machine learning algorithms based on style markers have been used for identifying a group of 73 poets, and yielded to an accuracy of 98.63%. In [15], the authors have focused on the usefulness of rhythm in poems for teaching purpose. Indeed they argue that most English native speakers that wish to learn Arabic have to analyze Arabic poetry, which is different from the English poetry.

3 Data

Arabic poetry is the oldest and the most prominent form of Arabic literature today. Ancient Arabic poetry is probably the primary source for describing the social, political and intellectual life in the Arab world at that time. Modern poetry has gone through major changes and shifts both in the form and in the topics. The Arabic Poetry Dataset, used in this work, includes over 58 K poems from the 6th to the 21st century. It includes also poem metadata such as poet name, the period of the poem and its category. We downloaded this dataset from Kaggle[1].

As our main work is focused on the problem of era classification, we opted to keep only a fraction of the dataset corresponding to four eras: Pre Islamic era (PI), Ummayad era (Um), Abbasid era (Ab) and Andalusian era (An). The statistics of the resulted dataset is shown in Table 1.

Table 1. Statistics of the used dataset.

	PI era	Um era	Ab era	An era	Total
# Poems	1,461	3,700	19,410	6,295	30,866
# Verses	14,977	41,137	236,722	89,514	382,350
# Unique Verses	14,906	41,062	235,503	89,304	380,600
# Words	143,878	395,059	2,282,718	868,145	3,689,800
# Unique Words	46,065	86,434	249,124	128,993	323,995

4 Preprocessing and Features

This phase consists in converting the corpus to a suitable format by removing all worthless information and passing our corpora of poetry data through a data cleaning process and taking off all punctuation's marks, diacritics, numbers and non-Arabic letters. In addition of normalizing some writing forms such as replacing آ إ أ with ا which is the form of writing adopted by most of people. Finally, changing our text corpus format into UTF-8 encoding is a necessary step. We have faced some difficulties to load all poems in the WEKA, so we did import all the corpus into an oracle database tables, then create an OJDBC

---

[1] https://www.kaggle.com/fahd09/arabic-poetry-dataset-478-2017.

connection. This really helped us to load all data so we can take benefit of the Weka-friendly ARFF format that is necessary to enable text classification and data mining. The classifiers that we adopted are: kNN, J48, Bagging classifier, NB, MNB, MCC and RF. We used the StringToWordVector Filter in order to fully use the WEKA's different parameters and functionalities like the stop words handler and different tokenizer methods. In one set of experiments, the *Word tokenizer* method was used to tokenize and text-mine all the words in the corpus and then the *N-Gram tokenizer* was used to improve the results, for both experiments we have used one time the Python NLTK standard Arabic stop words and other time without any stop words.

5 Results and Discussions

As aforementioned, the experiments were conducted using Waikato Environment for Knowledge Acquisition (WEKA). We conducted a classification process over a set of classifiers, using 66% of the dataset for training and 34% for test. The results are shown in Table 2. The best results are obtained by SVM, MNB and MCC.

Table 2. Classifiers' accuracy. The three best scores are in bold

	J48	kNN	NB	SVM	MNB	MCC	RF	Bag
Avg Precision	55.6%	47.6%	57.1%	66.4%	68.4%	66%	64.8%	63.2%
Avg Recall	59.3%	48.4%	51.2%	68.5%	70%	67.5%	63.8%	64.9%
Avg F-Measure	56.7%	47.6%	53.2%	65.7%	68.4%	65.7%	51.3%	55.6%
Accuracy	59.34%	48.44%	51.20%	**69.70%**	**70.21%**	**68.07%**	64.14%	64.93%
Kappa	0.17	0.04	0.19	**0.34**	**0.40**	**0.35**	0.07	0.12

Note that training has been carried out by considering four preprocessing setups: Word and Ngram tokenization with and without Stop words. We present the results in term of Precision, Recall and F1-Score in Fig. 1 for MNB and MCC and for SVM in Fig. 2. Furthermore, accuracy for the three classifiers is displayed in Fig. 3. In Fig. 1, we can note that the best performance has been achieved by the MNB classifier in the four setups, either in term of F1-Measure or Kappa Score. We can see also that the use of a stop words Filter has decreased somehow the performance. Note that WrdTok_StpWord, WrdTok_Wt_StpWord, NgramTok_StpWord, NgramTok_Wt_StpWord stand respectively for: Word tokenizer with stop words, Word tokenizer without stop words, Ngram tokenizer with stop words, and Ngram tokenizer without stop words. For the SVM classifier, the same conclusion could be inferred in term of the negative impact of the stop Words Filter on its performance (-see Fig. 3). This is why we try to find which model performed well for this task. Figure 3 presents a comparison of the

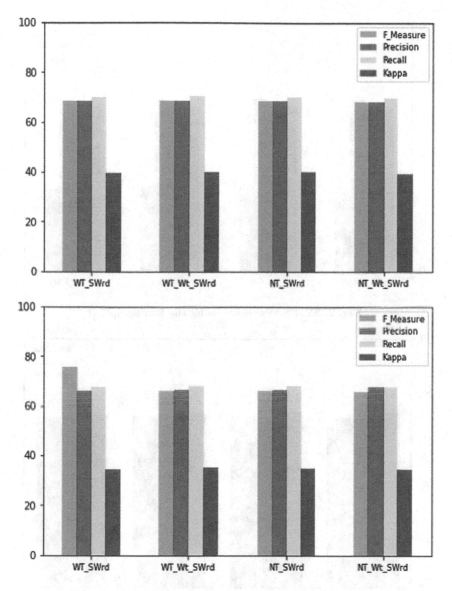

Fig. 1. MNB (**above**) and MCC (**below**) performance

three classifiers in accordance to the four setups. What we can note is that the MNB classifier has scored the best results in all setups in comparison to SVM and MCC. Applying Word tokenizer without filtering stop Words using MNB, yielded the best accuracy (70.21%).

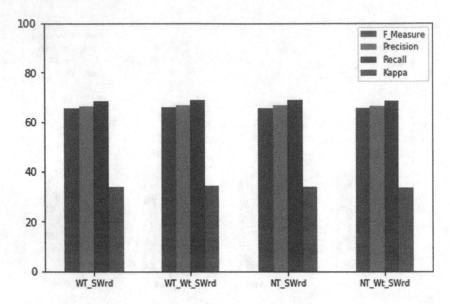

Fig. 2. SVM performance using the four setups.

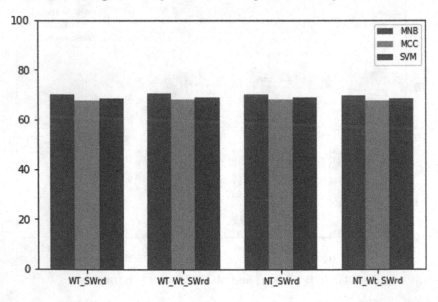

Fig. 3. Accuracy Comparison between the four setup using the three best Models.

6   Conclusion and Future Work

This work addressed the poetry categorization problem for the Arabic language. It started by selecting four of the most known poetry eras (categories) from our Arabic poetry dataset. Additionally, we used four different preprocessing setups, namely Word and Ngram tokenizers with and without stop words. We conducted several experiments on this dataset via WEKA then we presented the best models. We found that with word tokenizer and without stop words, results are much better than if using stop words. In the opposite, Ngram tokenizer with stop words gave better results than without stop words. The highest accuracy model was the Multinomial Naïve Bayes with Word tokenizer and without stop words which yielded a score of 70.21%. Consequently, we conclude that removing stop words is not necessary the right pre-processing step in some cases. We have shown in our experiments that word tokenization with stop words, in Arabic poetry classification, is useless, and this was confirmed with all the top three classifiers. In perspective, in order to improve classification performance, we plan to use lemmatization and Named Entity Recognition as well as enrichment of our stop words list.

References

1. Tizhoosh, H.R., Sahba, F., Dara, R.: Poetic features for poem recognition: a comparative study. J. Pattern Recognit. Res. **3**(1), 24–39 (2008)
2. Sahin, D.O., Kural, O.E., Kilic, E., Karabina, A.: A text classification application: poet detection from poetry (2018). arXiv preprint arXiv:1810.11414
3. Lou, A., Inkpen, D., Tanasescu, C.: Multilabel subject-based classification of poetry. In: Twenty-Eighth International Florida Artificial Intelligence Research Society Conference, pp. 187–192, April 2015
4. Kaur, J., Saini, J.R.: Punjabi poetry classification: the test of 10 machine learning algorithms. In: Proceedings of the 9th International Conference on Machine Learning and Computing, pp. 1–5. ACM, February 2017
5. Liang, J.F.: Research on the classification algorithms for the classical poetry artistic conception based on feature clustering methodology. In: 2nd International Conference on Electrical, Computer Engineering and Electronics, pp. 423–427, June 2015
6. Wahbeh, A.H., Al-Kabi, M.: Comparative assessment of the performance of three WEKA text classifiers applied to arabic text. Abhath Al-Yarmouk: Basic Sci. Eng. **21**(1), 15–28 (2012)
7. Al-Harbi, S., Almuhareb, A., Al-Thubaity, A., Khorsheed, M.S., Al-Rajeh, A.: Automatic Arabic text classification. In: Proceedings of The 9th International Conference on the Statistical Analysis of Textual Data, pp. 77–83, March 2008
8. Alsharif, O., Alshamaa, D., Ghneim, N.: Emotion classification in Arabic poetry using machine learning. Int. J. Comput. Appl. **65**(16) (2013)
9. Almuhareb, A., Alkharashi, I., Saud, L.A., Altuwaijri, H.: Recognition of classical Arabic poems. In: Proceedings of the Workshop on Computational Linguistics for Literature, pp. 9–16 (2013)
10. Almuhareb, A., Almutairi, W.A., Al-Tuwaijri, H., Almubarak, A., Khan, M.: Recognition of modern Arabic poems. JSW **10**(4), 454–464 (2015)
11. Mohammad, I.A.: Naïve Bayes for classical Arabic poetry classification. J. Al-Nahrain Univ.-Sci. **12**(4), 217–225 (2009)
12. Can, F., Can, E., Sahin, P.D., Kalpakli, M.: Automatic categorization of Ottoman poems. Glottotheory **4**(2), 40–57 (2013)

13. Ahmed, A.F., Mohamed, R., Mostafa, B., Mohammed, A.S.: Authorship attribution in Arabic poetry. In: 2015 10th International Conference on Intelligent Systems: Theories and Applications (SITA), pp. 1–6. IEEE, October 2015
14. Ahmed, A., Mohamed, R., Mostafa, B.: Machine learning for authorship attribution in Arabic poetry. Int. J. Future Comput. Commun. 6(2), 42–46 (2017)
15. Ahmed, M.A., Trausan-Matu, S.: A program for analyzing classical Arabic poetry for teaching purposes. Rom. J. Hum.-Comput. Interact. 10(4), 331–344 (2017)

A Page-Based Reject Option for Writer Identification in Medieval Books

Nicole Dalia Cilia, Claudio De Stefano, Francesco Fontanella[✉],
Claudio Marrocco, Mario Molinara, and Alessandra Scotto di Freca

Department of Electrical and Information Engineering (DIEI),
University of Cassino and Southern Lazio, Via G. Di Biasio, 43, Cassino, FR, Italy
{nicoledalia.cilia,destefano,fontanella,c.marrocco,m.molinara,
a.scotto}@unicas.it

Abstract. One main goal of paleographers is to identify the different writers who wrote a given manuscript. Recently, paleographers are starting to use digital tools which provide new and more objective ways to analyze ancient documents. On the other hand, in the last few years, deep learning techniques have been applied to many domains and to overcome its requirement of a large amount of labeled data, transfer learning has been used. This latter approach uses previously trained large deep networks as starting points to solve specific classification problems. In this paper, we present a novel approach based on deep transfer learning to implement a reject option for the recognition of the writers in medieval documents. The implemented option is page-based and considers the row labels provided by the trained deep network to estimate the class probabilities. The proposed approach has been tested on a set of digital images from a Bible of the XII century. The achieved results confirmed the effectiveness of the proposed approach.

1 Introduction

Digital palaeography uses computer-based approaches to analyze and represent ancient and medieval documents and its main purpose is to support the paleographical analysis of these documents by the paleographers [2]. These approaches can be used either to replace traditional qualitative measurements with modern computer-vision tools or by using the recently emerged AI and pattern recognition based approaches which have shown proved to be effective in processing the many currently available high-quality digital images of ancient and medieval manuscripts [6–8]. These approaches can be categorized according to the two types of features taken into account: global or local. The first are focused on measures from the whole page, whereas the second are based on the analysis of the single words, letters and signs of the written trace. In this framework, one of the most important problems faced by paleographers is to identify the writers who participated in the handwriting process of a given manuscript.

In the last few years, due to their ability to deal with complex and hard image classification tasks, deep learning (DL) based approaches have been receiving increasing attention from researchers and have been successfully applied

© Springer Nature Switzerland AG 2019
M. Cristani et al. (Eds.): ICIAP 2019 Workshops, LNCS 11808, pp. 187–197, 2019.
https://doi.org/10.1007/978-3-030-30754-7_19

to numerous real-world applications [20], and they have shown to be able to learn high-level features from mass data. These features are typically extracted from the available data by using unsupervised or semi-supervised feature learning algorithms and hierarchical feature extraction. On the contrary, traditional machine learning methods [4] need a preliminary feature engineering step involving the expert of the application field, increasing the cost of the development of the application. Although DL-based approaches have proven to be effective in many computer vision problems, their performance strongly depends on the availability of massive training data. Unfortunately, the insufficient training data problem cannot be easily solved in many application domains. This because the collection of labeled data may require a long and expensive process.

In order to overcome the problem of insufficient data, the transfer learning approach can be used. According to this approach, pre-trained networks, typically trained on huge datasets containing millions of images and thousands of classes, are used as starting points for the learning process of new networks. At present, the transfer learning paradigm is widely applied to computer vision and natural language processing tasks.

Previous DL approaches for ancient document analysis have been mainly used for identifying elements of interest inside document pages. In [11], for example, the authors use a Fully Convolutional Neural Network (FCNN) to locate handwritten annotations in historic German documents. In [16], instead, the authors introduced a database containing annotated pages of medieval manuscripts. They also tested the performance of a Convolutional Auto Encoder in the layout analysis of the database pages. In [14], Oliveira et al. addressed the problem of performing multiple tasks simultaneously; they considered tasks such as page extraction, baseline extraction and layout analysis.

Also transfer learning-based approaches have been used for document analysis. In [1], for example, the authors used a deep Convolutional Neural Network (CNN) based approach based on ImageNet to recognize ads, forms and scientific writings. As concerns historical documents, in [9] the authors used a FCCN for word spotting. The works presented in [21] and [5], instead, were devoted to optical character recognition (OCR). In particular, in [21] the authors used a transfer learning-based approach to recognize Hindi, Arabic, and Bangla handwritten numerals in ancient documents. As for the work presented in [5], it aimed at recognizing Chinese characters by using a deep neural network pretrained on Latin characters. Finally, at the best of our knowledge, there are no DL-based works for writer identification in ancient documents. However, in [13], the authors identify writers in ancient handwritten documents by using a DL-based technique for denoising and hand-crafted descriptor features for the writer identification task.

In many fields, the loss caused by a wrong prediction may be substantially greater than the advantage due to the correct one. Generally, these problems are usually solved by using learning procedures that, given an unseen sample, allows estimating the related class-probabilities vector, which i-th element represents

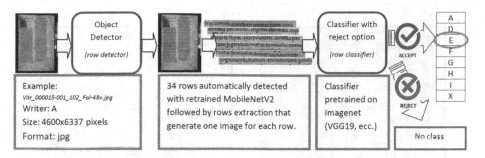

Fig. 1. The general structure of the computational chain

the probability that the sample belongs to the i-th class of the problem at hand. Once these probabilities have been learned, a reject option can be implemented: samples whose probability to belong to the assigned class is below a certain threshold are rejected, i.e. the classifier withdraws its decision and the sample is sent to a different automatic processing system or to a human expert. As for the threshold value, it depends on the problem at hand and it is set according to the error-reject curve, which shows the relationship between the error and reject rates when the threshold value is varied. When the class probabilities are well-estimated, this option allows a classification system to strongly reduce the error rate for the accepted samples, at the cost of a low reject rate.

In this paper, we present a novel approach based on deep transfer learning for the recognition of the writers in ancient documents. The proposed solution is an enhancement of a previously devised system, presented in [3]. That system first uses an object detection system to detect rows in document page images, then it classifies the detected rows producing the classification of the entire page. The enhancement proposed here consists in the addition of a class-based reject option. More specifically, given a page p in which n_p rows have been detected, the probability that the page p belongs to the i-th writer is computed as the ratio n_i/n_p, where n_i is the number of rows written by the i-th, according to the classifier output. The proposed system is shown in Fig. 1. In order to test the effectiveness of the proposed approach we considered the "Avila Bible", a medieval Bible written in Italy during the 12th century, and afterwards sent in Spain where it was completed.

The remainder of the paper is organized as follows: in Sect. 2, we will detail the materials and methods used to develop the proposed system, while, in Sect. 3, we will illustrate the experimental results. Finally, in Sect. 4 some conclusions are drawn.

(a) **(b)**

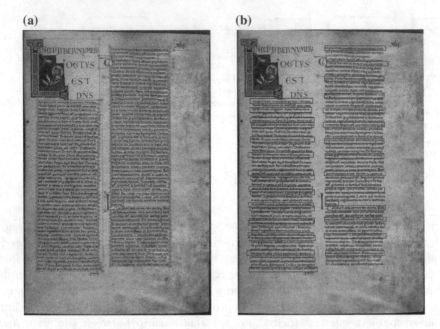

Fig. 2. (a) An example of manually annotate page. (b) An example of page with automatically detected rows

2   The Proposed System

In the following subsections, the dataset used to test the proposed approach, the models adopted as starting points of the learning process, the architecture of the new classifier, as well as the preprocessing and the training procedure, are detailed.

2.1   Data Construction

The Avila Bible consists of 870 two-column pages, manually labeled by expert paleographers. In our experiments, we considered only 749 pages where the paleographic analysis has individuated the presence of at least eight scribal hands. Since the rubricated letters might be all the work of a single scribe, we have removed them during a pre-processing step, thus considering only eight writers to be identified.

Starting from the Avila images, 96 pages have been manually annotated, twelve for each writer, in order to re-train both the object detector and the row classifier. For each page, a single annotation file has been manually generated (see Fig. 3). Each annotation file contains information about the bounding boxes identifying the rows. The object detector has been re-trained by using pages (png files) with annotations (xml files). An example of manually annotated image is shown in Fig. 2(a) while an example of page with automatically detected rows is shown in Fig. 2(b).

Fig. 3. Procedure for dataset generation: xml+png for object detection, single rows for row classifier

Starting from the xml file associated with a page, an image for each bounding box identifying a row has been extracted (see Fig. 3). For each writer, the related pages have been divided in three subsets: training (7 pages), validation (2 pages) and test (3 pages). From these subsets, a total of 12099 rows have been generated. The final test has been conducted on the remaining 653 page images by using the entire chain (see Fig. 1).

2.2 Row Detection and Classification

During the last years different models of Deep Neural Networks (DNNs) for object detection have been trained on public datasets like MS-COCO [12]. One of the most promising and versatile model is the MobileNetV2 [15], a Single Shot Detector fully scalable network ready to run on different targets, from workstation to mobile device.

As regards row classification, we used a transfer learning approach. In particular we considered five models: VGG19 [17], ResNet50 [10], InceptionV3 [19], InceptionResNetV2 [18], NASNetLarge [22]. The five DNNs adopted are characterized by two main sections: a section for Feature Extraction (FE) that receives the images as input and produces features as output in correspondence of the (so-called) bottleneck; and a section for classification (C) realized with some kind of fully connected network. This two-steps architecture has been modified by replacing the original classifier (C) with a unique classifier as described below.

Images have been resized from the original size to the maximum input size $w \times h$ of the network (see Table 1); after that, a simple rescaling has been adopted, by dividing each pixel for 255. Data has been augmented by changing: rotation (angle in $[0, 30]$); zoom (ratio in $[0, 30\%]$; width and heigth (shift in $[0, 30\%]$).

2.3 The Architecture of the New Row Classifier

Has mentioned above, for each network adopted, the original classifier has been substituted with a new classifier based on two fully connected layers with 2048 nodes, an intermediate dropout introduced to improve the generalization capability of the network and a softmax layer that generates the confidence degrees of the output class in the range $[0, 1]$.

Table 1 reports the size of the input image ($w \times h$) and the size n of the bottleneck (number of features extracted) for each of the models, as well as the number of the parameters of the classifiers. As for the number of parameters N_p, it depends on the size at bottleneck n and in general is: $N_p = n * 2048 + 2048 * 2048 + 2048 * 8$. As an example, for VGG19 where $n = 512$, the number of classifier parameters become $5,261,312$ (see Table 1).

Table 1. Number of parameters of the new classifier, maximum image input size and number of features extracted at bottleneck.

Model	Parameters of the classifier	Input size ($w \times h$)	Bottleneck Size (n)
VGG19	5.261.312	256×256	512
ResNet50	8.407.040	224×224	2.048
InceptionV3	8.407.040	299×299	2.048
InceptionResNetV2	7.358.464	299×299	1.536
NASNetLarge	12.470.272	331×331	4.032

2.4 Training: Transfer Learning and Fine-Tuning for the Row Classifier

The training of the row classifier models has been performed in two ways: Transfer Learning (TL) and Fine-Tuning (FT). As for the TL approach, all the parameters of the module FE are frozen whereas the parameters of the classifier C are randomly initialized and trained. When using the FT approach, instead, both modules (FE and C) are involved in the training, thus all the parameters are unfrozen. The FT assumes that the parameters are initialized with the ImageNet training for FE and the final values of TL for C. As training strategy we used the Stochastic Gradient Descent (SGD) method, while as a measure of performance we used the accuracy on the validation set. The hyper-parameters used in our experiments are shown in Table 2. The patience parameter represents the maximum number of epochs to perform without any improvement of the accuracy on the validation set. An epoch, instead, represents one pass of the full training set and is made of a number of iterations equal to *epochs/batch*.

3 Experiments and Results

The experiments were performed by using an Intel Core i7-7700 CPU @ 3.60 GHz 256 GB of RAM with a GPU Titan Xp. As framework, we used Keras 2.2.2 with TensorFlow 1.10.0 as backend. A time ranging from 2 h to 24 h was involved in TL and FT phases with a maximum of 24 h on NASNetLarge during the FT where there were 97 millions of parameters to learn. The final test has been made on 653 Avila pages. By applying the object detector a mean of about 40% of the

Table 2. Values of the hyper-parameters.

Parameter	Value
Learning rate	0.0001
Momentum	0.9
Max epochs	2,000
Patience	200
Batch size	16

Table 3. Best classification performance of five models taken into account.

	Type		A	D	E	F	G	H	I	X	Average
ResNet50	*TL*	Acc	0.82	0.89	0.58	0.82	0.58	0.90	0.58	0.69	0.73
		F1	0.84	0.68	0.71	0.73	0.50	0.93	0.72	0.61	0.72
Inception ResNetV2	*FT*	Acc	0.90	1.00	0.86	0.82	0.88	0.97	0.67	0.63	0.84
		F1	0.92	0.81	0.93	0.81	0.52	0.88	0.82	0.68	*0.80*
Num of pages by class			93	77	82	80	88	77	81	75	Tot 653

total rows are correctly identified page by page. These rows are submitted to the row classifier (one of the five selected in turns). A page is assigned according to the majority vote mechanism. In practice, the page is assigned to the writer to which the largest number of rows has been assigned.

Applying the overall system to these 653 images, we obtained a Confusion Matrix (CM) that reports, for each cell $CM_{i,j}$, the number of rows classified by the model as class j and belonging to class i as suggested by the ground truth. A CM summarizes the results of testing on different classes and the ideal case is a diagonal matrix. From the CM, it is possible to evaluate the Accuracy Acc and the F1-score $F1$, both class by class and globally. We used these measures to compare the five considered models on the test set. The Acc_i for the i-th class was computed as:

$$Acc_i = \frac{CM_{i,i}}{\sum\limits_{j=1}^{8} CM_{i,j}} \tag{1}$$

while the F1-score for the i-th class was computed by using the $precision_i$ and $recall_i$ of the same class. Not that for multiclass problem, the $precision_i$ is equal to the $accuracy_i$ while the $recall_i$ is:

$$recall_i = \frac{CM_{i,i}}{\sum\limits_{i=1}^{8} CM_{i,j}} \tag{2}$$

$$F1_i = 2 * \frac{precision_i * recall_i}{precision_i + recall_i} \tag{3}$$

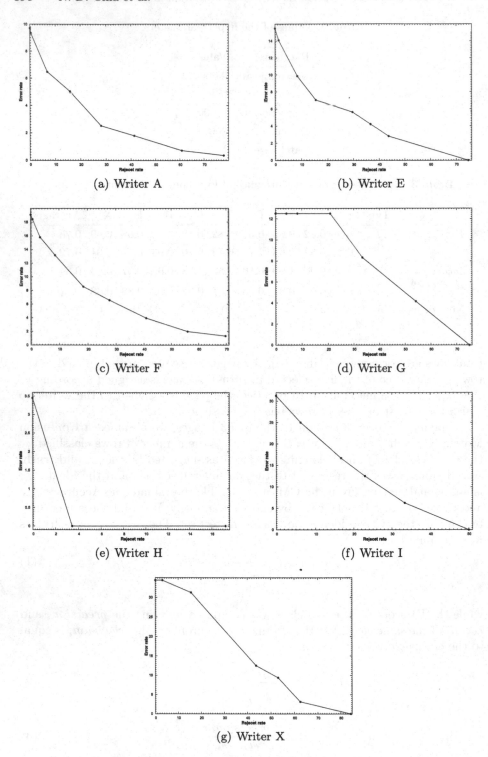

(a) Writer A

(b) Writer E

(c) Writer F

(d) Writer G

(e) Writer H

(f) Writer I

(g) Writer X

Fig. 4. Error- reject curves for the different writers.

Global Acc and $F1$ was evaluated as mean of the values associated with each class.

The best performance achieved by the five models taken into account are shown in Table 3. From the table it can be observed that: (i) there is generally an important improvement by passing from TL to FT; (ii) the best results have been produced with InceptionV3 after FT where Acc and $F1$ reach 88% and 83%, respectively; (iii) the best results with TL only, have been produced with ResNet50 where Acc and $F1$ reach 73% and 72%, respectively.

3.1 Testing the Reject Option

Once the models for the page classification have been tested, we used the top-performing one (Inception ResNetV2, trained with the fine-tuning method, see Table 3) to evaluate the effectiveness of the proposed rejection rule. This rule is based on the page classification method mentioned above, which assigns a page p to the writer whose number of rows is the largest one in p. More specifically, if n_p rows have been detected and classified in p, then the probability that the page p belongs to the i-th writer is computed as the ratio n_i/n_p, where n_i is the number of rows written by the i-th, according to the classifier output.

To test our rule, for each writer, we plotted the error-reject curve. These curves show the trends of the error and rejection rates when the acceptance threshold varies and allows estimating the effectiveness of the adopted rejection rule. Typically, good curves are those where the error rate rapidly decreases while the reject rate does not increase too much. These curves also allow setting the proper threshold value, according to the requirements of the problem at hand. The error-reject curves for seven of the eight writers are shown in Fig. 4. Note that the plot for the writer D is not shown because all his pages were correctly classified, even without setting any reject threshold.

From the figure, for the different writers, we can see that both the error rate without reject option (the most left points in the plots, we will refer to it in the following as e_0) and the error-reject curves differ widely. For instance, for the writer A e_0 is about 10%, while accuracy close to 2% can achieved by rejecting less than 30% of the test samples (pages). As for the writer H e_0 is about 3.5% and rejecting less than 4% of the samples allows achieving 0% of error rate. Finally, as for the writers I and X, e_0 is about 30% and the error rate decreases slowly, while error rates around the 10% are obtained only rejecting at least about 25% of the samples (writer I), or even about the 50% (writer X). From these results it is clear that the performance of the proposed reject option depends on that of the classifier, thus providing satisfactory results only when the latter achieves accuracy at least around 10%.

4   Conclusions

In this paper, we presented a novel approach, based on deep transfer learning, for the identification of the writers in medieval manuscripts. The proposed approach consists of three modules. The first uses an object detection system to detect the rows in the page images. The second one, instead, classifies the extracted rows. Finally, the third module implements a page-based reject option which takes into account the row labeled by the classifier to estimate the class probabilities for a given page. The proposed approach has been tested on the "Avila Bible", an XII century manuscript.

From the experimental results, the following conclusions can be drawn: (i) transfer learning without fine-tuning generally produces a weak classifier; (ii) the proposed page-based reject option works well when the classifier achieves satisfactory results.

Future work will include the extensions of test experiments on other datasets and with other intra and inter database training/testing.

Acknowledgment. The authors gratefully acknowledge the support of NVIDIA Corporation for the donation of the Titan Xp GPUs.

References

1. Afzal, M.Z., et al.: Deepdocclassifier: document classification with deep convolutional neural network. In: 2015 13th International Conference on Document Analysis and Recognition (ICDAR), pp. 1111–1115, August 2015
2. Antonacopoulos, A., Downton, A.C.: Special issue on the analysis of historical documents. IJDAR **9**(2–4), 75–77 (2007)
3. Bria, A., et al.: Deep transfer learning for writer identification in medieval books. In: 2018 IEEE International Conference on Metrology for Archaeology and Cultural Heritage (2018). (in press)
4. Bria, A., Marrocco, C., Molinara, M., Tortorella, F.: A ranking-based cascade approach for unbalanced data. In: 2012 21st International Conference on Pattern Recognition (ICPR), pp. 3439–3442. IEEE (2012)
5. Ciresan, D.C., Meier, U., Schmidhuber, J.: Transfer learning for latin and chinese characters with deep neural networks. In: The 2012 International Joint Conference on Neural Networks (IJCNN), pp. 1–6 (2012)
6. De Stefano, C., Maniaci, M., Fontanella, F., di Scotto Freca, A.: Layout measures for writer identification in mediaeval documents. Measurement **127**, 443–452 (2018)
7. De Stefano, C., Maniaci, M., Fontanella, F., di Freca, A.S.: Reliable writer identification in medieval manuscripts through page layout features: the avila bible case. Eng. Appl. Artif. Intell. **72**, 99–110 (2018)
8. De Stefano, C., Fontanella, F., Maniaci, M., Scotto di Freca, A.: A method for scribe distinction in medieval manuscripts using page layout features. In: Maino, G., Foresti, G.L. (eds.) ICIAP 2011. LNCS, vol. 6978, pp. 393–402. Springer, Heidelberg (2011). https://doi.org/10.1007/978-3-642-24085-0_41
9. Granet, A., Morin, E., Mouchère, H., Quiniou, S., Viard-Gaudin, C.: Transfer learning for handwriting recognition on historical documents. In: International Conference on Pattern Recognition Applications and Methods, Madeira, Portugal, January 2018. https://hal.archives-ouvertes.fr/hal-01681126
10. He, K., Zhang, X., Ren, S., Sun, J.: Deep residual learning for image recognition. CoRR arXiv:1512.03385 (2015). http://dblp.uni-trier.de/db/journals/corr/corr1512.html#HeZRS15

11. Kölsch, A., Mishra, A., Varshneya, S., Liwicki, M.: Recognizing challenging hand-written annotations with fully convolutional networks. CoRR arXiv:1804.00236 (2018)
12. Lin, T.-Y., et al.: Microsoft COCO: common objects in context. In: Fleet, D., Pajdla, T., Schiele, B., Tuytelaars, T. (eds.) ECCV 2014. LNCS, vol. 8693, pp. 740–755. Springer, Cham (2014). https://doi.org/10.1007/978-3-319-10602-1_48
13. Ni, K., Callier, P., Hatch, B.: Writer identification in noisy handwritten documents. In: 2017 IEEE Winter Conference on Applications of Computer Vision (WACV), pp. 1177–1186, March 2017. https://doi.org/10.1109/WACV.2017.136
14. Oliveira, S.A., Seguin, B., Kaplan, F.: dhsegment: A generic deep-learning app-roach for document segmentation. CoRR arXiv:1804.10371 (2018)
15. Sandler, M., Howard, A., Zhu, M., Zhmoginov, A., Chen, L.C.: Mobilenetv 2: inverted residuals and linear bottlenecks. In: The IEEE Conference on Computer Vision and Pattern Recognition (CVPR), June 2018
16. Simistira, F., Seuret, M., Eichenberger, N., Garz, A., Liwicki, M., Ingold, R.: Diva-hisdb: a precisely annotated large dataset of challenging medieval manuscripts. In: 2016 15th International Conference on Frontiers in Handwriting Recogni-tion(ICFHR), pp. 471–476, October 2016
17. Simonyan, K., Zisserman, A.: Very deep convolutional networks for large-scale image recognition. CoRR arXiv:1409.1556 (2014). http://dblp.uni-trier.de/db/journals/corr/corr1409.html#SimonyanZ14a
18. Szegedy, C., Ioffe, S., Vanhoucke, V.: Inception-v4, inception-resnet and the impact of residual connections on learning. CoRR arXiv:1602.07261 (2016). http://dblp.uni-trier.de/db/journals/corr/corr1602.html#SzegedyIV16
19. Szegedy, C., Vanhoucke, V., Ioffe, S., Shlens, J., Wojna, Z.: Rethinking the incep-tion architecture for computer vision. CoRR arXiv:1512.00567 (2015). http://dblp.uni-trier.de/db/journals/corr/corr1512.html#SzegedyVISW15
20. Trovini, G., et al.: A deep learning framework for micro-calcification detection in 2d mammography and c-view. In: Progress in Biomedical Optics and Imaging - Proceedings of SPIE.,vol. 10718 (2018)
21. Tushar, A.K., Ashiquzzaman, A., Afrin, A., Islam, M.R.: A novel transfer learn-ing approach upon hindi, arabic, and bangla numerals using convolutional neural networks. CoRR arXiv:1707.08385 (2017). http://arxiv.org/abs/1707.08385
22. Zoph, B., Vasudevan, V., Shlens, J., Le, Q.V.: Learning transferable architectures for scalable image recognition. CoRR arXiv:1707.07012 (2017). http://dblp.uni-trier.de/db/journals/corr/corr1707.html#ZophVSL17

Minimizing Training Data for Reliable Writer Identification in Medieval Manuscripts

Nicole Dalia Cilia, Claudio De Stefano, Francesco Fontanella[✉],
Mario Molinara, and Alessandra Scotto di Freca

Department of Electrical and Information Engineering (DIEI),
University of Cassino and Southern Lazio, Via G. Di Biasio, 43, Cassino, FR, Italy
{nicoledalia.cilia,destefano,fontanella,m.molinara,a.scotto}@unicas.it

Abstract. Palaeography aims to study ancient documents and the identification of the people who participated in the handwriting process of a given document is one of the most important problems. To this aim, expert paleographers typically analyze handwriting features such as letter heights and widths, distances between characters and angles of inclination. With the aim of achieving more precise measures and also thanks to the availability of high-quality digital images, paleographers are starting to use digital tools. In this context, in previous studies, we proposed a pattern recognition system for distinguishing the writers of mediaeval books and also investigated which is the minimum amount of training data needed to achieve satisfactory results in terms of accuracy. In this paper, we present a reject option that allows us to implement a highly-reliable system for writer identification, trained on a reduced set of data. The experimental results, performed on two sets of digital images from medieval Bibles, show that rejecting only a few samples it is possible to strongly reduce the error rate.

Keywords: Digital palaeography · Writer identification · Reject option

1 Introduction

Palaeography aims at studying medieval manuscripts and has among its main tasks the identification of the different people who worked together for the production of a given manuscript. This identification was traditionally performed manually, by measuring quantities such as letter heights and widths, distances between characters and angles of inclination. In the last decade, there has been a growing interest in the use of digital tools in palaeographic analysis. The aim has been twofold, from one hand to perform better quantitative analysis of ancient manuscripts and on the other hand to manage huge masses of data [1,6,21].

Such tools have been used either to perform traditional measurements more rapidly and systematically than in the past or to apply pattern-recognition-based approaches for the automatic processing of the manuscripts, which are

© Springer Nature Switzerland AG 2019
M. Cristani et al. (Eds.): ICIAP 2019 Workshops, LNCS 11808, pp. 198–208, 2019.
https://doi.org/10.1007/978-3-030-30754-7_20

able to fully exploit the potentiality of the currently available high-quality digital images. Typically these latter approaches are subdivided into two wide categories, depending on the type of measures performed, that can be either *local* or *global*. As for local measures, they are based on the analysis of individual letters and signs as well as of their composing strokes [20, 22, 26]. As concerns global measures, instead, they are focused on the global, automated observation of the handwritten page, by using texture features and/or layout analysis [4, 19, 23].

In previous studies [15, 16, 18] we proposed a pattern recognition system for distinguishing the writers of a medieval Bible. The proposed system was based on features derived from the analysis of page layout according to the suggestions of palaeographic researchers. In these studies, we also analyzed the proposed features by using the approaches discussed in [5, 8, 14]. However, those results were achieved by training the system on about half of the available dataset, thus limiting its practical use, because the manual labelling by expert paleographers is a very expensive process.

In many real-life problems, e.g. medical field or security-related decisions, the loss caused by a wrong prediction may be substantially greater than the advantage due to the correct one. In the pattern recognition field, these problems are usually solved by using classifiers that provide an estimate of the probability that the input sample belongs to the class it has been assigned to. This probability may be assumed as a measure of classification reliability. Once this probability is available, a reject option can be implemented by rejecting those samples whose probability to belong to the assigned class is below a certain threshold, set according to the trade-off between the cost of a wrong prediction and that of rejection for a given sample. When the class probabilities are well-estimated, this option allows a classification system to strongly reduce the prediction error for the accepted samples, delegating the decision for the reject samples to a different automatic processing system or to a human expert.

In this paper, in order to find the minimum quantity of training data needed to achieve satisfactory results, we performed two sets of experiments, each one performed by using an increasing number of training samples. As for the datasets, we used data extracted from two medieval bibles: the "Avila Bible" and the "Trento Bible". The first one was written in Italy by at least nine scribes within the third decade of the 12th century and then sent to Spain, where its text and decoration were completed by local scribes. Because of the presence of contemporary and not contemporary scribal hands, this manuscript represents a severe testbed for evaluating the effectiveness of our approach. As for the "Trento Bible", it is an Atlantic volume assigned to the first half of the 12th century, and it was written by at least five different scribes. Given the availability of full digitization of acceptable quality, these Bibles can be used as an effective test bench of our tool for automatic scribe distinction. Moreover, in order to improve the reliability of the classification results of our system, we implemented a reject option, based on the class probabilities provided by the adopted classifiers. The experimental results show that by using only 15% of the available samples to train a random forest classifier the error rate on unseen samples is less than 3%.

Moreover, the reject option implemented allowed us, for both datasets, to further reduce this error rate, on the accepted samples, to less than 1% by rejecting no about 10% of the test samples.

The remainder of the paper is organized as follows: Sect. 2 presents the architecture of the system, Sect. 3 illustrates and discusses the experimental results, while some discussions and conclusions are eventually left to Sect. 4.

2   The System Architecture

The proposed system receives as input RGB images of single pages of the manuscript to be processed, and performs for each page the following steps: *pre-processing, segmentation, feature extraction*, and *scribe distinction*. These steps are detailed in the following subsections.

2.1   Pre-processing and Segmentation

In the pre-processing step noisy pixels, such as those corresponding to stains or holes onto the page, or pixels included in the frame of the image, are detected and removed. Also, the red out-scaling capital letters are removed. Afterwards, the original RGB images are transformed into grey-level ones and then in binary images. In the segmentation step, in each page, columns and rows are detected. The two Bibles taken into account are in a two-column format and each column may have a slightly variable number of rows. The detection of both columns and rows is performed by computing pixel projection histograms on the horizontal and the vertical axis, respectively.

2.2   Feature Extraction

The features extracted have been devised in collaboration with expert palaeographers, mainly concerning the layout of the page. The first set relates to properties of the whole page and includes the upper and the lower margin of the page and the inter-column distance.

The second set of features concerns the columns: we have considered the number of rows in the column and the column exploitation coefficient [2]. The exploitation coefficient is a column-based measure and evaluates how much a column C is filled with ink, and is computed as $N_{BP}(C)/N_P(C)$, where the functions $N_{BP}(C)$ and $N_P(C)$ return the number of black pixels and the total number of pixels in C, respectively. Both features vary according to different factors, among which the expertise of the writer.

The third set of features characterizes the rows and includes the following features: weight, modular ratio, interline spacing, modular ratio/interline spacing ratio and peaks. The weight is analogous to the exploitation coefficient mentioned above, but in this case, it measures how much a row is filled with ink. A for the modular ratio, it is a typical palaeographic feature and estimates the dimension of handwriting characters. It is computed by measuring the height of the "centre zone" of the words each, then the interline spacing is the distance in pixels between two consecutive rows. It is worth noting that these last three features can be used both to characterize the handwriting of the single writers and also for geographical and/or chronological distinctions [24]. Since computing the inter-character space and the number of characters in a row, is a difficult task because it implies extracting the single characters contained in each word, we have chosen to estimate the number of characters in a row by counting the number of peaks in the horizontal projection histogram of that row.

2.3 Scribe Distinction

The last block of the proposed system, by using the features detailed in the previous subsection, implements a classification scheme, e.g. Random forest or decision trees, to distinguish the rows written by the different writers who participated the handwriting process of the manuscript. Moreover, in order to compute features such as the interlinear spacing (third group) each sample to be classified represents a group of M consecutive rows.

3 Experimental Results

In the experiments detailed in the following, we used two datasets of digital images obtained from two medieval bibles: the "Avila Bible" and the "Trento Bible". In order to investigate which is the minimum amount of data to effectively train the considered classifiers, so as to allow them to distinguish the different scribal hands, for each bible, we randomly selected half of the available samples and used them as test set; then we varied the amount of training data, adding new samples until all the remaining ones were included in the training set. The maximum percentage of samples used for the training was set to 50% of the entire database. In a further experiment, we tested the implemented reject option plotting the error-reject curve for each of the classifier taken into account. Finally, we performed twenty runs with different random seeds, averaging the corresponding results.

The databases used for testing the proposed approach, the considered classification schemes and the results of the experiments performed are detailed in the following subsections.

3.1 Avila Bible

The "Avila Bible" was written in Italy by at least nine scribes within the third decade of the 12th century and then sent to Spain, where its text and decoration were completed by local scribes; in a third phase (during the 15th century) additions were made by another writer. Because of the presence of contemporary and not contemporary scribal hands, this manuscript represents a severe test for evaluating the effectiveness of our approach. To the best of our knowledge, at present, no standard database with the same characteristics is available (high-quality full reproductions and a limited number of recognizable recurring hands), and this is the first study in which digital palaeography techniques have been applied to Romanesque Bibles, and particularly to the "Avila Bible". This is mainly due to the fact that Giant Bibles, being very large and difficult to handle, have not been often digitized in recent times and the available microfilms are not good enough to perform pattern recognition analysis (low quality of the images, cut off page margins, etc.).

The "Avila Bible" consists of 870 two-column pages, but we considered in this study only 800 pages of acceptable quality. The palaeographic analysis has individuated the presence of at least thirteen scribal hands. The pages written by each scribe are not equally numerous (they range from 1 to 143) and there are cases in which parts of the same page are written by different scribes. This implies that the classification problem to be solved is characterized by a strongly imbalanced distribution of the number of samples per class. Since the rubricated letters might be all the work of a single scribe, we have removed them during a pre-processing step, thus considering only twelve writers to be identified. As for the parameter M (see Subsect. 2.3), we set its value to four. This value represents the best compromise between two opposite requirements: on the one hand, high M values allows us to obtain, for each extracted sample, significant average values for the devised features. On the other hand, small M values ensure that the rows included in the pattern are written by a single scribe, thus allowing us to capture the distinctive aspects of his hand. Once the value of M has been fixed, we extracted from the images 20,867 samples.

3.2   Trento Bible

The second ancient document taken into account is the "Trento Bible", which is an Atlantic volume assigned to the first half of the 12th century, whose decoration was convincingly attributed to the so-called Master of the "Avila Bible" and his atelier. The extant portion of the Bible was written by at least three different scribes. Given the availability of a full digitization of acceptable quality, this Bible can be used as a test bench of our method for scribe distinction, based on layout features. It is useful to remark that the digital images of the "Trento Bible" are not publicly available. Finally, it is worth noticing that the number of scribes who participated to the production of the "Trento Bible" is significantly smaller than "Avila Bible", that the volume history is less intricate and concentrated in a more limited time span, without later additions and changes. Nonetheless, it represents a complex classification task, and the very high recognition rate also obtained in this second experiment confirms the effectiveness of our approach. From the available images, we extracted 6,048 samples.

3.3   The Classification Schemes

As for the classification algorithm, we considered three effective and widely used classification schemes, namely Decision Tree (DT), Random Forest (RF) and K-Nearest Neighbour (K-NN).

A **Decision Tree** is a decision support tool with a tree graph structure. In a DT, the internal nodes represent attribute tests, where each branch yields the outcome of the test, whereas leaf nodes represent class labels. The paths from the root node to the leaves represent classification rules [25]. As for the tree learning, we used C4.5 algorithm. This algorithm builds a decision tree with a top-down approach, by using the concept of information entropy. Given a training set S, it breaks down S into smaller and smaller subsets while at the same time an associated decision tree is incrementally developed. At each node of the tree, C4.5 chooses the attribute that most effectively splits the corresponding sample subsets. The splitting criterion is the normalized information entropy gain which measures how much the subsets are homogeneous, in terms of class labels, with respect to the split set. The algorithm then recurs on the smaller subsets.

Random Forest is a method for building decision tree ensembles, which combines bagging methods in order to maximize the diversity among the trees making up the ensemble [3]. In practice, in the RF algorithm, each ensemble tree is built by using both a different training set (because of bagging) and a different feature subset (because of Random Subspace). Once the ensemble has been built, unknown samples are labelled according to the majority vote rule. The Random Forest approach does not refer to a single algorithm, but rather to a family of algorithms. In this study, we have used the original algorithm proposed by Breiman in [3], usually referred to in the literature as *Forest-RI*. For its effectiveness, this algorithm was used as a reference method in most of the papers dealing with random forest methods. It has been also shown that RF outperforms both bagging and boosting.

The **K-Nearest Neighbor** algorithm is a well known non-parametric method that can be used for both classification and regression. According to this approach, an unknown sample is labelled with the most common label among its k nearest neighbours in the training set. The rationale behind the k-NN classifier is that, given an unknown sample $\mathbf{x}$ to be assigned to one of the c_i classes of the problem at hand, the a-posteriori probabilities $p(c_i|\mathbf{x})$ in the neighborhood of $\mathbf{x}$ may be estimated by looking at the class labels of the k nearest neighbors of $\mathbf{x}$. Nonetheless its simplicity, k-NN has shown to be able to obtain very accurate results [9]. As for the parameter k, we performed some preliminary experiments achieving the best results setting the value $K = 1$. Thus, we used this value for all the experiments.

3.4   Training Data Minimization

As mentioned above, in our experiments we used one half of the available samples as a test set, and then we created several training sets containing an increasing number of samples according to the following procedure: for the first training set,

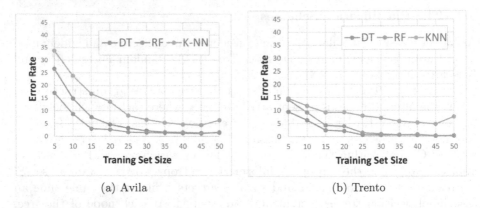

(a) Avila   (b) Trento

Fig. 1. Percentage of errors on the "Avila Bible" and on the "Trento Bible" respectively, in the first set of experiments as a function of the percentage of samples included in the training set.

a number of samples corresponding to 5% of the entire database were randomly selected among those not included in the test set; in the same way, for the second training set, we selected a number of samples corresponding to 10%, and so on for the other training sets, adding a number of samples equal to 5% each time, until the maximum percentage of 50% was reached. Therefore, the last training set consisted of all the samples not included in the test set. We used these sets to train the considered classification schemes and, for each of them, we computed the corresponding classification results on the test set.

The purpose of these experiments was to estimate the minimum training needed to achieve satisfactory classification performance on unseen samples. The results are summarized in Figs. 1(a) and (b), which refer to the "Avila Bible" and the "Trento Bible", respectively. The data in the plots show that the best results were obtained by using RF classifiers, which also demonstrated to be less sensitive to the size of the training set: in this case, in fact, using only 15% of the available samples for training, the overall reduction of the recognition rate is less than 2%. Furthermore, including about 25% of the available samples in the training set, there is in practice no reduction of the classification performance. DT classifiers exhibit worse results for smaller dimensions of the training set, achieving performances almost identical to those of RF with training sets that include at least 30% of available data. Finally, the performance of K-NN classifiers is far worse than those of the other classification schemes considered, and they seem also more sensitive to the size of the training set.

3.5   Reject Option Evaluation

Once we have investigated the relationship between the training set size and the classification performance for our system, we have tested the implemented reject rule for the three classification schemes considered. As concerns the amount of

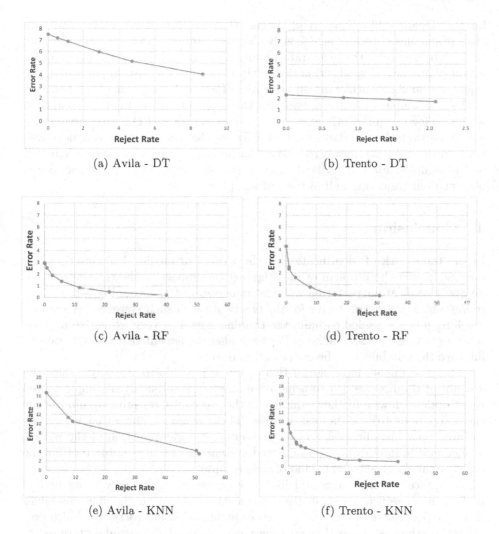

Fig. 2. Error-reject curves. These curves have been obtained by using 15% of the dataset to train the classifier.

training data, we chose 15%, because as discussed above, this is the minimum amount that allowed us to achieve satisfactory results.

To test our rule, we plotted the error-reject curves. These curves show the trends of the error and rejection rates when the acceptance threshold varies and allows estimating the effectiveness of the adopted rejection rule. Typically, good curves are those where the error rate rapidly decreases while the reject rate does not increase too much. These curves also allow setting the proper threshold value, according to the requirements of the problem at hand.

The error-reject curves are shown in Fig. 2. From the Figs. 2(a) and (b), we can see that for the DT classifier the error rate decreases slowly, especially for the Trento Bible. This trend suggest that by this classifier provided high class probabilities also for erroneously classified samples. As for the RF classifier (Figs. 2(b) and (c)), the error rate rapidly decreases, thus suggesting that this classifier provided a good estimation of the class probabilities. In particular, the reject option allows achieving an error rate of about 1% rejecting less than 10% of the test samples. Finally, as concerns the K-NN classifier (Figs. 2(c) and (d)), which achieved significantly worse results than the RF and DT, the curves differ widely between the two datasets: for the Trento dataset, the error rate decreases very slowly and a significant reduction is achieved only rejecting more than 15% of the samples; for the Avila dataset, a strong reduction of the error rate is obtained only rejecting half of the test samples.

4   Conclusions

In the framework of identification of the writers of medieval manuscripts, we have addressed the problem of investigating the impact of the training set size on the classification performance. The dimension of the training set, in fact, represents an important factor for the practical use of such systems, because the labelling process needed to build the training data is a very expensive process, requiring expert palaeographers. We have also implemented a reject option to improve the reliability of the classification results.

The experiments have shown that: (i) it is possible to strongly reduce the amount of training needed to achieve satisfactory results; (ii) the implemented reject option allows a further reduction of the error rate, rejecting, in most of the cases, less than 10% of the test samples. These results confirm that is possible to build up a classification tool for the automatic identification of the writers of medieval manuscripts. The proposed system can be a valuable tool for the paleographic analysis of this kind of manuscripts.

As a future work, we would like to improve our system by using better-performing classification strategies, such as those based on classifier ensembles [7,12,13,17]. The use of Learning Vector Quantization networks could also provide interesting results, as they are generally considered a powerful pattern recognition tool and give the advantage of providing an explicit representation of the prototypes of each class [10,11] (in our case, a prototype represents the specific feature values for a scribe).

References

1. Antonacopoulos, A., Downton, A.C.: Special issue on the analysis of historical documents. IJDAR **9**(2–4), 75–77 (2007)
2. Bozzolo, C., Coq, D., Muzerelle, D., Ornato, E.: Noir et blanc. Premiers résultats d'une enquête sur la mise en page dans le livre médiéval. In: Il libro e il testo, Urbino, pp. 195–221 (1982)
3. Breiman, L.: Random forests. Mach. Learn. **45**(1), 5–32 (2001)

4. Bulacu, M., Schomaker, L.: Text-independent writer identification and verification using textural and allographic features. IEEE Trans. Pattern Anal. Mach. Intell. **29**(4), 701–717 (2007)
5. Cilia, N., De Stefano, C., Fontanella, F., Scotto di Freca, A.: A ranking-based feature selection approach for handwritten character recognition. Pattern Recogn. Lett. **121**, 77–86 (2018)
6. Ciula, A.: The palaeographical method under the light of a digital approach. In: Rehbein, M., Sahle, P., Schaßan, T. (eds.) Kodikologie und Paläographie im digitalen Zeitalter-Codicology and Palaeography in the Digital Age, pp. 219–237. Bod, Norderstedt (2009)
7. Cordella, L.P., De Stefano, C., Fontanella, F., Scotto di Freca, A.: A weighted majority vote strategy using bayesian networks. In: Petrosino, A. (ed.) ICIAP 2013. LNCS, vol. 8157, pp. 219–228. Springer, Heidelberg (2013). https://doi.org/10.1007/978-3-642-41184-7_23
8. Cordella, L.P., De Stefano, C., Fontanella, F., Marrocco, C., Scotto di Freca, A.: Combining single class features for improving performance of a two stage classifier. In: 20th International Conference on Pattern Recognition (ICPR 2010), pp. 4352–4355. IEEE Computer Society (2010)
9. Cover, T., Hart, P.: Nearest neighbor pattern classification. IEEE Trans. Inf. Theor. **13**(1), 21–27 (2006)
10. De Stefano, C., D'Elia, C., Marcelli, A.: A dynamic approach to learning vector quantization. In: Proceedings of the 17th International Conference on Pattern Recognition (ICPR 2004), vol. 4, pp. 601–604 (August 2004)
11. De Stefano, C., D'Elia, C., Marcelli, A., Scotto di Freca, A.: Improving dynamic learning vector quantization. In: Proceedings of the 18th International Conference on Pattern Recognition (ICPR 2006), vol. 2, pp. 804–807 (August 2006)
12. De Stefano, C., Folino, G., Fontanella, F., Scotto Freca, A.: Using bayesian networks for selecting classifiers in GP ensembles. Inf. Sci. **258**, 200–216 (2014)
13. De Stefano, C., Fontanella, F., Folino, G., di Freca, A.S.: A bayesian approach for combining ensembles of GP classifiers. In: Sansone, C., Kittler, J., Roli, F. (eds.) MCS 2011. LNCS, vol. 6713, pp. 26–35. Springer, Heidelberg (2011). https://doi.org/10.1007/978-3-642-21557-5_5
14. De Stefano, C., Fontanella, F., Marrocco, C.: A GA-based feature selection algorithm for remote sensing images. In: Giacobini, M., et al. (eds.) EvoWorkshops 2008. LNCS, vol. 4974, pp. 285–294. Springer, Heidelberg (2008). https://doi.org/10.1007/978-3-540-78761-7_29
15. De Stefano, C., Maniaci, M., Fontanella, F., Scotto Freca, A.: Layout measures for writer identification in mediaeval documents. Measurement **127**, 443–452 (2018)
16. De Stefano, C., Maniaci, M., Fontanella, F., Scotto di Freca, A.: Reliable writer identification in medieval manuscripts through page layout features: The Avila Bible case. Eng. Appl. Artif. Intell. **72**, 99–110 (2018)
17. De Stefano, C., D'Elia, C., Scotto di Freca, A., Marcelli, A.: Classifier combination by bayesian networks for handwriting recognition. Int. J. Pattern Recogn. Artif. Intell. **23**(05), 887–905 (2009)
18. De Stefano, C., Fontanella, F., Maniaci, M., Scotto di Freca, A.: A method for scribe distinction in medieval manuscripts using page layout features. In: Maino, G., Foresti, G.L. (eds.) ICIAP 2011. LNCS, vol. 6978, pp. 393–402. Springer, Heidelberg (2011). https://doi.org/10.1007/978-3-642-24085-0_41

19. Dhali, M.A., He, S., Popovic, M., Tigchelaar, E., Schomaker, L.: A digital palaeographic approach towards writer identification in the dead sea scrolls. In: Proceedings of the 6th International Conference on Pattern Recognition Applications and Methods, ICPRAM, pp. 693–702 (2017)
20. Dinstein, I., Shapira, Y.: Ancient hebraic handwriting identification with runlength histograms. IEEE Trans. Syst. Man Cybern. **12**(3), 405 409 (1982)
21. Gurrado, M.: "Graphoskop", uno strumento informatico per l'analisi paleografica quantitativa. In: Rehbein, M., Sahle, P., Schaßan, T. (eds.) Kodikologie und Paläographie im digitalen Zeitalter-Codicology and Palaeography in the Digital Age, pp. 251–259. Bod, Norderstedt (2009)
22. He, S., Samara, P., Burgers, J., Schomaker, L.: Image-based historical manuscript dating using contour and stroke fragments. Pattern Recogn. **58**, 159–171 (2016)
23. Liang, Y., Fairhurst, M.C., Guest, R.M., Erbilek, M.: Automatic handwriting feature extraction, analysis and visualization in the context of digital palaeography. IJPRAI **30**(4), 1653001 (2016). 1–26
24. Maniaci, M., Ornato, G.: Prime considerazioni sulla genesi e la storia della bibbia di avila. In: Miscellanea F. Magistrale (2010)
25. Quinlan, J.R.: C4. 5 Programs for Machine Learning. Morgan Kaufmann Series in Machine Learning. Morgan Kaufmann, San Francisco (1993)
26. Schomaker, L., Franke, K., Bulacu, M.: Using codebooks of fragmented connected-component contours in forensic and historic writer identification. Pattern Recogn. Lett. **28**(6), 719–727 (2007). Pattern Recognition in Cultural Heritage and Medical Applications

e-BADLE: First International Workshop on eHealth in the Big Data and Deep Learning Era

Fusion of Visual and Anamnestic Data for the Classification of Skin Lesions with Deep Learning

Simone Bonechi[1], Monica Bianchini[1], Pietro Bongini[1,5], Giorgio Ciano[1,5],
Giorgia Giacomini[1,2], Riccardo Rosai[1], Linda Tognetti[3,4], Alberto Rossi[1,5],
and Paolo Andreini[1(✉)]

[1] Department of Information Engineering and Matemathics, University of Siena,
Siena, Italy
paolo.andreini@unisi.it
[2] Department of Biotechnology, Chemistry and Pharmacy, University of Siena,
Siena, Italy
[3] Department of Medicine, Surgery and Neuroscience, University of Siena,
Siena, Italy
[4] Department of Medical Biotechnologies, University of Siena, Siena, Italy
[5] Department of Information Engineering, University of Florence, Florence, Italy

Abstract. Early diagnosis of skin lesions is essential for the positive outcome of the disease, which can only be resolved with surgical treatment. In this manuscript, a deep learning method is proposed for the classification of cutaneous lesions based on their visual appearance and on the patient's anamnestic data. These include age and gender of the patient and position of the lesion. The classifier discriminates between benign and malignant lesions, mimicking a typical procedure in dermatological diagnostics. Good preliminary results on the ISIC Dataset demonstrate the importance of the information fusion process, which significantly improves the classification accuracy.

1 Introduction

Recently, the results obtained by Deep Learning techniques, and in particular by Convolutional Neural Networks (CNNs), have had a devastating impact on the field of image processing [1, 2]. *"Also the medical image analysis community has taken notice of these pivotal developments"* although *"the transition from systems that use handcrafted features to systems that learn features from the data has been gradual"* [3]. Many applications have been developed based on CNNs, ranging from automatic analysis reporting [4], to age estimation based on brain NMRs [5] and to skin lesion prognostic classification [6,7].

In this paper, we propose a new CNN–based tool, capable of classifying skin lesions, which can help dermatologists in the diagnosis of malignant pathologies. Skin cancer is one of the most common tumors in the world and its incidence is increasing worldwide. The main types of skin cancer are Non Melanoma Skin

© Springer Nature Switzerland AG 2019
M. Cristani et al. (Eds.): ICIAP 2019 Workshops, LNCS 11808, pp. 211–219, 2019.
https://doi.org/10.1007/978-3-030-30754-7_21

Cancer (NMSC) and Malignant Melanoma (MM) [8]. NMSC includes Basal Cell Carcinoma (BCC) and Squamous Cell Carcinoma (SCC), which usually develop in the epidermis, the outermost layer of the skin. Both tumors, BCC and SCC, tend to occur in over–65 patients, on healthy skin or precancerous skin lesions. In contrast to melanoma, BCC and SCC have a low grade of malignancy and rarely spread to other parts of the body [9]. BCC clinically appears as ulcerations, nodules, reddish plaques or scars. Although BCC is a low-invasive skin cancer, with reduced metastatic potential and, if diagnosed early and treated appropriately, in almost all cases it is easily resolved [10]. SCC is the second most common skin cancer after BCC. SCC usually starts as a small nodule and grows until it becomes an ulcered lesion. It may present as papules or cutaneous horns. The metastasis incidence of SCC is estimated between 0.5–16% [11]. Unlike BCC and SCC, melanoma is an aggressive form of cancer, triggered by an uncontrolled proliferation of melanocytes, pigment–producing cells of neuroectodermal origin. Cutaneous melanoma is the 20th most common cancer worldwide. It occurs most frequently in adults aged between 40 and 60, while it is rarely observed before puberty [12]. It is slightly more common in men than in women. Although cutaneous melanoma comprises less than 5% of all skin tumor cases, it causes the majority (75%) of skin cancer deaths. The worldwide incidence of this pathology has risen sharply over the last decades [13]. Globally, 287,723 new cases of cutaneous melanoma have been reported in 2018, and 466,914 new cases are expected to occur until 2040, according to the estimates of Globocan [14]. Furthermore, the incidence trends vary significantly across different geographic locations and ethnic groups [15]. Figure 1(a) shows the estimated incidence and mortality of cutaneous melanoma in different areas of the World. According to data from Globocan, the highest incidence rate worldwide is recorded in Australia and New Zealand, where melanoma is the third most common form of cancer. In Europe, as shown in Fig. 1(b), the highest incidence rates occur in Norway and Denmark, with 29.6 and 27.6 cases per 100,000 people per year, respectively. Regular clinical screenings and head–to–toe self–examinations are recommended to detect melanoma in its earlier stages, when the lesion is smaller than 2 mm and can be easily removed with surgery. If melanoma is diagnosed in a more advanced stage, in which the cancer has already spread to lymph nodes, the excision is insufficient. To treat these cases, surgery must be combined with radiotherapy, immunotherapy or targeted therapy [16]. The ABCDE rule is a common screening tool used to distinguish malignant melanoma from a benign mole. The characteristics of a lesion which can help in classifying it as a melanoma include asymmetry, border irregularity, color variegation, a diameter longer than 6 mm and an evolving shape. The development of cutaneous melanoma is a complex phenomenon. It is based on a series of interactions between environmental and endogenous factors, including phototype, number of nevi, presence of atypical nevi, genetic alterations and UV exposure, which is thought to be the major risk factor for this pathology [17]. In the diagnosis of melanoma, the dermatologist's expertise is a key element to recognize all the typical elements of a malignant lesion and put them together to set up a correct care path.

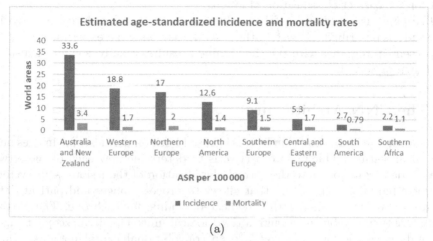

(a)

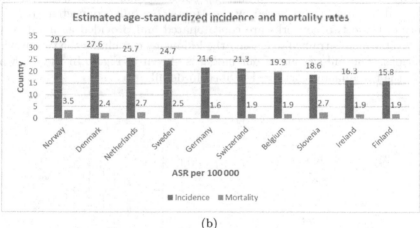

(b)

Fig. 1. Incidence and mortality of cutaneous melanoma. According to data from Globocan 2018 statistics, the barplots show the Age–Standardized Rate (ASR) of incidence and mortality caused by melanoma per 100,000 inhabitants, between different world areas, in (a), and in the ten European countries with higher incidence, in (b).

Recently, the results obtained by deep learning techniques and, in particular, by Convolutional Neural Networks (CNNs), in the field of image processing, have pushed the use of these methods to develop medical decision–making support tools. Therefore, our proposal is to implement a CNN–based tool capable of classifying lesion images, which can help dermatologists in diagnosing melanoma. More specifically, this study aims at improving the efficiency in the early detection of skin cancers, developing a classifier capable of integrating the information coming from both dermoscopic images and anamnestic data. Experimental tests were carried out on the freely downloadable International Skin Imaging Collaboration[1] (ISIC) Archive [18], showing the importance of the *exogenous* patient data for the correct classification of lesions.

The paper is organized as follows. In Sect. 2, the CNN architecture used in this study is described. In Sect. 3, the ISIC dataset and the experimental setup are presented, together with the the obtained results. Finally, some conclusions are drawn in Sect. 4.

2   The CNN Architecture

In our work, the analysis of skin lesions is based both on dermoscopic images and on clinical features. Our main objective is to determine how each of these two types of data contributes to the correct classification of the lesions. Our system has got a modular architecture that allows to process images and patient data separately and in parallel, with a dedicated module for each one. The partial results are then combined through a third logical unit. The dermoscopic images are analyzed with the *LesionNet*, a deep convolutional neural network, while the clinical features are processed by the *MetaNet*, a fully–connected MLP. The outputs of these two networks are concatenated and provided as input to the *MergedNet*, which is trained to classify the lesions by combining the two previous evaluations. The full schema of our model is shown in Fig. 2. In the following, each of the three main blocks is described in detail.

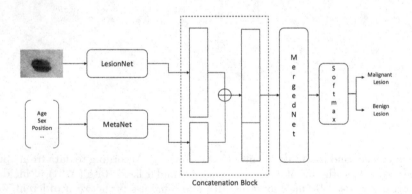

Fig. 2. Full schema of the deep architecture.

2.1   LesionNet

Due to data scarcity, a CNN pre–trained on ImageNet [19] was used to implement the *LesionNet*. To reach a good compromise between the performances and the computational cost of the experiments, the ResNet50 (with 50 convolutional

---

[1] https://isic-archive.com/.

layers) was chosen, which encodes a 2048 feature vector used for the binary classification of the lesions. The dermoscopic images were resized to a 224×224 resolution and normalized in the range [0, 1].

2.2 MetaNet

The *MetaNet* is a fully–connected three–layer network (with $128 \times 256 \times 128$ hidden neurons), which processes the vector of clinical features associated with each lesion. The input vector dimension is 80, based on the one–hot encoding of the features listed in the following.

- *Age:* the values were discretized by grouping them into 5–year ranges, going from 0 to 95.
- *Lesion location:* it indicates the body part in which the lesion occurs; a different code was assigned to each part: *anterior torso, upper extremity, lower extremity, lateral torso, palms/soles, head/neck.* A *null* value is used when this information is missing.
- *Gender:* a two–bit code indicates the gender of the patient.
- *Melanocytic:* a two–bit code indicates the presence or absence of melanocytes in the lesion.

2.3 MergedNet

The final classification is carried out by the *MergedNet*. The input of this network is built by concatenating the output of the last hidden layer of the two specialized networks. The main problem in concatenating these feature vectors is their different size and, in fact, the features extracted from images have a higher dimensionality than those obtained from clinical data. As a consequence, the *MergedNet* was expected to give more importance to the first category of features, taking less care to clinical data into its decision–making process. To balance the two contributions, a small fully–connected network was applied to the feature vector coming from the *LesionNet*, to reduce its size. This solution is not optimal, since the dimensionality reduction process (from 2048 to 128) leads to a loss of information. A better solution would have been represented by a *MetaNet* with a larger output dimensionality, and with larger hidden layers. Due to the limited computational resources available, though, the previous solution was preferred. The architecture of the *MergedNet* is very similar to that of the *MetaNet*, with three hidden layers plus a softmax output layer, composed of two units, which provide the binary classification of the lesion.

3   Experimental Setup and Results

3.1   The ISIC Dataset

The International Skin Imaging Collaboration [18] is a joint academia and industry project designed to facilitate the application of digital skin imaging to help reduce melanoma mortality. Besides, ISIC has developed an open source archive of skin images for the validation of new automated diagnostic systems. The dataset contains over 23,900 images of skin lesions divided into benign (about 19,300) and malignant (about 2200 images, most of which are melanomas while the rest are carcinomas). Some examples of the images collected in the ISIC dataset are given in Fig. 3.

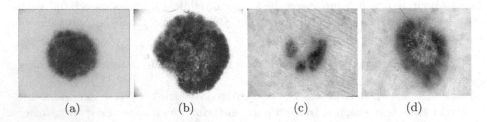

(a)   (b)   (c)   (d)

Fig. 3. Images of the ISIC dataset representing different skin lesions; (a) Mole, (b) Melanoma, (c) Basal Cell Carcinoma, and (d) Squamous Cell Carcinoma.

3.2   Experimental Setup

The ISIC dataset is split into training, validation and test sets, accounting respectively for 85%, 5%, 10% of the dataset size. To keep the classes balanced, the splitting procedure ensures that each set contains an equal number of benign and malignant cases. The training, validation and test sets are composed of 4840, 255, and 565 examples, respectively. Two different learning strategies were applied to our model: *local* training and *global* training. In the first case, the *LesionNet* and the *MetaNet* are trained on a separate basis, adding a softmax output layer to each network. This layer is removed after training, so that the *LesionNet* and the *MetaNet* can be seen as feature extractors. For each lesion, we get two intermediate representations, which are then concatenated and provided as input to the *MergedNet*. Global training, instead, means that the entire network—composed by the three sub–networks—is trained at once, backpropagating the error from the output layer of the *MergedNet* to the input layers of both the *LesionNet* and the *MetaNet*. Preliminary experiments showed that the *local* training strategy guarantees better performances. Thus, the results discussed in the following were all obtained with this method. Like most deep classifiers, our model makes use of the cross–entropy loss function. Given the number of classes C, the target Y, and the estimated probability of a given example to belong to the i–th class $\hat{Y}_i$, Eq. (1) defines the cross–entropy function as:

$$L = -\sum_{i=0}^{C} Y_i log\hat{Y}_i \tag{1}$$

The models were trained on a Nvidia GTX 1080 GPU. Due to memory limits, all the experiments were carried out with a batch size of 5. We employed Adam optimization algorithm [20], with an initial learning rate of 0.001. Dropout, with a forget rate of 0.5, was inserted before the softmax layer, to reduce overfitting. For the same purpose, we applied also early stopping. No other regularization method or image augmentation technique was used in this work. The test phase was then carried out on the model with the lowest validation loss. The importance of each clinical feature was also investigated in a dedicated set of experiments. In each of these, the network was trained on all but one of the features. The worse the performances of the model on the validation set, the more informative the excluded feature is.

3.3   Results

The results provided in Table 1 show that, in general, image–based models perform better than models based only on anamnestic features. This corresponds to the standard medical practice in the diagnosis of melanoma, which is mainly based on the visual inspection of the lesion.

Table 1. Results obtained with different experimental setups

Model	Validation accuracy	Test accuracy
LesionNet	87.00%	83.44%
MetaNet	83.00%	80.6%
MergedNet	91.00%	88.34%

In fact, the *LesionNet* exceeds the *MetaNet* by 2.84% accuracy points. Moreover, we can see how our *local* training strategy on the *MergedNet* is particularly effective in combining images and clinical features, outperforming classification accuracy of the *LesionNet* and the *MetaNet* by 4.9% and 7.74%, respectively. Finally, with respect to the informativity of each feature, *melanocytic* was found to be the most important one, allowing an accuracy improvement around 5% (the *MetaNet* gets down to 78% and 76% on the validation and test set respectively when this feature is removed), which confirms the importance of the presence of melanocytic cells in the melanoma diagnosis.

4   Conclusions

Using the anamnestic data of the patient together with the visual inspection of the skin lesion is the standard procedure in dermatological diagnostics. In fact, it has proven to be fundamental even in the case of the automatic analysis of dermoscopic images with CNNs. Actually, the proposed modular architecture was trained separately with respect to the two types of data—making each module act as an informed feature extractor—whose responses can be properly merged to define the prognosis. The impact of using also clinical data is clearly evidenced by our preliminary experimental results, which show a significant improvement in performance. It is a matter of future work to test our proposed architecture on a new, non publicly available, data repository. This new dataset [21] is being built by the Dermatology unit of the Siena Hospital "Le Scotte" and houses data coming from seven leader dermatological centers in Southern Europe.

References

1. He, K., et al.: Deep residual learning for image recognition. In: Proceedings of the IEEE Conference on Computer Vision and Pattern Recognition, pp. 770–778 (2016)
2. Chen, L.C., et al.: Rethinking atrous convolution for semantic image segmentation. arXiv preprint arXiv:1706.05587 (2017)
3. Litjens, G., et al.: A survey on deep learning in medical image analysis. Med. Image Anal. **42**, 60–88 (2017)
4. Andreini, P., Bonechi, S., Bianchini, M., Mecocci, A., Scarselli, F.: A deep learning approach to bacterial colony segmentation. In: Kůrková, V., Manolopoulos, Y., Hammer, B., Iliadis, L., Maglogiannis, I. (eds.) ICANN 2018. LNCS, vol. 11141, pp. 522–533. Springer, Cham (2018). https://doi.org/10.1007/978-3-030-01424-7_51
5. Rossi, A., et al.: Analysis of brain NMR images for age estimation with deep learning
6. Esteva, A., et al.: Dermatologist-level classification of skin cancer with deep neural networks. Nature **542**(7639), 115 (2017)
7. Yap, J., Yolland, W., Tschandl, P.: Multimodal skin lesion classification using deep learning. Exp. Dermatol. **27**(11), 1261–1267 (2018)
8. Leiter, U., Eigentler, T., Garbe, C.: Epidemiology of skin cancer. Adv. Exp. Med. Biol. **810**, 120–140 (2014)
9. Apalla, Z., et al.: Skin cancer: epidemiology, disease burden, pathophysiology, diagnosis, and therapeutic approaches. Dermatol. Ther. **7**(1), 5–19 (2017)
10. Paolino, G., et al.: Histology of non-melanoma skin cancers: an update. Biomedicines **5**(4), 71 (2017)
11. Apalla, Z., et al.: Epidemiological trends in skin cancer. Dermatol. Pract. Conceptual **7**(2), 1 (2017)
12. Rastrelli, M., et al.: Melanoma: epidemiology, risk factors, pathogenesis, diagnosis and classification. Vivo **28**(6), 1005–1011 (2014)
13. Schadendorf, D., Hauschild, A.: Melanoma in 2013: melanoma—the run of success continues. Nat. Rev. Clin. Oncol. **11**(2014), 75–76 (2013)
14. Globocan. https://gco.iarc.fr/. Accessed 06 June 2019
15. Matthews, N.H., et al.: Epidemiology of melanoma (2017)
16. Domingues, B., et al.: Melanoma treatment in review. ImmunoTargets Ther. **7**, 35 (2018)
17. Gandini, S., et al.: Meta-analysis of risk factors for cutaneous melanoma: II. Sun exposure. Eur. J. Cancer **41**(1), 45–60 (2005)
18. Codella, N.C., et al.: Skin lesion analysis toward melanoma detection: a challenge at the 2017 International Symposium on Biomedical Imaging (ISBI), hosted by ISIC. In: 15th International Symposium on Biomedical Imaging, pp. 168–172. IEEE (2018)

19. Russakovsky, O., et al.: ImageNet large scale visual recognition challenge. Int. J. Comput. Vis. (IJCV) **115**(3), 211–252 (2015)
20. Kingma, D.P., Ba, J.: Adam: a method for stochastic optimization. arXiv preprint arXiv:1412.6980 (2014)
21. Tognetti, L., et al.: An integrated clinical-dermoscopic risk scoring system for the differentiation between early melanoma and atypical nevi: the iDScore. J. Eur. Acad. Dermatol. Venereology **32**(12), 2162–2170 (2018)

Slide Screening of Metastases in Lymph Nodes via Conditional, Fully Convolutional Segmentation

Gianluca Gerard$^{(\boxtimes)}$ [ID] and Marco Piastra [ID]

Dipartimento di Ingegneria Industriale e dell'Informazione,
Università degli Studi di Pavia, Via Ferrata 5, 27100 Pavia, Italy
`cvml@unipv.it`

Abstract. We assess the viability of applying a conditional algorithm to the segmentation of Whole Slide Images (WSI) for human histopathology. Our objective is designing a deep network for automatic screening of large sets sentinel lymph-nodes of WSIs to detect those worth inspecting by a pathologist. Ideally, such system should modify and correct its behavior based on a limited set of examples, to foster interactivity and the incremental tuning to specific diagnostic pipelines and clinical practices and, not the least, to alleviate the task of collecting a suitable annotated dataset for training. In contrast, 'classical' supervised techniques require a vast dataset upfront and their behavior cannot be adapted unless through extensive retraining. The approach presented here is based on *conditional* and fully convolutional networks, which can segment a *query* image by conditioning on a *support* set of *sparsely* annotated images, fed at inference time. We describe the target scenario, the architecture used, and we present some preliminary results of segmentation experiments conducted on the publicly-available Camelyon16 dataset.

Keywords: Deep convolutional neural networks · Few-shot learning ·
Segmentation · Sparse annotation · Lymph nodes ·
Histopathological images

1 Introduction

Breast cancer is the most common form of cancer among women in the Western world. The prognosis depends on whether the cancer has spread to other organs. Sentinel lymph-nodes are the organs which are primarily reached by metastasizing cancer cells. Therefore their diagnosis is of critical importance to decide patients treatment. In clinical practice, the preparation of diagnostic samples is conducted through a pipeline: slices are cut from the sentinel lymph nodes, fixed on glass slides, then stained and finally digitized to obtain *Whole Slide Images* (WSIs). WSIs are visually inspected by pathologists to achieve the diagnosis.

© Springer Nature Switzerland AG 2019
M. Cristani et al. (Eds.): ICIAP 2019 Workshops, LNCS 11808, pp. 220–227, 2019.
https://doi.org/10.1007/978-3-030-30754-7_22

Objectives. Our goal is to design an automated lesion segmentation method that could help the pathologist in screening those WSI areas which are worth an accurate inspection. To do so we apply a novel deep learning method that can adapt its behavior based on a very limited set of examples. Deep learning, in fact, has achieved remarkable successes in the classification and segmentation of biomedical images [5]. However supervised deep learning, which entails training on large annotated datasets of images, does not adapt easily to handle images acquired through different protocols, unless the dataset is properly extended and a full training is performed again [7].

Target Scenario. We aim to achieve a system supporting the following working cycle:

- the deep network for segmentation is trained in supervised mode on an initial dataset of annotated WSIs;
- the trained network is applied to other WSIs to propose a segmentation of the areas that might contain relevant lesions;
- the human pathologist reviews such proposed segmentations and corrects them whenever necessary;
- the corrected segmentations are fed back incrementally to the network, at inference time and without retraining, to guide subsequent segmentation tasks;
- once enough corrected segmentations become available, a full retraining of the network is performed.

Potential Advantages. In the above perspective, few-shots learning deep networks could provide a significant advantage since:

- the behavior of the network at inference time, i.e. the lesion segmentation produced on each input *query image*, can be conditioned by a *support set* of annotated images;
- for the support set, the network allows using *sparse* annotations, namely sets of class-representing pixels instead of polyline-enclosed regions (i.e. *dense* annotations).

To the best of our knowledge, conditional networks have only been applied to detect new classes of generic objects which were unseen during the training process. The capability of the method to fit our scenario has yet to be assessed.

Relevance of This Work. In this preliminary work we study the application of few shots networks to the task of incremental, inference time improvement of the automatic segmentation of sentinel lymph-nodes WSIs. We focus on assessing how the network presented can change its output in response to different annotations (sparse and dense) and different support sets.

2   Related Works

The work described here is based on the few-shot segmentation method devised
by [3]. We use the *late fusion* variant of the algorithm, in which images in the
support set are kept separate from (sparse) annotations until inference time as
opposed to *early fusion*, in which the same images and annotations are merged
in a pre-processing step. As the authors report, and in agreement with our
preliminary tests, the latter variant is slightly less effective. The objective of
the original work was segmenting objects from classes unseen at training time
through the guidance of a few, *sparsely annotated*, input examples which are
provided at inference time.

Another relevant idea for the purposes of this work is annotating images
via *sparse annotations* [1], as opposed to *dense annotations*. Sparse annotations
were originally introduced for easing the interactive segmentation of natural
images [9].

3   Methods

3.1   Few-Shots Learning

The paradigm for few-shot learning is based on *episodic training* [8]. Networks
are trained in s-shot, K-way *episodes*, each created by selecting a subset of K
classes from a set of classes C_{train} and then selecting [4]:

- a *support* set $\mathsf{S} = \{(\boldsymbol{x}_1, \boldsymbol{L}_1), (\boldsymbol{x}_2, \boldsymbol{L}_2), \ldots, (\boldsymbol{x}_{s \times K}, \boldsymbol{L}_{s \times K})\}$ with s examples
  from each of the K classes;
- a *query* set $\mathsf{Q} = \{(\boldsymbol{x}_1^*, \boldsymbol{L}_1^*), (\boldsymbol{x}_2^*, \boldsymbol{L}_2^*), \ldots, (\boldsymbol{x}_t^*, \boldsymbol{L}_t^*)\}$ of t different examples from
  any of the K classes.

where, in our case, $\boldsymbol{x}_i$ is a WSI patch with shape $[h, w, 3]$ and $\boldsymbol{L}_i$ represents its
annotation. Annotations are sets of pixel-label pairs, $(\boldsymbol{p}, l)$, where $\boldsymbol{p}$ represents
the coordinates and $l \in K$ the corresponding label:

$$\boldsymbol{L}_i := \{(\boldsymbol{p}_j, l_j)\}_{j=1}^p \ , \ l \in \{1 \ldots K\}$$

where p is the number of annotated pixels. In a *dense* annotation, $p = h \times w$,
i.e. all pixels are labeled, whereas in a *sparse* annotation, p is much smaller [1].

In few shots learning and in our case, annotations in the support set are sparse
whereas those in the query set are dense. In each training episode the query
images and the support set are fed to the network, then query annotations are
used to compute the loss from the output segmentation and update the weights
in the network.

3.2   co-FCN Architecture

The overall architecture adopted is that of conditional, fully convolutional networks (co-FCNs), originally introduced by [3]. As shown in Fig. 1, such network
has two main branches:

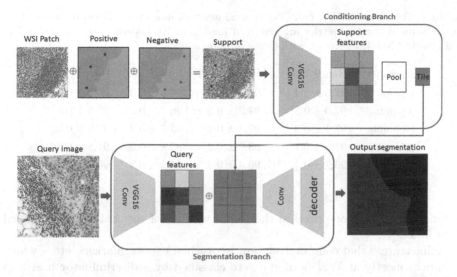

Fig. 1. co-FCN architecture. The conditioning branch (top row) is fed with the of WSI patches with their (sparse) annotations. The segmentation branch (bottom row) conditions on the output of the top branch to segment the query image. The two branches are learned jointly and end to-end.

1. a *conditioning* branch, which extracts a *latent representation* of the annotated support set;
2. a *segmentation* branch, which receives the latent representation of the support set and produces the segmentation of the query image.

Network weights are learned end-to-end by computing the loss between the predicted and the actual (dense) segmentation of the query image. Once trained, the behavior of the network can be conditioned by changing the support set at inference time, without further retraining.

The original co-FCN architecture was proposed for segmenting generic objects and to recognize classes that were unseen during the training process. In contrast, we do not aim to recognizing new classes but to improve incrementally, and at inference time, the segmentation behavior.

3.3   Dataset Selection and Preparation

The Camelyon16 dataset of histopathological images was used to create both training and validation datasets[1].

We converted each WSI into a set of patches of size 448×448, selected with stride 224. The set of resulting patches was filtered to eliminate those that were mostly background[2]. Each patch was classified to be either *lesion*, *non-lesion* or *artifact*:

---

[1] We used in fact 55 of the 110 WSIs with lesion available in the original dataset.

[2] Background was removed by converting each WSI from the RGB color space to HSV and then binarizing each HSV channel through Otsu's thresholding. We discarded

Table 1. Recall and IoU of co-FCNs trained and validated with different annotations on the same datasets. Metrics are reported for L and NL classes. The last row refers to a classic FNC-32s network with dense annotations.

Annotation	Recall NL (%)	Recall L (%)	IoU NL (%)	IoU L (%)
1 point	97.5 ± 0.4	93.1 ± 0.3	94.6 ± 0.2	90.5 ± 0.5
5 points	97.0 ± 0.3	97.3 ± 0.2	95.7 ± 0.2	93.8 ± 0.6
10 points	97.1 ± 0.3	97.1 ± 0.2	95.7 ± 0.2	93.9 ± 0.5
dense	97.9 ± 0.1	93.9 ± 0.2	95.8 ± 0.2	91.8 ± 0.3
FCN-32s	96.7 ± 0.4	96.4 ± 0.4	94.9 ± 0.2	90.7 ± 0.4

- lesion: if at least one pixel in the center window of size 224×224 is labeled as lesion [2];
- artifact: areas that contain irrelevant items (black spots, markers, etc. – which appear mostly at WSI borders) were classified by a discriminator based on logistic regression hence discarded;
- non-lesion: everything else.

Due to the heavy imbalance between lesions and non-lesion patches we decimated the final dataset at random to rebalance the two classes. The final training and validation dataset was composed by 17920 patches (47% lesion patches)[3].

4   Preliminary Results and Discussion

4.1   Validation Set Performances, Sparse Annotations Influence and Baseline Comparison

The initial experiments were conducted to evaluate the Recall and Intersection Over Union (IoU) of the network output on the balanced validation set described in the Sect. 3.3. Tests were performed with support sets containing 5 images each, with either dense annotations or sparse annotations with 1, 5 and 10 points per class, respectively.

The results for the two classes, lesion (L) and non-lesion (NL), are summarized in Table 1. All the measurements were taken as the average over 4 validation sets of 1120 query images each. Inter validation sets errors are reported as half the min-max range.

For comparison, we also trained a FCN-32s network [6] in fully supervised mode and with dense annotations. On the lesion class, the co-FCNs with 5 and 10 points sparse annotations achieved the highest recall and IoU performances, while maintaining comparable results on the non-lesion class.

---

patches in which the amount of binarized background (lesion) was greater than 95% in the S and V channels.

[3] Such dataset was split randomly into training and validation subsets with a 3:1 ratio.

Table 2. Recall, Precision and F1 score obtained with the same co-FCN on a reference query dataset, with different support sets.

Support set	Recall NL (%)	Recall L (%)	Prec. NL (%)	Prec. L (%)	F1 L
$RT.L^5$	89.7	85.0	99.8	8.9	0.161
$RT.L^{20}$	90.3	83.9	99.8	9.3	0.167
$RT.L^{40}$	90.0	84.4	99.8	9.2	0.165
$RT.NL^5$	91.7	81.9	99.8	10.4	0.185
$RT.B^{20}$	90.9	83.2	99.8	9.8	0.175
$RT.B^{40}$	91.1	82.9	99.8	10.0	0.178
$RT.B^{60}$	91.0	83.0	99.8	9.9	0.177
$SQ.B_0^{40}$	89.1	86.6	99.8	8.6	0.156
$SQ.B_1^{40}$	90.7	83.6	99.8	9.6	0.172

4.2 Influence of the Support Set

The influence of the support set on the co-FCN segmenting behavior, as function of selected images and set size, was assessed in two stages. We applied the co-FCN, trained with 5 shots and 5 points sparse annotations, on a previously unseen and heavily imbalanced query dataset, having only 1.2% of the pixels belonging to the L class. We first considered three kinds of support sets, chosen at random (R) from the training dataset (T):

- $RT.L^{(n)}$: n patches with over 95% of the pixels in the L class, sampled uniformly from T;
- $RT.NL^{(n)}$: n patches with over 95% of the pixels in the NL class, sampled uniformly from T;
- $RT.B^{(2n)} := RT.L^{(n)} \cup RT.NL^{(n)}$.

In a second stage we considered the segmentations obtained with the query dataset using the co-FCN with $RT.B^{(n)}$ support set and we constructed two further kinds of support sets by selecting (S) patches from the query dataset (Q) itself:

- $SQ.B_0^{(2n)}$: of n patches with the highest number of false positives and n patches with the highest number of false negatives, both selected from Q;
- $SQ.B_1^{(2n)}$: union of $RT.B^{(n)}$ with $n/2$ patches with the highest number of false positives and $n/2$ patches with the highest number of false negatives, both selected from Q.

In other words, in $SQ.B_0^{(2n)}$ we replaced the original support set completely while in $SQ.B_1^{(2n)}$ we just added several 'corrective' patches. Table 2 summarizes the numerical results obtained by testing the same co-FCN on the same query dataset with different kinds of support set. From this table, we observe that:

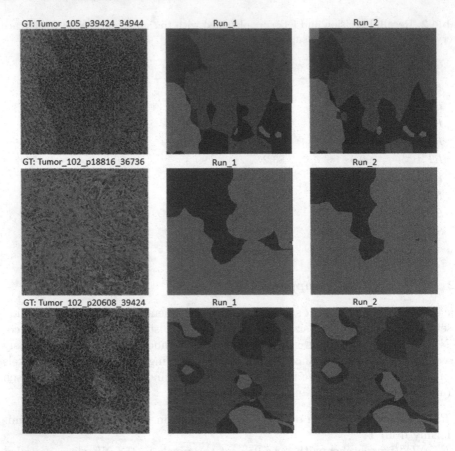

Fig. 2. Three densely annotated patches (left column) compared with the segmentation produced by the same co-FCN with $RT.B^{(40)}$ support set (center, Run_1) and $SQ.B_0^{(40)}$ support set (right, Run_2). True positives (L) are in red, true negatives (NL) in green, false positives in brown and false negatives in blue. (Color figure online)

- the behavior of the co-FCN varies across different support sets;
- an increase in size in the support set using images already seen during training does not improve the critical indicator, Recall L;
- on the other hand, a support set constructed with images that were *not* seen during training, as in the two $SQ.B_i^{(2n)}$ can produce an improvement on Recall L;
- yet, the best results in this direction are achieved when using unseen images only in the support set (i.e. $SQ.B_0^{(40)}$).

Figures in the previous table were computed globally, as pixel-wise counts. A better, qualitative account can be seen in Fig. 2, which shows the changes in the co-FCN behavior produced by switching from a $RT.B^{40}$ support set to a $SQ.B_0^{40}$

support set. As it can be seen, the support set $SQ.B_0^{40}$ produces an increase in the regions that are classified correctly as lesion, while increasing only slightly the false positive areas.

5   Conclusions and Future Work

In the perspective of using conditional, fully convolutional networks for the screening of histopathological WSIs with interactive and incremental improvement of the segmentation produced, we showed that the behavior of a co-FCN can be guided by acting on its conditioning support sets. Preliminary results show that by conditioning on previously unseen, corrective images, the recall of lesion areas can be improved.

As future work, apart from further experiments and comparison to other state of the art techniques, we are going to introduce better and more application-oriented indicators, in particular for measuring the capability of the network to signal the presence of small and isolated lesions, crucial for the diagnostic process.

References

1. Glocker, B., Zikic, D., Konukoglu, E., Haynor, D.R., Criminisi, A.: Vertebrae localization in pathological spine CT via dense classification from sparse annotations. In: Mori, K., Sakuma, I., Sato, Y., Barillot, C., Navab, N. (eds.) MICCAI 2013. LNCS, vol. 8150, pp. 262–270. Springer, Heidelberg (2013). https://doi.org/10.1007/978-3-642-40763-5_33
2. Liu, Y., et al.: Detecting cancer metastases on gigapixel pathology images. Technical report, arXiv (2017). arXiv:1703.02442
3. Rakelly, K., Shelhamer, E., Darrell, T., Efros, A.A., Levine, S.: Few-shot segmentation propagation with guided networks, May 2018. arXiv:1806.07373
4. Ren, M., et al.: Meta-learning for semi-supervised few-shot classification, March 2018. arXiv:1803.00676
5. Ronneberger, O., Fischer, P., Brox, T.: U-Net: convolutional networks for biomedical image segmentation. In: Navab, N., Hornegger, J., Wells, W.M., Frangi, A.F. (eds.) MICCAI 2015. LNCS, vol. 9351, pp. 234–241. Springer, Cham (2015). https://doi.org/10.1007/978-3-319-24574-4_28
6. Shelhamer, E., Long, J., Darrell, T.: Fully convolutional networks for semantic segmentation, May 2016. arXiv:1605.06211
7. Shen, D., Wu, G., Suk, H.I.: Deep learning in medical image analysis. Ann. Rev. Biomed. Eng. **19**, 221–248 (2017). http://www.ncbi.nlm.nih.gov/pubmed/28301734www.pubmedcentral.nih.gov/articlerender.fcgi?artid=PMC5479722
8. Vinyals, O., Blundell, C., Lillicrap, T., Kavukcuoglu, K., Wierstra, D.: Matching Networks for One Shot Learning, June 2016. arXiv:1606.04080
9. Xu, N., Price, B., Cohen, S., Yang, J., Huang, T.: Deep Interactive Object Selection, March 2016. arXiv:1603.04042

A Learning Approach
for Informative-Frame Selection
in US Rheumatology Images

Maria Chiara Fiorentino[1]([✉]) [iD], Sara Moccia[1,2] [iD], Edoardo Cipolletta[3] [iD],
Emilio Filippucci[3] [iD], and Emanuele Frontoni[1] [iD]

[1] Department of Information Engineering, Università Politecnica delle Marche,
Ancona, Italy
mariachiarafiorentino921@gmail.com
[2] Department of Advanced Robotics, Istituto Italiano di Tecnologia,
Genoa, Italy
[3] Department of Rheumatology, Università Politecnica delle Marche, Ancona, Italy

Abstract. Rheumatoid arthritis (RA) is an autoimmune disorder that
causes pain, swelling and stiffness in joints. Nowadays, ultrasound (US)
has undergone an increasing role in RA screening since it is a powerful tool to assess disease activity. However, obtaining a good quality US
frame is a tricky operator dependent procedure. For this reason, the purpose of this paper is to present a strategy to the automatic selection of
informative US rheumatology images by means of Convolutional Neural
Networks (CNNs). The proposed method is based on VGG16 and Inception V3 CNNs, which are fine tuned to classify 214 balanced metacarpal
head US images (75% used for training and 25% used for testing). A
repeated 3 fold cross validation for each CNN was performed. The best
results were achieved with VGG16 (area under the curve = 90%). These
results support the possibility of applying this method in the actual clinical practice for supporting the diagnostic process and helping young
residents' training.

Keywords: Frame selection · Deep learning · Fine tuning ·
Ultrasound images · Arthritis

1 Introduction

Rheumatoid arthritis (RA) is a chronic systemic inflammatory disease that
involves both large and small joints leading to patient disability and deterioration of quality of life. To prevent the worsening of the RA inflammatory process,
screening campaign able to identify early signs of RA are becoming more and
more spread. In this regards, ultrasound (US) is playing an increasing role, providing the detection and semi-quantitative assessment of (a) sub-clinical signs of
joint and tendon inflammation, (b) early signs of joint and tendon damage [1].

© Springer Nature Switzerland AG 2019
M. Cristani et al. (Eds.): ICIAP 2019 Workshops, LNCS 11808, pp. 228–236, 2019.
https://doi.org/10.1007/978-3-030-30754-7_23

Moreover, US is widely accessible, minimally expensive, safe/free of radiation hazard and well accepted by patients, making its use more convenient when compared to other imaging systems, such as computed tomography (CT) or plain radiography (X-ray).

Focusing on the metacarpal head which is one of the most affected by the disease, obtaining a good quality US frame may be a tricky operator-dependent procedure. An US frame can be considered as informative if (i) the hyperechogenic osteochondral interface is present, even in fairly damaged cartilages, (ii) the hyperechogenic chondrosynovial interface is visible in healthy subject (it may not be visible in damaged cartilage, though). Figure 1 shows relevant visual samples for US images of metacarpal head hyaline cartilage.

At present, there is still a lack of international guidelines for appropriate US training of residents in rheumatology [2]. Developing a computer-assisted strategy to select informative frames could potentially help in young residents' training, in quality-control standardization and detection of the cartilage damage.

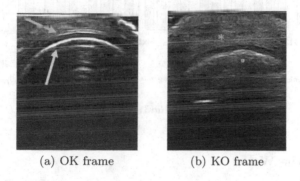

(a) OK frame   (b) KO frame

Fig. 1. (a) Informative frame (OK) of metacarpal head: both the interfaces between cartilage and bone (osteochondral interface, yellow arrow) and cartilage and overlying soft tissue (chondrosynovial interface, blue arrow) are sharp and clearly visible. (b) Non-informative frame (KO) of the same joints: the two interfaces are not visible (green asterisk and circle). (Color figure online)

1.1 Related Work

Considering the importance of automatic frame selection, several studies have been proposed in the years, even if not only specifically focused on US images. Most of them focused on simple uniform frame sampling to reduce the amount of data to pre-process (e.g. [3] for endoscopic bladder images). Two main issues however arise: (a) there is no guarantee that informative frames are extracted from all semantically important video segments, and (b) redundant frames could be selected if long segments with identical content are considered.

To tackle the variability encoded in medical images, more advanced approaches based on supervised machine learning (ML) are becoming more and more spread. The work in [4] classifies conoloscopy patch-based features, which are computed with the discrete cosine transform, using the random forest classifier. In [5] and [6], support vector machines are used for classification. Specifically, [5] uses local color histogram features for grastrointestinal endoscopic images, while [6] uses intensity, keypoint and image spatial content features for multiclass laryngoscopic frame classification. More recently, Convolutional Neural Networks (CNNs) showed promising results, outperforming standard and ML-based approaches [7]. The most recent work on the topic is [8], in which colonscopy informative frames are identified using a custom-built CNN with binarized weights.

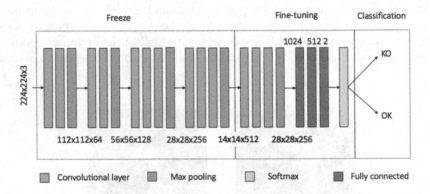

Fig. 2. VGG16 fine-tuning strategy.

1.2 Aim of the Work

In this paper, inspired by recent work in literature, we specifically address the problem of informative-frame classification in metacarpal head US images using CNNs. The availability of our training samples influenced the choice of the training strategy. As a matter of fact, training a net from scratch requires to have a large amount of labeled training data (difficult requirement in the medical domain in which expert annotation is expensive). It has been shown in [9] that the fine-tuning of a CNNs that has been trained using a large labeled dataset from a different application outperforms or, in the worst case, performs as well as a CNN trained from scratch, either using medical images. For this reason, we decided to fine-tune CNNs pre-trained on ImageNet[1], an image database that includes hundreds and thousands of pictures.

2   Methods

The proposed method is based on the fine-tuning of VGG16 and Inception V3 CNNs. These architectures are chosen for two main reasons: (1) they won the

---

[1] http://www.image-net.org/.

ImageNet challenge, (2) they are relatively simple (i.e. not too deep), allowing to obtain low level features for fine-tuning.

Hereafter, a short overview of the original architectures of the two CNNs is provided. In the original VGG16 implementation, the input RGB image is processed through 13 convolutional (conv) layers that extract image features. Each conv block has filters with a very small receptive field (3×3 pixels) and is followed by a rectified linear unit (ReLU) activation function. Max pooling layers are used after 2 or 3 convolutional blocks, depending on the layer, for CNN-parameter dimensionality reduction. Finally, 3 fully-connected layers - 4096 neurons in the first two layers and 1000 neurons in the last one - followed by a softmax layer are used to predict a probabilistic label map.

The Inception V3 architecture involves 11 inception modules including convolutions, average pooling, max pooling, concats, with ReLU as activation function. The Inception modules are different in terms of convolutional-kernel size, number of filters and depth. This allows to process the input image at varying scales. Finally, an average pooling, a dropout function, one fully-connected layers - 1000 neurons - followed by a softmax layer are used to predict the CNN classification output.

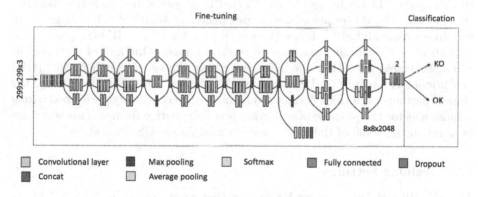

Fig. 3. Inception V3 fine-tuning strategy.

2.1 Fine-Tuning Strategy

In order to fine tune the proposed architectures, the Imagenet pre-trained weights were transferred to the CNNs. As regards the VGG16 fine-tuning, 4 conv blocks were frozen and the 3 fully connected layers were modified - 1024 neurons in the first layer, 512 neurons in the second and 2 neurons in the last one - and added to the remaining conv block (Fig. 2).

As regards Inception V3, all the modules were fine tuned and the last fully connected layer modified (from 1000 to 2 neurons) (Fig. 3).

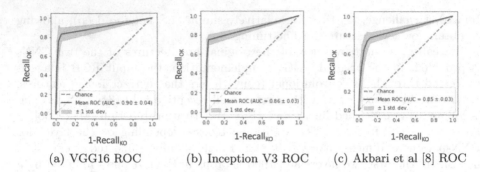

(a) VGG16 ROC   (b) Inception V3 ROC   (c) Akbari et al [8] ROC

Fig. 4. Receiving operating characteristics (ROC) obtained with the (a) fine-tuned VGG16, (b) fine-tuned Inception V3, (c) Akbari et al. CNN [8]. The mean and standard deviation of the area under the ROC (AUC) are reported, too.

3   Experimental Protocol

3.1   Dataset

In this study, 214 US images of metacarpal head joints, in which the chondrosine interface should be present, were prospectively analyzed. The images were acquired with a MyLab^{TM}Twice (Esaote ®) with a 10–22 MHz US probe. The MyLab Desk (Esaote ®) was used to retrieve images. One half of pictures has 800×608 pixels, the other one 860×808 pixels. The sets of informative (OK) and non-informative (KO) US images were balanced. To build the dataset, the clinical partners performed correct acquisitions and consciously performed wrong acquisitions for the purpose of collecting non-informative frames. This was done by reproducing some of the most common mistakes in US acquisition.

3.2   Training Settings

The VGG16 was feeded using US images that were resized to 224×224 pixels to match the Imagenet input dimension. Intensity mean was removed from each image. Then mini-batch stochastic gradient descend (SGD) as optimizer [10] and a categorical cross-entropy as loss function for 200 epochs were used. The batch size was set to 32 as a balance between training speed and gradient convergence, with a learning rate of 0.0001. Inception V3 was trained using US images resized to 299×299 pixels with the same settings of VGG16 network.

The dataset was split in a balanced way using the 75% of images as training and the 25% as test. The training set was augmented flipping each images. The training set was further divided in 3 folds for cross validation: one subsample is retained as the validation data for testing the model, and the remaining 2 subsamples are used as training data. The process is then repeated 3 times, with each of the 3 subsamples used exactly once as the validation data. The whole procedure was repeated twice for increased robustness, obtaining 6 models for each network.

The best CNN model for each fold was then selected according to the highest accuracy (*Acc*) on the validation set, for each network:

$$Acc = \frac{\sum_i TP_i}{n}, i \in C : [OK, KO] \tag{1}$$

where: C represents the classes set, TP_i represents the correctly classified sample and n is the total number of samples.

All experiments were implemented using Keras library[2] on Google Colaboratory[3]: a free GPU cloud platform.

Table 1. Classification metrics are reported in terms of mean values (standard deviation) for precision (*Prec$_i$*), recall (*Rec$_i$*) and f1-score (*f1$_i$*), with $i \in C$: [OK, KO].

	i	$Prec_i$	Rec_i	$f1_i$
VGG16	OK	0.95 (0.03)	0.82 (0.03)	0.88 (0.05)
	KO	0.89 (0.03)	0.97 (0.02)	0.93 (0.02)
Inception V3	OK	0.96 (0.02)	0.74 (0.03)	0.83 (0.03)
	KO	0.86 (0.02)	0.98 (0.01)	0.91 (0.01)
Akbari et al. [8]	OK	0.89 (0.06)	0.75 (0.05)	0.81 (0.04)
	KO	0.85 (0.02)	0.94 (0.03)	0.89 (0.02)

3.3   Performance Analysis

For classification performance evaluation, we computed the mean Receiver Operating Characteristic (ROC) and the mean classification Precision (*Prec$_i$*) (Eq. 2), Recall (*Rec$_i$*) (Eq. 3), and f1−score (*f1$_i$*) (Eq. 4) for the i-th class, with i ∈ C : [OK, KO].

$$Prec_i = \frac{TP_i}{TP_i + FP_i} \tag{2}$$

$$Rec_i = \frac{TP_i}{TP_i + FN_i} \tag{3}$$

$$f1_i = \frac{2 \times Prec_i \times Rec_i}{Prec_i + Rec_i} \tag{4}$$

where FP_i, FN_i are the false positives and the false negatives, respectively.

Since it has already been shown in [11] that deep learning overcomes handcrafted features for analyzing medical images, for the sake of comparison, we implemented only the CNN based method proposed in [8]. We used the same settings of the other two CNNs with the exception of image size (118×118 pixels as specified in [8]) and epochs that were set to 700.

---

[2] https://keras.io/.

[3] https://colab.research.google.com/notebooks/welcome.ipynb#recent=true.

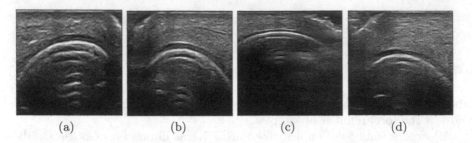

     (a)   (b)   (c)   (d)

Fig. 5. Examples of classification taking into account the best model of each net. (a) OK frames classified wrongly by all the nets, (b) OK frame only correctly classified by VGG16, (c) OK frame classified wrongly by Akbari et al., (d) KO frame classified wrongly by Akbari et al.

4   Results

Figure 4 shows the mean ROC curves obtained with the fine-tuned VGG16, the fine-tuned Inception V3 and the Akbari et al. CNN [8], reaching an area under the curve (AUC) of 0.90 (0.04), 0.86 (0.03) and 0.85 (0.03), respectively. Table 1 shows the classification results for both OK and KO frames, for each network. The fine-tuned networks performed better in all the metrics. In particular, VGG16 obtained the best values of Rec (0.82) and $f1$ (0.88) considering the OK frames and the best $Prec$ (0.89) and $f1$ (0.93) for the KO frames. Inception V3 outperformed the other networks in OK frames $Prec$ (0.96) and KO frames Rec (0.97). Visual samples of the classification results for OK and KO US frames considering the best model of each network are shown in Fig. 5.

5   Discussion and Conclusions

In this work, we presented a method to identify metacarpal head US informative frames in which the chondrosynovial interface should be present based on CNNs. In particular, we addressed fine-tuning of VGG16 and Inception V3 models, since limited training data were available. Comparing the proposed fine-tuned networks with the network trained from scratch of Akbari et al. [8], we showed that the fine tuning of pre-trained networks is a valid choice to accomplish our task. Overall, VGG16 resulted to be the best model, reaching satisfactory performance (AUC = 90%). This may be due to the fact that VGG16 is less deep than InceptionV3, resulting to be more effective considering the size of our training set and the low variability of our images. However, there are cases in which the classification failed, such as borderline cases in which the chondrosynovial interface is not clearly visible (Fig. 5). Nevertheless, VGG16 network was able to classify more blurred and decentralized images than the other two networks. A cross validation in the test set could be performed in order to get the results more robust. Moreover, a future development could be to increase the dataset using the Generative Adversarial Network, considering challenges in collecting large and labeled dataset [12].

As a next step, pathological images could also be included in the dataset to encode further challenges in the actual clinical practice.

To conclude, the proposed approach is a valuable tool to perform informative frame selection that can be processed by computer-assisted algorithms for supporting the diagnostic process and potentially applied also in different anatomical districts and imaging modalities (e.g. endoscopy) to support young clinicians in training.

Compliance with ethical standards

Conflict of interest. No conflict of interest to declare.

Ethical approval. All procedures performed in studies involving human participants were in accordance with the ethical standards of the institutional and/or national research committee and with the 1964 Helsinki Declaration and its later amendments or comparable ethical standards.

Informed consent. Informed consent was obtained from all individual participants included in the study.

References

1. Filippucci, E., et al.: Ultrasound imaging in rheumatoid arthritis. La Radiologia Medica, pp. 1–14 (2019)
2. Filippucci, E., et al.: Ultrasound imaging for the rheumatologist (2006)
3. Behrens, A.: Creating panoramic images for bladder fluorescence endoscopy. Acta Polytech. **48**(3), 50–54 (2008)
4. Tajbakhsh, N., et al.: Automatic assessment of image informativeness in colonoscopy. In: Yoshida, H., Näppi, J., Saini, S. (eds.) International MICCAI Workshop on Computational and Clinical Challenges in Abdominal Imaging, vol. 8676, pp. 151–158. Springer, Cham (2014). https://doi.org/10.1007/978-3-319-13692-9_14
5. Bashar, M.K., et al.: Automatic detection of informative frames from wireless capsule endoscopy images. Med. Image Anal. **14**(3), 449–470 (2010)
6. Moccia, S., et al.: Learning-based classification of informative laryngoscopic frames. Comput. Methods Programs Biomed. **158**, 21–30 (2018)
7. Nasr-Esfahani, E., et al.: Melanoma detection by analysis of clinical images using convolutional neural network. In: International Conference of the IEEE Engineering in Medicine and Biology Society, pp. 1373–1376. IEEE (2016)
8. Akbari, M., et al.: Classification of informative frames in colonoscopy videos using convolutional neural networks with binarized weights. In: International Conference of the IEEE Engineering in Medicine and Biology Society, pp. 65–68. IEEE (2018)
9. Tajbakhsh, N., et al.: Convolutional neural networks for medical image analysis: full training or fine tuning? IEEE Trans. Med. Imaging **35**(5), 1299–1312 (2016)
10. Mandt, S., et al.: Stochastic gradient descent as approximate bayesian inference. J. Mach. Learn. Res. **18**(1), 4873–4907 (2017)

11. Litjens, G., et al.: A survey on deep learning in medical image analysis. Med. Image Anal. **42**, 60–88 (2017)
12. Goodfellow, I., et al.: Generative adversarial nets. In: Advances in Neural Information Processing Systems, pp. 2672–2680 (2014)

A Serious Game to Support Decision Making in Medical Education

Ersilia Vallefuoco$^{(\boxtimes)}$, Michele Mele$^{(\boxtimes)}$, and Alessandro Pepino$^{(\boxtimes)}$

University of Naples Federico II, 08544 Naples, Italy
{ersilia.vallefuoco,michele.mele,pepino}@unina.it

Abstract. The patient safety is one of the most important element to guarantee a good quality of healthcare and to satisfy the required standard. As shown in several recent studies, the technological development facilitated the growth and the diffusion of the simulation in healthcare education. In particular, many different serious games have been developed to educate medical professionals and to improve the learning of the medical procedures. In this paper we present the design of an educational game to train the medical students in order to deal with cardiology cases. A multidisciplinary methodology was adopted in order to make the medical knowledge, the biomedical technical skills and the mathematical approach converging. The serious game was designed to support the decision making process, formulated as an integer programming mathematical model that also evaluates the game performance. Moreover, the serious game was developed in a 3D environment and was implemented by Scrum framework.

Keywords: Serious game · Decision making · Medical education · Healthcare simulation · IP formulation

1 Introduction

The healthcare is a complex process involving numerous variables, dynamics and pressures; in fact, the medical doctors has to make several choices, sometimes with lack of time, to manage emergencies and to work under pressure. The World Health Organization estimates that medical errors are registered in 8–12% of European hospitalizations [1], while a recent study indicates the medical errors as the third cause of death in US [2]. In addition, the technological improvement determined different changes in both the diagnosis and the cure so the education of healthcare professionals has to be continuously upgraded. Thus, new strategies have been adopted to train the healthcare professionals in order to guarantee the patient safety and to decrease the risk of adverse events. In particular, the simulation has become an innovative tool used both for the training and for the assessment in healthcare field [3].

Gaba [4] defined the simulation as a technique that allows reproducing real events and experiences in an interactive way. In particular, in the medical simulation the disciple can value his skills in different environments as the clinic, the surgery or the emergency room but he can also take on rare clinical cases or difficult medical procedures [5]. Moreover, the learner can meditate on his actions, decisions and mistakes through a feedback system, the latter is considered the cornerstone of the medical

M. Cristani et al. (Eds.): ICIAP 2019 Workshops, LNCS 11808, pp. 237–243, 2019.
https://doi.org/10.1007/978-3-030-30754-7_24

simulation [6, 7]. Therefore, in order to enhance the patient safety, the disciple can train in learning settings to acquire medical techniques and procedures, but also improve the problem solving and decision making processes [8]. The desired scenarios can be recreated either in real rooms with dummies and medical devices, or within virtual environments using virtual, augmented and mixed reality [9].

Different simulation applications of virtual reality can be classified as serious games because they allow to develop and to train skills, knowledge or attitudes, that can be transferred in real context, by entertaining the player [10]. Due to the large use of serious games, various taxonomies have been proposed based on different criteria [11–14]. Following the classification by player proposed in [11], the serious games for the healthcare professionals are part of the non-patient category. In particular, these games can support the development of technical skills, the not technical skills or the education and they are addressed to all healthcare professionals [15–18].

The current study presents the design and the development of a serious game prototype for medical students aimed to study and train medical procedures on cardiology cases. The medical treatment is interactive, in fact, the player can evaluate in real time the physiological responses of patient depending on his diagnostic-therapeutic choices. Scrum was adopted as framework of agile development and a mathematical formulation was elaborated to analyse the decision making process in the game session.

2   Materials and Methods

In healthcare, the development of serious game requires a multidisciplinary team because of the different game aspects as the contents, the design, the dynamics and their implementations [19]. Following this approach, we formed a project team that focused on three linked components:

- Medical knowledge and experience to individuate the realistic scenarios and the medical procedures to face them.
- Biomedical technical skills to effectively implement the settings and the dynamics of the real case and to adapt them in a game oriented focus.
- Mathematical formulation of the decision making process to model the correct procedure to follow and the different situations caused by mistakes and their effects.

Therefore, a Game Design Document [20] was drawn out identifying the main features of the game, namely, the purpose, the scenarios, the game dynamics, the feedback system and the software.

2.1   Game Description

The serious game is a 3D life simulation game aimed to provide an efficient training for medical professionals in order to support the decision making process and the choice of medical procedures in peculiar situations.

At the game start, the player can select the clinical case to simulate through a game menu. The clinical cases are related to cardiology treatments and reproduce pathologies as the heart attack, the heart failure or the arrhythmia. After the case choice, the player receives all information about the patient and his medical conditions in order to explain the clinical case. The game takes place in a cardiac ward of a hospital, especially, the game environment is the patient room (see Fig. 1). The player can move into the room and he can interact with the patient and the all useful objects for the diagnosis and the treatment. In particular, different game dynamics were implemented depending on the type of the object; e.g. when the player wants to do an electrocardiogram (ECG), he has to position the electrodes on the patient and control the ECG on the monitor. Table 1 reports the main medical procedures and the related interactions with the game elements.

Table 1. Checklist of main game elements and related game dynamics.

Game elements	Procedures related game dynamics
Electrocardiogram	The player can position the electrodes and monitor the ECG
Blood pressure monitor	The player can monitor the patient pressure
Thermometer	The player can evaluate the patient temperature
Pulse oximeter	The player can measure the oxygen saturation
Drugs	The player can indicate a pharmacological treatment
Medical record	The player can evaluate the medical record of the patient and prescribe medical examinations

The patient is animated with sounds and motions but his appearance and animation change by case to case. The sound effects and the music are included in the game; moreover, the feedback system is displayed via sounds and text messages. In particular, at the simulation end, the player can evaluate his game performance via a report of his actions based on his decision making process. A brief tutorial about the game instructions is provided to the players in the first session of the game.

Fig. 1. Screenshot of the patient room, from player prospective, in the heart attack case.

2.2   Game Design

The agile framework Scrum [21] was adopted to manage the development of the serious game in order to support a multidisciplinary approach. In fact, Scrum can promote the communication and the cooperation between the different team members, but also the control of the implementation [22]. In particular, we followed the framework process proposed by [23] to apply Scrum in the game development.

Unity and Autodesk Character Generator has been used to develop the prototype of the serious game. The game provides only a player in first person that can be controlled by two input devices: keyboard with mouse and joystick controller (Xbox 360).

The actions the player is allowed to vary from case to case represent a range of possible steps and decisions that the medical professional is going to face in real context. In order to develop a game feedback system, it is fundamental to analyse the player's game performance, namely, the evaluation of the choices the player made during the game session. The choice of the correct medical procedures to establish an effective plan of treatment can be compared to a complex decision process. Then, a mathematical model was formulated in order to evaluate the player's decision making process. In fact, an integer programming formulation not only allows to take into account all the possible action schemes, not only the best one, but also it unambiguously gives a measure of the player's performance. Therefore, the game feedback system is based on the output by the mathematical model.

Mathematical Model for the Decision Making Process. The decision making process can be formulated as a one-to-one shortest path problem [24]. Let $G = (V, E)$ be a directed graph, with a cost c_{ij} defined for each edge $(i, j) \in E; i, j \in V$. Let s and t be two distinguished vertices in V. The one-to-one shortest path problem requires to find the minimum cost path from s to t in G, namely the path for which the sum of the costs of the related edges is minimum.

Denote with $FS(i)$ and $BS(i)$ the set of edges exiting from a vertex i and the set of edges entering in i respectively. In order to formulate a mathematical model, we introduce for each edge (i, j) the Boolean decision variables x_{ij} assuming value 1 when (i, j) is taken in the solution and 0 otherwise.

$$\min \sum_{(i,j)\in E} c_{ij}x_{ij} \tag{1}$$

s.t.

$$\sum_{j\in FS(i)} x_{ij} - \sum_{j\in BS(i)} x_{ji} = 0 \qquad \forall i \in V\setminus\{s,t\} \tag{2}$$

$$\sum_{j\in FS(s)} x_{sj} - \sum_{j\in BS(s)} x_{js} = 1 \tag{3}$$

$$\sum_{j\in FS(t)} x_{tj} - \sum_{j\in BS(t)} x_{jt} = -1 \tag{4}$$

$$x_{ij} \in \{0, 1\} \tag{5}$$

The objective function (1) requires to minimize the total cost of the path. The constraints (2–4) assure that for each vertex exactly one edge of the path enters and exactly one edge exits from it, apart from s and t: in fact, no edge enters in s and no edge exits from t.

The decision making process consists of finding the best (with minimum cost) sequence of actions (identified as the edges) and intermediate steps (represented by vertices), among all possible sequences (regarded as paths) in the graph $G = (V, E)$ (including all the possible sequences), moving from a starting situation (represented by s) to an aimed one (identified as t). Clearly, the shortest path in the graph represents the best sequence of actions indicated by the medical guidelines. A graph can be built for each scenario in the game: all the possible consecutive choices by the player are made up of the actions and the results of those ones, respectively represented by the directed edges and the vertices that form the entire graph. Every edge is associated to a cost, so as every action by the player is related to a feedback. The sum of these costs generates the value of the objective function; thus, the latter also expresses an evaluation of the choices that the player makes. Smaller the value of the objective function (1) is, more suitable the procedure performed by the player is. Moreover, to cope with real world situations, it can be modelled as a one-to-one shortest path problem in which the costs c_{ij} are time dependent [25], leading to an NP-hard problem.

3 Discussion

In the last decades, the simulation established itself an important training tool for the healthcare professionals in order to improve the treatment and the safety of the patient [26]. In fact, the learner can prove his skills and knowledge in a learning environment without real consequences on the patient life. With reference to the virtual simulations, several studies have been investigated the serious game efficacy to train healthcare professionals [14].

The present study introduces the design and the development of a 3D serious game aimed to train medical students on the cardiology treatments. In particular, we proposed a methodology based on the construction of all possible action schemes that the player can execute and the analysis of the game performance via an IP mathematical model. Moreover, the 3D game environment is more effective because the underlaying graph is of a greater size as the number of possible decision is larger. The use of agile framework facilitated the development of the game prototype in brief time, but also the management of the multidisciplinary project.

In order to guarantee the efficacy of simulation with serious game, we recommend to follow the best practices for the medical simulation [6] and to accurately introduce the simulation in the circle of the learning [27]. In particular, a debriefing meeting has to be provided after the game session in order to analyse the simulation and to discuss the performance evaluating the choices and decisions. In this way the serious game report can be the starting point of the debriefing aiming to critically debate the simulation session and to understand the best way to operate in the specific case. Moreover, the serious game also allows to reproduce other aspects of the medical work, as the time management and the work rates, and to support a slow medical education [28].

In the future work the prototype of serious game will be tested by medical students in a cardiology course to evaluate the possible changes and to complete the game development.

References

1. WHO.   http://www.euro.who.int/en/health-topics/Health-systems/patient-safety/data-and-stat istics
2. Makary, M.A., Daniel, M.: Medical error-the third leading cause of death in the US. BMJ **3**, 353 (2016)
3. Satava, R.M.: The revolution in medical education-the role of simulation. J. Grad. Med. Educ. **1**(2), 172–175 (2009)
4. Gaba, D.: The future vision of simulation in health care. Qual. Saf. Health Care **13**, 2–10 (2004)
5. Datta, R., Upadhyak, K., Jaideep, C.: Simulation and its role in medical education. Med. J. Aimed Forces India **68**(2), 167–172 (2012)
6. Motola, I., Devine, L.A., Chung, H.S., Sullivan, J.E., Issenberg S.B.: Simulation in healthcare education: A best evidence practical guide. AMEE Guide No. 82. Med Teach **35** (10), e1511–e1530 (2013)
7. Doerr, H., Murray, W.: How to build a successful simulation strategy: the simulation learning pyramid. In: Kyle, R., Murray, W. (eds.) Clinical Simulation: Operations, Engineering and Management. Elsevier, New York (2008)
8. Rosen, K.: The history of simulation. In: Levine, Adam I., DeMaria, S., Schwartz, Andrew D., Sim, Alan J. (eds.) The Comprehensive Textbook of Healthcare Simulation, pp. 5–49. Springer, New York (2013). https://doi.org/10.1007/978-1-4614-5993-4_2
9. Al-Elq, A.H.: Simulation-based medical teaching and learning. J. Fam. Community Med. **17** (1), 35–40 (2010)
10. Abt, C.C.: Serious Games. Viking Press, New York (1970)
11. Wattanasoontorn, V., Hernández, R.J.G., Sbert, M.: Serious games for e-health care. In: Cai, Y., Goei, S.L. (eds.) Simulations, Serious Games and Their Applications. GMSE, pp. 127–146. Springer, Singapore (2014). https://doi.org/10.1007/978-981-4560-32-0_9
12. Sawyer, B.: From cells to cell processors: the integration of health and video games. IEEE Comput. Graph. Appl. **28**(6), 83–85 (2008)
13. McCallum, S.: Gamification and serious games for personalized health. Stud. Health Technol. Inform. **177**, 85–96 (2012)
14. Wang, R., DeMaria, S., Goldberg, A., Katz, D.: A systematic review of serious games in training health care professionals. Simul. Healthc.: J. Soc. Simul. Healthc. **11**(1), 41–51 (2016)
15. Graafland, M., Schraagen, J.M., Schijven, M.P.: Systematic review of serious games for medical education and surgical skills training. Br. J. Surg. **99**, 1322–1330 (2012)
16. Cook, N.F., McAloon, T., O'Neil, P., Beggs, R.: Impact of a web based interactive simulation game (PULSE) on nursing student's experience and performance in life support training- a pilot study. Nurse Educ. Today **32**(6), 714–720 (2011)
17. Ricciardi, F., De Paolis, L.T.: A comprehensive review of serious games in health professions. Int. J. Comput. Games Technol. **24**, 1–11 (2014)
18. Kleinert, R., Wahba, R., Chang, D., Plum, P., Hölscher, A.H., Stippel, D.L.: 3D immersive patient simulators and their impact on learning success: a thematic review. J. Med. Internet Res. **17**(4), e-91 (2015)

19. Korhonen, T, Halonen, R., Ravelin, T, Kemppainen, T., Kyösti, K.: A multidisciplinary approach to serious game development in the health sector. In: 11th Mediterranean Conference on Information Systems (MCIS), Genoa, Italy (2017)
20. Bethke, E.: Game Development and Production. Wordware Publishing, Texas (2003)
21. Abrahamsson, P., Salo, O., Ronkainen, J., Warsta, J.: Agile Software Development Methods: Review and Analysis. VTT Publication 478, Espoo (2002)
22. Schwaber, K., Sutherland, J.: The Scrum Guide. (2017). https://www.scrumguides.org/docs/scrumguide/v2017/2017-Scrum-Guide-US.pdf#zoom=100
23. Alcover, E.A., Jaume-i-Capó, A., Moyà-Alcover, B.: PROGame: a process framework for serious game development for motor rehabilitation therapy. PLoS ONE **13**(5), e0197383 (2018)
24. Dreyfus, S.E.: An appraisal of some shortest-path algorithms. Oper. Res. **17**(3), 395–412 (1969)
25. Madkour, A., Aref, W.G., Rehman, F.U., Rahman, M.A., Basalamah, S.M.: A Survey of Shortest-Path Algorithms. ArXiv (2017)
26. Aggarwal, R., et al.: Training and simulation for patient safety. BMJ Qual. Saf. **19**, 34–43 (2010)
27. Sautter, M., Eikeland, H.: The circle of learning in emergency medicine and healthcare education. Laerdal (2008)
28. Wear, D., Zarconi, J., Kumagai, A., Cole-Kelly, K.: Slow medical education. Acad. Med. **90**(3), 289–293 (2015)

Nerve Contour Tracking for Ultrasound-Guided Regional Anesthesia

Xavier Cortés, Donatello Conte[(✉)], and Pascal Makris

Laboratoire d'Informatique Fondamentale et Appliquée de Tours (LIFAT - EA 6300),
Université de Tours, 64 Avenue Jean Portalis, 37000 Tours, France
{xavier.cortes,donatello.conte,pascal.makris}@univ-tours.fr

Abstract. Ultrasound-Guided Regional Anesthesia is a technique to provide regional anesthesia aided by ultrasound visualization of the region on which the anesthesia will be applied. A proper detection and tracking of the nerve contour is necessary to decide where anesthesia should be applied. If the needle is too far from the nerve contour, the anesthesia could be ineffective, but if it touch the nerve could harm the patient. In this paper we address a model to track nerve contours in ultrasonic videos to assist the doctors during Ultrasound-Guided Regional Anesthesia procedures. The experimental results show that our model performs good within an acceptable margin of error.

Keywords: Nerves · Contour tracking ·
Ultrasound-Guided Regional Anesthesia

1 Introduction

Regional anesthesia is an interesting alternative to general anesthesia during surgical procedures. It reduces pain scores and postoperative complications. Typically, this technique has been performed by blind guidance of the needle to the target nerve. However, this method of needle guidance increases the risk of block failure, nerve trauma and local anesthetic toxicity [13]. To reduce these complications, the current trend is to use the Ultrasound-Guided Regional Anesthesia (UGRA) technique. The UGRA technique has had an enormous impact on the practice of regional anesthesia during the last years [10] becoming an emerging and an innovative technique for anesthesia procedures.

The key problems with UGRA practice is the nerve localization and tracking in ultrasound videos [15]. Some works have been published that address this issue, in particular the detection of the nerve in a ultrasound image [4–6,12]. Morevoer, nerve detection is typically a very time-consuming task, therefore is not suitable in practice for UGRA, where real-time processing is needed. Besides, to reduce the risk of trauma caused by touching nerves with the needle, the nerve

---

This work is part of the DANIEAL2 project supported by a Region Centre-Val de Loire (France) grant. We gratefully acknowledge Region Centre-Val de Loire for its support.

M. Cristani et al. (Eds.): ICIAP 2019 Workshops, LNCS 11808, pp. 244–251, 2019.
https://doi.org/10.1007/978-3-030-30754-7_25

contour tracking has to be fast and precise. Therefore, classic object tracking algorithms that provide only bounding box of targets, are not sufficient to be used in practice.

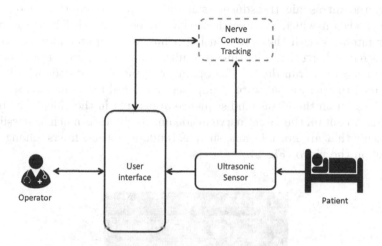

Fig. 1. General scheme of our framework.

For this reason, in this paper, we propose an attempt to solve the nerve contours tracking problem in ultrasound images aiming to assist the doctors during UGRA procedures. The proposed solution is real-time and quite precise. Even if each step of the approach are well-known image processing techniques, at the best of our knowledge, this is the first time that the whole framework is designed for nerve contour tracking in ultrasound images.

The rest of the paper is organized as follow: in Sect. 2, we describe the context within the tracking algorithm is situated; Sect. 3 presents the proposed method; in Sect. 4, we evaluate the method; finally, the paper ends with some conclusions and future perspectives (Sect. 5).

2 Framework Description

The model presented in this paper aims to aid UGRA procedures by highlighting the contour of the nerve that we want to anesthetize.

The elements involved in the procedure addressed in this paper are: an ultrasonic transducer to scan the local region of the patient's body where the anesthesia must be injected, the user interface that allows to the human operator to impose the initial bounding box and the nerve tracking module, which is the one that we propose here (see Fig. 1).

An accurate detection of the contour is fundamental because the region that surrounds the nerves is the one where the anesthesia must be injected. If it is too far from the nerve, it may be ineffective, while if it is inside the nerve, it could harm the patient.

The way in which this module works is related to a set of steps that are assisted by a human operator.

First, the ultrasonic transducer is manually placed on the region of the patient's body on which the anesthesia has to be injected. Then, the human operator interacts with the system using a human-computer interface consisting of a screen, showing in real-time, the ultrasound video sequence that comes from the ultrasonic transducer. The operator, typically a doctor who has specific training to operate the system, imposes the initial bounding box where the nerve is located on the ultrasound sequence appearing in the video. The bounding box must contain the target nerve inside and exclude, as much as possible, all the elements that are not relevant, such as tendons, muscle fibers among others appearing in the video (Fig. 2).

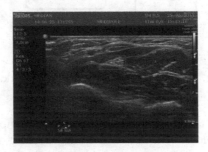

Fig. 2. An example of a bounding box (blue) limiting the region where the nerve contour is located. (Color figure online)

3   Proposed Model

To track the nerve contour we propose a procedure divided into three different steps that are processed iteratively for each frame of the video sequence after an initialization step in which the human operator imposes the bounding box. The first step consists in tracking the region inside the bounding box through the frames sequence. The second step is to reduce the noise of the region detected by the tracker in order to increase the quality of the contour detection and finally, the third step aims to detect the contour points inside the region bounded by the imposed box. In Fig. 3 we show a general scheme of the model.

3.1   Bounding Box Tracking

The first step after the initialization of the bounding box by a human operator, is to track the region in the video where the nerve is located. This region is affected by different deformations and translations because the shape and position of the nerves is not static in time.

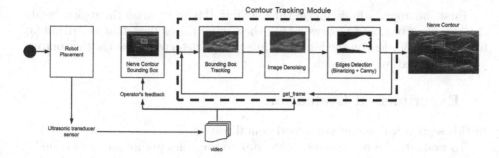

Fig. 3. General scheme of the contour tracking module.

The robustness of the tracking algorithm is crucial for the performance of the model. For this reason, we propose to evaluate our model using different state-of-the-art tracking algorithms in the experimental section.

3.2 Image Denoising

Ultrasonic transducers may not be entirely accurate because of the intrinsic noise in the data captured by the sensors. Due to this, we propose to apply the *Fast Non-Local Means* (FNLM) [14] algorithm, before the detection of the nerves contour, in order to improve the performance of the method. FNLM is an algorithm that reduces the computational complexity of the original *Non-Local Means* (NLM) [1] algorithm, for smoothing the image. This complexity reduction is necessary if we want to apply the entire process in real-time.

To give the basic principles and the complexity of NLM and FNLM, the denoiser algorithm applies, for each pixel of the image, a specific local filter built upon a neighborhood window. The computational complexity of the original NLM algorithm is $O(M^2 \cdot n^4)$ where M is the filter size and n is the number of pixels of the image. The fast version FNLM takes benefit of the Integral Image representation to reduce the number of computations needed for the filtering. Its complexity is $O(n^4)$, therefore it is independent from the filter size. Please, refer to [14] for more details.

We apply the denoiser algorithm only on the pixels within the bounding box provided by the previous step (tracking), because, by hypothesis, there is no nerve outside the box. This further reduces the computational cost of the processing.

3.3 Contour Detection

The final step is to detect the points belonging to the nerve contour. To do this we propose a combination of thresholding and edges detection.

First, we apply a basic image thresholding [11] to binarize the region inside the bounding box, and next we apply the Canny Edges detection algorithm [3] to detect the borders on the binarized image. The detected edges are the contour points returned by the model.

4   Experimental Evaluation

In this section we present the experimental results.

To evaluate the performance we compare the contours found by our model with the ground-truth contours that has been manually labeled by a human expert frame by frame on a grey-scale video of 659 frames captured by an ultrasonic transducer.

The metric used to evaluate the error between the contour found by the model and the ground-truth contour is the Mean Euclidean Distance (MED) defined as the mean distance in pixels between each point of the first contour with respect to the closest point of the second contour. Since this metric is not symmetric we evaluate the distance in both senses and calculate the mean.

We have compared the performance of our model using the following tracking algorithms (Sect. 3.1), that are know to be among the best in the scientific literature: *Online Multiple Instance Learning* (MIL) [2], *Median Flow* (MF) [16], *Kernel Correlation Filter* (KCF) [8,9] and *Real-time Tracking via On-line Boosting* (RTB) [7].

In Table 1 we show the mean, the maximum and the minimum MED results using different combinations of denoising and tracking algorithms. The performance are similar in terms of accuracy for MIL, KCF and RTB algorithms while for MF is significantly worse. Using the FNLM algorithm to eliminate noise (Sect. 3.2) we increase performance in all cases. By way of illustration in Fig. 4, we show some ultrasound images and the tracked contours in order to show the behavior of our model with different configurations.

Table 1. Comparative table of results with different tracking algorithms. Best results highlighted in bold.

Tracking algorithm	Mean	Max	Min
MIL	4.30	6.12	3.41
MIL + Denoising	3.95	6.10	2.14
MF	6.09	11.06	3.32
MF + Denoising	5.76	11.27	**2.13**
KCF	4.20	6.36	3.23
KCF + Denoising	**3.73**	6.15	**2.13**
RTB	4.18	6.04	3.21
RTB + Denoising	3.75	**6.01**	2.15

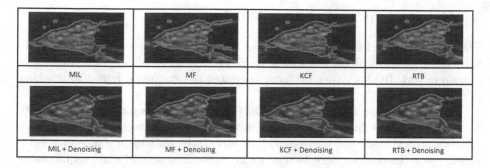

Fig. 4. Nerve contour examples using different configurations. Green: ground-truth contour. Blue: contour found by the algorithm. (Color figure online)

The second requirement that our model must satisfy is to be able to operate in real time or close to it. For this reason, in Fig. 5, we show frame rate comparison for different tracking algorithms with and without denoising application. We have executed our experiments using a Python interpreter running on Windows 10, with an Intel i7 processor at 2.6 GHz and 16 GB of RAM. The vertical bars represent the average number of Frames Per Second (FPS) that each configuration can process in our experiments.

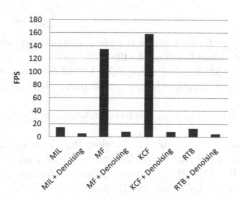

Fig. 5. Average number of Frames Per Second using different configurations.

On one hand, we observe that applying the FNLM in order to eliminate the noise increases significantly the runtime required to process each frame. On the other hand we see that the fastest algorithms are the MF and the KFC, while the MIL and the RTB have worse performance. The configurations that are able to process all the frames in real time assuming videos at 25 FPS in our hardware configuration are the MF and KCF when the noise is not removed using the FNLM algorithm (Sect. 3.2).

5   Conclusions and Future Work

The work presented in this paper is part of a bigger project aiming to provide anesthesia to medical patients in a framework supervised and operated by a human expert. In this paper we have presented the module referred to tracking of nerves contours.

Due to the design specifications of the project we have two main requirements to accomplish. The first one is to minimize the error as much as possible since this is a critical task that may result in injury to the patient or make anesthetic ineffective if the contour detection is not accurate. The second main requirement is to be able to track the contour in real time.

On one hand, the preliminary experimental results are very hopeful in terms of accuracy using different tracking algorithms. On the other hand, the runtime experiments show that when we remove the noise appearing in the frame we are far to be able to run the model in real-time using our hardware configuration.

As future work we propose to create a complete database with several videos and its ground-truth contour correspondences in order to exhaustively validate the model providing to the community a new benchmark to compare contour tracking algorithms. We plan also to define a new contour tracking algorithm, based on spatio-temporal continuity, in order to increase accuracy and to decrease runtimes.

References

1. Buades, A., Coll, B., Morel, J.M.: A review of image denoising algorithms, with a new one. Multiscale Model. Simul. **4**, 490–530 (2005)
2. Babenko, B., Yang, M.-H., Belongie, S.J.: Visual tracking with online multiple instance learning. In: Computer Vision and Pattern Recognition, CVPR, pp. 983–990. IEEE (2009)
3. Canny, J.: A computational approach to edge detection. Pattern Anal. Mach. Intell. **8**, 679–698 (1986)
4. Hadjerci, O., Hafiane, A., Conte, D., Markis, P., Vieyres, P., Delbos., A.: Ultrasound median nerve localization by classification based on despeckle filtering and feature selection. In: 2015 IEEE International Conference on Image Processing, ICIP 2015, Quebec City, QC, Canada, 27–30 September 2015, pp. 4155–4159 (2015)
5. Hadjerci, O., Hafiane, A., Makris, P., Conte, D., Vieyres, P., Delbos, A.: Nerve detection in ultrasound images using median Gabor binary pattern. In: Campilho, A., Kamel, M. (eds.) ICIAR 2014. LNCS, vol. 8815, pp. 132–140. Springer, Cham (2014). https://doi.org/10.1007/978-3-319-11755-3_15
6. Hadjerci, O., Hafiane, A., Vieyres, P., Conte, D., Makris, P., Delbos, A.: On-line learning dynamic models for nerve detection in ultrasound videos. In: 2016 IEEE International Conference on Image Processing (ICIP), pp. 131–135. IEEE (2016)
7. Grabner, H., Grabner, M., Bischof, H.: Real-time tracking via on-line boosting. In: British Machine Vision Conference, BMVC, vol. 1 (2006)
8. Henriques, J.F., Caseiro, R., Martins, P., Batista, J.: Exploiting the circulant structure of tracking-by-detection with Kernels. In: Fitzgibbon, A., Lazebnik, S., Perona, P., Sato, Y., Schmid, C. (eds.) ECCV 2012. LNCS, vol. 7575, pp. 702–715. Springer, Heidelberg (2012). https://doi.org/10.1007/978-3-642-33765-9_50

9. Danelljan, M., Khan, F.S., Felsberg, M., van de Weijer, J.: Adaptive color attributes for real-time visual tracking. In: Computer Vision and Pattern Recognition, CVPR, pp. 1090–1097. IEEE (2014)
10. Marhofer, P., Willschke, H., Kettner, S.: Current concepts and future trends in ultrasound-guided regional anesthesia. Curr. Opin. Anesthesiol. **23**(5), 632–636 (2010)
11. Sezgin, M., Sankur, B.: Survey over image thresholding techniques and quantitative performance evaluation. Electron. Imaging **13**, 146–168 (2004)
12. Thouin, E., Hafiane, A., Vieyres, P., Xylourgos, N., Triantafyllidis, G., Papadourakis, G.: Nerve region segmentation for ultrasound guided local regional anaesthesia (LRA). In: Mediterranean Conference on Information Systems (2011)
13. Tsui, B.C., Suresh, S.: Ultrasound imaging for regional anesthesia in infants, children, and adolescentsa review of current literature and its application in the practice of extremity and trunk blocks. Anesthesiol. J. Am. Soc. Anesthesiol. **112**(2), 473–492 (2010)
14. Karnati, V., Uliyar, M., Dey, S.: Fast non-local algorithm for image denoising. In: International Conference on Image Processing, ICIP, pp. 3873–3876 (2009)
15. Woodworth, G.E., Chen, E.M., Horn, J.L.E., Aziz, M.F.: Efficacy of computer-based video and simulation in ultrasound-guided regional anesthesia training. J. Clin. Anesth. **20**(3), 212–221 (2014)
16. Kalal, Z., Mikolajczyk, K., Matas, J.: A computational approach to edge detection. In: International Conference on Pattern Recognition, ICPR, pp. 2756–2759. IEEE (2010)

Skin Lesions Classification: A Radiomics Approach with Deep CNN

Gabriele Piantadosi[1]([✉]), Giampaolo Bovenzi[1], Giuseppe Argenziano[2],
Elvira Moscarella[2], Domenico Parmeggiani[3], Ludovico Docimo[3],
and Carlo Sansone[1]

[1] Dip. di Ingegneria Elettrica e delle Tecnologie dell'Informazione,
University of Naples Federico II, Naples, Italy
{gabriele.piantadosi,giampaolo.bovenzi,carlo.sansone}@unina.it
[2] Dip. di Salute Mentale e Fisica e Medicina Preventiva,
University of Campania Luigi Vanvitelli, Caserta, Italy
{giuseppe.argenziano,elvira.moscarella}@unicampania.it
[3] Dip. di Scienze Mediche e Chirurgiche Avanzate,
University of Campania Luigi Vanvitelli, Caserta, Italy
{domenico.parmeggiani,ludovico.docimo}@unicampania.it

Abstract. Supporting the early diagnosis of skin cancer is crucial for the sake of any kind of treatment or surgery. This work proposes to improve the outcome of automatic diagnoses approaches by using an ensemble of pre-trained deep convolutional neural networks and a suitable voting strategy. Moreover, a novel patching approach has been deployed. The proposal has been fairly evaluated with the literature proposals demonstrating good preliminary results.

1 Introduction

The skin cancers can be roughly divided into two categories: melanoma and non-melanoma. The most common skin cancer belongs to the category of non-melanoma tumours and is the basal cell carcinoma and squamous cell carcinoma representing the 5th most commonly occurring cancer in men and women, with over 1 million diagnoses worldwide in 2018, although this is likely to be an underestimate [2]. Skin cancer diagnosis is a non-trivial challenge for several reasons: this disease is usually underestimated. Due to these factors, it is likely that the reported global incidence of skin cancer is an underestimate to the extent that some people with cancer do not consult a physician; moreover there are different sub-types of skin cancer, leading to issues in data collection; for example, non-melanoma skin cancer may be not completely tracked by cancer registries.

According to the American Cancer Society, each year, more than 60000 people in the United States were diagnosed with melanoma and more than 8000 Americans died of disease [2]. Melanoma is the most aggressive form of skin cancer and the surgical treatments are the main approach. However, patients

M. Cristani et al. (Eds.): ICIAP 2019 Workshops, LNCS 11808, pp. 252–259, 2019.
https://doi.org/10.1007/978-3-030-30754-7_26

who undergo late treatment may develop metastasise to regional lymph nodes or distant metastases. The median survival date in that conditions is about 6–9 months, and the five-year survival rate is less than 5%. As a consequence, it is important to rely on more effective strategies to decrease mortality rates from melanoma such as early detection. In recent years, Deep learning (DL) approaches, and in particular deep Convolutional Neural Networks (CNNs), obtain wide popularity in many pattern recognition tasks thanks to their ability to autonomous learn compact hierarchical features that best fit the specific input domain. The aim of this work is to support the skin lesion diagnosis by means of deep learning approaches with a suitable ensemble of deep CNN.

The paper is organised as follows: Sect. 2 outlines some traditional approaches and related works; Sect. 3 describes the proposal, introduces the dataset and illustrates the evaluation approach; Sect. 4 reports our results compared with those obtained by using some literature proposals; finally, Sect. 5 discusses the obtained results and provides some conclusions.

2 Related Works

Nowadays, detection of melanoma is strongly improved by means of novel approaches to support the visual inspection such as total body photography, dermoscopy, automated diagnostic systems and reflectance confocal microscopy. Dermoscopy is the most spread method for skin cancer detection. It consists of a non-invasive, *in-vivo* technique and it is performed by means of a manual instrument called dermatoscope. The procedure allows for the visualization of subsurface skin structures in the epidermis, at the dermoepidermal junction, and in the upper dermis; these structures are usually not visible to the naked eye [1,9,10]. An interesting aspect of such a technique is the possibility of the images to be digitised for storage, far transmission or sequential analysis. Thanks to this feature dermatologists have begun to incorporate novel imaging techniques into diagnostic algorithms.

The automatic skin cancer diagnosis techniques are traditionally based on computer vision approaches that implement one or more of the following approaches:

Geometry analysis: like all the tumour forms, the growth of the lesion has an irregular pattern which, in the case of skin tumour forms, leads to asymmetry in the shape. It is important, therefore, to rely on powerful descriptors such as area, perimeter, convexity, the major/minor-axis' length and angle, compactness, elongation, eccentricity (also known as ellipticity), roundness (or circularity) and sphericity [1,6].

Color analysis: the tonality of the skin when a tumour grows may change in a discriminant way. Therefore, automatic approaches may benefit from colour analysis. This descriptors are mainly histogram derived considerations and require the choice of a colour space such as RGB, Hue-Saturation-Value (HSV), YCrCb, and the novel Hue-Min-Max-Difference (HMMD). Among the common colour descriptors there are the Scalable Color Descriptor (SCD), defined by a fixed colour space quantization, and the Haar transform encoding; the dominant colour (DC) quantify the distribution of the salient colours in the image; the Color Layout Descriptor (CLD) captures the spatial layout of the dominant colours; and so on [8, 12, 13].

Texture analysis: texture, like colour, is a powerful low-level descriptor in skin tumour classification. Computer Vision literature is plenty of textural descriptors that can be roughly divided into local or global approaches operating in space or frequency domain [8, 12].

It is, therefore, necessary to rely on robust segmentation and feature extraction approaches that must be developed by domain experts.

While newer hand-crafted features for skin cancer detection are continuously proposed by domain experts, in the last years deep learning approaches have gained popularity in many pattern recognition and computer vision tasks, being able to outperform classical machine learning approaches in different fields [5]. Among these 'Deep Approaches', the most used are the Deep CNN (better discussed in the Sect. 3), composed of different convolutional layers stacked in a deep architecture meant to automatically learn the best data representation as composed by simpler concepts. They usually perform better than classifiers trained on hand-crafted features because are able to learn a compact and hierarchical representation of an image, that well fits the specific task to solve.

Among the deep approaches for skin cancer diagnosis Codella et al. [3] propose to feed a pre-trained network called AlexNet [7]. The pre-trained network was used as a feature-extractor (better discussed in Sect. 3) to map the images in a bigger feature-space (4096 features). The vectors in the new space were used to train a Support-Vector Machine (SVM) model.

Pomponiu et al. [11] propose a similar approach by applying data augmentation to feed a bigger number of images. This feeding approach consists of applying affine transformations to the input images during the training phase with the aim of improving generalization behaviour. The authors also change the classification model with a weaker k-Nearest Neighbors (k-NN) model.

A novel deep approach proposed by Haenssle et al. [4] consists of using a more complex pre-trained network called GoogLeNet Inception-v3 [7]. The difference consists in using the pre-trained network in a fine-tuning flavour (transfer learning approaches are better discussed in Sect. 3) to adapt the whole network for the skin cancer detection task.

3   Materials and Methods

In this work we propose to address the skin lesion classification by means of Convolutional Neural Networks (CNNs) using transfer learning as a training strategy.

Convolutional Neural Networks (CNNs) are machine learning models borrowed from traditional Neural Networks (NNs). Such architectures share most of the features: they are both made of neurons, usually organized in layers; layers are stratified to create a feed-forward network in which the output of a layer is the input of next layer. However, while traditional NNs operate on the features designed and extracted by a domain expert, CNNs use a hierarchy of convolution operations to autonomously design the features that better model the problem under analysis. Although this characteristic gives to CNNs a great representational ability, it also comes with a huge number of parameters to learn and, despite efforts made to design increasingly compact networks, CNNs tend to strongly focus on the input dataset (also know as overfit behaviour) when the training phase is limited to few training instances. The solution would be to provide a large number of input instances but, when these are not easily available, a valid solution is to transfer the knowledge from a previous trained CNN (also on a different domain) to the new input domain by training it to solve the new task with a proper amount of available training data. This approach is also known as *Transfer Learning* and can be obtained by following two approaches:

Fine-Tuning: consists in train only the last few layers of a pre-trained CNN (usually called fully connected layers). This fine-tuning of part of the weights not only address the novel input problem but also adapt the last layer of the network to the different output classes.

Feature-Extraction: uses the pre-trained CNN as is by relying on the output of the second/third layer; no further training is required to obtain a feature vector to be used as input of different models, such as traditional ML approaches, or a mapping function in a novel and bigger vectorial space. This approach is strongly promoted because the knowledge of the pre-trained network is able to efficiently map the instances for several tasks (also for very different domains).

Both the approaches aim to reduce the computational burden of to train a network from scratch but only the Feature-Extraction approach also performs a space transformation that may help to index a bunch of images efficiently and relying on visual peculiarity not easy to catch up with handcrafted features.

3.1   Proposed Approach

The proposed architecture is depicted in the Fig. 1.

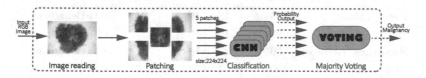

Fig. 1. Proposed approach.

The approach consists of four main stages organised as follows:

Image Reading: Since there are several tools and cameras for dermoscopy that can provide digital images suitable for computer vision aided analysis, it is required a suitable read, conversion and representation format able to be compliant with the subsequent steps. The formats accepted are JPEG, BMP, PNG, DICOM, NIFTI and the image is, therefore, converted into RGB matrices.

Patching: The whole image is divided into five patches extracted as big as half the dimensions. The position of each patch is: four from the corners and one in the centre. Each patch is, then, resized to the squared size of 224×224 to be compliant with the input of the subsequent stage (the input of the neural network).

Classification: Each patch undergoes a neural network to create an ensemble classification of the same lesion with five points of view. The result is obtained with a pre-trained Alexnet [7] fine-tuned on our dataset. The output of this stage is the probability of each patch to belong to malignant melanoma (a five element vector).

Voting: The five element vector is, therefore, combined to produce an ensemble decision by applying a weighted majority voting. The most probable class (malignant/non-malignant) is returned.

3.2 Dataset

The dataset was collected with the "Synergy-net: Research and Digital Solutions against Cancer" project (funded in the framework of the POR Campania FESR 2014–2020) and labelled by experienced dermatologists. The size consists of 200 patients (77 female and 123 male subjects) with several images per patient as described in Table 1. The table also shows the four different skin lesions included in the dataset and the relative class considered for the final aim of this article. Lesions belong to patients with age from 1 to 100 years old and are from different parts of the body.

Table 1. Dataset composition.

Lesion	Patients	Male	Female	Images	Class
Nevus (Mole)	23	13	10	24	(B) Benignant
Angioma	27	14	13	27	(B) Benignant
Seborrheic Keratosis	50	32	18	51	(B) Benignant
Melanoma	100	64	36	107	(M) Malignant
Total	**200**	**123**	**77**	**209**	$\frac{B}{M} = \frac{102}{107}$

The colour images composing the dataset have different resolutions ranging from a minimum of 1999×1333 pixel to a maximum of 5184×3456 and three RGB channels.

3.3   Experimental Setup

The proposed CNNs have been evaluated using the high-level neural networks API Keras (Python 3.6) with TensorFlow 1.6 as back-end. Python scripts have been executed on a physical server hosted in our university HPC center[1] equipped with 2 x Intel(R) Xeon(R) Intel(R) 2.13 GHz CPUs (4 cores), 32 GB RAM and a Nvidia Titan Xp GPU (Pascal family) with 12 GB GRAM.

All the competitors have been developed by strictly implementing the design published in their works and evaluated on the same set of data and configuration of cross-validation (fixing the seeds of the pseudo-random generators). To face the size limitation of the training dataset a data augmentation approach has been applied. Spatial affine transformations such as Left/Right flip, Top/Bottom flip, 90° rotations have been applied.

Finally, in order to train the proposed models, a cross-entropy loss has been minimized and the performance has been evaluated in 10-fold cross-validation considering the median values of the Area Under the Receiver Operating Characteristic (ROC) Curve or AUC-ROC.

4   Results

This section reports the results of the described approach compared with some literature proposals. Table 2 reports our approach by varying the training stage (with or without the augmentation). The subpatching strategy has been also evaluated by considering the baseline approach (whole image).

Table 2. Proposed approach variants comparison. AUC median values (obtained with a 10-folds CV).

Augmentation	SubPatch	Voting	AUC-ROC
Yes			84.19%
	Yes	OR	55.28%
	Yes	Majority	60.91%
Yes	Yes	OR	83.63%
Yes	Yes	Majority	**87.27%**

To evaluate the effectiveness of the proposed approach, our results were compared with those obtained by applying the algorithms described in Sect. 2, by using a 10-fold Cross Validation (CV) ensuring that, to obtain a reliable and fair evaluation, the lesion from the same subject are always separated across the CV folds. Since Table 2 clearly shows that a form of augmentation improves the model to generalise the problem and thus improves the final result, we evaluated competitors that did not already apply this approach using our own augmentation technique. Results are reported in Table 3.

---

[1] http://www.scope.unina.it.

Table 3. Our approach compared with the literature proposals. AUC median values (obtained with a 10-folds CV).

Approach	Methodology	AUC-ROC
Haenssle et al. [4]	Inception-v3 (FineTuning)	55.68%
Pomponiu et al. [11]	Alexnet (FeatureExtraction) + kNN	76.41%
Codella et al. [3]	Alexnet (FeatureExtraction) + SVM	78.06%
Haenssle et al. [4] + Augmentation	Inception-v3 (FineTuning)	80.91%
Codella et al. [11] + Augmentation	Alexnet (FeatureExtraction) + SVM	84.54%
Our approach	Ensamble of Alexnet (FineTuning)	**87.27%**

5 Discussions and Conclusions

The aim of this work was to apply deep convolutional neural networks to support the early diagnosis of skin cancer. Table 2 demonstrates how our novel patching approach and the suitable ensemble of pre-trained networks is able to produce a reliable diagnosis.

Table 3 compares the best CNN-based approach with other approaches presented so far in the literature and described in Sect. 2, showing that, even if we try to train the competitors in the best condition, our proposal achieves the best classification results in terms of AUC. Table 2 also makes it clear that our dataset, due to the size limitation, requires data augmentation approach to successful train the network. For this reason and for the sake of the fairness we also train the competitors with data augmentation (middle part of Table 3).

As part of the "Synergy-net: Research and Digital Solutions against Cancer" project, the data acquisition is currently going on providing novel data with the aim of retraining the model and further validating the insights. Moreover, we are currently investigating the data fusion of geometrical features, textural features and deep features to provide a more robust ML/DL approach in skin lesion diagnosis.

Acknowledgments. The authors gratefully acknowledge the support of the Calculation Centre SCoPE of the University of Naples Federico II and his staff. This work is part of the "Synergy-net: Research and Digital Solutions against Cancer" project (funded in the framework of the POR Campania FESR 2014–2020 - CUP B61C17000090007).

References

1. Argenziano, G., et al.: Dermoscopy of pigmented skin lesions: results of a consensus meeting via the internet. J. Am. Acad. Dermatol. **48**(5), 679–693 (2003)
2. Bray, F., Ferlay, J., Soerjomataram, I., Siegel, R.L., Torre, L.A., Jemal, A.: Global cancer statistics 2018: GLOBOCAN estimates of incidence and mortality worldwide for 36 cancers in 185 countries. CA Cancer J. Clin. **68**(6), 394–424 (2018)

3. Codella, N., Cai, J., Abedini, M., Garnavi, R., Halpern, A., Smith, J.R.: Deep learning, sparse coding, and SVM for melanoma recognition in dermoscopy images. In: Zhou, L., Wang, L., Wang, Q., Shi, Y. (eds.) MLMI 2015. LNCS, vol. 9352, pp. 118–126. Springer, Cham (2015). https://doi.org/10.1007/978-3-319-24888-2_15
4. Haenssle, H.A., et al.: Man against machine: diagnostic performance of a deep learning convolutional neural network for dermoscopic melanoma recognition in comparison to 58 dermatologists. Ann. Oncol. **29**(8), 1836–1842 (2018)
5. He, K., Zhang, X., Ren, S., Sun, J.: Deep residual learning for image recognition. In: Proceedings of the IEEE Conference on Computer Vision and Pattern Recognition, pp. 770–778 (2016)
6. Henning, J.S., et al.: The cash (color, architecture, symmetry, and homogeneity) algorithm for dermoscopy. J. Am. Acad. Dermatol. **56**(1), 45–52 (2007)
7. Krizhevsky, A., Sutskever, I., Hinton, G.E.: Imagenet classification with deep convolutional neural networks. In: Advances in Neural Information Processing Systems, pp. 1097–1105 (2012)
8. Manjunath, B.S., Ohm, J.R., Vasudevan, V.V., Yamada, A.: Color and texture descriptors. IEEE Trans. Circuits Syst. Video Technol. **11**(6), 703–715 (2001)
9. Marghoob, A.A., et al.: Instruments and new technologies for the in vivo diagnosis of melanoma. J. Am. Acad. Dermatol. **49**(5), 777–797 (2003)
10. Menzies, S., Ingvar, C., McCarthy, W.: A sensitivity and specificity analysis of the surface microscopy features of invasive melanoma. Melanoma Res. **6**(1), 55–62 (1996)
11. Pomponiu, V., Nejati, H., Cheung, N.M.: Deepmole: deep neural networks for skin mole lesion classification. In: 2016 IEEE International Conference on Image Processing (ICIP), pp. 2623–2627. IEEE (2016)
12. Yu, H., Li, M., Zhang, H.J., Feng, J.: Color texture moments for content-based image retrieval. In: Proceedings of International Conference on Image Processing, vol. 3, pp. 929–932. IEEE (2002)
13. Zalaudek, I., et al.: Three-point checklist of dermoscopy: an open internet study. Br. J. Dermatol. **154**(3), 431–437 (2006)

DeepRetail: Deep Understanding of Shopper Behaviours and Interactions in Intelligent Retail Environment

Semantic 3D Object Maps for Everyday Robotic Retail Inspection

Marina Paolanti[1]([✉]), Roberto Pierdicca[2], Massimo Martini[1],
Francesco Di Stefano[2], Christian Morbidoni[1], Adriano Mancini[1],
Eva Savina Malinverni[2], Emanuele Frontoni[1], and Primo Zingaretti[1]

[1] Dipartimento di Ingegneria dell'Informazione, Università Politecnica delle Marche,
Via Brecce Bianche 12, 60131 Ancona, Italy
{m.paolanti,m.martini,c.morbidoni,a.mancini,e.frontoni,
p.zingaretti}@univpm.it
[2] Dipartimento di Ingegneria Civile, Edile e dell'Architettura,
Università Politecnica delle Marche, Via Brecce Bianche 12, 60131 Ancona, Italy
{r.pierdicca,e.s.malinverni}@univpm.it

Abstract. In retail field, customer culture is shifting towards in-store researching, and retailers need to re-evaluate their location services to better assist customer. In-store mapping help retailers learn how their employees are interacting and it satisfies user intent to search for products, something that is often ignored by retailers especially for the secondary placement, which contains offers and promotions that change very often. In this paper, we describe a retail robot that moves autonomously inside a store and gathers points cloud data for a semantic store mapping. With all the data collected, it is possible to build a 3D map of the store with the exact product locations. This retail robot combines the features of both Robotics and Artificial Intelligence. Three classification approach have been compared in order to achieve the best performances: a machine learning technique, PointNet++ and a novel Reflectance PointNet++ especially designed for this task. Experiments are performed in a real retail environment that is an Italian supermarket, during business hours. A dataset has been built and made publicly available. The application of our approach yields good results in terms of precision, recall and F1-score and demonstrates the effectiveness of the proposed approach.

Keywords: 3D Point cloud · Reflectance PointNet · PointNet++ · Machine learning · Retail

1 Introduction

In retail field, customer culture is shifting towards in-store researching, and retailers need to re-evaluate their location services to better assist customer. More engaged shoppers are exceptionally valuable to retailers. For this reason, companies provide a consistent experience throughout all channels: shopping lists, live product reviews, maps to help find items on shopping lists, inventory

M. Cristani et al. (Eds.): ICIAP 2019 Workshops, LNCS 11808, pp. 263–274, 2019.
https://doi.org/10.1007/978-3-030-30754-7_27

information. All of these ideas build a better experience for customers. In-store mapping help retailers learn how their employees are interacting within the store and understand which areas of the store generate the most traffic, essentially giving them the information they need to better stock shelves, deploy associates to high-traffic areas and deliver exceptional customer service [11]. In comparison with the technologies already adopted in this context [20], indoor mapping satisfies user intent to search for products, something that is often ignored by retailers especially for the secondary placement, which contains offers and promotions that change very often. In these situations, a semantic map provides a qualitative description of the environment which a robot explores, with the aim to enhance the navigation ability, plan activities aimed at reaching a target and above all improve the interaction between robot and man [9]. So, a semantic map is an improved representation of the environment, which involves both geometric information and high-level qualitative characteristics. According to [1], a semantic map should not only assign labels or features relevant for the environments as in [3,7], but to provide a knowledge representation that the system can use. In [1], the authors, in fact, propose a formalization of a minimal general structure implemented in a semantic map, that has the task to interface its between all the semantic maps, with extensions and integration. A metric map allows the robot to navigate in the surrounding environment as it has all the geometric characteristics that the robot needs to move and so to navigate in human environments by calculating their position. While, a semantic map includes the features that shape human concepts so as to know the places, forms and relationships between them. In literature there are a lot of methods that use a metric map by adding semantic information. There also exist some works in particular based on vision that build a semantic map without the use of a geometric map [17]. In recent years, semantic maps have been used both for indoors and outdoors applications. Methods developed for indoors situations are distinguished into single-scene and large-scale ones. Moreover, taking into account the sensory input and the architecture that has been used, it is possible to introduce a further classification of methods for semantic mapping into scene annotation and point cloud based annotation. In the methods based on scene annotation, the recognition of a place is used as the only attribute to semantically increase a metric map. While the second method is commonly based on semantic partitioning and labeling of arranged point clouds that are acquired directly by laser scanners and RGB-D sensors or calculated from stereo images. The increasing need for a fast quantification and characterization of complex environments has created challenges deriving from different environments, including retail. Accurate 3D data acquisitions are crucial for choosing the right mapping approach for a retail store. In this regard, the use of points cloud technology to represent 3D objects and spaces is the most available annotation. Point clouds have proven to be useful in different robot related tasks, as path planning in indoor environments, resulting in advancements in smoothing the robot maneuver when compared to other approaches, and in objects grasping. This paper outlines an innovative approach that represents the semantic map of a store using the point clouds segmentation.

A robot moving inside a store, acquires points cloud using the kaarta Stencil tool. Each 3D point is characterized by four features: x, y, z coordinates and a factor called "reflectance". This last feature provides further information regarding the material, with which the laser interacts. Before the classification phase, we introduced a pre-processing phase to clean the points cloud and make it lighter, since the points cloud is computationally heavy. When dealing with a huge amount of data, deep learning approaches [6,9,14] have been proven to be more suitable compared to machine learning and feature-based approaches [10,12].

Then, three classification approach are compared, in order to evaluate their performances:

- Machine Learning with the comparison of state-of-art classifiers;
- PointNet++ [16];
- Reflectance-PointNet++.

In fact, we have designed a novel network architecture, the so-called Reflectance-PointNet++, that has been modified compared with the previous ones, introducing for each point the Reflectance information. Another difference from the PointNet++ is that we transformed the training phase as the test, or we passed the sphere on the whole training scene and therefore the whole scene was given as input to the network. In the experimental phase, in order to classify the objects of the store, we have made two experiments: the first considering 6 classes of objects and the second 13 classes of objects (5 of these are equals to the previous defined). Figure 1 represents the plant of the store in which we acquired the data and the objects classes considered in the classification process. In fact, our approach is validated using real data gathered from a real store which helps to make our results more confident and our experiments repeatable; used data are publicly available in an open dataset that is the first dataset based on extensive real data in this field.

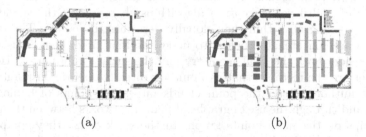

(a)   (b)

Fig. 1. (a) Represents the six classes of objects considered in the classification process. (b) Depicts the thirteen classes of objects. (Color figure online)

To briefly summarize, the main contributions of this work are: (i) a store map system for showing where everything is located indoors; (ii) a retail robot which brings deep learning to the store environment for helping retailers make their day-to-day ordering routines more efficient; (iii) a novel Reflectance PointNet++ designed for semantic segmentation; (iv) a challenging new dataset real data gathered from a real store. The application of our approach yields good results in terms of precision, recall and F1-score and demonstrates the effectiveness of the proposed approach.

The remainder of the paper is organized as follows: Sect. 2 describes the existing approaches of point cloud annotation or the store semantic mapping representation. Section 3 is focused on the description of the workflow and in particular the details of phases that compose the overall system. Results and experiments on a real store are discussed in Sect. 4. Finally, the Sect. 5 closes the paper, presenting also future developments.

2   Related Works

In the past, several efforts have been made to create semantic maps based on 3D point clouds [18]. The creation of such maps is a very complex process and involves the combination of different algorithms. In [8], the authors have associated the acquired 3D laser scans with the semantic characteristics, this in order to use the gradient between neighboring points by detecting three different classes of objects. In other works [19], the environment is a kitchen and the authors considered planar all the surfaces of a kitchen, so the 3D point clouds are segmented into planes. Then a learning algorithm was applied to classify the different kitchen objects. A similar work is proposed by [21], where the authors introduced a mapping technique based on feature also including on the map the positions of horizontal surfaces. In [4], the system used an RGB-D method to rebuild the surfaces in the 3D point clouds, detect different kinds of objects by estimating their position. The output is a representation of the environment with mesh curves, enhancing the scene with the CAD models of detected objects. In [15], the authors proposed PointNet method that directly operates on 3D point clouds. The basic idea is the extraction of features using a sequence of multilayer-perceptron algorithms that process the single points and a max-pooling algorithm that globally describes the points. The two representation are concatenated before to make the final prediction. This method did not consider both the local geometry and the surface information. However, many other are the methods that as PointNet directly operate on point clouds. In [5], the authors cluster the point clouds into super-points of homogeneous elements, and through the use of graphical neural networks between them define relationships on the super-points graph. In the work of [2], they compare the performances of a PointNet++ [16] (an extension of PointNet) where neighborhoods are statically defined by a metric distance, with their proposal that create the neighborhood on the basis of the feature space. In [22], the authors classify 3D point clouds of outdoor scenes. The aim of the authors is to propose a fully automated framework consisted of four components, by comparing a variety of approaches in terms of simplicity, efficiency and reproducibility.

In this paper, starting from previous works in this context [9,13], we propose a retail robot which combines robotics and artificial intelligence for detecting objects in store. The robot is equipped with an innovative instrument that allow, on the one hand, to build a map, on the other, to localize with respect to this map and, therefore, to determine their global position with considerable accuracy.

3   Materials and Methods

In this section, we introduce our system for localization and semantic classification of store furniture and good. The proposed approach is composed of three steps: (1) data acquisition, (2) data processing and (3) semantic classification.

The framework for semantic 3D store mapping, as well as the novel retail dataset used for evaluation, comprises three main components: point cloud data acquisitions, point cloud data processing and point cloud data classification.

Further details on the data processing and classification are given in the following sections. Details on the data collection and ground truth labelling are discussed in Subsect. 3.1.

3.1   Point Cloud Data Acquisition

The data acquisition is performed using a SLAM laser scanner mounted on a TurtleBot[1]. The ground-based photogrammetric survey of interior and exterior environments of the store is carried by Kaarta Stencil 2. We chose this instrument for its fast method and reducing time to obtain a completely survey. Stencil is a stand-alone, light weight and low-cost system delivering the integrated power of mapping and real-time position estimation. Stencil is based on scientific work and depends on LIDAR and IMU data for localization. The system uses Velodyne VLP-16 connected to a low-cost MEMS IMU and a processing computer for real-time mapping. A 10-Hz scan frequency is used for the data capture, and the "strongest" echo mode of the scanner is used to create the point observations from the LIDAR signal. VLP-16 has a 360° field of view with a 30° azimuthal opening using 16 scan lines. The progress of the mapping can be monitored on-line via an external monitor attached with a USB cable. The survey of the entirely indoor space of the store follows a closure trajectory.

The following step of data processing consist on first checking the quality of points cloud on CloudCompare software that permits the cleaning and the denoising. Then using Agisoft Photoscan we align selected frames of panoramic photos creating a RGB dense cloud and the final texture of some chosen parts of the store. Exporting the RGB points cloud, we open it on CloudCompare pasting on the points cloud made from Stencil Kaarta, so they have the same localization. Figure 2 shows an example of the points cloud acquired from the robot during its store inspection. The different colors depends on the value of the reflectance.

---

[1] http://www.turtlebot.com.

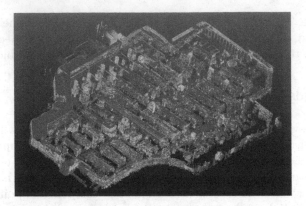

Fig. 2. Points cloud acquired by the retail robot. (Color figure online)

3.2   Point Cloud Data Processing

Since the points cloud is very burdensome, we introduced a pre-processing phase
to clean it and make it lighter. This, in order to improve the performances of
the next phases. The first phase is "Remove Outliner Points", where the outlier
points are removed (i.e. anomalous values generated by the acquisition instrument, perhaps even deriving from a sampling error). We use a CloudCompare
opensource software filtering tool. Subsequently, in the second pre-processing
phase, the under-sampling of the cloud is carried out, maintaining a tradeoff
between the size of the cloud and the geometric definition of the elements. This
procedure can be performed in two ways: via CloudCompare with octree filtering, eliminating various points in the cloud (decimation); or via a MATLAB
function based on a grid. The problem is that in this second case, the subsampling generates new points, starting from interpolation of the original points
that fall into that grid. We have applied the first method for the implementation
of PointNet++, because we want to keep the reflectance information for each
point, which otherwise would be lost with the second approach. Instead, the
second method generates the cloud for the Machine Learning phase.

3.3   Point Cloud Objects Classification

As stated in the introduction, the classification of different types of elements
(i.e. counter, cash register, shelf, and so on) was made by comparing the three
different approaches. The first Machine Learning approach consists of three subsequent phases: feature extraction, feature selection and classification based, as
described in [22]. We extract 21 features and other five values that represent
the eigenvalues of the 2D and 3D covariance matrices for each point. Then, the
features selection phase allowed to use only the most significant features. We
have also tested the univariate and multivariate analysis methods as in [22].
Five state-of-art classifiers are evaluated: k-NN, Decision Tree (DT), Random

Forest (RF), SVM and Multilayer Perceptron. The second approach is based on Deep Learning and PointNet++ [16] network was trained to classify objects. Furthermore, we introduce a novel modified architecture, the so called Reflectance-Pointnet++. This network has been modified compared to the previous ones at the input information. In particular, it receives as input the Reflectance feature acquired by kaarta. In this way the network will learn much more discriminating features, based not only on the geometry of the objects but also on the type of material with which they are made. The PointNet++ was a combination of three principles type of layers: Sampling Layer, Grouping Layer and PointNet Layer. We modified this architecture to get in input also the reflectance informations, then we improved the PointNet Layer to combine both geometrical and reflectance informations. This layer is responsible for learning the features for the final classification.

The described classification methods are all point-based, i.e. we have a predicted class for every point. For this reason, we performed a post processing phase to transform the predicted results into an object-based classification. We have used a Winner Take All (WTA) approach. As first step, we can isolate the single objects from the test scene by using their bounding boxes previously calculated. Then, we calculate the classification percentage of each predicted class for each individual object. If the classification percentage exceeds a certain threshold, then we will associate that "winning" class with that object.

4   Results and Discussions

In this section, we present the experimental results obtained using our approach. Referring to the preliminary cleaning cloud procedure, the robot has initially acquired a total number of points cloud equals to 28.619.314 for the training phase, by reducing to 7.349.311 total points, after the procedure of points cloud cleaning. The total number of points cloud equals to 7.106.000 for the testing phase, by reducing to 1.918.123 total points, after the procedure of points cloud cleaning.

In a second step, we manually labelled the various objects in the scene using the CloudCompare software. In total we have segmented 113 different objects, classified into 13 different classes.

The dataset is very unbalanced on some classes of objects. This would lead to low accuracy performance in network training, so we decided to balance the dataset by performing a subsampling of the classes that had too many points. Based on the class with the smallest number of points, we decided to sub-sample the other classes randomly. In this way, we have a tradeoff between the maintenance of the geometry of the objects and the balancing of the classes. This phase also allows an improvement in training times for both Machine Learning classifiers and neural networks.

In the original project of PointNet++ there is a sampler that gives in input to the network a portion of 8192 points of a scene. The network was trained by using the ScanNet dataset, taking a sample of each training scene for each epoch. Instead, for the test, the sampler was moved through all the scenes of the test-set. In our case instead we have only one scene to use as training, but this scene is much bigger than those of the Scannet dataset. As a first step, we have divided our point cloud into two parts, splitting with 80–20% to create our own training and test sets. The splitting was made while still maintaining a good balance between the various classes of objects. The first change we have made to the original PointNet++ design was to improve the training approach. When we have performed some tests we inferred that using the sampler in a random way on the scenes, the training of the network was unbalanced only on the classes of points that were actually fed to the network. Smaller objects were often not selected by the sampler and therefore often the network could not predict these classes in the testing phase. So we ensured that the sampler moved across our entire training scene. In this way, we will always be sure that all classes will be used to train the network. In addition, this 8192 point sampler has been designed in such a way that at each epoch it will be positioned in different positions from the previous ones, giving a contribution of randomness of input that allows to improve the training performance of the network.

All test was performed by PyTorch framework and python 2.7. Different types of experiments were performed for finetuning the network's hyper-parameters. We compared:

- Batch size: 4, 8, 16, 32;
- Sampler size: 8192, 4096, 2048;
- Data Augmentation: random rotation;
- Optimizer: Adam with different learning rates.

In a first experiment, we considered 6 classes for the classification phase of the shelves and specifically the system has to classify the following objects: counter, cash register, pillar, fridge, shelf, and bracket (Fig. 1a).

6 classes	Precision	Recall	F1-score
Counter	0.85	0.85	0.85
Cash register	0.84	0.93	0.88
Pillar	0.77	0.80	0.78
Fridge	0.37	0.43	0.40
Shelf	0.49	0.37	0.43
Bracket	0.48	0.45	0.46
Overall	0.64	0.65	0.63

In a second experiment, in order to refine the classification procedure we considered 13 classes for the classification phase of the shelves and specifically the system has to classify the following objects: counter, cash register, pillar, low fridge, tall fridge, counter fruit, shelf, low shelf, bracket, secondary stack (sec-stack), secondary-promotional (sec-promo), secondary shelf (sec-shelf) and secondary table (sec-table). These classes are depicted with different colours in Fig. 1b.

13 classes	Precision	Recall	F1-score
Counter	0.46	0.34	0.39
Cash register	0.62	0.80	0.70
Pillar	0.73	0.80	0.76
Low fridge	0.16	0.18	0.17
Tall Fridge	0.34	0.34	0.34
Counter fruit	0.43	0.64	0.52
Shelf	0.24	0.25	0.25
Low shelf	0.35	0.38	0.36
Bracket	0.33	0.45	0.38
Sec-stack	0.10	0.12	0.11
Sec-promo	0.16	0.05	0.08
Sec-shelf	0.32	0.20	0.25
Sec-table	0.28	0.17	0.21
Overall	0.33	0.35	0.34

Since the individual samples are points, we compare the true class and the predicted class of each point. The first one estimates the performance that can be made globally on all points. The second one considers the points as part of an object (shelf, counter, etc.). In this case, each object is represented by points cloud enclosed in a previously defined bounding-box. Using the WTA method, we indicate the most common class predicted of points within the bounding-box as the predicted class of the object. We define object-based accuracy as the ratio between the correctly predicted object classes and the total number of objects (Tables 1 and 2).

Table 1. Classification results for six classes

Approach	Accuracy	Precision	Recall	F1-score	Instance acc.
Machine Learning	0.64	0.63	0.64	0.63	9/13
PointNet++ [16]	0.63	0.58	0.64	0.56	10/13
Reflectance-PointNet++	0.65	0.64	0.65	0.63	11/13

The recognition of the six classes is much higher than the recognition of the thirteen classes and the reflectance has slightly higher performance for classification.

Table 2. Classification results for thirteen classes

Approach	Accuracy	Precision	Recall	F1-score	Object based acc.
Machine Learning	0.36	0.34	0.36	0.34	15/22
PointNet++ [16]	0.37	0.33	0.37	0.33	11/22
Reflectance-PointNet++	0.38	0.33	0.35	0.34	16/22

5   Conclusion and Future Works

In this paper, we have described a retail robot that moves autonomously inside a store and gathers points cloud data for a semantic store mapping by kaarta Stencil. This retail robot combines the features of both Robotics and Artificial Intelligence. Three classification approach have been compared in order to achieve the best performances: a machine learning technique, PointNet++ and a novel Reflectance PointNet++ especially designed for this task. Experiments are performed in a real retail environment, which is an Italian supermarket, during business hours. A dataset has been built and made publicly available. The application of our approach yields good results in terms of precision, recall and F1-score and demonstrates the effectiveness of the proposed approach.

Further investigation will be devoted to extend our approach for detecting and counting objects in stores with also adding the RGB feature. The robot will detect whether shelves are empty or products are missing. It will create a point cloud map from the surroundings and into that we connect the store images from the robot's cameras. With this information, we can produce a 360 3D environment with the indoor position points. All daily operations are run inside the robot with its GPU powered units.

References

1. Capobianco, R., Serafin, J., Dichtl, J., Grisetti, G., Iocchi, L., Nardi, D.: A proposal for semantic map representation and evaluation. In: 2015 European Conference on Mobile Robots (ECMR), pp. 1–6. IEEE (2015)
2. Engelmann, F., Kontogianni, T., Schult, J., Leibe, B.: Know what your neighbors do: 3D semantic segmentation of point clouds. In: Proceedings of the European Conference on Computer Vision (ECCV) (2018)
3. Goerke, N., Braun, S.: Building semantic annotated maps by mobile robots. In: Proceedings of the Conference Towards Autonomous Robotic Systems, pp. 149–156 (2009)
4. Günther, M., Wiemann, T., Albrecht, S., Hertzberg, J.: Building semantic object maps from sparse and noisy 3D data. In: 2013 IEEE/RSJ International Conference on Intelligent Robots and Systems, pp. 2228–2233. IEEE (2013)
5. Landrieu, L., Simonovsky, M.: Large-scale point cloud semantic segmentation with superpoint graphs. In: Proceedings of the IEEE Conference on Computer Vision and Pattern Recognition, pp. 4558–4567 (2018)

6. Liciotti, D., Paolanti, M., Pietrini, R., Frontoni, E., Zingaretti, P.: Convolutional networks for semantic heads segmentation using top-view depth data in crowded environment. In: 2018 24th International Conference on Pattern Recognition (ICPR), pp. 1384–1389. IEEE (2018)
7. Mozos, O.M., Mizutani, H., Kurazume, R., Hasegawa, T.: Categorization of indoor places using the kinect sensor. Sensors 12(5), 6695–6711 (2012)
8. Nüchter, A., Wulf, O., Lingemann, K., Hertzberg, J., Wagner, B., Surmann, H.: 3D mapping with semantic knowledge. In: Bredenfeld, A., Jacoff, A., Noda, I., Takahashi, Y. (eds.) RoboCup 2005. LNCS (LNAI), vol. 4020, pp. 335–346. Springer, Heidelberg (2006). https://doi.org/10.1007/11780519_30
9. Paolanti, M., Romeo, L., Martini, M., Mancini, A., Frontoni, E., Zingaretti, P.: Robotic retail surveying by deep learning visual and textual data. Robot. Auton. Syst. 118, 179–188 (2019)
10. Paolanti, M., Frontoni, E., Mancini, A., Pierdicca, R., Zingaretti, P.: Automatic classification for anti mixup events in advanced manufacturing system. In: ASME 2015 International Design Engineering Technical Conferences and Computers and Information in Engineering Conference, p. V009T07A061. American Society of Mechanical Engineers (2015)
11. Paolanti, M., Liciotti, D., Pietrini, R., Mancini, A., Frontoni, E.: Modelling and forecasting customer navigation in intelligent retail environments. J. Intell. Robot. Syst. 91(2), 165–180 (2018)
12. Paolanti, M., Romeo, L., Felicetti, A., Mancini, A., Frontoni, E., Loncarski, J.: Machine learning approach for predictive maintenance in industry 4.0. In: 2018 14th IEEE/ASME International Conference on Mechatronic and Embedded Systems and Applications (MESA), pp. 1–6. IEEE (2018)
13. Paolanti, M., Sturari, M., Mancini, A., Zingaretti, P., Frontoni, E.: Mobile robot for retail surveying and inventory using visual and textual analysis of monocular pictures based on deep learning. In: 2017 European Conference on Mobile Robots (ECMR), pp. 1–6. IEEE (2017)
14. Pierdicca, R., Malinverni, E., Piccinini, F., Paolanti, M., Felicetti, A., Zingaretti, P.: Deep convolutional neural network for automatic detection of damaged photovoltaic cells. In: International Archives of the Photogrammetry, Remote Sensing & Spatial Information Sciences, vol. 42, no. 2 (2018)
15. Qi, C.R., Su, H., Mo, K., Guibas, L.J.: PointNet: deep learning on point sets for 3d classification and segmentation. In: Proceedings of the IEEE Conference on Computer Vision and Pattern Recognition, pp. 652–660 (2017)
16. Qi, C.R., Yi, L., Su, H., Guibas, L.J.: PointNet++: deep hierarchical feature learning on point sets in a metric space. In: Advances in Neural Information Processing Systems, pp. 5099–5108 (2017)
17. Ranganathan, A., Dellaert, F.: Semantic modeling of places using objects. In: Proceedings of the 2007 Robotics: Science and Systems Conference, vol. 3, pp. 27–30. Georgia Institute of Technology (2007)
18. Rusu, R.B., Marton, Z.C., Blodow, N., Dolha, M., Beetz, M.: Towards 3D point cloud based object maps for household environments. Robot. Auton. Syst. 56(11), 927–941 (2008)
19. Rusu, R.B., Marton, Z.C., Blodow, N., Holzbach, A., Beetz, M.: Model-based and learned semantic object labeling in 3D point cloud maps of kitchen environments. In: 2009 IEEE/RSJ International Conference on Intelligent Robots and Systems, pp. 3601–3608. IEEE (2009)
20. Sturari, M., et al.: Robust and affordable retail customer profiling by vision and radio beacon sensor fusion. Pattern Recogn. Lett. 81, 30–40 (2016)

21. Trevor, A.J., Rogers, J.G., Nieto-Granda, C., Christensen, H.I.: Tables, counters, and shelves: semantic mapping of surfaces in 3D. Georgia Institute of Technology (2010)
22. Weinmann, M., Jutzi, B., Hinz, S., Mallet, C.: Semantic point cloud interpretation based on optimal neighborhoods, relevant features and efficient classifiers. ISPRS J. Photogram. Remote Sens. **105**, 286–304 (2015)

Collecting Retail Data Using a Deep Learning Identification Experience

Salvatore La Porta[1]([✉]), Fabrizio Marconi[1], and Isabella Lazzini[2]

[1] JEF Srl, Civitanova Marche, Italy
{salvatore.laporta,fabrizio.marconi}@jef.it
[2] Consumer Business Group Italia, Huawei, Milan, Italy
isabella.lazzini@huawei.com

Abstract. The aim of the paper is to present a part of an architecture realized by Huawei, that propose the first Christmas tree endowed with artificial intelligence. Its ability is to identify facial expressions from images acquired by a mobile application and then recognize the sentiment of the subject. So, basing on the prevailing sentiment the tree lights up itself with different special effects. Our task in the project was testing the performances of the neural networks employed in the mobile application for the recognition of facial emotion. We used a convolutional neural networks model-based and created a purposely dedicated dataset of images for testing the recognition performances.

Keywords: Facial emotion recognition · Deep learning ·
Convolutional neural networks · Sentiment analysis

1 Introduction

Over the past decades the detection of facial emotions received an ever increasing interest. Since recognizing the expressions of faces is an important aspect in social communication, studies concerning the automatic recognition of emotions are recently becoming subject of numerous researches. These studies mainly concern the commercial sphere, where it is essential for sales to understand the general feeling. [11,16,19]. It is possible to understand the feeling of people, as for example joy, unhappiness and anger, not only the tone of voice, but above all observing the expressions of the face [8]. The rapid development of technologies based on artificial intelligence, such as human-machine interaction, virtual reality, augmented reality and sentiment analysis have allowed an increase in automatic face recognition approaches [1,13,15,21,22]. However, in literature there are conventional methods applied to face recognize, as for example face region detection and geometrical features extraction [5], appearance features [6] or a combination of them [4]. The relationships between the components of the face are used to create a vector of functionality, in order to detect the geometric characteristics. The approaches used for the extraction of aesthetic characteristics are based not only on the entire face, but also take into consideration different

M. Cristani et al. (Eds.): ICIAP 2019 Workshops, LNCS 11808, pp. 275–284, 2019.
https://doi.org/10.1007/978-3-030-30754-7_28

regions of the face that contain different information. Hybrid approaches that combine geometric and appearance characteristics are intended to overcome any weakness in the two methods.

Recently, methods based on deep learning have been used in combination with traditional ones [18,23]. Compared with machine learning and feature-based approaches [14,17], their advantage is to really exploit complex nonlinear functions, learn representations of distributed and hierarchical features, and employ both labeled and unlabeled data [12,25]. Different are approaches based on deep learning, but the most popular is the Convolutional Neural Network (CNN) [7,9]. CNNs are not very recent, in fact was introduced thirty years ago, but only recently they have been widely used in application concerning image classification issues [2,20].

In fact, thanks to an increase in the computing power and to the optimization of the algorithms used to train the models, the very high number of parameters of the CNN networks is no longer a limiting factor for their application in real contexts, also considering the need for classify an ever-increasing amount of data. There are currently many problems with image classification using CNNs: object recognition, facial recognition, facial expression recognition and more. In models that use CNN, the input image is processed by a collection of filters in the convolution layers that provide in output a map of characteristics. The last layer of the network is completely connected and classifies the facial expression in a particular class.

In this paper we present a part of the overall project that, departing from facial emotions of images acquired and elaborated by a mobile application, light up a smart tree with different lights and colors according to the prevalent sentiment. Our task consisted of developing and testing a convolutional neural network to correctly recognize the sentiment of people that use the application. Moreover, we have collected a purposely created dataset of images to evaluate the performance of the system.

The CNN network we used is based on a modified CNN model [10], in which Local Binary Patterns (LBPs) were added to the implementation, which were initially used to classify image textures. The authors are the first to use LBP functions as input for CNN networks, with the aim of improving performance compared to models consisting only of RGB images. The idea on which this approach is based is to simplify the initial problem by eliminating the confounding factors from the input images, taking into account changes in image illumination. This, with the aim of reducing the amount of data required to effectively train deep CNN models.

The purpose of the entire project was to create a smart Christmas tree, adding artificial intelligence, installed in the most modern district of the city of Milan, the CityLife shopping district. The tree smartly changes its lighting colors, taking into account the prevailing feeling of the population, which uses the application.

The use of an architecture able to identify and show the emotions of people is important not only concerning the visual impact and the enjoyment, but especially for attractive purposes. In other words, the idea of a Christmas tree that lights up according to the feelings of different people has the task not only to fascinate and enjoy, but above all for a shopping center, to attract the greatest number of shoppers. In the big city of shopping, location where the smart tree has been installed, the collection of this great quantity of data is very important for future marketing research that have the aim to attract people to purchase. In fact, to know the possible consumer allows to also guide the sales.

2 Materials and Methods

The first Christmas tree with artificial intelligence that can recognize emotions and change color based on people's sentiment was proposed by Huawei. This smart tree was installed inside the CityLife Shopping District of Milan, in Piazza Tre Torri. This location represents the largest urban commercial district in Italy and is the symbol of technological innovation and design. The installation concerns the Christmas period and visitors can experience Huawei technology using three different methods: (i) taking a photo using the new Huawei Mate 20 Pro model provided by some Christmas elves in Piazza Tre Torri, (ii) using advertising totems in the City Shopping District; and (iii) at home, thanks to the "Take your happiness" application.

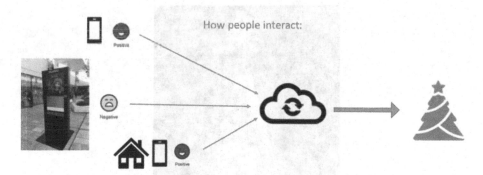

Fig. 1. Interaction of people with the system: (i) by taking a photo using the new model Huawei Mate 20 Pro; (ii) by using the advertising totems in the CityLife Shopping District; (iii) at home, thanks to a mobile application.

Figure 1 represents the implemented system, where during the Christmas season, people will be able to interact with the system, using three different methodologies:

- by taking a photo using the new model Huawei Mate 20 Pro,
- by using the advertising totems in the CityLife Shopping District;
- or at home, thanks to a mobile application.

All the pictures are sent to a Cloud service developed by Huawei where this service after having analysed the crowd identifies the predominant emotion of the people. In other words, every day, all the sentiments will be sent to the technological heart of the tree that, thanks to the Mate 20 Pro dual Artificial Intelligence, analyses the crowd identifying the emotions of the people, attributes one of the four colors available and light up accordingly. Every 15 min, therefore, the tree will show, with charming plays of colored light, the main sentiment detected by the shots received.

The general architecture is very simple, on the Huawei Mate 20 Pro phone there is kirin 980, a processor dedicated to artificial intelligence. An android application has been developed, that allows to take a selfie and by implementing the CNN-based model it estimates the sentiment of the users and transmits data to a server. This data have been aggregated by a server and, considering established time intervals, sends a command on a TCP socket to a lighting control unit which colors the led of the tree on the base of the prevailing emotion.

In order to evaluate the performances of the implemented system for the recognition of facial expression, the CNN was tested on a dataset of 152 images collected within our university. The sentiment is subdivided into four classes (four "Final Emotion"): two positives, happy and surprise, one negative, angry, and finally one neutral.

Fig. 2. First example of Christmas tree illuminated by an emotion (Color figure online)

Fig. 3. Second example of Christmas tree illuminated by an emotion (Color figure online)

The Figs. 2 and 3 show the special effects of the real installation, considering an example of two different color according the most experienced sentiment at a given moment.

2.1 Workflow Description

In this section we describe the workflow model of the implemented process. First, a CNN network takes in input Local Binary Patterns (LBP), that were originally developed for image texture classification. It is the first work that uses LBP functions as input to CNN networks, with the aim to improve the performances compared to models that are trained only using RGB images. This choice aims at simplifying the problem, with particular attention to variations in image illumination and for reducing the amount of data required to effectively train deep CNN models. During the preprocessing phase, the images are converted into gray scale and cropped to the region of the face, where faces are in-plane aligned. Each face image is processed as follows: (i) applying LBP encoding to the pixels using different values for the LBP radius parameter and then image intensity values to one of 256 LBP code values. So, we map these values to a 3D metric space and visualized as RGB colors. The original RGB images, along with the mapped code images, are then used to train multiple, separate CNN models to predict several emotion classes. We tested 4 different existing architectures, pretrained on ImageNet [3] dataset:

- VGG16 [24];
- VGG16-2048;
- VGG16-4096;
- GoogleNet [26].

For the final classification we realized a weighted average over the outputs of the network ensemble considering the predicted emotion class to be the one with the maximum average probability.

Figure 4 schematically shows that the architecture uses the combination of the output obtained from different implemented networks to establish the final sentiment ("Final Emotion"). Combining the results of different networks the system appear more robust since it overcomes possible errors deriving from a single incorrect classification.

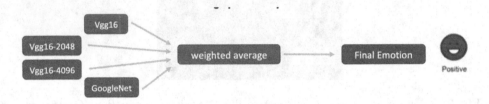

Fig. 4. Scheme of the implemented system.

Figure 5 schematically shows how, using kirin 980, a processor dedicated to artificial intelligence, the system based on the prevailing sentiment colors the Christmas tree on the shopping city. If as in the example, the system has in output positive as higher percentage sentiment, the overall sentiment will be positive and the tree will be colored with a color representative of that emotion.

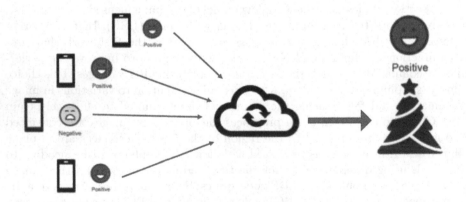

Fig. 5. Scheme of sentiment combination. (Color figure online)

3   Experimental Results

During the experimental procedure, an ad hoc dataset was used to verify the performance in a real case of the implemented CNN network. Figures 6, 7, 8 and 9 show some examples of different sentiment extracted from our dataset and the symbols indicate if the sentiment was correctly recognized (green tick icons show a correct classification) or not (red cross icons show a wrong classification).

Fig. 6. Examples of happy sentiment (Color figure online)

Fig. 7. Examples of angry sentiment (Color figure online)

Fig. 8. Examples of surprise sentiment (Color figure online)

Fig. 9. Examples of neutral sentiment (Color figure online)

Table 1. Results of sentiment classification by CNN

Sentiment	Images	Correct	Accuracy (%)
Happy	49	43	87.75%
Angry	26	14	53.84%
Surprise	21	11	52.38%
Neutral	56	42	75.00%

Observing the results in Table 1 we can note that considering "happy" and "neutral" sentiment, we obtained the best performances of recognition. While for "angry" and "surprise" sentiment, the results are not so good, in fact they appear more ambiguous and difficult to recognize.

In Table 1, in the first column are listed all the sentiment analyzed; in the second column are specified all the available images for each sentiment, and in the third the number of images correctly classified. In the last column, the value of the accuracy shows that the "happy" sentiment has a high rate of recognition corresponding to 87.75%.

4   Conclusion

The recognition of facial expressions is having a great interest particularly in the last decades, this is due to the development of approaches based on artificial intelligence methods and techniques that use machine learning approaches such as deep learning. In this ambit, the aim of our work is to create a mobile application able to add intelligence and make more attractive the shopping experience. The idea is to add intelligence to a Christmas tree installed in the CityLife shopping district of Milan, implementing an application that changes the color of the lighting basing on the sentiment of people that use the app. The app is able to automatically recognize the sentiment of people through the face detection analysis. The system that uses convolutional neural networks, an approach based on deep learning, consists of three sequences: face and facial features detection, features extraction and sentiment classification. Experimental results on a purposely created dataset gave encouraging results, mostly in the recognition of "happy" sentiment, which proved to be unambiguous.

In future our aim is to assure good performances also for other kinds of sentiment, better tuning the chosen network.

References

1. Bekele, M.K., Pierdicca, R., Frontoni, E., Malinverni, E.S., Gain, J.: A survey of augmented, virtual, and mixed reality for cultural heritage. J. Comput. Cult. Heritage (JOCCH) **11**(2), 7 (2018)
2. Cai, G., Xia, B.: Convolutional neural networks for multimedia sentiment analysis. In: Li, J., Ji, H., Zhao, D., Feng, Y. (eds.) NLPCC 2015. LNCS (LNAI), vol. 9362, pp. 159–167. Springer, Cham (2015). https://doi.org/10.1007/978-3-319-25207-0_14
3. Deng, J., Dong, W., Socher, R., Li, L.J., Li, K., Fei-Fei, L.: Imagenet: a large-scale hierarchical image database. In: 2009 IEEE Conference on Computer Vision and Pattern Recognition, pp. 248–255. IEEE (2009)
4. Ghimire, D., Jeong, S., Lee, J., Park, S.H.: Facial expression recognition based on local region specific features and support vector machines. Multimedia Tools Appl. **76**(6), 7803–7821 (2017)
5. Ghimire, D., Lee, J.: Geometric feature-based facial expression recognition in image sequences using multi-class adaboost and support vector machines. Sensors **13**(6), 7714–7734 (2013)
6. Happy, S., George, A., Routray, A.: A real time facial expression classification system using local binary patterns. In: 2012 4th International Conference on Intelligent Human Computer Interaction (IHCI), pp. 1–5. IEEE (2012)
7. Kim, Y.: Convolutional neural networks for sentence classification. arXiv preprint arXiv:1408.5882 (2014)
8. Ko, B.: A brief review of facial emotion recognition based on visual information. Sensors **18**(2), 401 (2018)
9. LeCun, Y., et al.: Backpropagation applied to handwritten zip code recognition. Neural Comput. **1**(4), 541–551 (1989)
10. Levi, G., Hassner, T.: Emotion recognition in the wild via convolutional neural networks and mapped binary patterns. In: Proceedings of the 2015 ACM on International Conference on Multimodal Interaction, pp. 503–510. ACM (2015)
11. Liciotti, D., Paolanti, M., Frontoni, E., Zingaretti, P.: People detection and tracking from an RGB-D camera in top-view configuration: review of challenges and applications. In: Battiato, S., Farinella, G.M., Leo, M., Gallo, G. (eds.) ICIAP 2017. LNCS, vol. 10590, pp. 207–218. Springer, Cham (2017). https://doi.org/10.1007/978-3-319-70742-6_20
12. Liciotti, D., Paolanti, M., Pietrini, R., Frontoni, E., Zingaretti, P.: Convolutional networks for semantic heads segmentation using top-view depth data in crowded environment. In: 2018 24th International Conference on Pattern Recognition (ICPR), pp. 1384–1389. IEEE (2018)
13. Naspetti, S., Pierdicca, R., Mandolesi, S., Paolanti, M., Frontoni, E., Zanoli, R.: Automatic analysis of eye-tracking data for augmented reality applications: a prospective outlook. In: De Paolis, L.T., Mongelli, A. (eds.) AVR 2016. LNCS, vol. 9769, pp. 217–230. Springer, Cham (2016). https://doi.org/10.1007/978-3-319-40651-0_17

14. Paolanti, M., Frontoni, E., Mancini, A., Pierdicca, R., Zingaretti, P.: Automatic classification for anti mixup events in advanced manufacturing system. In: ASME 2015 International Design Engineering Technical Conferences and Computers and Information in Engineering Conference, p. V009T07A061. American Society of Mechanical Engineers (2015)
15. Paolanti, M., Kaiser, C., Schallner, R., Frontoni, E., Zingaretti, P.: Visual and textual sentiment analysis of brand-related social media pictures using deep convolutional neural networks. In: Battiato, S., Gallo, G., Schettini, R., Stanco, F. (eds.) ICIAP 2017. LNCS, vol. 10484, pp. 402–413. Springer, Cham (2017). https://doi.org/10.1007/978-3-319-68560-1_36
16. Paolanti, M., Liciotti, D., Pietrini, R., Mancini, A., Frontoni, E.: Modelling and forecasting customer navigation in intelligent retail environments. J. Intell. Robot. Syst. **91**(2), 165–180 (2018)
17. Paolanti, M., Romeo, L., Felicetti, A., Mancini, A., Frontoni, E., Loncarski, J.: Machine learning approach for predictive maintenance in industry 4.0. In: 2018 14th IEEE/ASME International Conference on Mechatronic and Embedded Systems and Applications (MESA), pp. 1–6. IEEE (2018)
18. Paolanti, M., Romeo, L., Martini, M., Mancini, A., Frontoni, E., Zingaretti, P.: Robotic retail surveying by deep learning visual and textual data. Robot. Auton. Syst. **118**, 179–188 (2019)
19. Paolanti, M., Sturari, M., Mancini, A., Zingaretti, P., Frontoni, E.: Mobile robot for retail surveying and inventory using visual and textual analysis of monocular pictures based on deep learning. In: 2017 European Conference on Mobile Robots (ECMR), pp. 1–6. IEEE (2017)
20. Pierdicca, R., Malinverni, E., Piccinini, F., Paolanti, M., Felicetti, A., Zingaretti, P.: Deep convolutional neural network for automatic detection of damaged photovoltaic cells. In: International Archives of the Photogrammetry, Remote Sensing & Spatial Information Sciences, vol. 42, no. 2 (2018)
21. Pierdicca, R., Frontoni, E., Pollini, R., Trani, M., Verdini, L.: The use of augmented reality glasses for the application in Industry 4.0. In: De Paolis, L.T., Bourdot, P., Mongelli, A. (eds.) AVR 2017. LNCS, vol. 10324, pp. 389–401. Springer, Cham (2017). https://doi.org/10.1007/978-3-319-60922-5_30
22. Pierdicca, R., Paolanti, M., Frontoni, E.: eTourism: ICT and its role for tourism management. J. Hosp. Tour. Technol. **10**(1), 90–106 (2019)
23. Schmidhuber, J.: Deep learning in neural networks: an overview. Neural Netw. **61**, 85–117 (2015)
24. Simonyan, K., Zisserman, A.: Very deep convolutional networks for large-scale image recognition. arXiv preprint arXiv:1409.1556 (2014)
25. Sturari, M., Paolanti, M., Frontoni, E., Mancini, A., Zingaretti, P.: Robotic platform for deep change detection for rail safety and security. In: 2017 European Conference on Mobile Robots (ECMR), pp. 1–6. IEEE (2017)
26. Szegedy, C., et al.: Going deeper with convolutions. In: Proceedings of the IEEE Conference on Computer Vision and Pattern Recognition, pp. 1–9 (2015)

A Large Scale Trajectory Dataset
for Shopper Behaviour Understanding

Patrizia Gabellini, Mauro D'Aloisio, Matteo Fabiani, and Valerio Placidi(✉)

Grottini Lab S.R.L., Via Santa Maria in Potenza, 62017 Porto Recanati, Italy
patrizia.gabellini@grottinicommunication.com,
{mauro.daloisio,matteo.fabiani,valerio.placidi}@grottinilab.com
http://www.grottinilab.com

Abstract. In intelligent retail environment, Ultra Wideband (UWB) is suitable for applications where the positioning accuracy is a critical parameter. This technology provides the use of several UWB antennas properly positioned inside a predetermined area and powered battery tags free to move inside the area. This has been used to deploy a Real Time Locating System (RTLS), which gives complete oversight of the customers and employees in the store and improves the customer experience. In this paper, it is described a tracking system based on UWB technology. The installation, in stores in Germany and Indonesia became the basis for a trajectory dataset and results presented in this paper based on a two-year experience that measured 10.4 million shoppers. Through the analysis of the collected tracking data, it allows to derive several information on the shoppers behaviour inside a store. Behaviours that concern flows of walking, most visited areas inside the space dedicated to the shopping and average travel times. The collection of this great quantity of data is very important for future marketing research that have the aim to attract people to purchase.

Keywords: Ultra-Wide Band · RTLS ·
Shopper behaviour understanding · Intelligent retail environment

1 Introduction

The aim to apply artificial intelligence to the shopping centres is gaining increasing importance, as a consequent of the augmented complexity of retail environments and in order to raise awareness and loyalty of customers [12]. In this context, taking into account the latest advances on Computer vision and image understanding, several applications have developed for improving and personalising shopping experience [11,19,20]. This aspect is strictly related with the daily use of technology in every sector of everyday life. Almost all of the population has a smart phones and use its for several purposes and so they are familiar with technology. From the point of view of a smart store or multi-store, the aspect we want to investigate is the possibility of using smart devices and systems that

M. Cristani et al. (Eds.): ICIAP 2019 Workshops, LNCS 11808, pp. 285–295, 2019.
https://doi.org/10.1007/978-3-030-30754-7_29

provide different services to customers thanks to the intelligence the device is equipped with. An application that guarantees an intelligent service to the customer is for example their localization and tracking. The system that instantly knows their position and movement can provide to the customer real time information about discounted products, latest arrivals products, fashionable products and so on. Another important aspect that an intelligent device must have is its non-invasiveness, in the sense that interactions with customers must be such that the system adapts to users' needs without making any request to the user. The improvement of technologies like sensors, actuators and processing units that are ever less expensive and occupy ever less space allowed the developments of these applications.

Moreover, mainly in last decades the experience of the shopping is considerably changed. Just think that many years ago, the store was locations where the shoppers went only for searching and buying products they needed [17]. Now the situation is very different since the store is a place where people spend their time, can test products in real time and can know which is the current trends. This in particular occurs in a shopping center or multi-store that is the suitable location for product trying, seeing, touching, professional consulting and ambience shopping [16].

The main idea is to plan the paths of customers in a store starting from a design, configuration, structuring the store and coming to establish the correct position of products on the shelves. This approach concerns not only big shopping centres or multi-store but also small stores, taking into account the different challenges that involve them [4,5,18]. Different activities and aspects involve the operations as for example, sales, costumer services and merchandises, inventory and warehouse management and visual merchandising. This last is to attract, push and drive a customer to buy a particular product without being invasive.

Yamabe et al. [21] have before analyzed the behaviour of customers influencing them with economic incentives, adjusting the incentive mechanisms and how this modify their behaviour. Other similar works are [6,15].

An important aspect to be considered when the shopper behaviour is analyzed is the shopping time, about this the work [22] studied the relation between shopping time and buying. The authors divide the time that a customer use for the shopping activity and for the enjoyment. They use a phone-based system to perceive the shopping activities while they monitor the permanence time in the store.

The behaviour of customers while acting on their buying decision through promotional strategies is analyzed in another work [10]. In contrast to a previous approach, they make use of a WLAN system for determining which is the latest position of customers in the store with the aim to establish the interest in specific products [1] and then promote customized marketing strategies. To increase the number of visitors in the stores, they use a combination of NFC and WLAN system. In this work, it is described an UWB (Ultra-Wide Band) technology based system able to monitor the trajectories of customers in stores and send tracking data to a cloud server. Two UWB systems will be compared for indoor localization and will be described a software for data collection and upload via internet. The installation, in stores in Germany and Indonesia, became the basis for a trajectory dataset and results presented in this paper based on a two-year experience that measured 10.4 million shoppers. Through the analysis of the collected tracking data, it is possible to derive several information on the shoppers behaviour inside a store. Behaviours that concern flows of walking, most visited areas inside the space dedicated to the shopping and average travel times.

To briefly summarize, the main contributions of this work are: (i) solutions, for real retail environments with a great variability in data acquired, derived from a large experience over 10.4 million shoppers observed in two years in different types of stores and in different countries; (ii) a challenging new dataset of trajectories for the deep understanding of shopper behaviours that is publicly available to the scientific community for testing and comparing different approaches; (iii) statistical analysis different data collection for different store layout.

The remainder of the paper is organized as follows. In following Sect. 2 related works and methods for indoor localization and tracking are presented. Moreover the most important technologies used for localization and tracking system are summarized. Section 3 describe in detail the navigation system object of this work. The experimental results are presented in Sect. 4. Section 5 discusses the results, proposes some future developments and concludes the paper.

2   Localization Technique: A Literature Review

A localization system has to meet several performance criteria that according to [3] can be classified in different areas. They are:

- **Accuracy** is defined as the mean error distance between the estimated location and real location, and is the most important requirement for a positioning system. For a localization system, higher is the value of accuracy better are the performances.
- **Responsiveness** indicates how quickly the position of an object that is moving is updated. When a target is quickly moving, the updating must be fast.
- **Coverage** that can be local, scalable and global is strictly related to the accuracy and perform the network coverage for a specific area. This parameter is important to evaluate the performances of a positioning system and indicate the size of the considered region.
- **Adaptiveness** is the ability of a localization system to adapt itself when changes in the environment occur. A system is efficient when it is able to give a correct position without calibration even when the environment changes.
- **Scalability** is an important characteristic when a system is projected since this means that the system correctly works with requests of higher positions and wider coverage. A system to be scalable has to manage also a large number of variables.

- **Complexity** indirectly influences the performances of a positioning system as the complexity of the algorithms used represents a problem to be considered. Complexity and accuracy are two criteria that most influence the overall cost of the system.

However considering the study conducted in 2008 by the National Institute of Standards and Technology (NIST)[1], that reveals which are the most important features that a localization system must have, we can say that they are summarized as follows: the accuracy of positioning must have near 1 meter; training not required on site; functioning on all buildings; stability when structural changes occurs and obviously limited costs.

Taking into account several environments and locations, in the work [7], the authors synthesize which are the main problem and requirements for an indoor positioning system and they classify techniques on the base of their use. In several works proposed in the last years [14], that present indoor localization techniques different technologies have been analyzed: Global positioning system (GPS), Radio-Frequency IDentification (RFID), cellular based, WLAN based, Bluetooth, Ultra-Wide Band (UWB) and many more. One of the main and well-known positioning system is GPS. But one of the biggest problems with this technology is that it can not be used in indoor environments due to a lack of GPS signal. Moreover other problem is that the hardware is too expensive [23]. However, also in particular outdoor condition, GPS is not useful as for example in urban canyons for the lack of signal and where the position is not univocally determined.

Radio-Frequency IDentification (RFID) technology is usually used to store and retrieve data through an electromagnetic transmission sent to a RF compatible integrated circuit and now is considered as a tool to increase processes of data handling. This technology provides many basic components and has a passive or active role [14].

System based on cellular are mainly used to detect the location of user for outdoor applications. This method has a very low accuracy and depends on the dimension of cell. For indoor localization this kind of technology could be used if the building has different base stations or at least one base station with a strong RSS signal received from indoor mobile client.

In the recent years, Wireless Local Area Network (WLAN) has become a technology very popular in public hotspots and corporate locations. However for positioning applications this technology is not suitable since a typical WLAN that uses RSS signal has a very low accuracy and so it does not satisfy the performance criteria, and has also an updating range of a few seconds.

If we compare WLAn and Bluetooth technology, we obtain that this last has a lower gross bit rate and the range is shorter. Most phones and personal digital assistants (PDA) has Bluetooth technology and each device has a unique ID. In order to use Bluetooth technology, all devices must have Bluetooth signal actives, but not always this occurs. The technology used in this work is Ultra

---

[1] www.nist.gov, last accessed: March 7, 2016.

Wide Band (UWB), a radio frequency technology for short range (less than 1 ns), high-bandwidth communication with a low duty cycle and has the properties of multipath resistance. The advantages of this technology have been presented in the work of [8].

While RFID systems use single bands of radio spectrum, UWB at the same time transmit signals on multiple bands of frequencies (from 3.1 to 10.6 GHz). UWB signals are transmitted with a shorter duration than RFID, consuming less power and can operate in a wider area of the radio spectrum. Since UWB and RFID are different from the point of view of signal type and radio spectrum can operate without interference in the same area. A great advantage of UWB signal is that it can pass through walls, devices and clothes without interferences. The high value of accuracy of UWB in indoor environment (near to 20 cm) it makes that this technology is widely used for indoor application and applications that require high precision in real time for 2-D and 3-D localization, accuracy that can not be obtained using other conventional technologies (RFID, WLAN and others). An example of UWB application is the work of [9], employed in indoor tracking and location. Detecting the target position in a wireless system concerns the set of location information from radio signals that travel between the target and a number of reference nodes. For this purpose, time-based positioning technique determines travel times of signals among nodes and UWB technology is a very useful tool for wireless positioning thanks to its high resolution in the time domain.

3   System Overview

In this section, we describe the implemented architecture that developing and testing a system based on UWB technology, able to monitor the path of customers in stores and send the tracking data collected to a cloud server. Collected data have been processed and stored in a database and allow to know useful information about the behaviour of consumer during their visit in a store.

3.1   RTLS Technology and Localization and Tracking System

UWB technology has been used to deploy a Real Time Locating System (RTLS), in order to collect real time localization data from shopping carts and baskets. Tests performed in the store achieved an accuracy in the position measurement of 20 cm in terms of indoor positioning and due to a smart power management provides a high autonomy for the battery-powered tags. The UWB radio module DWM1000 advent (IEEE802.15.4-2011 UWB compliant) by decaWAVE, at a low price (10$ per 1000 unit), has given a great number of tracking solutions, developed by European companies.

The trajectories of store visitors are collected with information concerning attraction time in front of a shelf/category, average walking, interaction with the products on the shelves, all useful information for the retailers since they help to better know the customer and then to improve the shopping experience. The

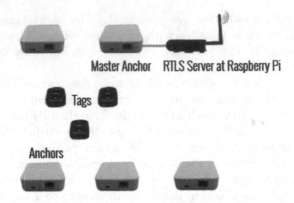

Fig. 1. Sewio UWB kit

parameters can be measured are: Time of arrival (ToA), Direction of Arrival (DoA), and the Received Signal Strength (RSS). These information are very important, because they indicate the way in which the consumer interacts with the store, which is the most visited zone, if there are some problems to find a product and which are the most efficient policies put in place for marketing, communication and space planning [2].

Figure 2 shows a scheme of the store with represented the components of Sewio kit.

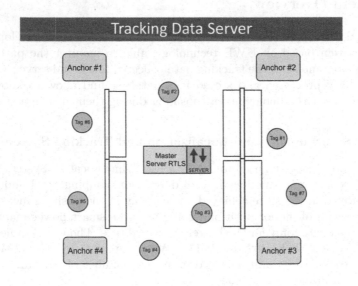

Fig. 2. System overview

The tracking system adopted consists of different module which are part of Sewio kit composed of 4 anchor, 1 master, 4 battery-powered tags and a Raspberry to elaborate 3D data for the tracking Fig. 1. Below are described the components:

- **Anchors** are static devices, antennas, that have known positions and placed on the ceiling of the store. They are positioned in order to represent a homogeneous grid that cover all the store. The anchors receive signals from the tags and forward this data (timestamps of received signals and tags related information such as ID and battery level) to the RTLS server. They are connected and powered through a PoE switch via Ethernet to the RTLS server. The anchors must share the same time and one of anchor is selected as master anchor to synchronize them.
- **Tags** are mobile devices that have to tracked. Using a specified transmission rate they send data to the anchors and also a broadcast message that is received by the anchors in a communication system. They have an accelerometer for the movement detection this for increase the lifetime of battery. In fact, in this way data are sent only when the tags overcome a chosen and also adaptable threshold.
- **RTLS Server** gathers data coming from the anchors, estimates 3D position of tags and then send all this information to the cloud server. Then Through a multilateration, a Time Difference of Arrival (TDOA) algorithm that only considers timestamps that simultaneously coming from at least three anchors, the tag position is estimated. The RTLS Server sends localization data on a TCP/IP socket. A software is developed to collect the information:
  - master ID;
  - tag ID;
  - 3D coordinates position (x, y, z);
  - battery level of the tag and timing information (such as tracking system and RTLS server timestamp).

3.2 Trajectories Dataset

In this work, we provided the first study on understanding shoppers' behaviours using UWB technology. As discussed in Sect. 1, we have collected a huge dataset of trajectories in different stores with different layout: one in Indonesia and two in Germany. An unique identification code (id) is associated with each subject that enters the store and this association ends when the subject exits from the store. The stores in which these trajectories are collected are:

- *Indonesia*: period of about six months (from 01 January 2019 to 06 June 2019) and a time slot from 7:00 to 21:59. Users data collected correspond to 1466367 id_people (with a mean value of 10327 each day).
- *Germany_store 1*: period of about six months (from 01 February 2019 to 30 June 2019) and a time slot from 7:00 to 20:59. Users data collected correspond to 69288 id_people (with a mean value of 468 each day).

– *Germany_store 2*: period of about six months (from 14 January 2019 to 30 June 2019) and a time slot from 7:00 to 20:59. Users data collected correspond to 181339 id_people (with a mean value of 1305 each day).

4   Experimental Results

In this section, we present some statistical evaluation on these trajectories in the stores target.

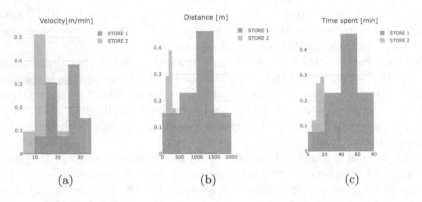

(a)   (b)   (c)

Fig. 3. Representation of the metrics used for the analysis of consumer behavior in two stores.

The Fig. 3 shows the values for different metrics used to study the behaviour of the shopper in different stores. In the first figure, we evaluate how fast the subject moves in the store, considering the velocity as the distance traveled divided by the time ($velocity = Distance/Time$). The second figure only considers the travelled distance in meters and finally, the last figure considers the permanence time in minutes. These indicators are important for the store staff to understand the shoppers behaviour, in order to evaluate their trade and marketing policy.

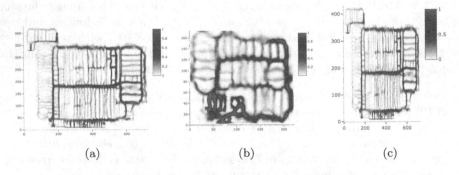

(a)   (b)   (c)

Fig. 4. Heat maps of the trajectories in three stores. (Color figure online)

Figure 4 shows the heat maps of trajectories in three different areas. The heat maps provide needful information about frequency of visiting of areas inside a store. The different colors of the map represent the most strategic information for the store staff and the sales, as well as important marketing indicators.

5 Conclusion and Future Works

In this paper, we presented a tracking system based on Ultra-wideband technology which found application in retail field. Our aim is developed a huge trajectories dataset for understanding shoppers behaviour. This dataset is publicly available. Through the analysis of the collected tracking data, the system allows to derive several information about the shoppers behaviour inside the stores target. The behaviours are flows of walking, most visited areas inside the space dedicated to the shopping and average travel times. The proposed architecture have the aim to scientifically demonstrate effectiveness of communication and general "call to action" in intelligent retail environment. Retailers are very interested of such a tools lays in the fact that, departing from the collected data, they can obtain information about their consumer behaviour. In this application, it is also possible to monitor areas of interest of the store by establishing the best arrangement and equipment of the store. In order to attract the shoppers attention, efficient marketing strategies can be adopted thanks to the metrics extracted from the system. Moreover, the low cost of employed components and the simple installation makes this solution suitable for all typologies of store. Very interesting are the results obtained during the experimental phase in a real environments. They allowed to extract different parameters to statistically evaluate the behaviour of shoppers inside the stores. Following the movement of each subject is very important to understand what are the points of interest and how they attract the visitor, creating in the future also a sort of "typical shopper".

In future, we will also prove the efficiency of the system in other different real store, where it is going to be installed permanently. Moreover, we also expect to merge data coming from Ultra-wide band with the data from RGB-D sensor in a top view configuration [13].

References

1. Cheng, Q.J., Ng, J.K.Y., et al.: A wireless LAN location estimation system using center of gravity as an algorithm selector for enhancing location estimation. In: 2012 IEEE 26th International Conference on Advanced Information Networking and Applications (AINA), pp. 261–268. IEEE (2012)
2. Contigiani, M., Pietrini, R., Mancini, A., Zingaretti, P.: Implementation of a tracking system based on UWB technology in a retail environment. In: 2016 12th IEEE/ASME International Conference on Mechatronic and Embedded Systems and Applications (MESA), pp. 1–6. IEEE (2016)
3. Farid, Z., Nordin, R., Ismail, M.: Recent advances in wireless indoor localization techniques and system. J. Comput. Netw. Commun. **2013** (2013)

4. Ferracuti, N., Norscini, C., Frontoni, E., Gabellini, P., Paolanti, M., Placidi, V.: A business application of rtls technology in intelligent retail environment: defining the shopper's preferred path and its segmentation. J. Retail. Consum. Serv. **47**, 184–194 (2019)

5. Frontoni, E., Mancini, A., Zingaretti, P.: Embedded vision sensor network for planogram maintenance in retail environments. Sensors **15**(9), 21114–21133 (2015)

6. Frontoni, E., Raspa, P., Mancini, A., Zingaretti, P., Placidi, V.: Customers' activity recognition in intelligent retail environments. In: Petrosino, A., Maddalena, L., Pala, P. (eds.) ICIAP 2013. LNCS, vol. 8158, pp. 509–516. Springer, Heidelberg (2013). https://doi.org/10.1007/978-3-642-41190-8_55

7. Fuchs, C., Aschenbruck, N., Martini, P., Wieneke, M.: Indoor tracking for mission critical scenarios: a survey. Pervasive Mob. Comput. **7**(1), 1–15 (2011)

8. Gezici, S., et al.: Localization via ultra-wideband radios: a look at positioning aspects for future sensor networks. IEEE Signal Process. Mag. **22**(4), 70–84 (2005)

9. Koyuncu, H., Yang, S.H.: A survey of indoor positioning and object locating systems. IJCSNS Int. J. Comput. Sci. Netw. Secur. **10**(5), 121–128 (2010)

10. Lam, K.Y., Ng, J.K.Y., Wang, J., Ho Chuen Kam, C., Wai-Hung Tsang, N.: A pervasive promotion model for personalized promotion systems on using WLAN localization and NFC techniques. Mob. Inf. Syst. **2015** (2015)

11. Liciotti, D., Paolanti, M., Frontoni, E., Mancini, A., Zingaretti, P.: Person re-identification dataset with RGB-D camera in a top-view configuration. In: Nasrollahi, K., et al. (eds.) FFER/VAAM -2016. LNCS, vol. 10165, pp. 1–11. Springer, Cham (2017). https://doi.org/10.1007/978-3-319-56687-0_1

12. Liciotti, D., Paolanti, M., Frontoni, E., Zingaretti, P.: People detection and tracking from an RGB-D camera in top-view configuration: review of challenges and applications. In: Battiato, S., Farinella, G.M., Leo, M., Gallo, G. (eds.) ICIAP 2017. LNCS, vol. 10590, pp. 207–218. Springer, Cham (2017). https://doi.org/10.1007/978-3-319-70742-6_20

13. Liciotti, D., Paolanti, M., Pietrini, R., Frontoni, E., Zingaretti, P.: Convolutional networks for semantic heads segmentation using top-view depth data in crowded environment. In: 2018 24th International Conference on Pattern Recognition (ICPR), pp. 1384–1389. IEEE (2018)

14. Liu, H., Darabi, H., Banerjee, P., Liu, J.: Survey of wireless indoor positioning techniques and systems. IEEE Trans. Syst. Man Cybern. Part C Appl. Rev. **37**(6), 1067–1080 (2007)

15. Mancini, A., Frontoni, E., Zingaretti, P., Placidi, V.: Smart vision system for shelf analysis in intelligent retail environments. In: ASME 2013 International Design Engineering Technical Conferences and Computers and Information in Engineering Conference, pp. V004T08A045–V004T08A045. American Society of Mechanical Engineers (2013)

16. Marin-Hernandez, A., de Jesús Hoyos-Rivera, G., Garcia-Arroyo, M., Marin-Urias, L.F.: Conception and implementation of a supermarket shopping assistant system. In: 2012 11th Mexican International Conference on Artificial Intelligence (MICAI), pp. 26–31. IEEE (2012)

17. Newman, A.J., Foxall, G.R.: In-store customer behaviour in the fashion sector: some emerging methodological and theoretical directions. Int. J. Retail. Distrib. Manag. **31**(11), 591–600 (2003)

18. Paolanti, M., Liciotti, D., Pietrini, R., Mancini, A., Frontoni, E.: Modelling and forecasting customer navigation in intelligent retail environments. J. Intell. Robot. Syst. **91**(2), 165–180 (2018)

19. Paolanti, M., Romeo, L., Martini, M., Mancini, A., Frontoni, E., Zingaretti, P.: Robotic retail surveying by deep learning visual and textual data. Robot. Auton. Syst. **118**, 179–188 (2019)
20. Paolanti, M., Sturari, M., Mancini, A., Zingaretti, P., Frontoni, E.: Mobile robot for retail surveying and inventory using visual and textual analysis of monocular pictures based on deep learning. In: 2017 European Conference on Mobile Robots (ECMR), pp. 1–6. IEEE (2017)
21. Yamabe, T., Lehdonvirta, V., Ito, H., Soma, H., Kimura, H., Nakajima, T.: Applying pervasive technologies to create economic incentives that alter consumer behavior. In: Proceedings of the 11th International Conference on Ubiquitous Computing, pp. 175–184. ACM (2009)
22. You, C.W., Wei, C.C., Chen, Y.L., Chu, H.H., Chen, M.S.: Using mobile phones to monitor shopping time at physical stores. IEEE Pervasive Comput. **2**, 37–43 (2011)
23. Zeimpekis, V., Giaglis, G.M., Lekakos, G.: A taxonomy of indoor and outdoor positioning techniques for mobile location services. ACM SIGecom Exch. **3**(4), 19–27 (2002)

An IOT Edge-Fog-Cloud Architecture for Vision Based Pallet Integrity

Raffaele Vaira[1], Rocco Pietrini[1], Roberto Pierdicca[2(✉)], Primo Zingaretti[1], Adriano Mancini[1], and Emanuele Frontoni[1]

[1] Dipartimento di Ingegneria dell'Informazione, Università Politecnica delle Marche, Via Brecce Bianche 12, 60131 Ancona, Italy
{r.vaira,r.pietrini}@pm.univpm.it,
{p.zingaretti,a.mancini,e.frontoni}@univpm.it
[2] Dipartimento di Ingegneria Civile, Edile e dell'Architettura, Università Politecnica delle Marche, Via Brecce Bianche 12, 60131 Ancona, Italy
r.pierdicca@univpm.it

Abstract. Improving the availability of products in a store in order to avoid the OOS (out-of-stock) problem is a crucial topic nowadays. The reduction of OOS events leads to a series of consequences, including, an increase in customer satisfaction and loyalty to the store and brand, the production of positive advertising with a consequent growth in sales, and finally an increase in profitability and sales for a specific category. In this context, we propose the Pallet Integrity system for the automatic and real-time detection of OOS on promo pallets and promo forecasting using computer vision. The system uses two cameras placed in top-view configuration; one equipped with a depth sensor used to determines the number of pieces on the pallet and the other, a very high resolution webcam, that is used for the facing recognition. The computer vision depth process takes place on edge, while the product recognition and promo OOS alarms runs on the fog, with a processing unit per store; the multi-promo forecasting service and the data aggregation and visualization is on cloud. The system was extensively tested on different real stores worldwide with accurate OOS detection and forecasting results.

Keywords: Out-of-stock · Fog-cloud architecture · RGB-D camera

1 Introduction

The term Out-of-Stock (also referred to as OOS) generally refers to the unavailability of a product in a store. Unfortunately, this is a phenomenon rather frequent in the retail sector, especially in the promo areas and promo pallets (Fig. 1). Out-of-stock rates vary greatly among retailers and their stores depending on several factors, but the majority tends to fall in the range of 5–10% with an average worldwide rate which amount at 8%. Furthermore, as mentioned in [6] for fast selling and/or promoted products (often placed on pallets in the store), the OOS regularly exceeds 10% with picks to the 25%.

© Springer Nature Switzerland AG 2019
M. Cristani et al. (Eds.): ICIAP 2019 Workshops, LNCS 11808, pp. 296–306, 2019.
https://doi.org/10.1007/978-3-030-30754-7_30

Due to these stock-outs, retailers can lose up to half of their expected sales [3] with both short-term and long-term losses. Short-term losses are generated when customers delay purchases or switch to a competing store [8]; long-term losses include loss of market share, loss of customers and negative word-of-mouth [19]. Several studies have highlighted that out-of-stock situations translate into sales losses of about 4% to 14% [3,6]. Furthermore, these out-of-stock situations undermine the consumer loyalty to a particular store, also producing a negative publicity and consequential business losses.

Conversely, reducing out-of-stock situations reduces the consumer's necessity to look for the products they need from competing retailers, thereby increasing consumer satisfaction, loyalty to the brand and, as shopper, loyalty to the store; finally, reducing OOS contributes to sales increasing and category profitability [2]. As Berger [1] declares, the customer satisfaction is often guaranteed by maintaining the shelves completely ranged, avoiding the out-of-shelf problem.

Fig. 1. An usual grocery retailer with promo pallets in different locations and different categories.

To ensure high levels of products availability, several methods are used to detect and resolve OOS events. Physical inspections have been widely used both in industry [15,18] and research [14], as a method for evaluating the products availability within the store [4]. Machine learning and classification methods used in literature can be useful also in this contex [13,16,17]. The audits are performed by humans, store staff or outside actors, that physically check the availability of a product through visual inspection or using a bar code scanner. In this way, the OOS is calculated in real time, thus allowing a fast refill as well as an understanding of the reasons why an item is no more available in the store. However, such a method is labour intensive, extremely expensive and does not provide a reliable evaluation for the out-of-stock as it depends on the visiting schedule of the auditors (in which annotations on OOS are logged) and because just a sample of products is chosen for audit (the choice falls on the most representative products, taking into account also the policy of the store).

However, nowadays, is crucial for the retail sector to have a method that estimates OOS without having to conduct physical store audits. In this scenario,
methods based on point-of-sale (POS) data and inventory data are commonly
used. The first method detect unusual low sales for specific products that may be
due to partial or total OOS status; the second make use of store inventory data
in order to calculate stock-outs as an approximation to OOS. These approaches
are inexpensive and provides a continuous measurements tool for out-of-stock
events but the accuracy of data extrapolated is not verified since, among the
other things, it's difficult to have accurate and updated inventory information.
For this reason, the OOS detection cannot rely only on inventory and POS data.

Finally, thanks to the joint effort of retailers and suppliers in the European
grocery retail sector, it was proposed the European OOS-Index [7]. This approach only considers fast moving items with constantly high sales; the index
monitors the sales of the corresponding products on a daily basis. If for a given
day a product sells zero items (or lower than a predefined threshold), then the
latter it is consider to be OOS. However, this approach loses generality as it only
applies to a very limited number of products, normally less than 5% of a typical
product assortment found in grocery retail stores.

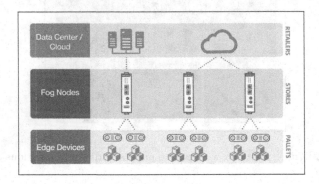

Fig. 2. The edge (pallets), fog (stores) and cloud (retailers and distribution centers)
data processing architecture.

We propose, with this work, a measurement system for the detection of out-
of-stock events for product placed on a pallet; our approach takes into account
the time variable thus knowing in real-time when the OOS events occur and
then promptly working to solve the problem. Using RGB-D camera for stock-out
detection is a brand new approach in the state-of-art. This is a new and effective
way to evaluate out-of-stock situation in the retail context. In fact, other studies
are focused for example on shelf real-time stock-out detection using proximity
sensor network [5] placed on shelves behind the products; however this approach
is not suitable for a pallet, where products are placed directly on the wooden
structure.

Several researches in the field of consumer behaviours are dealing with the OOS problem with the main scope of understanding how costumers react to this inefficiency [10, 14, 17], and [11].

In this context, the proposed IoT multimedia architecture (Fig. 2) is novel in terms of modern distributed computation design: The computer vision depth process takes place on edge, while the product recognition and promo OOS alarms runs on the fog, with a processing unit per store; the multi-promo forecasting service and the data aggregation and visualization is on cloud. The system was extensively tested on different real stores worldwide with accurate OOS detection and forecasting results.

Our approach has several positives: the top-view camera it's not intrusive in the retail store and it can be placed directly on dropped ceiling panels to control key situation [9]; the use of the depth sensor allow to measure height of facings of the entire pallet with a good percentage of success in order to estimate quantities (knowing the size of the product) thus predicting the occurrence of an OOS event; the proposed Edge-Fog-Cloud architecture is novel and suitable to monitor tens of pallets with high resolution image processing on low cost sensors with a distributed computing architecture.

In the next section, we first describe the hardware characteristics of the proposed solution, the Pallet Integrity System, and then its distributed software architecture characteristics and functionality. Finally, there are reported real store results and conclusions.

2 Materials and Methods

As above highlighted, OOS is an industry wide problem from the last 40 years with an estimated OSS average rate of 8.3%; in particular, these percentages become higher for promotional and fast selling products that are often placed on pallets. With this in mind, we propose the Pallet Integrity system with the aim of overcoming the problem of automatic detection of OOS, with particular regard to stock-out events occurring on pallets, trying to provide a robust measure system that could provide indisputable evidence and actionable data at a low cost. The Pallet Integrity system here proposed overcomes all issues discussed on OOS measurement, providing real time information by analyzing the stock on a pallet, computing in real-time the exact number of products stacked in each facing finally detecting possible stock-out situations.

2.1 Scenario and Hardware Architecture

From the hardware architecture point of view, the Pallet Integrity system consist of two different cameras placed in top-view configuration (Fig. 3) and one elaboration unit where the software runs. The cameras used are of two different types and perform two different tasks that will be better clarified in the continuation. In particular, the following cameras have been chosen:

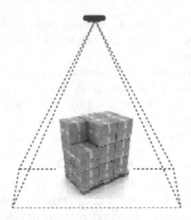

Fig. 3. Camera in top-view configuration on pallet.

1. Logitech C920 HD PRO
2. ASUS Xtion PRO (for depth)

The first is an high-definition camera used for facing recognition; the other is an RGB-D camera equipped with an on-board depth sensor used to compute the number of pieces per facings on the entire pallet. As mentioned before, using RGB-D camera in top-view configuration is a brand new approach in the state-of-art for the stock-out detection and has several positives:

1. the top-view camera it's not intrusive in a retail context
2. the camera can be placed directly on dropped ceiling panels to control key situation
3. the number of occlusions between camera and products are minimized

Usually in a store there are more than 50 promo areas or pallets and low cost solutions are mandatory. The local processing unit is an embedded vision processing unit. Finally, the fog processing unit, is a simple mini PC, is connected to the network via router for information exchange through APIs technology to the cloud for further processing. The overall hardware cost is limited thanks to this specific architecture design and to the decentralized processing specifically designed for retail stores and every highly distributed multimedia IoT networks.

2.2 Pallet Integrity Computer Vision Layer

This section illustrates the functioning of the software on which the Pallet Integrity system relies. In order to ensure the correct operating of the entire system, it is necessary to perform a preventive configuration phase. This setup procedure involves both the RGB-D and the RGB cameras and, for this reason, it is divided into two different steps. The first of these concerns the RGB-D camera and consists in specifying, through the use of a proper GUI, the points on the pallet that will then be taken as reference by the software. The procedure is performed on an empty pallet and the chosen points will be those that correspond to the center of each facing. In this phase, the camera-floor distance is also calculated, as well as the height of the product that will be placed on the pallet (this last measurement is obtained by positioning a first level of products thus calculating their height by difference starting from the camera-floor distance).

As Above described, the software evaluates static points manually selected in the setup phase in correspondence of each facing (center of facing) when just one product per facing is present on the pallet. At these points the height of the facing is calculated and therefore the number of products stacked, based on data coming from the centralized fog layer (where local knowledge about facing images and box dimensions are stored). However, due to the camera perspective, as the number of products stacked increases, the position of the chosen points will no longer correspond to the center of the facing (Fig. 4); in this case the measures obtained could be erroneous and in the processing phase the alignment is performed based on the image alignment.

Fig. 4. Static points in red in worst case scenario on record. The numbers positioned in correspondence of each facing represent the current reading of the number of pieces for each stack. (Color figure online)

To overcome this issue, a relocation of the previously mentioned points is necessary. Starting from the assumption that there is a connection between frame coordinates and real ones we convert coordinates related to the frame into real world coordinates (xyz) referred to the center of the camera; this conversion is performed through the dedicated functionality of OPENNI.

We can assume that the facings increase in height (number of stacked products) just vertically so the real world x and y coordinates set in the setup phase must be constant, within certain interval, whatever the height is. The OPENNI coordinate conversion functions (depth frame to real world and vice versa) can hence be used to look for the only possible matching between setup points and current points; this matching is performed by scanning all the possible values for height, using the z real world coordinate, together with x and y, converting them to frame coordinates and check for their admissibility. In this way, the only admissible point per facing will be found, and will be certainly located in the center of the facing. Finally, the algorithm plots on-screen dynamic dots just retrieved (Fig. 5).

Fig. 5. Deviation between static and dynamic points. As can be seen from the figure, the dynamic points (in green) remain positioned in the center of the facing even when the height of the stack increases. (Color figure online)

Through the use of the alignment function, the coordinates transformation does not require more sophisticated computer vision technique to detect facings and their center of mass allowing faster computation.

Table 1 summarize results coming from test conducted on a video recording showing typical operation on a pallet. Maximum pixel deviation and percentage of deviation (related to the frame size) from starting (static) points has been calculated.

Table 1. Test result showing higher deviation for facing number corresponding to the tallest one for the correction procedure.

Facing number (height)	Max deviation (pixel)	Percentage deviation
1	34.7131	8.67828%
2	7.0711	1.76777%
3	7.2111	1.80278%
4	14.3178	3.57946%
5	1.41421	0.353553%
6	4	1%

As you can see from the obtained results, the tallest stack (facing number 1) causes the highest deviation(>8% of deviation). In the case of static point (manually selected), the high value of deviation could have caused the shift of this point outside the relative facing thus causing a false stock-out situation.

The second step in the setup phase involves the RGB camera and consists in specifying for each product level the corresponding ROI (region of interest). For each layer a file will be created in which the coordinates, relative to the frame, for each of the indicated ROI will be stored. The entire procedure is performed through a dedicated GUI that provides a view of what, in real time, is placed on the pallet.

After the setup phase has been completed, the algorithm proceeds with the reading of the depth map corresponding to the current scene. In this way, for each stack, the height and the corresponding number of pieces are obtained.

In order to establish not only the quantity but also the product type, for each stack the file (generated during the setup phase) corresponding to the height detected is selected and from this the coordinates relative to the position of the stack are fetched. From these coordinates a portion of the current frame is extracted and compared with a series of model images (pre-loaded) representing the several products that can be placed on pallet. The comparison is made up by using the OPENCV libraries and in particular the SIFT [12] algorithm. Through this algorithm the key-points and the relative descriptors, for the current cropped image, are obtained; after that, using a FLANN (Fast Approximate Nearest Neighbor) based algorithm, matches between key-points of the current cropped image and those of the different models are found. Finally, according to the following expression:

$$\frac{\#\ \text{of key-points correspondence}}{\max\left(\text{actual key points, model key points}\right)} \tag{1}$$

a score to each model is assigned. This score represents the probability that the product shown by the model is actually the one on the pallet. In this way, not only the number of pieces but also the corresponding SKU (Stock Keeping Unit) can be detected for each stack.

2.3 Pallet Integrity Store Level Fog Layer

The fog layer, with a centralized processing unit per store, is responsible of the local storage of the SKUs packaging images and dimensions and is the feature matching unit (SIFT features extracted from the edge layer and compared with the whole packaging image data set). The fog layer is updated daily from the Cloud layer APIs that allow to download new SKU images and dimensions. The fog layer is finally responsible of the maintenance of the multimedia IoT network and it is responsible of the quality control on every device on edge and of data quality of the single images obtained from cameras during the initial switch on. Maintenance alarms are managed by this layer sending mails and messages to the store manager.

2.4   Pallet Integrity Forecasting and Data Analytic Cloud Layer

The entire software described above is integrated into an application that runs on a tablet and through which it is possible to remotely control the system with a given frequency, accessing to the fog layer via a http interface. All the data obtained from the latter are sent to the cloud infrastructure, processed for forecasting estimation and displayed on a dashboard that provides an overview of the current status of the pallet.

The forecasting procedure use time series from promo pallet counting system to forecast the promo effectiveness and to predict OOS events in advance using basic machine learning methods on these data. This forecasting cloud layer investigates the effectiveness of probability forecasts output by standard machine learning techniques (Neural Network, C4.5, K-Nearest Neighbours, Naive Bayes, SVM and HMM) when tested on time series data sets from various problem domains. Raw data was converted into a pattern classification problem using a sliding window approach, and the respective target prediction was set as some discredited future value in the time series sequence. Experiments were conducted in the online learning setting to model the way in which time series data is presented. The performance of each learner's probability forecasts was assessed using ROC curves, square loss, classification accuracy and Empirical Reliability Curves (ERC). Our results demonstrate that effective probability forecasts can be generated on time series data and we discuss the practical implications of this.

3   Experimental Results

As mentioned above, it is possible to run the entire software as a tablet application, thus displaying the results of the processing on a proper dashboard. The first and most immediate data that can be accessed through this dashboard is that which indicates the number of pieces per pallet. The scenario we have considered consists of four different pallets on which different interactions are made.

For each pallet is returned the information about the SKU and the corresponding number of pieces. Six columns with a maximum of six layers of product each are considered for each pallet.

In this way it is possible to periodically monitor the state of the pallet; for our tests we have chosen an hourly rate for the measurements. Be $s(h)$ the stock on pallet relative to a certain hour and $s(h-1)$ that relative to the previous hour; the hourly selling it is obtained as: $v(h) = s(h) - s(h-1)$. In so doing, it is possible to obtain the trend of hourly sales as shown in Fig. 6.

In the event that the hourly selling assumes a value greater than zero, this means that a pallet refill has been made by the staff of the store; in this case, the sold is set to 0 for that particular hour.

Starting from the information about the hourly sold, through an average operation, it is possible to obtain information concerning the average hourly sold. Knowing the average hourly sales and the number of items on pallets at a

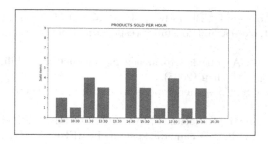

Fig. 6. The figure shows the number of items sold per hour.

given time of day, it is possible to make an estimate of the time remaining before a given pallet goes into stock-out condition.

4 Conclusion

In this paper, we have proposed a measurement system for the detection of OOS events for product placed on a pallet. The approach presented has involved the use of an RGB-D camera for stock-out detection. This is a new and effective way to evaluate out-of-stock situation in the retail context. Through the Pallet Integrity system, it is possible to obtain other useful data such as daily sales and daily average sales. The system was extensively tested on different real stores worldwide with accurate OOS detection and forecasting results. All this information, which can be displayed through the dedicated application, contributes to the maintenance of sufficient availability of products in the store, thus avoiding OOS events with a certain advantage for the store and for the brand.

Acknowledgments. This work was funded by Grottini Lab (www.grottinilab.com).

References

1. Berger, R.: Full-shelf satisfaction, reducing out-of-stocks in a grocery channel. Grocery Manufacturers of America (GMA) (2002)
2. Colacchio, F., Tikhonova, O., Kisis, J.: Consumer response to out-of stock: decision making process and influencing factors. In: ECR European Conference (2003)
3. Corsten, D., Gruen, T.: Stock-outs cause walkouts. Harv. Bus. Rev **82**, 26–28 (2004)
4. Ferracuti, N., Norscini, C., Frontoni, E., Gabellini, P., Paolanti, M., Placidi, V.: A business application of rtls technology in intelligent retail environment: defining the shopper's preferred path and its segmentation. J. Retail. Consum. Serv. **47**, 184–194 (2019)
5. Frontoni, E., Mancini, A., Zingaretti, P.: Real time out of shelf detection using embedded sensor network. IEEE/ASME 10th International Conference on Mechatronic and Embedded Systems and Apllications (MESA) (2014)

6. Gruen, T.W., Corsten, D., Bharadwaj, S.: Retail out of stocks: a worldwide examination of extent, causes, and consumer responses. Grocery Manufacturers of America (2002)
7. Hausruckinger, G.: Approaches to measuring on-shelf availability at the point of sale. ECR Europe, Mnchen (2005)
8. Kim, M., Lennon, S.: Consumer response to online apparel stockouts. Psych. Mark. **28**, 115–144 (2011)
9. Liciotti, D., Zingaretti, P., Placidi, V.: An automatic analysis of shoppers behaviour using a distributed RGB-D cameras system. In: IEEE/ASME 10th International Conference on Mechatronic and Embedded Systems and Apllications (MESA), pp. 1–6 (2014)
10. Liciotti, D., Paolanti, M., Frontoni, E., Zingaretti, P.: People detection and tracking from an RGB-D camera in top-view configuration: review of challenges and applications. In: Battiato, S., Farinella, G.M., Leo, M., Gallo, G. (eds.) ICIAP 2017. LNCS, vol. 10590, pp. 207–218. Springer, Cham (2017). https://doi.org/10.1007/978-3-319-70742-6_20
11. Liciotti, D., Paolanti, M., Pietrini, R., Frontoni, E., Zingaretti, P.: Convolutional networks for semantic heads segmentation using top-view depth data in crowded environment. In: 2018 24rd International Conference on Pattern Recognition (ICPR). IEEE (2018)
12. Lowe, D.G.: Distinctive image features from scale-invariant keypoints. Int. J. Comput. Vis. **60**, 91–110 (2004)
13. Paolanti, M., Frontoni, E., Mancini, A., Pierdicca, R., Zingaretti, P.: Automatic classification for anti mixup events in advanced manufacturing system. In: ASME 2015 International Design Engineering Technical Conferences and Computers and Information in Engineering Conference, pp. V009T07A061–V009T07A061. American Society of Mechanical Engineers (2015)
14. Paolanti, M., Liciotti, D., Pietrini, R., Mancini, A., Frontoni, E.: Modelling and forecasting customer navigation in intelligent retail environments. J. Intell. Robot. Syst. **91**(2), 165–180 (2018)
15. Paolanti, M., Romeo, L., Felicetti, A., Mancini, A., Frontoni, E., Loncarski, J.: Machine learning approach for predictive maintenance in industry 4.0. In: 2018 14th IEEE/ASME International Conference on Mechatronic and Embedded Systems and Applications (MESA), pp. 1–6. IEEE (2018)
16. Paolanti, M., Romeo, L., Martini, M., Mancini, A., Frontoni, E., Zingaretti, P.: Robotic retail surveying by deep learning visual and textual data. Robot. Auton. Syst. **118**, 179–188 (2019)
17. Paolanti, M., Sturari, M., Mancini, A., Zingaretti, P., Frontoni, E.: Mobile robot for retail surveying and inventory using visual and textual analysis of monocular pictures based on deep learning. In: 2017 European Conference on Mobile Robots (ECMR), pp. 1–6. IEEE (2017)
18. Sturari, M., Paolanti, M., Frontoni, E., Mancini, A., Zingaretti, P.: Robotic platform for deep change detection for rail safety and security. In: 2017 European Conference on Mobile Robots (ECMR), pp. 1–6. IEEE (2017)
19. Zinn, W., Liu, P.: Consumer response to retail stockouts. J. Bus. Logis **22**, 49–71 (2001)

The Vending Shopper Science Lab: Deep Learning for Consumer Research

Fioravante Allegrino[1], Patrizia Gabellini[2], Luigi Di Bello[2], Marco Contigiani[2], and Valerio Placidi[2(✉)]

[1] Sogeda S.R.L., Via Volturno, 10, 66020 San Giovanni Teatino, Chieti, Italy
[2] Grottini Lab S.R.L., Via Santa Maria in Potenza, 62017 Porto Recanati, Italy
patrizia.gabellini@grottinicommunication.com,
{luigi.dibello,marco.contigiani,valerio.placidi}@grottinilab.com,
http://www.grottinilab.com

Abstract. To understand human behavior, a fundamental aspect is the analysis of the face and movement. This aspect is particularly important in the context of sales, where to know the shopper also means to guide purchases. A major challenge for vending environment is to predict the shopper behavior, with the aim to influence and increase purchases. In this ambit, vending machine industry is actually an interesting and growing data-driven marketing area of research. In this context, the aim of this paper is to propose an innovative architecture that is able to integrate face and movement understanding in a common strategy for real time consumer modeling. The vending machine and the decision support system process multimedia data to smartly respond with dynamic pricing and product proposal to the particular shopper which is in front of a vending machine. The aim is to build an intelligent vending machine which in real time is able to suitably propose products to a labelled shopper. The results come from real environments vending lab with 30 locations and about 1 million consumers in Italy, and have the aim to demonstrate the good performances and high efficiency of our solution in recognizing the age and the gender of consumer and different interactions with the vending machine.

Keywords: Human behaviour understanding · Face detection · Machine learning · Vending machine

1 Introduction

In many retail fields, the use of big data analytics is a widely used practice [12,19,22], while there are not many the works that deals this argument in the vending machines (VM) industry. However, since technological revolution proceeds, the new technologies solutions also involved VM market, as in other domains [24,25]. In fact, the new generation of VMs offer functionality such as face and voice recognition and are known as intelligent VMs. The intention is to increase their intelligence using machine learning [17,20] and deep learning

© Springer Nature Switzerland AG 2019
M. Cristani et al. (Eds.): ICIAP 2019 Workshops, LNCS 11808, pp. 307–317, 2019.
https://doi.org/10.1007/978-3-030-30754-7_31

[13,23,28] approaches in order to attract more shoppers. Moreover, understanding sentiment and emotions is extremely important for improving the customer experience [15,18]. As in retail environment, the industry growth forecasts are stimulated by the integration of face recognition in VMs allowing the communication among consumer and VM [21]. By adding these features, the VM systems will be equipped with an intelligence capable of obtaining information on consumer preferences and behavior and therefore offering a visual experience with targeted promotions.

In this context, our work intends to provide existing VM of a non-intrusive additional hardware, placed entirely inside the machine itself, adding a visible low cost commercial camera. By combining the vision algorithms and the information coming from the VM telemetry it is possible to obtain a complete view of the customers, and therefore provide information related to sales such as: the number of people passing in front of the VM, the number of those who stop and make a purchase, time spent, and more. All this information is also linked to a breakdown of the customer by gender and age group.

The system guarantees the privacy of individuals, a feature required for current systems, maintaining real-time processing, without storing images and/or videos. The information collected by the vision algorithms and the VM telemetry are anonymously sent to the cloud. So the choice was to implement algorithms that allow fast calculations on low-cost hardware, also considering the limited space available within a VM to install additional hardware. All this to create a fast and almost real-time architecture.

Experiments are performed considering a VM in Florence, Italy and the brand new VM lab with 30 real location all over Italy. The data collected covered a period of three months (from August to October). The experimental results demonstrated the efficiency of the proposed system, highlighting its effectiveness especially in the real environment considered in the experimental phase. Furthermore, at this stage it is also possible to assess the impact that new products, new offers and new promotions have on customers.

We can summarize the main contributions of this paper as follows: (i) the machine learning approach for face detection and behaviour understanding; (ii) a process of identifying and reacting shoppers to boost sales and promotional offers; (iii) the contribution to the practice by supporting VM retailers to carry out knowledge discovery processes more effectively; iv) the real-world testing process based on real world VM location and more than one million shoppers per year.

The remainder of the paper is organized as following: Sect. 2 presents a review of the literature of face detection applied to shopper analysis. Section 3 describes the architecture implemented and the research method, deepening the system technology and the algorithms adopted. Section 4 presents the experimental results obtained considering a real environment. Finally, in Sect. 5, we draw conclusions and discuss future directions for the research.

2   Related Works

Recent researches in the face recognition field demonstrate that it has been widely used in large-scale commercial applications [4,14]. The principal component analysis (PCA) algorithm, that transforms the input high-dimensional feature space to a low-dimensional subspace where the dominant feature energy is maintained with generalization capability, are largely applied for face recognition purpose [11]. Even if PCA ensures the maximum variance, not always is better for classification purpose in fact, linear discriminant analysis [3], a supervised statistical learning method displays superior performance in classification over PCA. In [31], the authors present the sparse representation classification algorithm (SRC) a representative classification-based method for face recognition. The characteristic of SRC algorithm is to consider a test sample as a representation of a linear combination of training samples of the same person, and allows classifying the test sample to the class that has the minimal residual between the test sample and its collaborative representation. Xu et al. [32,33], in their works use a coarse-to-fine K nearest neighbor (KNN) classifier, which considers a small number of training samples that are close to the test sample and succes sively identifies the kNNs of the test sample. Wiskott et al. [30] propose a face recognition algorithm based on elastic bunch Graph matching (EBGM). The face image in EGBM is represented using the labeled graph. The local feature matching and recognition of corresponding facial parts are realized by the difference among several face images labeling graph. In real-world scenarios, many are issues that can affect the systems of face recognition as for example facial expressions, poses, illuminations, and occlusion [6,7,26,29,34], moreover often, the available training samples are very limited, and can happen to have a single face image per subject. When the sample size is smaller than the sample dimensionality, there is the problem of the small sample size (SSS) problem [8,9]. Since this problem is a great obstacle in the case of face recognition, many algorithms have been proposed for addressing SSS in the presence of significant variations in illuminations, poses and facial expressions, an example is presented in [5]. A new supervised learning method named two-dimensional CCA (2DCCA) is presented to address SSS in [35].

Unlike previous works presented in literature, our approach has the aim to integrate face and behaviour analysis based on supervised learning computer vision methods. Moreover, we propose a clustering algorithm for consumer segmentation and automatic vending machine response with specific consumer based promo and cross merchandising activities. We consider a real scenario and a modern, affordable and scalable cloud infrastructure for big data and machine learning, with the aim to implement the first open and real world lab of VMs.

3   Materials and Methods

The VM has been equipped with a low-cost commercial camera, model Hercules HD Twist, directly mounted above the VM keypad and connected to a dedicated elaboration unit. This last is also connected to the VM which reveal a text file having logged keypad events. Human Behaviour Analysis in VM systems want to associate all the data deriving from different sources, such as the camera and the VM. The task of the elaboration unit is to gather all the data and then send them to the cloud, where the integration happens. The main problem is split into the following sub-problems: people detection, face detection, age and gender classification and data integration. We combined two different algorithms in cascade, where the output of the previous is the input of the following. Figure 1 reports computer vision and data aggregation organization. Different layers are following described, with the aim to put in evidence the main novelty of our proposal: the integration of machine learning algorithms and feature based approaches that are efficiently elaborated on edge with low cost hardware and a mix of edge and cloud processing power. A unique ID is generated for each shopper that pass with other defined characteristic: gender, age, the stopping time, entering and exiting direction, time spent in front of the VM, number of people interacting at the same time (groups), interactions with the VM, payment methods, sell-out.

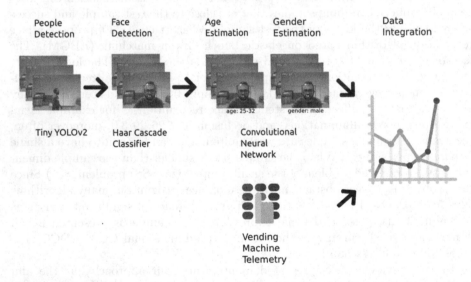

Fig. 1. Computer Vision Architecture: a multi model ML classifier is used to perform people detection, face detection, age and gender estimation, joining all data with the data coming from the VM.

3.1   People Detection

For people detection is applied a Convolutional Neural Network (CNN), in particular a real-time Neural Network (Tiny YOLOv2), that is able to classifies objects in 20 different classes. It is a smaller version of the more complex full YOLOv2 network and consisted of 9 convolutional layers and 6 max-pooling layers. In particular a pretrained model on the PASCALVOC 2007 and 2012 dataset [27] is applied.

3.2 Face Detection

For a previous detecting phase, the Haar Feature-based Cascade Classifier trained for frontal faces using the OpenCV library [2] was applied, and it is useful to reveal the actual VM customers and so to detect people who really approach the VM. Then there is a subdivision among people that "passing by" and "stopping", that occurs when a face is detected and it is in the "interaction area" with the VM (usually 3mt around the VM). This procedure is also effective for multi-face detection for understanding shoppers acting in a group of people.

3.3 Age and Gender Classification

In the last face processing step, the age and gender are estimated. The output of the previous layer was the input of a Deep CNN developed by Gil Levi and Tal Hassner [10]. We used the same network for both tasks obtaining two classes for gender (M,F) and eight interval classes for age (0−2, 4−6, 8−13, 15−20, 25−32, 38−43, 48−53, 60+). For computational performances we have obtained a classification rate of 10 frames per second.

3.4 Data Integration

The data processing layer performs data aggregation on a bottom up strategy that store and use data starting from the row data level and moving up the the insight and the real-time user profiling for dynamic promotion in every VM connected to the cloud services. The architecture is a novel way of managing data that allows to store and use at the same time data at different aggregation level to optimize performances.

In the cloud platform the information coming from the vision system are integrated with VM telemetry on a user ID basis. This combination provides an overall view of the shopper, knowing the age and gender estimation, behaviours and interactions with the keypad. The list of features derived from our architecture can be summarized in the Table 1.

They are processed by an unsupervised classification algorithm [1] which provides in output a classification of different behaviours and automatically react giving different purposely input. While the clusters number are automatically selected applying the distortion metric for the choice of the optimal global scale [16].

4 Results and Discussion

In the following section we reports the results obtained in a real world lab in Italy, and then the performances of the integrated architecture based on a real test case are presented.

Table 1. Data aggregation: starting from gender and age obtained by face analysis, behaviour features are added for the target unsupervised classification. (*Age segments = 0−2, 4−6, 8−13, 15−20, 25−32, 38−43, 48−53, 60+)

Feature type	Feature name	Feature values
Face analysis	Gender	Man, female or not classified
Face analysis	Age	Age segments*
Behaviours	Time	Time stamp entering the VM area
Behaviours	Group	Contemporary people in the VM area
Behaviours	Stopping	Avg stopping time
Behaviours	Entering direction	Entering from left, right or front of the VM
Behaviours	Groups	People IDs that are contemporary in the VM area
Behaviours	Interactions	Total number of interactions with the VM interface
Transactions	Buy actions	Total number of products bought at the VM
Transactions	Payment	Payment type (money, credit card, e-key)

The Fig. 2 schematically presents the vending machine lab in Italy. There are 30 vending machines distributed in different target cities and monitored in real time for one year. The VMs are classified considering high, medium and low traffic location and high, medium and low sell-out. These aspects are able to make comparison between different locations and to obtain significant data for better future solution. The total number of people passing by the VMs is about 1 million per year. The VM lab is the first devoted to this particular aspect in the European scenario and is designed together with companies to increase the global performances of the vending industry.

Fig. 2. The Italian vending lab with 30 locations and 1 million consumers per year

We reported the results of a test related to a VM positioned in Florence, where gathered data referred to a period of three months (August, September and October). In order to show several examples of different data collected by our architecture, Figs. 3, 4 and 5 show different distribution at different layers. Figure 3 presents the distribution of people passing in front of the vending and a plot of people stopping and purchasing, Fig. 4 indicates the weekly and hourly distribution of total purchases and Fig. 5 reports a mix of face and behaviour showing age and gender distribution of stopping.

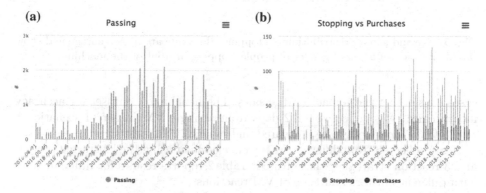

Fig. 3. (a) Distribution of people passing in front of the vending (from camera with NN); (b) Plot of people stopping and purchasing

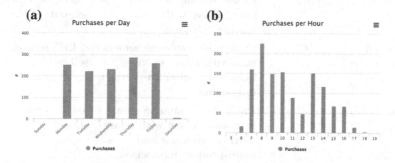

Fig. 4. (a) Weekly distribution of total purchases; (b) Hourly distribution of total purchases

The second result, that we presented, has the aim to show the real-time face and behaviour analysis classification and reaction taking into account an enhancement in term of attracting and sells. There are really three important results: (i) a public dataset for accuracy evaluation and improvements; (ii) the accuracy of the proposed computer vision methods on the feature set evaluation; (iii) the application of the proposed reaction strategy on 3 real testing

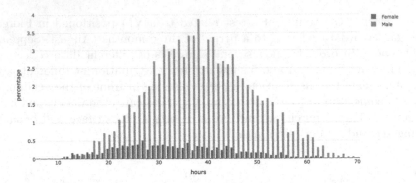

Fig. 5. Age and gender distribution of stopping: the value are in percentage and show the distribution of age and gender of people stopping in front of the machine.

cases considering the impact on the sales. The benchmark dataset for accuracy measurement was collected for 2 days from a single VM in a real scenario. A total of 235 shoppers where measured and manually annotated.

Data collected from different VMs were classified using the clustering process and 3 reaction strategies where tested. Table 2 reports results for different tests with different clusters and type of VM reactions.

Table 2. VM reaction strategies and sales impact.

Test type	Shoppers	Reaction strategy	Sales variation
Healthy food	372	Promo healthy snack on young ladies with a fast moving behaviour	+3.7% on category sell-out
Coffee and chocolate combo	167	Promo the combo on seniors man with a slow moving behaviour and multi-product interaction	+4.1% on combo sell-out
Combo Beverage and snack	231	Promo the combo on young man and woman with a fast moving behaviour and multi-product interaction	+4.1% on combo sell-out

The joined face/behaviour classification with a clustering approach is a fast and efficient way to design shopper segmentation and apply specific reactions with relevant impact on VM business performances.

The approach allow to test and evaluate the return of investment of special promo or new promo material before rolling out the solution worldwide.

Data driven marketing solutions can be easily implemented and tested in the first open lab for the Vending Industry.

5 Conclusions and Future Work

The aim of this paper is to present our study that wants to integrate face and behaviour understanding of shopper in front of VM introducing a new purpose created architecture. The VM and the cloud architecture (the decision support system) process the data together in order to react with dynamic pricing and intelligent product proposal to the target shopper in front of the VM.

Experimental results are obtained considering 30 real vending labs and about 1 million consumers around Italy, demonstrating the efficiency and the considerable developments of our proposal. Moreover, the analysis of reaction in front of a VM opens new frontiers for VM management policy.

In future, our scope is to enhance the classification algorithm to a supervised approach, to collect and share big open data on the field, to increase the property to automatically compose reactions useful for a particular target.

Acknowledgement. This work was funded by Grottini Lab (www.grottinilab.com) and partially supported by EVA (European Association for the coffee service and Vending industry) and CONFIDA (Italian Association of Automatic Distribution). The authors want to thank Dr. Davide Manco for his contribution in the software development process.

References

1. Atev, S., Miller, G., Papanikolopoulos, N.P.: Clustering of vehicle trajectories. IEEE Trans. Intell. Transp. Syst. **11**(3), 647–657 (2010)
2. Bradski, G.: The OpenCV library. Dr. Dobb's J. Softw. Tools **25**, 120–125 (2000)
3. Chen, X., Yang, J., Zhang, D., Liang, J.: Complete large margin linear discriminant analysis using mathematical programming approach. Pattern Recogn. **46**(6), 1579–1594 (2013)
4. Fan, Z., Xu, Y., Zhang, D.: Local linear discriminant analysis framework using sample neighbors. IEEE Trans. Neural Netw. **22**(7), 1119–1132 (2011)
5. He, X., Yan, S., Hu, Y., Niyogi, P., Zhang, H.J.: Face recognition using laplacianfaces. IEEE Trans. Pattern Anal. Mach. Intell. **27**(3), 328–340 (2005)
6. Jun, B., Kim, D.: Robust face detection using local gradient patterns and evidence accumulation. Pattern Recogn. **45**(9), 3304–3316 (2012)
7. Kautkar, S.N., Atkinson, G.A., Smith, M.L.: Face recognition in 2D and 2.5D using ridgelets and photometric stereo. Pattern Recogn. **45**(9), 3317–3327 (2012)
8. Kim, S.-W.: On using a dissimilarity representation method to solve the small sample size problem for face recognition. In: Blanc-Talon, J., Philips, W., Popescu, D., Scheunders, P. (eds.) ACIVS 2006. LNCS, vol. 4179, pp. 1174–1185. Springer, Heidelberg (2006). https://doi.org/10.1007/11864349_107
9. Kyperountas, M., Tefas, A., Pitas, I.: Weighted piecewise LDA for solving the small sample size problem in face verification. IEEE Trans. Neural Netw. **18**(2), 506–519 (2007)
10. Levi, G., Hassner, T.: Age and gender classification using convolutional neural networks. In: Proceedings of the IEEE Conference on Computer Vision and Pattern Recognition Workshops, pp. 34–42 (2015)

11. Li, L., Liu, S., Peng, Y., Sun, Z.: Overview of principal component analysis algorithm. Optik-Int. J. Light Electron Optics **127**(9), 3935–3944 (2016)
12. Liciotti, D., Paolanti, M., Frontoni, E., Zingaretti, P.: People detection and tracking from an RGB-D camera in top-view configuration: review of challenges and applications. In: Battiato, S., Farinella, G.M., Leo, M., Gallo, G. (eds.) ICIAP 2017. LNCS, vol. 10590, pp. 207–218. Springer, Cham (2017). https://doi.org/10.1007/978-3-319-70742-6_20
13. Liciotti, D., Paolanti, M., Pietrini, R., Frontoni, E., Zingaretti, P.: Convolutional networks for semantic heads segmentation using top-view depth data in crowded environment. In: 2018 24th International Conference on Pattern Recognition (ICPR), pp. 1384–1389. IEEE (2018)
14. Lu, J., Yuan, X., Yahagi, T.: A method of face recognition based on fuzzy c-means clustering and associated sub-NNs. IEEE Trans. Neural Netw. **18**(1), 150–160 (2007)
15. Naspetti, S., Pierdicca, R., Mandolesi, S., Paolanti, M., Frontoni, E., Zanoli, R.: Automatic analysis of eye-tracking data for augmented reality applications: a prospective outlook. In: De Paolis, L.T., Mongelli, A. (eds.) AVR 2016. LNCS, vol. 9769, pp. 217–230. Springer, Cham (2016). https://doi.org/10.1007/978-3-319-40651-0_17
16. Ng, A.Y., Jordan, M.I., Weiss, Y.: On spectral clustering: analysis and an algorithm. In: Advances in neural information processing systems, pp. 849–856 (2002)
17. Paolanti, M., Frontoni, E., Mancini, A., Pierdicca, R., Zingaretti, P.: Automatic classification for anti mixup events in advanced manufacturing system. In: ASME 2015 International Design Engineering Technical Conferences and Computers and Information in Engineering Conference, pp. V009T07A061–V009T07A061. American Society of Mechanical Engineers (2015)
18. Paolanti, M., Kaiser, C., Schallner, R., Frontoni, E., Zingaretti, P.: Visual and textual sentiment analysis of brand-related social media pictures using deep convolutional neural networks. In: Battiato, S., Gallo, G., Schettini, R., Stanco, F. (eds.) ICIAP 2017. LNCS, vol. 10484, pp. 402–413. Springer, Cham (2017). https://doi.org/10.1007/978-3-319-68560-1_36
19. Paolanti, M., Liciotti, D., Pietrini, R., Mancini, A., Frontoni, E.: Modelling and forecasting customer navigation in intelligent retail environments. J. Intell. Rob. Syst. **91**(2), 165–180 (2018)
20. Paolanti, M., Romeo, L., Felicetti, A., Mancini, A., Frontoni, E., Loncarski, J.: Machine learning approach for predictive maintenance in industry 4.0. In: 2018 14th IEEE/ASME International Conference on Mechatronic and Embedded Systems and Applications (MESA), pp. 1–6. IEEE (2018)
21. Paolanti, M., Romeo, L., Martini, M., Mancini, A., Frontoni, E., Zingaretti, P.: Robotic retail surveying by deep learning visual and textual data. Rob. Auton. Syst. **118**, 179–188 (2019)
22. Paolanti, M., Sturari, M., Mancini, A., Zingaretti, P., Frontoni, E.: Mobile robot for retail surveying and inventory using visual and textual analysis of monocular pictures based on deep learning. In: 2017 European Conference on Mobile Robots (ECMR), pp. 1–6. IEEE (2017)
23. Pierdicca, R., Malinverni, E., Piccinini, F., Paolanti, M., Felicetti, A., Zingaretti, P.: Deep convolutional neural network for automatic detection of damaged photovoltaic cells. Int. Arch. Photogram. Remote Sens. Spat. Inf. Sci. **42**(2) (2018)

24. Pierdicca, R., Frontoni, E., Pollini, R., Trani, M., Verdini, L.: The use of augmented reality glasses for the application in industry 4.0. In: De Paolis, L.T., Bourdot, P., Mongelli, A. (eds.) AVR 2017. LNCS, vol. 10324, pp. 389–401. Springer, Cham (2017). https://doi.org/10.1007/978-3-319-60922-5_30

25. Pierdicca, R., Paolanti, M., Frontoni, E.: eTourism: ICT and its role for tourism management. J. Hosp. Tourism Technol. **10**(1), 90–106 (2019)

26. Pishchulin, L., Gass, T., Dreuw, P., Ney, H.: Image warping for face recognition: from local optimality towards global optimization. Pattern Recogn. **45**(9), 3131–3140 (2012)

27. Redmon, J., Farhadi, A.: Yolo9000: better, faster, stronger. In: Proceedings of the IEEE Conference on Computer Vision and Pattern Recognition, pp. 7263–7271 (2017)

28. Sturari, M., Paolanti, M., Frontoni, E., Mancini, A., Zingaretti, P.: Robotic platform for deep change detection for rail safety and security. In: 2017 European Conference on Mobile Robots (ECMR), pp. 1–6. IEEE (2017)

29. Wang, J., You, J., Li, Q., Xu, Y.: Orthogonal discriminant vector for face recognition across pose. Pattern Recogn. **45**(12), 4069–4079 (2012)

30. Wiskott, L., Fellous, J.-M., Krüger, N., von der Malsburg, C.: Face recognition by elastic bunch graph matching. In: Sommer, G., Daniilidis, K., Pauli, J (eds.) CAIP 1997. LNCS, vol. 1296, pp. 456–463. Springer, Heidelberg (1997). https://doi.org/10.1007/3-540-63460-6_150

31. Wright, J., Yang, A.Y., Ganesh, A., Sastry, S.S., Ma, Y.: Robust face recognition via sparse representation. IEEE Trans. Pattern Anal. Mach Intell. **31**(2), 210–227 (2009)

32. Xu, Y., Zhu, Q., Fan, Z., Qiu, M., Chen, Y., Liu, H.: Coarse to fine k nearest neighbor classifier. Pattern Recogn. Lett. **34**(9), 980–986 (2013)

33. Xu, Y., Zhu, X., Li, Z., Liu, G., Lu, Y., Liu, H.: Using the original and 'symmetrical face' training samples to perform representation based two-step face recognition. Pattern Recogn. **46**(4), 1151–1158 (2013)

34. Zhang, D.: Advanced pattern recognition technologies with applications to biometrics, IGI Global (2009)

35. Zou, C., Sun, N., Ji, Z., Zhao, L.: 2DCCA: a novel method for small sample size face recognition. In: IEEE Workshop on Applications of Computer Vision 2007, WACV 2007, pp. 43–43. IEEE (2007)

Industrial Session

Boosting Object Recognition in Point Clouds by Saliency Detection

Marlon Marcon[1,2,3](✉)[iD], Riccardo Spezialetti[3][iD], Samuele Salti[3][iD],
Luciano Silva[2][iD], and Luigi Di Stefano[3][iD]

[1] Federal University of Technology - Paraná, Dois Vizinhos, Brazil
marlonmarcon@utfpr.edu.br
[2] Federal University of Paraná, Curitiba, Brazil
luciano@inf.ufpr.br
[3] University of Bologna, Bologna, Italy
{riccardo.spezialetti,samuele.salti,luigi.distefano}@unibo.it

Abstract. Object recognition in 3D point clouds is a challenging task, mainly when time is an important factor to deal with, such as in industrial applications. Local descriptors are an amenable choice whenever the 6 DoF pose of recognized objects should also be estimated. However, the pipeline for this kind of descriptors is highly time-consuming. In this work, we propose an update to the traditional pipeline, by adding a preliminary filtering stage referred to as saliency boost. We perform tests on a standard object recognition benchmark by considering four keypoint detectors and four local descriptors, in order to compare time and recognition performance between the traditional pipeline and the boosted one. Results on time show that the boosted pipeline could turn out up to 5 times faster, with the recognition rate improving in most of the cases and exhibiting only a slight decrease in the others. These results suggest that the boosted pipeline can speed-up processing time substantially with limited impacts or even benefits in recognition accuracy.

Keywords: Local descriptors · RGB-D images ·
Salient object detection

1 Introduction

Application of computer vision techniques aimed at object recognition is gathering increasing attention in industrial applications. Among others, prominent applications in this space include robot picking in assembly lines and surface inspection. To address these tasks, the vision system must estimate the 6 DoF (degrees-of-freedom) pose of the sought objects, which calls for a 3D object recognition approach. Moreover, in industrial settings robustness, accuracy as well as run-time performance are particularly important.

Reliance on RGB-D sensors providing both depth and color information is conducive to 3D object recognition. Yet, typical nuisances to be dealt with in

© Springer Nature Switzerland AG 2019
M. Cristani et al. (Eds.): ICIAP 2019 Workshops, LNCS 11808, pp. 321–331, 2019.
https://doi.org/10.1007/978-3-030-30754-7_32

3D object recognition applications include clutter, occlusions and the significant degree of noise which affects most RGB-D cameras. Many studies, such as [6,8], have investigated on these problems and highlighted how local 3D descriptors can effectively withstand clutter, occlusions and noise in 3D object recognition.

The local descriptors pipeline for 3D object recognition is however quite slow. Indeed, RGB-D cameras generate a high amount of data (over 30 MB/s) and, as this may hinder performance in embedded and real-time applications, sampling strategies are needed. To reduce processing time, keypoint extraction techniques are widely used. In addition, some solutions propose to assign higher priority to specific image areas, like, for example, in the foveation technique [5]. Another approach, inspired by human perception and widely explored for 2D image segmentation, consists in saliency detection, which identifies the most prominent points within an image [2]. Unlike the foveation, which processes arbitrary regions, the use of saliency allows for highlighting image regions that are known to be more important.

This work proposes a solution to improve the performance of the standard local descriptors pipeline for 3D object recognition from point clouds. The idea consists in adding a preliminary step, referred to as Saliency Boost, which filters the point clouds using a saliency mask in order to reduce the number of processed points and consequently the whole processing time. Besides, by selecting only salient regions, our approach may yield a reduction in the number of false positives, thereby often also enhancing object recognition accuracy.

2 Related Works

3D object recognition systems based on local descriptors typically deploy two stages, one carried out offline and the other online, referred to as training and testing, respectively. The training stage builds the database of objects, storing their features for later use. In the testing stage, then, features are extracted from scene images. Given a scene, the typical pipeline, depicted in Fig. 1 and described, e.g. in [4], consists of the following steps (1) Keypoints extraction; (2) Local descriptors calculation; (3) Matching; (4) Grouping correspondences; and (5) Absolute orientation estimation. The first two, described in more details below, are those which really differentiate the various approaches and impact performance most directly.

2.1 Keypoints Extraction

This step concerns selecting some surface points, either from images or point clouds. According to [18], keypoint extraction must reduce data dimensionality without losing discriminative capacity. In this work, we explore techniques which work in 3D, as Uniform sampling and Intrinsic Shape Signatures (ISS), and 2D alike, i.e. SIFT and FAST.

Uniform Sampling downsamples the point cloud segmenting it in voxels based on a certain leaf size, and selects as keypoint each nearest neighbor point to a voxel centroid [13]. ISS [19] selects keypoints based on a local surface saliency criterion, so as to extract 3D points that exhibit a large surface variation in their neighbourhood.

The keypoint detector proposed in SIFT [11] is arguably the prominent proposal for RGB images. It is based on the detection of blob-like and high contrast local features amenable to compute highly distinctive features and similarity invariant image descriptors. The FAST keypoint extractor is a 2D corner detector based on a machine learning approach, which is widely used in real-time computer vision applications due to its remarkable computational efficiency.

2.2   Local Descriptors

A local 3D descriptor processes the neighborhood of a keypoint to produce a feature vector discriminative with respect to clutter and robust to noise. Many descriptors have been proposed in recent years and several works, e.g. [6], have investigated on their relative merits and limitations. In this work, we explore both descriptors which process only depth information, such as Signatures of Histograms of OrienTatIons (SHOT) [16] and Fast Point Feature Histogram (FPFH) [14], as well as depth and color, like Point Feature Histogram for Color (PFHRGB) [15] and Color SHOT (CSHOT) [16].

Introduced by [16], SHOT describes a keypoint based on spatial and geometric information. To calculate the descriptor, first 3D Local Reference Frame (LRF) around the keypoint is established. Then, a canonical spherical grid is divided into 32 segments. Each segment results in a histogram that describes the angles between the normals at the keypoint and the normal at the neighboring points. The authors also proposed a variation to work with color at the points, called CSHOT. The color value is encoded according to the CIELab color space and added to the angular information deployed in SHOT. This descriptor is known to yield better results than SHOT when applied to colored point clouds.

PFHRGB [15] is based on the Point Feature Histogram (PFH) and stores geometrical information by analyzing the angular variation of the normal between each pair of combination in a set composed by the keypoint and all its k-neighbors. PFHRGB works on RGB and stores also the color ratio between the keypoint and its neighbors, increasing its efficiency on RGB-D data [1]. In order to speed-up the descriptor calculation, [14] proposed a simplified solution, called FPFH, which considers only the differences between the keypoint and its k-neighbors. Also, an influence weight is stored, resulting in a descriptor which can be calculated faster while maintaining its discriminative capacity.

2.3   Saliency Detection

Salient object detection is a topic inspired by human perception, which affirms that the human being tends to select visual information based on attention mechanisms in the brain [9]. Its objective is to emphasize regions of interest in a scene [2]. Many applications benefit from the use of saliency, such as object tracking and recognition, image retrieval, restoring and segmentation.

The majority of recent works perform saliency detection using either RGB [2,7] or RGB-D [3,10] images and are based on Deep Learning algorithms.

3   Proposed Approach

We present a way to improve significantly the time performance and also the memory efficiency of the standard pipeline described above, by adding an additional step to the original pipeline. We refer to this step as *saliency boost*. It leverages the RGB scene image by detecting salient regions within it, which are then used to filter the point cloud and to execute the local descriptors' pipeline only on salient regions. In particular, we use the saliency mask to reduce the search space for 3D keypoints by letting them run on the part of the point cloud which corresponds to the salient regions of the image. To project saliency information from the 2D domain of the RGB image to the point cloud we leverage the registration information provided by RGB-D cameras. Figure 1 presents a graphical overview of the approach. In the case of 2D keypoint detectors, instead, we run them on the full RGB image and we then filter out keypoints not belonging to the salient regions: we do not filter the image before the keypoint extraction step because 2D detectors exploit also pixels from the background to define blobs and edges/corners to detect keypoints. In the 3D case, instead, points from the background are usually far away and outside the sphere used to define the keypoint neighborhood, so it is possible to filter them before without affecting the detector performance.

Our approach is not dependent from a specific saliency detection technique. In this work, we choose the DSS algorithm [7], and we detect salient areas by running the trained model provided by the authors.

4   Experimental Results

4.1   Dataset

The experiments were performed on the Kinect dataset from the University of Bologna, presented in [16]. This dataset has sixteen scenes, and six models with pose annotation. Each model is represented as a set of 2.5D views from different angles and has from thirteen to twenty samples. Figure 2 depicts some examples of models and scenes in this dataset.

4.2   Local Descriptors Pipeline

In the local feature pipeline for object recognition, the choice of the keypoint extraction and description methods is key, and depends on the applications, the kind of 3D representation available and their resolution, the sensor noise, etc. In

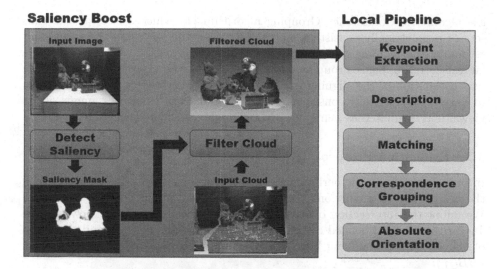

Fig. 1. Local descriptor pipeline with saliency boost. (Color figure online)

Fig. 2. Examples of models and scenes from Kinect dataset [16]. Models of Mario and Rabbit (leftmost figures), and scenes (rightmost figures).

order to evaluate the performance of the proposed approach in an application-agnostic scenario, we test combinations of several descriptors and detectors. The selected descriptors are: SHOT and CSHOT (Color SHOT) [16], FPFH [14] and PFHRGB [15]. The keypoint detectors working on 3D data are Uniform sampling (with leaf sizes ranging from 2 to 5 cm with step of 1 cm) and ISS [19], while on images we test SIFT [11] and FAST [12], run on the RGB image and projected on the point cloud, as discussed.

The matching step is performed by nearest neighbor (NN) search implemented by the FLANN library, integrated in the Point Cloud Library (PCL) [13]. A KdTree is built for each view of each model in the database and each keypoint on the scene is matched to only one point of one view of one model in the database by selecting the closest descriptor among views and models. After this process, all matches pointing to a view of a model are processed by the Geometric Consistency Grouping algorithm [4], which selects all the sub-sets of geometrically consistent matches between the view and the scene, and estimates the aligning transformation. The transformation obtained from the largest correspondence group among all the views of an object is considered the best estimation of the aligning transformation for that object. If an object fails to have a geometrically consistent subset with at least 3 matches among all its views, it is estimated as being not present in the considered scene.

4.3 Evaluation Protocol

In order to evaluate the performance of the proposed object detection pipeline, the correctness of predictions both of object presence and pose are evaluated. We adopt the Intersection over Union (IoU) metric (Eq. 1), also known as the Jaccard index, and defined as the ratio between the intersection and the union of the estimated bounding box (BB_{Est}) and the ground truth bounding box (BB_{GT}).

$$IoU = \frac{BB_{GT} \cap BB_{Est}}{BB_{GT} \cup BB_{Est}} \tag{1}$$

A detection is evaluated as correct if its IoU with the ground truth is greater than 0.25, as in [17]. Given detections and ground truth boxes, we calculate precision and recall (Eqs. 2 and 3) by considering a correct estimation as True Positive (TP), i.e. $IoU \geq 0.25$, an estimation of an absent object as False Positive (FP), and misdetections or detections with $IoU < 0.25$ as False Negative (FN).

$$precision = \frac{TP}{(TP + FP)} \tag{2}$$

$$recall = \frac{TP}{(TP + FN)} \tag{3}$$

To calculate precision-recall curves (PRC), we varied the threshold on the number of geometrically consistent correspondences to declare a detection, increasing it from the minimum value of 3 up to when no more detections are found in a scene. The area under the PRC curve (AUC) is then computed for each combination detector/descriptor and used to compare and rank the pipelines.

4.4 Implementation Details

Tests were performed on a Linux Ubuntu 16.04 LTS machine, using the Point Cloud Library (PCL), Version 1.8.1, OpenCV 3.4.1 and the VTK 6.2 library. For comparison purposes, all trials were performed on the same computer, equipped with an Intel Core i7-3632QM processor and 8 GB of RAM. When available in PCL, the parallel version of each descriptor was used (e.g. for SHOT, CSHOT, and FPFH).

As for parameters of detectors, the ISS Non-Maxima Suppression radius was set to 0.6 cm and the neighborhood radius to 1 cm, while for SIFT and FAST we used the default values provided in OpenCV. As for descriptors, to estimate the normals we used the first ten neighbors of each point while the description radius was set to 5 cm for all the considered.

4.5   Results

In this section, we present the results obtained in the experiments. All trials were performed on the Kinect dataset, comparing the original pipeline (blue part in Fig. 1) with the proposed pipeline with saliency boosting. For each descriptor and each pipeline we tested seven keypoint extractors, totaling 56 trials. The scene processing time, which comprises the saliency detection (only for boosted pipeline), keypoint extraction, description, matching correspondences, clustering and pose estimation, was measured to verify the impact of the proposed modification also on processing time.

Results in terms of the number of keypoints extracted are presented in Table 1. The saliency filtering reduces significantly the average number of keypoins extracted by each detector: reduction using saliency boost ranges from 24.58% to almost 80% with an average of 56%.

Table 1. Average number of keypoints extracted from scenes in the trials with the traditional local pipeline (LP) and boosted by saliency (Boost). The column "%" represents the variation between them. Best value in bold.

Keypoints	LP	Boost	%
FAST	489.71	369.36	−24.58
ISS	4201.16	846.75	**−79.84**
SIFT	282.79	199.79	−29.35
$US_{0.02}$	4559.80	1457.86	−68.03
$US_{0.03}$	2144.07	731.36	−65.89
$US_{0.04}$	1266.00	446.29	−64.75
$US_{0.05}$	820.57	303.71	−62.99
Average	–	–	−56.49

The number of keypoints extracted impacts directly the running time of the pipeline, mainly by two factors: the number of descriptors that have to be computed and the time it takes to match them. The SHOT and CSHOT descriptors are calculated relatively fast but due to their length (352 and 1344 bins respectively), the matching phase is slower, accounting for 97 and 99% of the processing time, respectively. The PFHRGB and FPFH are shorter descriptors (250 and 33 bins respectively), but the description is slower and requires 94 and 89% of the overall time, respectively. As shown in Table 2, the extraction of keypoints only in salient regions reduces drastically the processing time for both kinds of descriptors.

In the best case, reductions in processing time is as high as 80%, i.e. the boosted pipeline is 5 times faster due to the proposed saliency boosting. For all the considered detector/descriptor combinations, deployment of the saliency boosting step always reduces the processing time significantly, from the 22% obtained by FAST/SHOT to 83% for ISS and $US_{0.05}$ with FPFH.

Table 2. Average scene processing time (s) in the trials with the traditional Local Pipeline (LP) and boosted by saliency (Boost). The column "%" represents the variation between them. Best value in each column in bold.

Keypoints	CSHOT			SHOT			PFHRGB			FPFH		
	LP	Boost	%	LP	Boost	%	LP	Boost	%	LP	Boost	%
FAST	244.0	174.8	−28.36	59.1	45.9	−22.31	351.4	238.8	−32.06	46.6	19.0	−59.14
ISS	226.1	**47.7**	**−78.90**	72.4	**17.1**	**−76.45**	2580.4	489.1	−81.05	141.9	24.3	−82.92
SIFT	**132.2**	94.5	−28.50	**34.3**	25.7	−25.29	**195.3**	138.2	−29.24	**31.3**	17.7	−43.39
$US_{0.02}$	2167.9	668.8	−69.15	505.7	174.5	−65.50	2100.9	455.5	−78.32	150.6	29.6	−80.32
$US_{0.03}$	988.0	335.6	−66.04	238.8	88.0	−63.16	913.2	191.5	−79.03	137.4	24.1	−82.47
$US_{0.04}$	583.4	205.2	−64.83	139.7	54.1	−61.29	506.1	103.5	−79.56	130.9	22.2	−83.08
$US_{0.05}$	378.1	139.9	−63.01	90.7	37.2	−58.99	304.3	**62.1**	−79.61	128.7	20.9	**−83.76**
Average			−56.97			−53.29			−65.55			−73.58

Reducing processing time is only beneficial if it doesn't harm recognition and localization performance. Interestingly, deployment of the saliency boosting step very often improves AUC with respect to the traditional pipeline, as shown in Table 3. In particular, for 19 of the 28 trials which included the saliency boosting step, the pipeline boosted by saliency performed better also on AUC, with massive improvements by more than 50% for PFHRGB and FPFH. Viceversa, when the AUC decreases due to the deployment of the saliency boost, it does it usually marginally, by 1 or 2%, with the worst decrease in AUC being greater than 10% only once, when using the SIFT detector.

Table 3. AUC results in the trials with the traditional Local Pipeline (LP) and boosted by saliency (Boost). The column "%" represents the variation between them. Best value in each column in bold.

Keypoints	CSHOT			SHOT			PFHRGB			FPFH		
	LP	Boost	%	LP	Boost	%	LP	Boost	%	LP	Boost	%
FAST	0.946	0.874	−7.61	0.915	0.892	−2.45	0.743	0.761	2.43	0.631	0.668	5.89
ISS	0.868	0.881	1.52	0.866	0.912	**5.30**	**0.745**	**0.900**	20.68	0.491	**0.752**	**53.04**
SIFT	0.864	0.889	2.83	0.903	0.820	−9.15	0.472	0.549	16.41	0.529	0.476	−10.13
$US_{0.02}$	**0.949**	**0.948**	−0.07	**0.941**	**0.938**	−0.31	0.739	0.807	9.19	**0.641**	0.728	13.48
$US_{0.03}$	0.861	0.905	5.08	0.875	0.843	−3.58	0.731	0.814	11.37	0.488	0.621	27.26
$US_{0.04}$	0.832	0.875	5.23	0.824	0.817	−0.92	0.564	0.700	24.22	0.289	0.368	27.14
$US_{0.05}$	0.582	0.619	**6.19**	0.682	0.644	−5.64	0.373	0.599	**60.76**	0.145	0.162	11.77
Average			1.88			−2.39			20.72			18.35

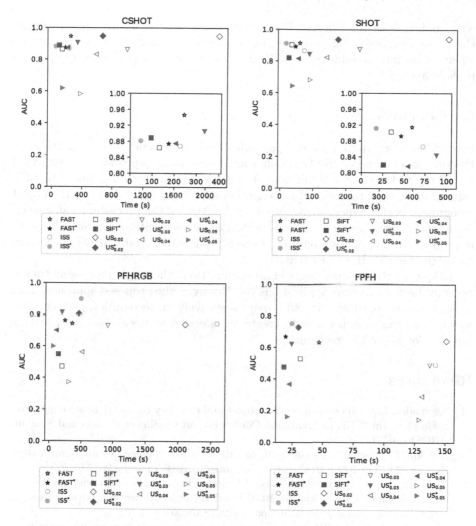

Fig. 3. AUC × Time Results for the descriptors: (a) CSHOT, (b) SHOT, (c) PFHRGB and (d) FPFH. Boosted pipeline denoted by an asterisk (*) next of the keypoint name.

While the AUC generally increases with the boosted pipeline, it doesn't do so on average when deployed with the SHOT descriptor. However, it does increase by 5% in the very relevant case of combining SHOT with the ISS detector, the combination that delivers the fastest running time among all the tested variants (as shown in Table 2).

Finally, in Fig. 3, we report a Pareto analysis on the data for all descriptors. We can see how points (i.e. detector/descriptor pairs) closer to the ideal point (that is $AUC = 1$ and Time as low as possible) are obtained by the execution of the boosted pipeline. In this analysis, the CSHOT, SHOT and FPFH obtained the best performance when paired with the boosted ISS (ISS*), while PFHRGB when paired with the Boosted Uniform Sampling at $r = 3\,\mathrm{cm}$ ($US^*_{0.03}$). Hence, the boosting pipeline outperforms the traditional one for all tested descriptors when taking into account the combined effect of processing time and recognition performance.

5   Conclusion

In this work, we presented an approach based on saliency detection to boost the processing time of the traditional local descriptor pipeline. It was verified for all the tested cases a significant processing time reduction, from 22 to 83%. Interestingly, the processing time reduction didn't generally decrease the object recognition performance, as measured by the AUC of the precision recall curves. Actually, an improvement on the performance recognition was found for all descriptors in at least one pairing, up to 5% for SHOT and CSHOT, and more than 50% for FPFH and PFHRGB.

In spite of the improvements in processing time, the whole processing time is not suitable for real-time applications yet. However, the proposed approach offers a considerable speed-up without impact negatively on recognition performance, which brings us a step closer to create an effective and real-time local feature pipeline for 3D object recognition.

References

1. Alexandre, L.A.: 3D descriptors for object and category recognition: a comparative evaluation. In: IEEE International Conference on Intelligent Robots and Systems (IROS) (2012)
2. Aytekin, C., Iosifidis, A., Gabbouj, M.: Probabilistic saliency estimation. Pattern Recogn. **74**, 359–372 (2018). https://doi.org/10.1016/j.patcog.2017.09.023
3. Chen, H., Li, Y., Su, D.: Multi-modal fusion network with multi-scale multi-path and cross-modal interactions for RGB-D salient object detection. Pattern Recogn. (2018). https://doi.org/10.1016/j.patcog.2018.08.007
4. Chen, H., Bhanu, B.: 3D free-form object recognition in range images using local surface patches. Pattern Recogn. Lett. **28**(10), 1252–1262 (2007). https://doi.org/10.1016/j.patrec.2007.02.009
5. Gomes, R.B., da Silva, B.M.F., de Medeiros Rocha, L.K., Aroca, R.V., Velho, L.C.P.R., Gonçalves, L.M.G.: Efficient 3D object recognition using foveated point clouds. Comput. Graph. **37**(5), 496–508 (2013). https://doi.org/10.1016/j.cag.2013.03.005
6. Guo, Y., Bennamoun, M., Sohel, F., Lu, M., Wan, J., Kwok, N.M.: A comprehensive performance evaluation of 3D local feature descriptors. Int. J. Comput. Vis. **116**(1), 66–89 (2015). https://doi.org/10.1007/s11263-015-0824-y
7. Hou, Q., Cheng, M., Hu, X., Borji, A., Tu, Z., Torr, P.H.S.: Deeply supervised salient object detection with short connections. IEEE Trans. Pattern Anal. Mach. Intell. **41**(4), 815–828 (2019). https://doi.org/10.1109/TPAMI.2018.2815688
8. Johnson, A., Hebert, M.: Using spin images for efficient object recognition in cluttered 3D scenes. IEEE Trans. Pattern Anal. Mach. Intell. **21**(5), 433–449 (1999). https://doi.org/10.1109/34.765655

9. Kastner, S., Ungerleider, L.G.: Mechanisms of visual attention in the human cortex. Annu. Rev. Neurosci. **23**(1), 315–341 (2000). https://doi.org/10.1146/annurev. neuro.23.1.315

10. Li, Z., Lang, C., Feng, S., Wang, T.: Saliency ranker: a new salient object detection method. J. Vis. Commun. Image Represent. **50**, 16–26 (2018). https://doi.org/10. 1016/j.jvcir.2017.11.004

11. Lowe, D.G.: Object recognition from local scale-invariant features. In: 7th IEEE International Conference on Computer Vision, vol. 2, pp. 1150–1157, September 1999. https://doi.org/10.1109/ICCV.1999.790410

12. Rosten, E., Drummond, T.: Machine learning for high-speed corner detection. In: Leonardis, A., Bischof, H., Pinz, A. (eds.) ECCV 2006. LNCS, vol. 3951, pp. 430–443. Springer, Heidelberg (2006). https://doi.org/10.1007/11744023_34

13. Rusu, R.B., Cousins, S.: 3D is here: Point cloud library (PCL). In: 2011 IEEE International Conference on Robotics and Automation, pp. 1–4, May 2011. https:// doi.org/10.1109/ICRA.2011.5980567

14. Rusu, R.B., Blodow, N., Beetz, M.: Fast point feature histograms (FPFH) for 3D registration. In: IEEE International Conference on Robotics and Automation (ICRA). IEEE, May 2009. https://doi.org/10.1109/robot.2009.5152473

15. Rusu, R., Blodow, N., Marton, Z., Beetz, M.: Aligning point cloud views using persistent feature histograms. In: IEEE International Conference on Intelligent Robots and Systems (IROS). IEEE, September 2008. https://doi.org/10.1109/iros. 2008.4650967

16. Salti, S., Tombari, F., Di Stefano, L.: SHOT: unique signatures of histograms for surface and texture description. Comput. Vis. Image Underst. **125**, 251–264 (2014). https://doi.org/10.1016/j.cviu.2014.04.011

17. Song, S., Xiao, J.: Deep sliding shapes for Amodal 3D object detection in RGB-D images. In: IEEE Conference on Computer Vision and Pattern Recognition (CVPR). IEEE, June 2016. https://doi.org/10.1109/cvpr.2016.94

18. Tombari, F., Salti, S., Di Stefano, L.: Performance evaluation of 3D keypoint detectors. Int. J. Comput. Vis. **102**(1–3), 198–220 (2012). https://doi.org/10.1007/ s11263-012-0545-4

19. Zhong, Y.: Intrinsic shape signatures: a shape descriptor for 3D object recognition. In: 12th IEEE International Conference on Computer Vision (ICCV) Workshops. IEEE, September 2009. https://doi.org/10.1109/iccvw.2009.5457637

Hand Gesture Recognition for Collaborative Workstations: A Smart Command System Prototype

Cristina Nuzzi$^{(\boxtimes)}$ (iD), Simone Pasinetti (iD), Roberto Pagani (iD),
Franco Docchio (iD), and Giovanna Sansoni (iD)

Università degli Studi di Brescia, Via Branze 38, 25123 Brescia, BS, Italy
c.nuzzi@unibs.it

Abstract. Human-machine collaboration is a key aspect in modern industries, which must be compliant to the Industry 4.0 paradigm. Although the collaboration can be achieved using a Collaborative Robot in a purposely designed workstation, this solution is not always neither feasible nor affordable for the specific task to be carried out in the workstation. On the other hand, using a smart HMI to make an industrial robot a "smart" robot can be a better and affordable solution depending on the task. In this work we present the preliminary development and characteristics of an experimental HMI for smart manufacturing developed in MATLAB and ROS Industrial. The collaboration between humans and robots is achieved by leveraging the Faster R-CNN Object Detector to robustly detect and recognize the hand gestures performed in real-time. The system is based on a state machine to carry out simple tasks such as the repeated movement of the robot following a given trajectory and a pick and place task where the robot interactively reaches a given point and a jog modality.

Keywords: Human-Machine Interface · Gesture recognition · Object Detector

1 Introduction

In recent years, the advances of Computer Vision research have brought exciting results and applications in different fields, especially thanks to the rise of Deep Learning. The ability to see and interpret visual information is of utmost importance in the complex task of creating smart applications, which will therefore be able to interact with humans in a more natural and straightforward way.

A perfect example of this is the industrial world, which nowadays must quickly cope up with new technological advances in order to adhere to the Industry 4.0 paradigm [1]. Industrial machines and robots are intensively used in industrial plants, but not every machine needs to cooperate with humans. Human-machine cooperation is, in fact, only needed for those tasks which still require human intervention, but can be eased and/or sped up with the aid of a smart robot [2].

In this context, smart manufacturing can be achieved in two ways: (i) by using a Collaborative Robot [3], which can safely cooperate with humans at the cost of reduced

M. Cristani et al. (Eds.): ICIAP 2019 Workshops, LNCS 11808, pp. 332–342, 2019.
https://doi.org/10.1007/978-3-030-30754-7_33

speed and force, or (ii) by using the existing machines and robots of the plant, which are "made smart" by a purposely designed Human-Machine Interface (HMI) [4].

To design an HMI with these properties, it is fundamental to have in mind how humans cooperate and interact: by using voice and by using body language [5]. Body language has been studied for long time and interesting results have been accomplished, both focused on the whole body pose [6] and on the hands pose only [7, 8]. Speech recognition, on the other hand, can be tricky especially if used in industrial plants, where loud noises are usually in the background; therefore, we decided to focus on hand gesture recognition as a first approach to the problem.

In this work we explored these concepts, intensely leveraging existing Deep Learning models and techniques to interpret a purposely designed set of hand gestures. Hence, we aim to build a smart HMI which can interpret these commands and translate them to the robot, which will therefore execute them.

2 Gestures Analysis

To design the gesture recognition portion of the system, we used a well-known Deep Learning model called "Faster Region Proposal Convolutional Neural Network", or Faster R-CNN [9]. The model has been developed and trained in MATLAB 2017b, the details of the structure detailed in [10], on a Linux machine equipped with a GPU Nvidia GeForce 1060 6 GB, a CPU Intel i7 6700 and 16 GB RAM.

2.1 Experimental Dataset

The dataset used for this work has been manually acquired using different smartphones. A person moved around the actor with the device, acquiring the gestures with different angles. A total of 15 actors have been registered performing the gestures, 5 females and 10 males (Fig. 1). Different backgrounds where chosen for each actor, in order to increase the variability of the dataset and prevent the network to learn how to recognize the background instead of the hands. It is worth noting that 5 actors presented a solid bright green color background; in particular two of them have the hands segmented out from the rest of the body by a green frame (Fig. 1k and l).

The dataset has been augmented using a random combination of 3 augmenting techniques:

- **Random spatial distortion:** applies a virtual zoom to the original HD image and a dimensional distortion, thus losing the original aspect ratio. The distorted images have been then cropped to the standard size of 224×224 px (Fig. 2a and b);
- **Random color distortion:** multiplies the channels of the image for a random numerical value. To increase variability, the program selects randomly the color space on which perform this distortion (RGB, HSV). Speckle noise is added afterwards with intensity randomly chosen (Fig. 2a and b);
- **Artificial background:** 5 actors have been purposely acquired with a solid bright green color background. This color is easily selected by the program and substituted

with a random background downloaded from the internet, followed by a low-pass filtering step to obtain a more realistic fusion between the actor and the new background (Fig. 2c).

The total number of images is 39584 for the training dataset and 5739 for the test dataset, both randomly shuffled.

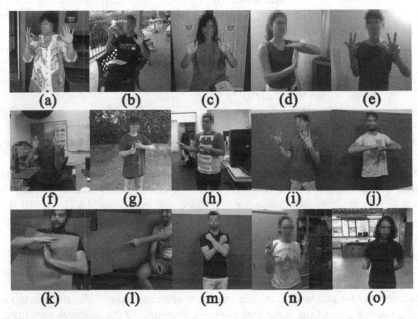

Fig. 1. Examples taken from the dataset for every actor. Actors from (a) to (l) have been used for training, while actors from (m) to (o) have been used for testing.

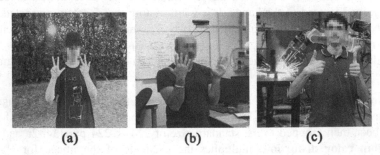

Fig. 2. Examples of the augmenting techniques. (a) Spatial distortion along the y-axis, RGB distortion and speckle noise added on top, (b) spatial distortion along the y-axis, HSV distortion and speckle noise added on top, (c) artificial background added, random crop and zoom, speckle noise added on top.

2.2   Selection of the Gestures

The gestures chosen for the experiment are shown in Fig. 3. As a first approach, we wanted to understand if the model was able to properly recognize left-hand and right-hand gestures and, at the same time, back-hand and front-hand gestures. Because of this, gestures from Fig. 3a to m have 4 variants. Gestures from Fig. 3n to q have only left and right variants, while gestures in Fig. 3r and s have four variants since these both are intended as "*directional gestures*". Finally, gestures from Fig. 3t to v are two-hand gestures, thus having only one variant.

Table 1 shows the results obtained from a training made by using only back-hand and front-hand gestures of the same hand (left or right only). The parameters used are: (i) the number or true positives (TP), (ii) the number of true negatives (TN), (iii) the number of false positives (FP), (iv) the number of false negatives (FN), (v) the total accuracy, (vi) the positive predicted value or precision (PPV), (vii) the true negative rate or specificity (TNR), (viii) the true positive rate or recall (TPR) and (ix) the F1-Score, which is an harmonic average of PPV and TPR.

This first experiment highlights that back-hand and front-hand gestures are often misclassified with each other by the model, and that gestures from "*Six*" to "*Nine*" are extremely hard to be recognized, given their similarities. The results for the other variants are supposed to be similar to the abovementioned ones, hence were not computed.

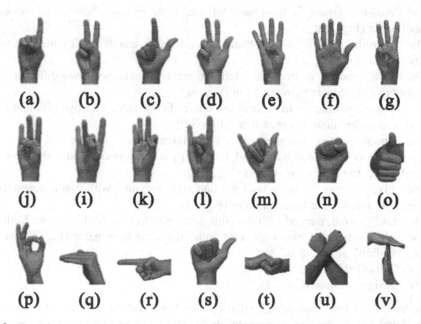

Fig. 3. Experimental gestures proposed. (a) One_FR, (b) Victory_FR, (c) Two_FR, (d) Three_FR, (e) Four_FR, (f) Five_FR, (g) Six_FR, (j) Seven_FR, (i) Eight_FR, (k) Nine_FR, (l) Rock_FR, (m) Span_FR, (n) Punch_FR, (o) Thumb_R, (p) Ok_R, (q) Vel_R, (r) OneH_FR, (s) ThumbH_FR, (t) Collab, (u) XSign, (v) TimeOut.

Table 1. Evaluation results of the first experiment test dataset.

TP	TN	FP	FN	Accuracy	PPV	TNR	TPR	F1-Score
3347	0	2392	1205	48%	58%	0%	74%	65%

2.3   Selected HMI Commands

Given the results of the first experiment, we (i) removed almost every back-hand gesture and (ii) used only a limited number of gestures, some of which have been merged in a single class even if they were intended as different classes or with different meaning with respect to the original one. The modified gestures are: (i) the *"Thumb"* gesture, used to represent number one because the latter is frequently classified as the *"Two"* or the *"Victory"* gestures due to the fingers positions, or as the *"Punch"* gesture because of the presence of the knuckles; (ii) the *"Span"* gesture, used to represent number four because the *"Five"* and *"Four"* gestures are frequently misinterpreted due to a wrong placing of the bounding box, which cuts off the thumb of the hand. This issue may be fixed by adopting a different model (i.e. the RFCN model, which adopts a voting method inside the bounding box to correctly place it around the object of interest [11]). Finally, (iii) the *"Nine"* gesture has been merged with the *"Ok"* gesture because the two can be considered the same gesture according to how much the "o" shape of the gesture is shown to the camera.

In conclusion, the selected gestures chosen after this evaluation are:

- The **"Punch"** gesture, in front-hand left and right variants, both under the same label name (Fig. 3n);
- The **"Thumb"** gesture, in front-hand left and right variants, both under the same label name (Fig. 3o);
- The **"Two"** gesture, in front-hand left and right variants, with two different label names to differentiate between them (Fig. 3c);
- The **"Three"** gesture, in front-hand left and right variants, with two different label names to differentiate between them (Fig. 3d);
- The **"Span"** gesture, necessary since the original "Four" gesture was often misclassified. Both front and back-hand, left and right variants are used under the same label name, to increase robustness (Fig. 3m);
- The **"Five"** gesture, in front-hand left and right variants, with two different label names to differentiate between them (Fig. 3f);
- The **"Ok"** gesture, merged with the Nine gesture to form a single gesture. Both left and right front-hand variants are used under the same label name (Fig. 3k and p);
- The **"Collab"** gesture (Fig. 3t);
- The **"TimeOut"** gesture (Fig. 3v);
- The **"XSign"** gesture (Fig. 3u).

A second final test has been carried out on them, and the results are reported in Table 2 and Fig. 4. For this experiment, both right-hand and left-hand gestures have been used for the selected gestures, for a total of 29542 images for training and 4066 for testing.

Table 2. Evaluation results of the second experiment test dataset.

TP	TN	FP	FN	Accuracy	PPV	TNR	TPR	F1-Score
2955	0	929	278	71%	76%	0%	91%	83%

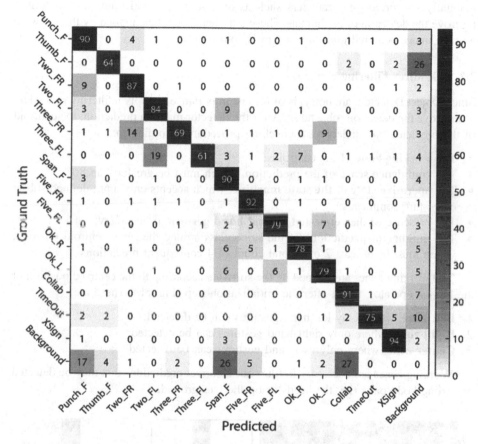

Fig. 4. Normalized confusion matrix of the results of the second experiment test dataset.

3 Command System Interface

The core functionalities of the proposed experimental Command System Interface have been developed as part of a state machine. The system is based on MATLAB 2017b for the recognition of gestures and for the description of the state machine, and on ROS Industrial [12] for the communication between the system and the robot controller.

3.1 Initialization Procedure

To improve the detection performances and to filter out the incorrect predictions, it is necessary to perform an initialization procedure at the start of the system. The operator position is found in the image by performing the *"XSign"* gesture. After 15 successful acquisitions of the gesture, the final centroid position is calculated as the mean of the centroids of the boxes. To ease the process, after the first successful acquisition of the gesture the area on the left and right of the box is rendered in black, hence removing distracting portions of the image such as the background (Fig. 5a). It is also possible to manually set correction parameters such as hue, saturation and brightness to further improve the detection of the human. These parameters are then applied by the software to each image acquired until the system is shut down.

3.2   Gestures Filtering

Since Object Detectors are noisy, is of utmost importance to apply a filtering procedure to improve the detection robustness. After the detector makes a prediction, the centroid of the predicted box undergoes a checking procedure according to:

- The **working zone** of the centroids;
- The **confidence score** of the prediction, which must be greater than 80%;
- The **operative state of the state machine**, which accepts only a pre-defined subset of gesture commands;
- The presence of the **requested second hand gesture**, if necessary;
- The **number of predictions** of the same class around the same centroid position, which must be at least 2 on a total count of 4 consequent predictions.

The working zones are defined by the software according to the centroid position of the human operator, found after the initialization step (Fig. 5b). These are:

1. **Left zone**, where only left-hand gestures can be detected;
2. **Right zone**, where only right-hand gestures can be detected;
3. **Center zone**, where only two-hand gestures can be detected.

Working zones are necessary to filter out incorrect predictions that may be detected on wrong body parts (i.e. the head) or on the background.

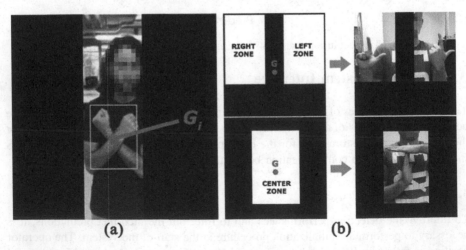

(a)   (b)

Fig. 5. Initialization procedure. (a) Centroid detection, (b) working zones definitions.

It is worth noting that since the number of selected gestures is less than the number of initial gestures, we expand the number of commands by using both single-hand commands and two-hands commands, obtained as a combination of single-hand gestures. This approach has been already explored in our previous publications [13, 14], which has been proved successful. Commands are then subdivided by their meaning and usage in the Command System as follows:

1. **Numerical commands:** gestures from "*Punch*" to "*Five*", indicating numbers from 0 to 5. These are performed with a single hand;
2. **Interface commands:** these are used to confirm, cancel or undo the given commands, thus avoiding giving the robot the wrong command by mistake (Fig. 6). Each command is performed with both hands to create a more robust instruction. To confirm an instruction the "*Punch*" gesture must be performed by both hands at the same time. To delete an instruction and re-enter it in the system, the "*Five*" gesture must be performed with one hand and the "*Punch*" gesture with the other. To cancel an instruction, the "*Five*" gesture must be performed by both hands at the same time;
3. **System commands:** these commands are used to send precise instructions to the robot or to the Command System. The "*XSign*" gesture is used both for starting the communication with the system and for closing the communication. To start a robot execution the "*Punch*" gesture must be performed with both hands, while to stop it is enough to show to the camera a single hand "*Five*" gesture. The emergency stop is obtained by using both hands to perform the "*Five*" gesture. The "*TimeOut*" gesture is used to pause a robot execution (i.e. a Loop task), that can be re-started by the start command. The "*Collab*" gesture is used to display the instructions available in that particular state of the state machine. The "*Ok*" gesture is used to change the velocity of the robot: it is expressed as a percentage, obtained as the slope of the segment having the extremes in the centroids of the boxes of the two hands both performing the "*Ok*" gesture.

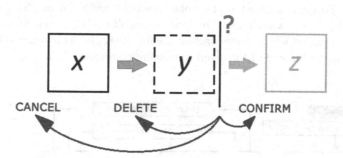

Fig. 6. Example of the Interface commands. When the user is prompted with an Interface command request, it is possible to confirm the instruction and proceed with the operation, or to delete (thus returning to a previous state and re-enter the command) or cancel the operation.

Each state uses only a specific subset of gestures depending on the state, thus filtering out the possible mistakes the detector can make. In addition, only predictions with a confidence score greater than 80% are detected and at the same time a command is sent to the robot only after 4 complete commands are checked and, among these, at least 2 commands are of the same class/combination and are detected in correspondence of the same position.

Considering all the filtering procedures taken into account when sending a command, in this configuration is possible to work and move the hands freely, avoiding the risk of sending a command by accident.

3.3 Proposed System Structure

The proposed structure of the System is represented in Fig. 7. The core functionalities are carried out by using MATLAB 2017b installed on the machine. Images are acquired from the Kinect v2 camera leveraging the *libfreenect2* and *iai_kinect2* open source libraries for ROS: when a new frame is available from the camera, it is written on several topics according to the resolution of the sensor. In our case, we continuously read HD frames from the */kinect2/hd/image_color* topic, with a rate of 5 FPS.

The **Gesture Recognition** node reads the images, crops and resizes them to fit a 224×224 px resolution and applies the hue, saturation and brightness corrections set during the initialization phase. The processed image is then sent to the trained detector, which is defined as an object in the MATLAB environment. The detector outputs a set of predictions, filtered by several functions which apply consecutive filtering policies.

If, at the end of the process, the survived predictions compose a valid command, then this command is used by the **State Machine** to perform transitions or different tasks. When there is a trajectory instruction ready to be sent to the robot, it is embedded in a *trajectory_msgs/JointTrajectory* message and written on the */joint_path_command* topic.

The joints positions and velocities are read by the **Robox Driver** written in ROS Industrial and are translated for the robot controller, which finally moves the robot accordingly. To get a feedback on the robot positions and velocities for each joint in real time, these are written as a *trajectory_msgs/JointTrajectory* message in the */joint_states* topic, which the State Machine continuously checks in order to know if the robot has reached the end of the given movement command.

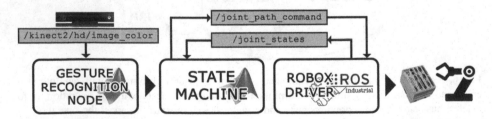

Fig. 7. Proposed structure of the Command System. The nodes are represented as white boxes, while the topics are represented as gray boxes.

The State Machine has 4 operative states:

1. The **Points Definition State:** where the user can manually add points coordinates to the list, which is saved afterwards in a file to keep track of saved points;
2. The **Loop State:** where the user can command the robot to execute the same operation a given number of times (i.e. perform the circle trajectory 5 times);
3. The **Pick&Place State:** where the user can interactively command the robot to perform different movements according to its needs (i.e. going first to point A, pick up an object, go to point B, release the object);
4. The **Jog State:** where the user can move the robot one joint at a time (selected by using a numerical gesture) at a reduced velocity.

The **Emergency State** is a special state, which intervenes when either an emergency stop triggers or a time out happens or a dangerous position is reached. In each case, the state completely stops the robot and the Command System until a total system restart.

4 Conclusions

The proposed HMI is still an experimental prototype, and evaluation tests and performance analysis have yet to be carried out. Even so, the careful study conducted on the gesture recognition system is promising and the filtering policies adopted to further refine the predictions have shown interesting performances. The study also highlighted some useful details on how to build a complex system such as the one presented here, especially on how to design an interactive command system and a new language. In this case we adopted a reduced set of gestures and combined them to create a more robust and vast command list but, as future development, we want to address more carefully this aspect and design a gesture dictionary that better suit human needs according to the task.

This work also highlights that even if it is possible to use MATLAB and ROS in parallel on the same machine, it will be surely better to develop the whole system on the same platform to increase speed and optimize the resources usage. ROS also allows the creation of a modular system that can be gradually expanded with more functionalities, an aspect that we think is the backbone of a good, flexible and "smart" HMI.

MATLAB has shown to be a good platform on which try out Deep Learning models and experiment with them but is still limited compared to more mature frameworks such as TensorFlow or Caffe, which also support the deployment of the models on embedded systems.

In conclusion, we think that this prototype is a stepping stone for a more refined control system than can successfully substitute traditional command systems such as the teach pendants, and that it is not necessary to think of Co-Bots as the only mean to obtain a collaborative workstation compliant with Industry 4.0 directions.

References

1. Rojko, A.: Industry 4.0 concept: background and overview. Int. J. Interact. Mobile Technol. (iJIM) **11**(5), 77–90 (2017)
2. Cherubini, A., Passama, R., Crosnier, A., Lasnier, A., Fraisse, P.: Collaborative manufacturing with physical human–robot interaction. Robot. Comput.-Integr. Manuf. **40**, 1–16 (2016)
3. Colgate, J.E., Wannasuphoprasit, W., Peshkin, M.A.: Cobots: robots for collaboration with human operator. In: Proceedings of the ASME Dynamic Systems and Control Division (1996)
4. Peruzzini, M., Pellicciari, M., Gadaleta, M.: A comparative study on computer-integrated set-ups to design human-centred manufacturing systems. Robot. Comput. Integr. Manuf. **55**, 265–278 (2018)
5. Fong, T., Thorpe, C., Baur, C.: Collaboration, dialogue, human-robot interaction. In: Jarvis, R.A., Zelinsky, A. (eds.) Robotics Research. Springer Tracts in Advanced Robotics, vol. 6, pp. 255–266. Springer, Heidelberg (2003). https://doi.org/10.1007/3-540-36460-9_17
6. Zimmermann, C., Welschehold, T., Dornhege, C., Burgard, W., Brox, T.: 3D human pose estimation in RGBD images for robotic task learning. In: IEEE International Conference on Robotics and Automation (ICRA) (2018)
7. Arenas, J.O.P., Moreno, R.J., Murillo, P.C.U.: Hand gesture recognition by means of region-based convolutional neural networks. Contemp. Eng. Sci. **10**(27), 1329–1342 (2017)
8. Avola, D., Bernardi, M., Cinque, L., Foresti, G.L., Massaroni, C.: Exploiting recurrent neural networks and leap motion controller for the recognition of sign language and semaphoric hand gestures. IEEE Trans. Multimedia **21**(1), 234–245 (2019). https://doi.org/10.1109/TMM.2018.2856094
9. Ren, S., He, K., Girshick, R.B., Sun, J.: Faster R-CNN: towards real-time object detection with region proposal networks. In: Proceedings of the 28th International Conference on Neural Information Processing Systems - Volume 1, pp. 91–99. MIT Press (2015)
10. Mathworks. Object Detection Using Faster R-CNN Deep Learning. https://it.mathworks.com/help/vision/examples/object-detection-using-faster-r-cnn-deep-learning.html
11. Dai, J., Li, Y., He, K., Sun, J.: R-FCN: object detection via region-based fully convolutional networks, arXiv preprint arXiv:1605.06409 (2016)
12. Edwards, S.M., Lewis, C.L.: ROS-industrial - applying the robot operating system (ROS) to industrial applications. In: Presented at the International Conference on Robotics and Automation/Robot Operating System Developer Conference (ICRA/ROSCon), St. Paul, Minnesota (2012)
13. Nuzzi, C., Pasinetti, S., Lancini, M., Docchio, F., Sansoni, G.: Deep learning based machine vision: first steps towards a hand gesture recognition set up for collaborative robots. In: Proceedings of the 2018 IEEE International Workshop on Metrology for Industry 4.0 and IoT, Brescia, Italy (2018)
14. Nuzzi, C., Pasinetti, S., Lancini, M., Docchio, F., Sansoni, G.: Deep learning-based hand gesture recognition for collaborative robots. IEEE Instrum. Meas. Mag. **22**(2), 44–51 (2019)

In-Line Burr Inspection Through Backlight Vision

Matteo Fitti[1], Paolo Castellini[1], Nicola Paone[1(✉)], Marco Zannini[2], Saverio Zitti[2], Marco Gambini[3], and Paolo Chiariotti[1]

[1] Università Politecnica delle Marche, via Brecce Bianche, 60131 Ancona, Italy
n.paone@staff.univpm.it
[2] Zannini SpA, Via Che Guevara, 63, 60022 Castelfidardo, Italy
[3] Zannini Poland, Wojkowicka 60, 41-250 Czeladź, Poland

Abstract. This paper presents a vision-based quality control system for detecting burrs (miniature metal filaments) in transverse holes of high precision turned hollow cylinders. The system performs 100% in-line quality control at the turning station. It exploits a camera with telecentric optics framing the sample from the outside in back-light condition. A specifically developed cylindrical illuminator provides radial diffuse back-light illumination over 360° and can be inserted within the part to be inspected. The possibility to detect burrs placed on both the outer and the inner surface of target holes is achieved by exploiting a customized rotating device integrated to a commercial gripping device. Overall, the system mimics the manual inspection normally performed by operators. Burrs are detected as modifications of the circular shape of each hole, through algorithms that identify the holes on grayscale images, perform circle identification by geometric matching and identify burrs through analysis of local deviations of the edge from circularity. Results acquired in a real production line over a batch of 2000 parts showed no false-positive or false-negative diagnosis.

Keywords: In line quality control · Back light illumination · Burr inspection

1 Introduction

1.1 The Role of Vision for in Line Quality Control

In-line quality control is recognized as one of the pillars of digital factories, according to the paradigm of Industry 4.0; indeed, early detection of defects and anomalies allows preventing defects to propagate to downstream processes and allows to develop adaptive control strategies which may compensate for deviations from nominal specifications by feed-back at single process or feed-forward at following stages of a multi-stage manufacturing system. Therefore, quality control is intimately connected to process control [1], in the perspective of Zero Defect Manufacturing (ZDM).

Vision plays a very relevant and increasing role for in-line quality control, because vision systems can be designed to mimic a variety of visual inspections normally done by expert operators. Vision systems for in-line quality control span over a wide range of complexity, from a single fixed camera and steady illumination, to moving cameras

M. Cristani et al. (Eds.): ICIAP 2019 Workshops, LNCS 11808, pp. 343–351, 2019.
https://doi.org/10.1007/978-3-030-30754-7_34

on robot arms in eye-in-hand configuration [2], with adaptive illumination [3], or structured illumination [4], just to mention a few solutions that can be found in manufacturing lines.

An image contains a variety of quantitative and qualitative information that can be extracted by suitable image processing algorithms: to this extent, a vision system can be considered a measurement system, composed by a series of functional blocks, which, all together, determine system metrological performance. The optical block (illumination, light-object interaction, imaging optics), in series to the sensor block (camera), and to the acquisition block generate the raw image, which is the primary dataset. Then processing algorithms can be implemented, to extract the characteristic features of the image which allow to measure physical quantities in the 2D image plane domains, for example lengths, areas, positions, etc., or physical quantities related to the image intensity domain for example infrared radiation for thermal related quantities. Sets of two or more images, and suitable illumination, either structured in space or time or both, can provide kinematic quantities, deformation, in 2D or in 3D.

It is important to notice that the overall uncertainty of measurement systems based on vision will primarily depend on the quality achieved in the image acquisition phase, that provides the raw image/s; the following processing steps are certainly relevant, but their result will be better if a higher quality raw image is acquired.

Bearing in mind this thought, when considering a quality control system based on vision for in-line inspections, the first and most important step is the design of the system lay-out, including illumination, imaging optics, camera and image acquisition. In real industrial applications of vision in production lines, which are noisy, sometimes dirty, environments, with variable lightning conditions, variable optical characteristics of target surfaces, this is of the utmost importance for the achievement of the final result. The algorithmic part is as important, but it is necessarily the second step to be addressed.

In the following paragraphs an automatic system for burr inspection, based on a vision system, is presented. A patent application is pending to protect the solution developed [5].

The research work presented in this paper has been developed within the European Project GO0DMAN [6, 7], which aims to develop ZDM strategies supported by smart quality control systems (QCS).

1.2   The In-Line Quality Control of Burrs: Problem and State of Art

Several industrial sectors make large use of high precision turned components. Relevant examples are the sleeves for hydraulic actuators, widely used in automotive industry for automatic gear shifts Fig. 1. These components are hollow cylinders, a few mm diameter and about a mm thickness, with a series of transverse holes at different angular and longitudinal axial positions. Functionality of these components is strictly related to geometric tolerance. Such parts are produced in batches, often in several thousand sequences.

Fig. 1. Typical high precision turned component: a sleeve of a hydraulic actuator.

Concerning manufacturing of high precision turned components, dimensional measurements are required for conformity assessment; for this purpose quality control takes place either on a sample based procedure, which exploits specific instruments in the metrologic laboratory of the plant, or on 100% production, by in-line measurement equipment, at the cost of lower metrologic performance [8, 9]. At the same time, a proper working condition of these turned parts can be achieved if no burrs are present in the functional holes, i.e. the transversal holes on the cylinder. Therefore, it is of extreme importance to detect the presence of burrs. Indeed, the part can be either reworked, whenever it is possible, or can be rejected, but no parts non-compliant to functional standards are released to the end-user. Therefore in-line quality control on 100% of production is now becoming mandatory, in the perspective of ZDM.

Burrs are metal pieces approximately 1 mm long and 0.05–0.10 mm thick. Figure 2 (left) shows typical burrs that can be detected in turned components. A common method to highlight the presence of these unwanted elements is visual inspection in quality laboratory by a trained operator. Visual inspection is performed using image magnification systems and rotating the sample so that the operator can identify the presence of eventual burrs either in the inner or the outer surface of the sample under test (Fig. 2 right).

Fig. 2. Typical visual inspection of burrs performed manually by an operator.

If burrs are detected the sample is reworked, the defect is eliminated, at the cost of increasing production time and cost. The presence of burrs is a rather deterministic defect, due to several causes, such as tool wear, lubrication problems, vibrations: therefore, when burrs start forming, it is highly probable that most parts produced in a sequence will exhibit the same defect [10]. Being a manual control, this inspection cannot be performed on a 100% basis, therefore the risk of missing samples not compliant for the presence of burrs is high. Moreover, a sample-based quality control performed off-line risks to provide a feed-back to the process with an excessive delay, during which many parts may have been produced with defects and may have reached the following stages of production, thus determining a series of negative effects and associated costs, due the non-compliance to specifications.

If the operator-based visual inspection is replaced by an automated system exploiting machine vision, the 100% inspection target can be reached.

2   Design of the Vision System

2.1   System Lay-Out

The idea underlying the system is to somehow mimic, in an automated way, the operations that an operator would do in checking a part, i.e. rotating it and observing the circular shape of each hole. To ease burr visibility, the part is inspected under backlighting; backlight illumination is generated by a light stick inserted into the cylindrical part.

All these features are reproduced in the system, whose lay-out is reported in Fig. 3: it is composed by two cylindrical illuminators which can be inserted axially inside the hollow cylinder under inspection, mounted on a gripper for fixing the part and rotating it axially. The backlit image of the lateral holes is taken through telecentric optics aligned orthogonally to the axis of the part under inspection. Each component is described hereafter.

Fig. 3. Lay-out of the system (left) and laboratory prototype (right). You can see: camera, telecentric optics, gripper with backlit internal illuminator and rotating actuator.

The Backlight Diffuse Illuminator
It is a transparent polymeric cylinder with a rough surface; light is fed to the light stick by a LED source glued on its base and travels along the cylinder. Due to light source divergence and to light scattering within the core of the polymeric cylinder, light reaches the rough surface of the cylinder which acts as a diffuser. Hence light is

diffused radially and, once the illuminator is inserted inside the hollow cylinder to be inspected, its inner surface is illuminated over the full length over the 360°.

This allows an external observer to see the light exiting from the lateral holes; burrs will appear as black shades oved a luminous circle.

The LED light source is RGB+W, for colour control. This feature enables image optimization (contrast enhancement) with respect to environmental light and the optical characteristics of the part.

The illuminator is 5 mm diameter.

Fig. 4. The "light stick" illuminator on the gripper.

The Gripper

In order to automate the system, the diffuse internal illuminator is realized in two parts, which can be inserted from the two opposite sides of the hollow cylinder. Each part is mounted on one finger of a robot gripper, which allows insertion of the illuminator inside the hollow cylinder. Two conic elements allow centering the hollow cylinder with respect to the internal diffuse illuminator.

The conic elements can rotate axially, under the action of a step motor mounted on one of the fingers. Once the fingers are closed, and the conic parts block the hollow cylinder, the step motor can rotate it. This allows a fixed camera to observe in sequence all the outer surface of the cylinder; lateral holes will appear as luminous circles over a black surface, thanks to the inner backlit diffuse illuminator.

Loading and unloading of the hollow cylinder onto the gripper is done by a robot arm; however, the system can also be operated by a human operator.

The Camera and Lens

The hollow cylinder under inspection is positioned orthogonal to the optical axis of the objective and with its own axis horizontal (see Fig. 4).

We have selected a telecentric optics having a field of view of 34.98 mm 29.18 mm; this allows inspection of parts whose dimension is lower than 30 mm over a depth of field of 11 mm. The contrast transfer function (CTF @ 70 lp/mm) is larger than 40%, thus assuring an optical spatial resolution better than $a_{opt} < 0,014$ mm.

We have selected a CMOS camera having a 2/3″ chip, with 2464 × 2056 pixels. The camera is operated in ROI mode; this is cone with the purpose to reduce the image size and speed up the frame rate (current frame rate; 200 fps).

Overall the system allows for a spatial resolution of less than $a_{sens} < 0.015$ mm (no sub-pixeling considered).

Camera resolution combined to optical resolution limit detectable burr size to $a < 0.02$ mm: however, burrs are expected to always exceed this dimension.

3   Image Processing for Burr Detection

3.1   Typical Images

The images are acquired and processed in the pre-defined Region of Interest identified by the green rectangle in Fig. 5. Two further ROIs, indicated by the red and yellow rectangles have been also identified. These latter two ROIs are functional to the identification of burrs lying on the inner surface of the sample in case the central ROI does not provide results reliable enough. It is worth recalling that, in the central ROI, burrs are identified as deviations from a circular shape given by each hole.

Fig. 5. ROIs used for hole inspection (Color figure online)

The following Fig. 6 reports a typical image acquired on holes which are close to orthogonal to the optical axis of the telecentric vision system within the central ROI. On the right a zoom allows to see a burr highlighted by a red circle.

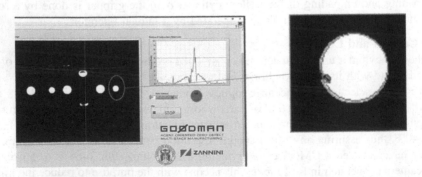

Fig. 6. Typical image and zoom on a hole with a burr (Color figure online)

3.2   The Algorithms

Burrs recognition is based on a geometric pattern matching algorithm [11]. Indeed, this algorithm is exploited to highlight dissimilarity with respect to known geometric shapes (circles in the central ROI; ellipses in the top and bottom ROIs). With respect to standard pattern matching approaches, in which pixel intensity levels in the template image are used for matching on the final image, the algorithm exploits geometric information present in the template image as primary features (e.g. low-level features, like edges or curves, or higher-level features, such as the geometric shapes made by the curves in the image) for matching. Deviations from known geometric features are then compared to a threshold: if some data falls above the threshold, these data, very likely, correspond to burrs on the hole.

Being a system in which detection of burrs relies on a comparison with a threshold, it is important to periodically check/update this threshold. This can be done by using a reference part with burrs of known extensions in known locations. Once the reference part is mounted on the system, the capability of the QCS to correctly detect and locate the burrs can be checked. Since the part is a reference tool, it has to be worked to have a reference hole (e.g. smaller hole) easily detectable, from which the nominal location of holes with burrs can be recovered.

The measurement sequence is made in steps. The system waits for an external trigger event; in the automatic version, it will be a hardware trigger provided by the robot (and exchanged using TCP-IP communication protocol) placing the hollow cylinder onto the gripper; in the manual operating mode, the part is charged onto the gripping system by the operator, and trigger is provided via a push button on the system's HMI (Human Machine Interface). Once this trigger has been received, the part is then closed by the gripping system and the internal illuminator inserted accordingly. The colour of the illuminator light is adjusted depending on environmental light and/or the part finishing; this is a smart behaviour which aims to keep image contrast as high as possible. After this adjustment the part is brought to rotation and the measurement starts. If data are not consistent to predefined confidence level after one rotation (e.g. clockwise), rotation direction is inverted (e.g. counter clockwise) and inspection is performed again.

4   Results

A validation testing campaign, which aimed to ensure equal/superior performance of the QCS to the inspection strategy currently used in ZANNINI, has been performed in ZANNINI Poland' facility. A batch of 2000 parts was tested using manual charge/discharge onto the burrs inspection system. Inspection was performed on 100% of the batch and double-checked by the standard burrs inspection approach adopted by ZANNINI Poland's quality operators. Before the validation phase, the threshold to be used in the algorithm was identified running dedicated tests on a batch of healthy parts (batch of 100 parts).

The validation test identified no damaged parts among the batch produced. Actually, 5/2000 false positives came out after an initial screening. However, it turned out that these false positives were due to a wrong charging of parts onto the gripping system. Consequently, a further test of these 5/2000 parts with the burrs inspection system revealed their healthy nature.

The system is currently exploited in a bigger demonstration phase (overall batch production: 20000 parts) running in ZANNINI Poland within the GO0D MAN project.

5 Concluding Remarks

We have presented an automated quality control system based on vision, designed to detect burrs in hollow cylinders with transverse holes. The system is designed to operate on 100% production in-line. The paper has introduced the industrial relevance of this problem and the need to overcome the present state of art, which consist in visual inspection by operators.

The system developed mimics the way an operator does the inspection; the part is rotated and holes are inspected from the outside, under backlight illuminations. For the purpose we developed a dedicated gripper, whose fingers host two cylindrical diffuse illuminators, which can be inserted inside the hollow cylinder. The part is placed orthogonal to the optical axis of the vision system and rotated around its axis, so that all the holes can be imaged.

A CMOS camera equipped with a telecentric lens collects images within a ROI; the holes will appear as luminous circles over a dark background. If burrs are present, their shade will appear.

Image processing is based on geometric pattern matching algorithms, which recognize circles; once a circle is identified, then deviations of its circularity are interpreted as burrs. For the purpose, deviations are analyzed versus a threshold established experimentally.

Image contrast is continuously controlled by varying the colour and intensity of the illumination, so to compensate environmental light variations typical of the factory.

Results from validation tests demonstrated the capability of the system to substitute the approach currently used by operators in assessing the health status of parts produced. Further tests currently running aim to show how a vision-based approach can improve the identification of burrs and therefore ease the path to Zero Defect Production.

Acknowledgements. This research is part of the European Project GO0DMAN-"aGent Oriented Zero Defect Multi-Stage Manufacturing". GO0D MAN project has received funding from the European Commission under the EU Framework Programme for Research and Innovation Horizon 2020 (2014–2020) within the FoF – Technologies for Factories of the Future initiative. Contract no. H2020-FOF-03-2016-723764.

References

1. Cristalli, C., et al.: Integration of process and quality control using multi-agent technology. In: ISIE 2013-22nd IEEE International Symposium on Industrial Electronics, Taipei, 28–31 May 2013 (2013). ISBN 978-146735194-2. https://doi.org/10.1109/isie.2013.6563737
2. Montironi, M.A., Castellini, P., Stroppa, L., Paone, N.: Adaptive autonomous positioning of a robot vision system: application to quality control on production lines. Robot. Comput. Integr. Manuf. **30**(5), 489–498 (2014). https://doi.org/10.1016/j.rcim.2014.03.004
3. Stroppa, L., Castellini, P., Paone, N.: Self-optimizing robot vision for on-line quality control. Exp. Tech. **40**(3), 1051–1064 (2015). https://doi.org/10.1007/s40799-016-0103-z
4. Castellini, P., Bruni, A., Paone, N.: Design of an optical scanner for real-time on-line measurement of wood-panel profiles. In: Osten, W., Gorecki, C., Novak, E.L. (eds.) 18th International Congress on Photonics in Europe, Optical Metrology, Munich, Germany, 18–21 June 2007. Optical Measurement Systems for Industrial Inspection V, Proceedings of SPIE, vol. 6616, p. 66164E, (2007). ISBN 0277-786X/07/$18. https://doi.org/10.1117/12.725042
5. Italian patent application pending: Sistema per rilevamento di bave di lavorazione in componenti meccanici. No. 102018000003929, filing date 26/03/2018
6. GO0DMAN project website. http://go0dman-project.eu/. Accessed 17 June 2019
7. Chiariotti, P., et al.: Smart measurement systems for zero-defect manufacturing. In: IEEE-INDIN-18: IEEE 16th International Conference on Industrial Informatics, pp. 534–539, IEEE Catalog Number: CFP18INI-USB, Porto, Portugal, July 2018. ISBN 978-1-5386-4828-5/18
8. Chiariotti, P., Fitti, M., Castellini, P., Zitti, S., Zannini, M., Paone, N.: High-accuracy dimensional measurement of cylindrical components by an automated test station based on confocal chromatic sensor. In: IEEE International Workshop on Metrology for Industry 4.0 & IoT, pp. 58–62, IEEE Catalog Number: CFP18N49-USB, Brescia, April 2018 (2018). ISBN 978-1-5386-2496-8. https://doi.org/10.1109/metroi4.2018.8428340
9. Chiariotti, P., Fitti, M., Castellini, P., Zitti, S., Zannini, M., Paone, N.: Smart quality control station for non-contact measurement of cylindrical parts based on confocal chromatic sensor. Instrum. Meas. Mag. **21**(6), 22–28 (2018). https://doi.org/10.1109/mim.2018.8573589
10. Aurich, J.C., Dornfeld, D., Arrazola, P.J., Franke, V., Leitz, L., Min, S.: Burrs—analysis, control and removal. CIRP Ann. – Manuf. Technol. **58**, 519–542 (2009)
11. Gavrilov, M., Indyk, P., Motwani, R., Venkatasubramanian, S.: Geometric pattern matching: a performance study. In: Proceedings of Symposium on Computational Geometry, Proceedings of the Fifteenth Annual Symposium on Computational Geometry, Miami Beach, Florida, USA, 13–16 June 1999, pp. 79–85 (1999)

Segmentation Guided Scoring of Pathological Lesions in Swine Through CNNs

Luca Bergamini[1(✉)] , Abigail Rose Trachtman[3] , Andrea Palazzi[1] ,
Ercole Del Negro[2], Andrea Capobianco Dondona[2], Giuseppe Marruchella[3],
and Simone Calderara[3]

[1] AImageLab, University of Modena and Reggio Emilia, Modena, Italy
{luca.bergamini24,andrea.palazzi}@unimore.it
[2] Farm4Trade, Chieti, Italy
{ercole,andrea}@farm4trade.com
[3] University of Teramo, Teramo, Italy
abigailrose.trachtman@studenti.unite.it, gmarruchella@unite.it,
simone.calderara@unimore.it

Abstract. The slaughterhouse is widely recognised as a useful check-point for assessing the health status of livestock. At the moment, this is implemented through the application of scoring systems by human experts. The automation of this process would be extremely helpful for veterinarians to enable a systematic examination of all slaughtered livestock, positively influencing herd management. However, such systems are not yet available, mainly because of a critical lack of annotated data.

In this work we: *(i)* introduce a large scale dataset to enable the development and benchmarking of these systems, featuring more than 4000 high-resolution swine carcass images annotated by domain experts with pixel-level segmentation; *(ii)* exploit part of this annotation to train a deep learning model in the task of pleural lesion scoring.

In this setting, we propose a segmentation-guided framework which stacks together a fully convolutional neural network performing semantic segmentation with a rule-based classifier integrating *a-priori* veterinary knowledge in the process. Thorough experimental analysis against state-of-the-art baselines proves our method to be superior both in terms of accuracy and in terms of model interpretability.

Code and dataset are publicly available here:
https://github.com/lucabergamini/swine-lesion-scoring

Keywords: Swine lesions recognition ·
Slaughterhouse scoring system · Computer vision · Deep learning

1 Introduction

The slaughterhouse can be defined as "an establishment used for slaughtering and dressing animals, the meat of which is intended for human consumption"

M. Cristani et al. (Eds.): ICIAP 2019 Workshops, LNCS 11808, pp. 352–360, 2019.
https://doi.org/10.1007/978-3-030-30754-7_35

(Reg. CE 853/2004 of the European Parliament). Therefore, the *postmortem* inspection of slaughtered animals is mainly meant to target public health risks [18]. In addition, the abattoir is also widely recognised as a key checkpoint for monitoring the health status of livestock, representing a useful source of data for epidemiological investigations [20].

Motivations. The systematic analysis of lesions at the abattoir is a helpful feedback to the farm to assess the health status of livestock and to improve herd management: biosecurity measures, welfare, vaccination strategies, the rational administration of antimicrobial drugs. The latter is crucial to limit antibiotic-resistance [14,21] which has been indicated as a paramount threat to human health in the upcoming future [1]. Moreover, the slaughterhouse can be useful to evaluate the economic impact of diseases, which negatively affect the profitability of farming [2,6]. This is especially true for pigs, as their "short" productive cycle prevents the full healing of lesions, which are still visible at market weight [20].

Currently, the registration of lesions at the abattoir is performed voluntarily, at the request of the stakeholders, and it is very challenging in terms of time and economic resources. As a consequence, large amounts of informative and relevant data are frequently lost [11].

Pleurisy Scoring Systems. Pleurisy is frequently observed at necropsy or during the *post-mortem* inspection at the abattoir, its prevalence often being close to 50% [16]. Over the years, a number of methods have been developed to score pleurisy [20]. Among these, the Slaughterhouse Pleurisy Evaluation System (SPES [18]) is widely considered as the most informative method under field conditions. Recently, an alternative method (Pleurisy Evaluation on the Parietal Pleura, PEPP [5,12,13]) has been developed. The PEPP method provides well matching results when compared with SPES and, differently from SPES, it can be efficiently performed on digital images.

Automatic Swine Analysis. To the best of our knowledge, this is the first work addressing pleural lesion scoring in pigs in an automatic, data-driven fashion. Still, methods have been proposed for tasks related to swine welfare, productivity and diseases prevention. As an example, Chung et al. [3] proposes an automatic system for the detection and the recognition of multiple pig wasting diseases analysing audio data. Shao and Xin [19] employ computer vision techniques for the assessment of thermal comfort for group-housed pigs.

Contributions. Our contribution is twofold. On the one hand, we introduce a large pixel-level segmentation dataset comprised of more than 4000 images of pig carcasses. Our dataset is annotated by two sectorial experts after agreeing upon the annotation procedure. We believe this data can enable the development of new automatic methods for real-time and systematic analysis of animal health, production and welfare parameters.

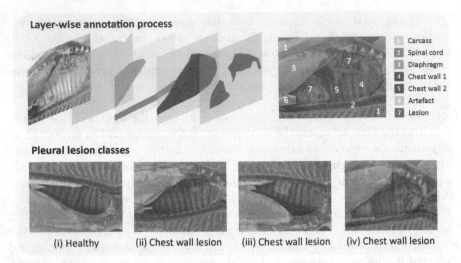

Fig. 1. Top left: different segmentation layers; some of them were collapsed for clarity. Top right: correspondence between colours and structure names. See Sect. 2 for further details. Bottom: visual examples of the four classes for pleurisy scoring. (Color figure online)

On the other hand, we introduce one such method, based on deep learning techniques, which requires only a single RGB image of a pig chest wall to score pleural lesions according to PEPP [5,12,13]. This method could be employed in the slaughter chain to provide a systematic, real time and cost effective diagnosis. Moreover, it could produce a continuous stream of data suitable for epidemiological investigations as well as to classify farms according to risk categories.

2   Dataset

Our dataset is comprised of 4444 high-resolution images of pig carcasses from four independent slaughterhouses. The images taken are from the end of the slaughter chain after the removal of internal organs and washing the carcass. Two experts annotate four anatomical structures; namely *carcass*, *spinal cord*, *diaphragm*, *chest wall*[1], as well as two anomalous structures: *artefacts* and *lesions* (see Figs. 1 and 2). The experts follow a depth-wise fashion during the annotation process. In particular, artefacts and lesions are annotated after the anatomical structures, which are thus entirely annotated even when covered by another structure. In the following, we focus on the pleural lesion scoring task only.

Pleurisy Scoring. We simplify the scoring methodology presented in PEPP into a four class problem. Two domain experts classify each dataset image as:

---

[1] According to PEPP [5,12,13], we consider the area between the first and the fifth intercostal space as *chest wall 1* and the rest of the chest wall as *chest wall 2*.

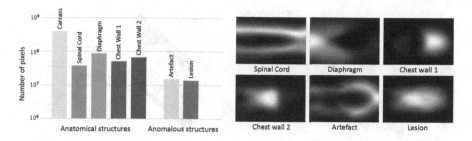

Fig. 2. Left: number of annotated pixels per category (in log scale). Right: spatial localisation of the segmented classes, computed as the average of the annotations on the training set. A symmetry is introduced by the two halves of the carcass.

(i) absence of lesions; (ii) lesions on the first chest wall; (iii) lesions on the second chest wall; (iv) lesions on both chest wall areas. To allow an evenhanded evaluation we provide an independent test set of 200 images. The four classes distribution for the two sets is shown in Table 1. It is worth noting how the distribution of the classes in the train set is skewed towards class i (healthy swine). This reflects what is stated in [16]. Contrarily, we artificially ensure an even distribution for the test set to allow for a focus on the different pathological classes.

3   Method

Here we first discuss four classification baseline methods from state-of-the-art literature for the task of pleural lesion scoring (Sect. 3.1). We then introduce our segmentation-based method, which leads to higher accuracy and interpretability by explicitly exploiting task-specific prior information (Sect. 3.2).

3.1   Classification Baselines from State-of-the-Art

End-to-end Classification Network. Our first two baselines rely on ResNet-34 architecture [7]. A first network (*ResNet*) is trained from scratch on our dataset. For the second one (*ResNet$_{PT}$*) we initialise the convolutional layers with pretrained weights from ImageNet [4]. In both networks we replace the last fully connected layer to address a four classes problem.

Table 1. Number of images annotated for each class, in each dataset split.

	Class i	Class ii	Class iii	Class iv	total
Train set	2347	381	498	1018	4244
Test set	50	50	50	50	200

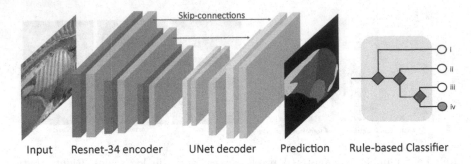

Input   Resnet-34 encoder   UNet decoder   Prediction   Rule-based Classifier

Fig. 3. Overview of our model for pleural lesion scoring. An encoder-decoder network is trained for the *proxy* task of semantic segmentation; a rule-based classifier is then used to discern the class from the segmentation. In Sect. 4 we show how this architecture is more interpretable and outperforms competitive end-to-end classification baselines.

Deep Features and Shallow Classifiers. Similarly to [9,15], we train two shallow classifiers in the task of pleural lesion scoring, starting from ResNet-34 activations. The first one (SVM) is a Support Vector Machine with Gaussian kernel and C regularisation set to 1. The second one (RF) relies on a Random Forest classifier with 50 estimators and entropy split criterion.

3.2   Segmentation Guided Network for Pleural Lesions

Our proposed method leverages experts' pixel-level annotation as a *proxy* for the pleural lesion scoring. Indeed, according to PEPP [5,12,13], the three different pathological classes of pleural lesions (i.e. ii, iii and iv) are discerned by the lesion's location over the chest wall. Consequently, a faithful segmentation always leads to a reliable classification of the image.

With this premise, we propose to train a network for semantic segmentation and to leverage a rule-based classifier to translate the predicted maps into a pleural lesion score, see Fig. 3. Besides the performance gain (see Sect. 4), this framework has the desirable property of enabling an immediate interpretation of the model prediction.

Network. Our network architecture derives from UNet [17]. To ensure consistency with the baselines (Sect. 3.1), we rely on pre-trained ResNet architecture as encoder; the decoder path is based on four Transposed Convolutions blocks [10], each one with the same number of channels of the corresponding ResNet layer in the encoder path. Long skip-connections promote the flow of information between the encoder and the decoder.

For training, we optimise a set of Binary Cross Entropy (BCE) losses. In particular, given the l-th channel of the output map $\tilde{\mathbf{y}}_l \in \mathbb{R}^{N \times W \times H}$ and the corresponding ground truth channel $\mathbf{y}_l \in \mathbb{R}^{N \times W \times H}$:

$$BCE_{(\mathbf{y_1},\tilde{\mathbf{y}_1})} = -\frac{1}{N}\sum_i^N \mathbf{y}_i \cdot \log_2(\tilde{\mathbf{y}}_i) + (1 - \mathbf{y}_i) \cdot \log_2(1 - \tilde{\mathbf{y}}_i) \qquad (1)$$

Were N is the number of images and W, H are the width and the height of each image respectively. By doing that, we effectively decouple each segmentation label from the others to avoid their competition over a pixel, reflecting the annotation methodology of our dataset.

Classifier. Then, the rule-based classifier C_{RB} performs connected component analysis on the segmentation output to compute the overlap between each lesion and the two chest walls. C_{RB} assigns images to class (ii) or (iii) if there is an overlap between a lesion area and the first or second chest wall areas respectively. When a lesion overlaps with both chest walls the image is assigned to class (iv). Due to this small set of rules, it becomes trivial to understand why a certain decision was taken: this in turn leads to a full interpretability of the result.

4   Experiments

In this section we report quantitative results for all methods presented in Sect. 3.

Implementation Details. Our model is trained for 40 epochs with batch size 6. We resize the image to 400×300 px and perform extensive data augmentation including random horizontal or vertical flip, translation and rotation. We use Adam [8] optimiser with initial learning rate 0.001 and halve it every 15 epochs.

Results. Classification results are reported in terms of accuracy and confusion matrix. Fig. 4(a) illustrates the test set accuracy scores of methods from Sect. 3. Both *RF* and *SVM* perform poorly with respect to end-to-end methods. This suggests that even though ImageNet features may provide a good representation, fine-tuning the features extractor is still required to achieve good results.

Method	Accuracy				
	i	ii	iii	iv	*Avg*
RF	0.92	0.3	0.1	0.44	0.44
SVM	0.8	0.56	0.24	0.46	0.52
ResNet	0.90	0.64	0.58	0.72	0.71
ResNet_{PT}	0.92	**0.70**	0.62	0.68	0.73
ours	**0.98**	0.68	**0.78**	**1.00**	**0.86**

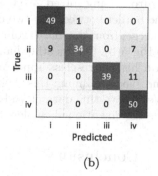

(a)   (b)

Fig. 4. (a) Class-wise accuracy score on the test set for each method in Sect. 3. (b) Confusion matrix on the test set for our proposed method (Sect. 3.2).

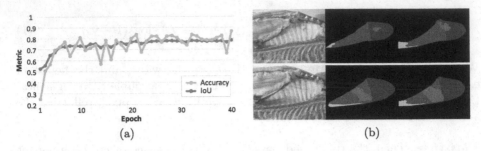

Fig. 5. (a) Correlation between accuracy and IoU during training. (b) Two failure cases for our methods (see Sect. 4).

In fact, end-to-end training gives to *ResNet$_{PT}$* a significant performance boost over shallower models. *ResNet* closely follows but loses 2% accuracy, suggesting that even though a domain shift between ImageNet and our dataset is certainly present, features learned on the former still provide a suitable initialisation.

Eventually, we need to steer towards a segmentation guided approach to get an additional significant performance improvement. Since pathological classes are discerned by the position of lesions, segmentation is crucial to preserve this spatial information in the output. Then, the rule based classifier translates this localised information into a discrete label by applying rules that derive from experts' knowledge. As shown in Fig. 5(a), classification accuracy increases steadily as IoU improves. This highlights how segmentation is indeed an optimal *proxy* for pleural lesion scoring.

The confusion matrix for our method is shown in Fig. 4(b). Notably, anti-diagonal entries of the confusion matrix are all zero, highlighting the absence of healthy examples associated with the most severe pathological class and *vice-versa*. Furthermore, very few examples are misidentified even between the two less represented classes (i.e. ii and iii).

Discussion. Despite the encouraging results, the pleural lesion scoring task is far from being solved. We believe this is due to various factors. On the one hand, the border between the two chest walls is crucial for the final classification. This emerges from the fourth column of Fig. 4(b), and this kind of failure case is shown in Fig. 5(b). On the other hand, organic nature of lesions and artefacts is reflected in a high intra-class appearance variance, including cuts and bruises in tissues and blood staining: this makes the two classes particularly hard to distinguish. We believe this dataset will bolster future efforts from the community to solve the aforementioned challenges.

5   Conclusions

In this work we propose a large visual dataset for the pixel-level segmentation of swine carcasses. This dataset includes 4444 images annotated by domain experts with four anatomical and two anomalous structures. Furthermore, we show how these annotations can be leveraged to tackle the *post-mortem* diagnosis and scoring of pleurisy. Our segmentation-guided method enables a much higher interpretability of the output and outperforms competitive baselines on an independent test set by a large margin. Future works will exploit our segmentation dataset for the analysis of other diseases of pigs and will focus on applying the same methodology to pathological conditions affecting other anatomical structures in swine and other livestock.

References

1. Aslam, B., et al.: Antibiotic resistance: a rundown of a global crisis. Infect. Drug Resist. **11**, 1645 (2018)
2. Bao, C., et al.: Establishment and comparison of actinobacillus pleuropneumoniae experimental infection model in mice and piglets. Microb. Pathog. **128**, 381–389 (2019)
3. Chung, Y., Oh, S., Lee, J., Park, D., Chang, H.H, Kim, S.: Automatic detection and recognition of pig wasting diseases using sound data in audio surveillance systems. Sensors **13**(10), 12929–12942 (2013)
4. Deng, J., Dong, W., Socher, R., Li, L.J., Li, K., Fei-Fei, L.: Imagenet: a large-scale hierarchical image database. In: 2009 IEEE Conference on Computer Vision and Pattern Recognition, pp. 248–255. IEEE (2009)
5. Di Provvido, A., et al.: Pleurisy evaluation on the parietal pleura: an alternative scoring method in slaughtered pigs. J. Swine Health Prod. (2019)
6. Gottschalk, M.: Diseases of Swine, 10th edn. vol. 2012, pp. 653–669. Wiley-Blackwell, Oxford (2012)
7. He, K., Zhang, X., Ren, S., Sun, J.: Deep residual learning for image recognition. In: Proceedings of the IEEE Conference on Computer Vision and Pattern Recognition, pp. 770–778 (2016)
8. Kingma, D.P., Ba, J.: Adam: a method for stochastic optimization. In: International Conference on Learning Representations (ICLR) (2015)
9. Lim, Y.K., Liao, Z., Petridis, S., Pantic, M.: Transfer learning for action unit recognition. arXiv preprint arXiv:1807.07556 (2018)
10. Long, J., Shelhamer, E., Darrell, T.: Fully convolutional networks for semantic segmentation. In: Proceedings of the IEEE Conference on Computer Vision and Pattern Recognition, pp. 3431–3440 (2015)
11. Marcato, P.S.: Patologia Suina: Testo E Atlante; a Colour Atlas of Pathology of the Pig. Edagricole (1998)
12. Marruchella, G., Odintzov Vaintrub, M., Di Provvido, A., Farina, E., Fragassi, G., Vignola, G.: Alternative scoring method of pleurisy in slaughtered pigs: Preliminary investigations. In: Proceedings of SIPAS, pp. 375–380 (2018)
13. Marruchella, G., Odintzov Vaintrub, M., Di Provvido, A., Farina, E., Vignola, G.: Scoring pleurisy in slaughtered pigs. In: Proceedings of SISVet, pp. 238–239 (2018)
14. Mathew, A.G., Cissell, R., Liamthong, S.: Antibiotic resistance in bacteria associated with food animals: a United States perspective of livestock production. Foodborne Pathog. Dis. **4**(2), 115–133 (2007)
15. McAllister, P., Zheng, H., Bond, R., Moorhead, A.: Combining deep residual neural network features with supervised machine learning algorithms to classify diverse food image datasets. Comput. Biol. Med. **95**, 217–233 (2018)

16. Merialdi, G., et al.: Survey of pleuritis and pulmonary lesions in pigs at abattoir with a focus on the extent of the condition and herd risk factors. Vet. J. **193**(1), 234–239 (2012)
17. Ronneberger, O., Fischer, P., Brox, T.: U-Net: convolutional networks for biomedical image segmentation. In: Navab, N., Hornegger, J., Wells, W.M., Frangi, A.F. (eds.) MICCAI 2015. LNCS, vol. 9351, pp. 234–241. Springer, Cham (2015). https://doi.org/10.1007/978-3-319-24574-4_28
18. Scollo, A., Gottardo, F., Contiero, B., Mazzoni, C., Leneveu, P., Edwards, S.A.: Benchmarking of pluck lesions at slaughter as a health monitoring tool for pigs slaughtered at 170 kg (heavy pigs). Prev. Vet. Med. **144**, 20–28 (2017)
19. Shao, B., Xin, H.: A real-time computer vision assessment and control of thermal comfort for group-housed pigs. Comput. Electron. Agric. **62**(1), 15–21 (2008)
20. Sorenson, V., Jorsal, S., Mousing, J.: Diseases of Swine, 9th edn. pp. 149–178. Blackwell Pubishing (2006)
21. Van Boeckel, T.P., et al.: Reducing antimicrobial use in food animals. Science **357**(6358), 1350–1352 (2017)

Intelligent Recognition of TCP Intrusions
for Embedded Micro-controllers

Remi Varenne[1], Jean Michel Delorme[2], Emanuele Plebani[1],
Danilo Pau[1(✉)], and Valeria Tomaselli[3]

[1] STMicroelectronics, Agrate B, Italy
danilo.pau@st.com
[2] STMicroelectronics, Grenoble, France
[3] STMicroelectronics, Catania, Italy

Abstract. IoT end-user devices are attractive and sometime easy targets for attackers, because they are often vulnerable in different aspects. Cyberattacks, started from those devices, can easily disrupt the availability of services offered by major internet companies. People that commonly get access to them across the world may experience abrupt interruption of services they use. In that context, this paper describes an embedded prototype to classify intrusions, affecting TCP packets. The proposed solution adopts an Artificial Neural Network (ANN) executed on resource-constrained and low-cost embedded micro controllers. The prototype operates without the need of remote intelligence assist. The adoption of an on-the-edge artificial intelligence architecture brings advantages such as responsiveness, promptness and low power consumption. The embedded intelligence is trained by using the well-known KDD Cup 1999 dataset, properly balanced on 5 types of labelled intrusions patterns. A pre-trained ANN classifies features extracted from TCP packets. The results achieved in this paper refer to the application running on the low cost widely available Nucleo STM32 micro controller boards from STMicroelectronics, featuring a F3 chip running at 72 MHz and a F4 chip running at 84 MHz with small embedded RAM and Flash memory.

Keywords: Intrusion detection · TCP packets · Neural networks · Micro controllers · STM32 · Automatic C code generation

1 Introduction

The widespread adoption of connected devices in the Internet of Things (IoT) paradigm has led to new threats to consumer and industrial systems. IoT devices often do not have the computational resources to run sophisticated antivirus or diagnostic software [1] and they are an easy target for attackers. Attacks on industrial control systems are especially dangerous, because they can cause physical damage to people or tools [2]. Moreover, as the distributed denial of service attack (DDoS) carried by the Mirai botnet [3] shows, compromised IoT devices may be a threat to the Internet at large. Among IoT systems, automotive devices are especially vulnerable. Over the years, cars have incorporated processors that are more powerful and network interfaces to implement

© Springer Nature Switzerland AG 2019
M. Cristani et al. (Eds.): ICIAP 2019 Workshops, LNCS 11808, pp. 361–373, 2019.
https://doi.org/10.1007/978-3-030-30754-7_36

advanced driver assistance systems (ADAS), self-driving capabilities and internet connections for on-vehicle entertainment. However, such features leave the car vulnerable to network attacks focused on getting access to private data or getting control of the steering systems.

The Controller Area Network (CAN) bus in particular has no-inbuilt encryption capabilities, and it is one of the most common attack interfaces [4]. While often, the internet-connected entertainment functionality runs on a separate subsystem, access to the CAN bus is sufficient to gain control of the driving control system and activate the car brakes, as shown by the successful attack on a Jeep Cherokee performed through its mobile connection [5].

Intrusion detection systems (IDS) [6] are algorithms which analyze the packet content and traffic patterns to detect potential attacks by an intruder, and they are key components of computer network security. In this paper, we propose a lightweight detection algorithm based on deep learning, which can run on micro-controllers (MCUs) and recognize five different attacks from the KDD Cup 1999 dataset with a false positive rate lower than 1%. We automatically ported and validated the model on STM32 microcontrollers using the STM32Cube.AI [7] tool and we developed a sample application to test the system on a stream of network packets.

The rest of the paper is organized as follows. In Sect. 2, we present a summary of the state of the art on IDS, with an emphasis on IoT and automotive applications; in Sect. 3, we describe in detail how we developed the demonstrator, including training and deployment on embedded MCUs; in Sect. 4, we analyze the accuracy, efficiency of the model validated on MCUs and in Sect. 5 we present our conclusions and future works.

2   State of the Art

Research on IDS approaches for IoT and automotive systems is relatively recent, driven by the increasing complexity of control devices, and Young et al. in [8] provide a recent review. IDS methods are broadly divided in signature-based, which rely on specific attack patterns, and anomaly-based, which are based on statistical properties of network packets and traffic; we focus on the latter class in this work.

Unsupervised deep learning approaches have been used for anomaly-based detection, for example deep belief networks [9] or auto encoder variants, such as the non-symmetric deep auto encoder in Shone et al. [10]. When annotated packet data is available, supervised methods may be used to further classify attacks into known patterns; for example, Kim et al. use a Long-Short Term Memory (LSTM) network [11] to recognize attacks in the KDD Cup 1999 dataset. Faker et al. [12] performed a comparative study of gradient boosting, random forest and neural networks for intrusion detection, showing that neural networks give the best classification performance. Unfortunately, no work is focused on simplifying the neural network complexity while preserving accuracy, up to the point of allowing the instantiation on resource-limited MCUs.

IoT devices pose additional constraints on IDS algorithms, because they are usually based on low-power microcontrollers, e.g. integrating the ARM Cortex M4 or M7 architecture, and they have limited storage capacity (e.g. FLASH memory) and working memory (e.g. RAM). On the other hand, security features are increasingly important to ensure the safety of IoT systems.

End-to-end encryption is by far the most common security measure, but IDS systems tailored for low-resource processors have been already investigated, such as the SVELTE system proposed by *Raza et al.* [13]. While SVELTE is based on a network of MCUs working in a cooperative scheme, we devoted our efforts to automatically shrink the neural network on which the IDS is designed to fit in a single simple MCU.

To map the model on the very broad STM32 family of microcontrollers, we relied on the STM32Cube.AI [7], an automatic pre trained neural network converter, which is described in detail in Sect. 3.1.

Popular toolboxes used for deep learning are not suitable for direct deployment NNs on limited resources MCUs, and thus several solutions to this problem have recently appeared.

For example, ARM released in 2018 the CMSIS NN library [14], a set of APIs implementing common neural network operations, such as convolution and pooling; the ARM NN tool was released in the same year, allowing the automatic mapping of neural networks on MCUs [15]. Renesas has released the automatic mapping tool *e-AI*, which maps neural networks to its microcontrollers [16]. Finally, Google has proposed a version of Tensorflow adapted to the resource constraints of MCUs, called Tensorflow Micro [17]. All of them are limited because they are not able to generate ANSI C code automatically and, without user intervention, they support a limited variety of MCU in term of computational and memory resources or they do not include code validation and on target profiling facilities. Moreover, the existing solutions do not interoperate with a variety of deep learning tools the AI community uses, nor they support the multiple Integrated Development Environments (IDEs) that embedded programmers use for compiling, linking, debugging and deploying C projects on MCUs.

3 Demonstrator

3.1 STM32 Platform

STM32

A MCU (Micro Controller Unit) is a small system on a single integrated circuit. It contains one or more processor cores, integrated with memory and programmable input/output peripherals. Microcontrollers, differently from general-purpose microprocessors, are usually tailored for low cost and low power embedded applications. MCUs have reduced size and cost, compared to systems using a separate microprocessor, memory and input/output (I/O) devices, and hence they are economically advantageous in digital control tasks. Moreover, they are also very popular edge devices in the growing Internet of Things domain, representing a cheap solution for increasing programmable computing of sensing and actuation chips, which interface the physical world.

STM32 is a family of 32-bit microcontrollers, based on the Arm® Cortex®-M processor. They are designed to offer very high performance, real-time capabilities, digital signal processing, low power and low-voltage operation, and connectivity, while maintaining full integration and ease of development. They are programmed in C with a variety of compilers, free and commercial.

In particular, STM32 Nucleo-32 boards NUCLEO-F303K8 (which incorporates a STM32F303K8T6 MCU) and NUCLEO-F411RE (containing a STM32F411RET6 MCU) have been used in this work, as non-limiting example of mapping. Both the STM32F303K8T6 and STM32F411RET6 microcontrollers incorporate the high-performance Arm® Cortex®-M4 32-bit RISC core with a single-precision Floating-Point Unit (FPU). They operate at frequencies up to 72 MHz and at up to 100 MHz, respectively. STM32F303K8T6 embeds high-speed embedded memories (up to 64 Kbytes of Flash memory, 16 Kbytes of SRAM with HW parity check), an extensive range of enhanced I/Os and peripherals connected to two Advanced Peripheral Buses (APBs). STM32F411 incorporates high-speed embedded memories (up to 512 Kbytes of Flash memory, 128 Kbytes of SRAM), and an extensive range of enhanced I/Os and peripherals connected to two APB buses, two Advanced High-performance Buses (AHBs) and a 32-bit multi-AHB bus matrix.

STM32Cube.AI

It is today very common to associate the execution of Deep Neural Networks to powerful Graphic Processing Units (GPUs) running on workstations. Although this is true for high-end applications such as image segmentation, pixel labelling and natural language processing, many other low-resource demanding applications can still be ported on less powerful and much cheaper systems, such as MCUs. With the aim of changing the Internet of Things (IoT) landscape by bringing neural networks to all STM32 devices and increase developer productivity in the open market, on January 2019 we publicly released STM32Cube.AI [7].

It is a tool automatically converting pre trained neural networks into optimized C code (in memory and computation) to run efficiently on any STM32 MCUs. STM32Cube.AI significantly extends the feature-set of the STM32CubeMX tool by enabling it to import any artificial neural network trained with many of the most popular libraries available for free today, such as Keras, TensorFlow, Caffe, Lasagne, or ConvnetJS. Through STM32Cube.AI, STM32CubeMX maps a neural network on any STM32 MCU and optimizes the resulting library by, for example, folding some of its layers in a single computational node and reducing its memory footprint. The C code generator then produces a library that embedded developers can instantiate in their application. The code generator includes a platform selection tool, which analyzes the complexity of the network to recommend a subset of STM32 MCUs with the proper amount of computational resources and memory. The STM32Cube.AI Expansion Package offers also several strategies to validate models both on x86 CPUs and STM32 MCUs, as well as to measure performance on STM32 devices without requiring the user to develop any ad-hoc C code.

3.2 The Dataset

Description

The dataset used is provided by the KDD Cup 1999 challenge [18], which is a widely known benchmark for intrusion detection in computer networks. It is a subset of the 1998 DARPA dataset made by the Lincoln Labs. The authors dumped nine weeks of TCP data from a local-area network (LAN) simulating a typical U.S. Air Force network hit by multiple attacks. The setup included a simulated military network consisting of three 'target' machines running various operating systems and services; additionally, three machines were used to spoof different IP addresses to generate traffic. Finally, a sniffer recorded all network traffic using the TCP dump format and useful packed features were extracted and saved in comma-separated values (.csv) files.

Composition

From one packet, Lincoln Labs extracted 41 features, separated in 4 main types:

1. Basic features are obtained from the packet header, without examining the content of the packet (duration, protocol type, service, flag and the number of bytes sent from the source to the destination and vice versa).
2. Content features are determined by analyzing the content of the TCP packet (number of unsuccessful attempts to login to the system)
3. Time features, which determine the duration of the connection from a source IP address to target IP addresses. The connection is a sequence of data packets starting and ending at some predefined times.
4. Traffic features are based on a window that has an interval of a given number of connections (not time intervals). This is suitable to describe attacks that last longer than the interval of the stipulated time features.

Each sample (packet) is also labelled as normal or with the name of the attack (*neptune*, *smurf*, etc.) to classify what kind of intrusion the sample belongs to. The size of the input features is around 100 bytes. There are approximately 5 million of samples with the distribution shown below:

classes	Number of samples		classes	Number of samples
normal	972,781		neptune	1,072,017
smurf	2,807,886		back	2,203
buffer_overflow	30		ftp_write	8
guess_passwd	53		imap	12
ipsweep	12,481		land	21
loadmodule	9		multihop	7
nmap	2,316		perl	3
phf	4		pod	264
portsweep	10,413		rootkit	10
satan	15,892		spy	2
teardrop	979		warezclient	1,020
warezmaster	20			

Intrusions patterns can be split in four categories:

1. *Probe:* the attacker collects information about the system or computer network, by scanning a machine or a networking device in order to determine weaknesses or vulnerabilities that may later be exploited in order to compromise the system.
2. *Denial of Service (DoS):* the attacker does not allow legitimate users to access computational resources or overloads them so that requests cannot be processed in real time. The result of this attack is the unavailability of resources, i.e. they are too busy or too full to serve legitimate networking requests and hence denying user's access to a machine.
3. *User-to-root (U2R):* the attacker explores vulnerabilities in order to acquire administrator privileges (root access to the system). The hacker starts on the system with a normal user account and looks for vulnerabilities in order to gain super user privileges.
4. *Remote-to-Local (R2L)*: the attacker tries to obtain access to a remote system without a user account on the target machine.

Modifications and Pre-processing
The KDD Cup 1999 dataset is very unbalanced and many classes have few (less than ten) training samples. Therefore, to train the model we restricted the dataset to the six most represented classes in order to have a large enough number of samples. We selected the classes *normal, neptune, smurf, ipsweep, portsweep* and *satan*. Moreover, we converted the string features to float single precision values in order to have all the features normalized in the range (0.0, 1.0).

To balance the dataset we oversampled the classes with the lowest number of samples, that is, we created copies of their samples. We used the randomOverSampler() function from the python library Scikit-learn[1] to serve that need. The method copies random samples of under-represented classes in order to have the same number of sample associated to each class.

Before training, we split the classes in train/test sets with a 90%–10% proportion. We use stratified sampling, so each class has the same proportion of samples in train and test.

After these modifications, the train dataset was composed of 2,807,890 samples for each class, amounting to approximately 16 million samples. We further split 90% of our train dataset to learn our neural network model and 10% to validate it. The following neural network models have also been evaluated on the test set.

3.3   Development of Artificial Neural Networks

We investigated different NN topologies with fully connected and convolutional layers. Being low complexity (with the high accuracy) the main concern, we started addressing few classes increasing them without increasing complexity still fitting computing constrained micro controllers and memory limited.

---

[1] https://scikit-learn.org/stable/.

The model chosen at the end of experimentations is a neural network with two dense layers. We add to the first dense layer ReLU activation, and 20% dropout, to avoid overfitting. For the second dense layer, we add softmax activation to output the class of a sample, between 6 chosen. The topology of the NN is shown in Fig. 1 using the Netron visualizer[2]. We have used this topology at the beginning, slightly changing it over different attempts, in order to understand which modifications allow to find the best model.

Fig. 1. NN visualized using Netron software

Floating Point Implementation

The first trained model has activations and weights values in single precision floating point (32 bits). Layer computations, such as multiplications and additions, are in floating point, which is natively implemented into STM32 MCUs since they feature the ARM Cortex M4-7 instruction sets.

Table 1. Accuracy achieved by NN in floating point precision (Model 1)

test loss: 0.0019						
test accuracy: 0.9997						
Confusion matrix						
		normal	neptune	smurf	ipsweep	portsweep	satan
predictions	normal	97,175	4	41	15	19	24
	neptune	3	107,193	0	0	1	5
	smurf	32	0	280,757	0	0	0
	ipsweep	1	0	0	1,247	0	0
	portsweep	0	0	0	0	1,041	0
	satan	5	0	0	0	1	1,583
		prediction	recall	f1-score	support		
	normal	1.00	1.00	1.00	97,278		
	neptune	1.00	1.00	1.00	107,202		
	smurf	1.00	1.00	1.00	280,789		
	ipsweep	0.99	1.00	0.99	1,248		
	portsweep	0.98	1.00	0.99	1,041		
	satan	0.98	1.00	0.99	1,589		
macro average		0.99	1.00	1.00	489,147		

---

[2] https://electronjs.org/apps/netron.

Table 1 shows accuracy very close to 1 in all cases, suggesting the dataset may be too simple for this network topology. Indeed, the loss is close to zero and the overall accuracy is almost perfect. The second part of Table 1 shows the confusion matrix, which allows to understand the achieved accuracy by looking at the values, which are not in the diagonal. There are just a few wrong samples for each class according to the reported confusion matrix. Table 1 reports also the F1-score as another measure of the accuracy achieved.

Fixed-Point Implementation

Fully connected neural networks have a very simple topology; however, they are very expensive in term of permanent storage memory (e.g. Flash read-only memory) due to a large number of floating point weights. In order to reduce this memory cost, we use a scalar quantizer on Model 1 (shown in Fig. 1) to reduce the weight size by four times, to 8 bits. Typically, there are two ways to quantize a neural network: as a post processing step of an already trained model or by training a model with fixed-point weights constraints (also known as quantizer in-loop training). We used the simpler first option to create the so-called Model 2.

Unfortunately, when we tried to quantize the Model 1, the accuracy dropped by 20%. Except for the *smurf* class and its F1-score of 1.00, each class has its score significantly reduced. Indeed, with Model 2, the second best F1-score (for the *normal* class) was 0.61.

To better understand which layer was responsible of the drop in accuracy, we tried to quantize one layer at a time. At first, we quantized only the weights and the last dense layer in 8 bits fixed point to create Model 3. Even if the results improved a little (average of 0.66 instead of 0.34) with a partial quantization, we were still far from the results of floating point Model 1. Indeed, there were many 2,661 *satan* attacks wrongly classified as *neptune* attacks. Moreover, for *portsweep*, there were more attacks classified as *neptune* attacks (885) than correct predictions (838). In the next step, we quantized the weights only (Model 4) to understand if the accuracy drop was linked to the quantization of the activations. Unfortunately, there was still an important difference between the floating model and the weight quantized model (average of 0.78 instead of 1.00); in particular for *portsweep* and *ipsweep* attacks the F1-score did not even reach 50%.

We tried to understand this drop of performances as the models are made of dense layers, where batch normalization is not used. We considered to insert normalization layers in-between, but we thought that once we merge them we'll get the same range problems. That means the matrix of the first dense layer is badly conditioned. Moreover after experiments we saw little differences between models with and without normalization.

Indeed by checking more carefully the configuration of the fully quantized model, we observed large range changes (e.g. from 3, 4 to 29, −22) after the first layer and this is probably the reason of the bad performances of quantized model since saturation cannot be avoided with such narrow 8 bit precision. Saturation than badly affect accuracy up to a point IDS (in our current shape) is not 8 bits quantization friendly.

We tried also to increase the number of outputs of the first dense layer to 100 (instead of 41) and without quantizing the first dense layer (Model 5). The performances of this last model are shown in Table 2.

Table 2. Confusion Matrix and F1-score of Accuracy of Model 5

test loss: 0.3637

test accuracy: 0.9904

Confusion matrix

		normal	neptune	smurf	ipsweep	portsweep	satan
predictions	normal	97,253	4	0	7	12	2
	neptune	135	103,521	0	0	885	2,661
	smurf	455	0	280,334	0	0	0
	ipsweep	44	0	0	1,203	1	0
	portsweep	129	69	0	0	838	5
	satan	94	139	0	0	54	1,302
		prediction	recall	f1-score	support		
	normal	0.99	1.00	1.00	97,278		
	neptune	1.00	0.97	0.98	107,202		
	smurf	1.00	1.00	1.00	280,789		
	ipsweep	0.99	0.96	0.98	1,248		
	portsweep	0.47	0.80	0.59	1,041		
	satan	0.33	0.82	0.47	1,589		
macro average		0.80	0.93	0.84	489,147		

Model 5 achieves results closer to the floating point model. We still have poor accuracy in two classes as shown in Table 2 and by the confusion matrix. Indeed, the precision of the *portsweep* and *satan* classes is not very high (barely 50%) but this is the best results we were able to achieve without a significant increase in complexity. As such, the network employs mixed precision; floating point for first layer and 8 bit fix point for second one.

The best accuracy was achieved with full floating-point precision, as reported on Table 3, while Table 4 reports computation and memory complexity as estimated by the STM32Cube.AI tool. We can see that the changes in Model 5 increase the number of parameters and as a result the complexity with respect to Model 3. 8bit fixed point quantization reduces the complexity at the cost of reduced accuracy as well.

Another way to compress the Model 1 was to use the scalar compression option provided by STM32Cube.ai. We loaded Model 1 into STM32Cube.ai and selected compression by a factor of 4. As result a limited number of floating point weights are stored in a look-up table (LUT) during off-line compression and during on-line computations, LUT values are retrieved and re instanciated into the neural network; as result of the discretization, accuracy could decrease. Table 5 shows the results for this new Model 6.

We can see at the bottom of Table 5 that we have reduced the complexity and the Flash memory by a factor of two and we also preserved Model 1 accuracy. As we have implemented Model 1 in the application, we are confident Model 6 will perform with almost the same performances of Model 1.

Table 3. Accuracy achieved by various models with different precisions: fp32 and 8fxp

		F1-score (accuracy representation)						
		normal	neptune	smurf	ipsweep	portsweep	satan	macro avg
Model 1	Weights and activations parameters in fp32	1.00	1.00	1.00	0.99	0.99	0.99	**1.00**
Model 2	Weights and activations parameters in 8fxp	0.61	0.02	1.00	0.31	0.08	0.00	**0.34**
Model 3	Weights and last dense layer quantized in 8fxp	0.99	0.93	1.00	0.88	0.10	0.07	**0.66**
Model 4	Only weights in 8fxp	1.00	0.97	1.00	0.91	0.29	0.53	**0.78**
Model 5	More resilient model with weights and last dense layer quantized	1.00	0.98	1.00	0.98	0.59	0.47	**0.84**

Table 4. Complexity of floating point NN as profiled by STM32Cube.AI. MACC = combined multiply and accumulation operations

	Model 1	Model 2	Model 3	Model 4	Model 5
Parameters	1,974	1,974	1,974	1,974	4,806
Computational complexity MACC	2,058	2,058	2,152	2,140	4,984
ROM Kbytes	7.90	1.98	7.90	7.90	19.22
RAM Bytes	192	137	328	328	568

Table 5. Confusion Matrix, accuracy and complexity of Model 6

test accuracy: 0.99							
Confusion matrix							
		normal	neptune	smurf	ipsweep	portsweep	satan
predictions	normal	10	0	0	0	0	0
	neptune	0	18	0	0	0	0
	smurf	0	0	18	0	0	0
	ipsweep	0	0	0	18	0	0
	portsweep	0	0	0	0	18	0
	satan	0	1	0	0	0	17
Computational complexity		2,058					
ROM		3.79 KB					
RAM		192 KB					

4 Performances

4.1 STM32 Results

Starting from the floating point pre-trained Model 1, we have been able to convert and test it with STM32Cube.AI tool. The goal was to check if our model can be validated both on x86 and on STM32. Firstly, we needed to setup the MCU project configuration using STM32CubeMX. We chose the F411RE MCU and STM32Cube.AI version 3.4.0, publicly available through STM32CubeMX update function. Then, we validated the Keras Model 1 converted by the tool using random values on x86 CPU. Next, we validated the model on F411RE and with a subset of test inputs, in order to profile the execution speed and memory occupation. With STM32F4RE11, we have 2,058 MACC per each NN inference run, 7.71 KB as Flash occupation and 192 Bytes as RAM size. Those results suggest that even the simplest STM32 MCU may host that complexity. The ANSI C project was automatically generated by STM32CubeAI tool and we have chosen TrueStudio as IDE. Then, we have built and installed the compiled project on the MCU, and debugged the program. With the STM32F4RE11 MCU running at 84 MHz, we achieved an execution time of 0.281 ms, 23,625 MCU cycles and 11,48 cycles per MACC operation on average.

We have also profiled the model on STM32F303K8, the simplest and cheapest MCU available with the ARM M4 architecture. We set the MCU clock to 72 MHz, the baud rate to 115200 (Table 6).

Table 6. Summary of NN Model 1 complexity profiles on selected STM32 MCUs

	Core frequency	Baud rate	Inference run duration (avg)	Cycles (avg)	Cycles by MACC (avg)
STM32 F411RE	84 MHz	115,200	0.281 ms	23,625	11.48
STM32 F303K8	72 MHz	115,200	0.527 ms	37,964	18.45

4.2 User Interface

As part of the application used for demonstration, we developed also a user interface. It offers basic capabilities such as loading a set of pre-labeled and preprocessed TCP features, streaming them via USB to STM32 MCU board attached to the PC and displaying the classes predicted by the NN model running on MCU.

To communicate between the UI and the Nucleo board, a specific module was written to connect the application and specifically the user interface to the MCU board. The user interface was written in Python with the graphic library Qt5.

The demonstration starts with the home window. The first action is to open a CSV file, which contains the input values to test. A progress bar will start and indicate the ratio of samples being processed by the MCU. When all inputs are processed, a new window, shown in Fig. 2, will be opened reporting the results.

Figure 2 is composed by a table with the number of samples for each class on the left, the intrusion ratio on the top right, the overall accuracy, the USB processing rate, the MCU processing rate, the inference time on MCU and finally the confusion matrix on the bottom-right side.

The number of inputs and the returned outputs are also shown. The green color means that the predicted class matches the ground truth one, the red color that it is not.

The intrusion ratio represents the number of intrusion label over the total number of samples.

The overall accuracy is the ratio of exact predictions over the total number of samples.

The USB rate is the number of packets that the application can process in one second, the CPU rate is the number of packets that the STM32 can process in one second. The latter is higher than the former as it measures the pure NN inference execution time without any communication overhead due to the USB connection. The inference time is the time needed by the MCU to process one input packet.

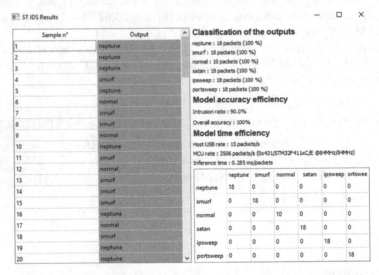

Fig. 2. User interface window with results after processing on STM32

5   Conclusions and Future Work

With this work we demonstrated that even a very simple intrusion detection algorithm based on neural networks can reach high accuracy while using very limited resources, with a throughput of up to 5,000 packets/second on a typical MCU (STM32 M4). Balancing the dataset has proven to be a key step to ensure accuracy while keeping the model complexity low.

Our different attempts to get the best compromises between accuracy and complexity allowed us to understand that the network variant were very sensitive to quantization, decreasing the accuracy for any model modification. For this reason we chose to not demonstrate the quantized models on the user interface, but only the Model 1 using floating point precision.

In the future we plan to expand the model to a larger number of attack patterns and to validate the approach on different IDS datasets, such as CICIDS 2017 [19].

Additionally, we will test the algorithm on other MCU platforms and in particular on the most powerful STM32 F7 and H7 processors, running respectively at 216 and 480 MHz.

References

1. Zhang, Z., Cho, M.C.Y., Wang, C., Hsu, C., Chen, C., Shieh, S.: IoT security: ongoing challenges and research opportunities. In: 2014 IEEE 7th International Conference on Service-Oriented Computing and Applications, Matsue, pp. 230–234 (2014)
2. Sadeghi, A., Wachsmann, C., Waidner, M.: Security and privacy challenges in industrial Internet of Things. In: 2015 52nd ACM/EDAC/IEEE Design Automation Conference (DAC), San Francisco, CA, pp. 1–6 (2015)
3. Kolias, C., Kambourakis, G., Stavrou, A., Voas, J.: DDoS in the IoT: mirai and other botnets. Computer 50(7), 80–84 (2017)
4. Buttigieg, R., Farrugia, M., Meli, C.: Security issues in controller area networks in automobiles. In: 2017 18th International Conference on Sciences and Techniques of Automatic Control and Computer Engineering (STA), Monastir, pp. 93–98 (2017)
5. Miller, C., Valasek, C.: Remote exploitation of an unaltered passenger vehicle. Black Hat USA 2015, 91 (2015)
6. Mukherjee, B., Heberlein, L.T., Levitt, K.N.: Network intrusion detection. In: IEEE Network, vol. 8, no. 3, pp. 26–41, May–June 1994
7. STM32Cube.AI. https://www.st.com/en/embedded-software/STM32Cube.AI.html
8. Young, C., Zambreno, J., Olufowobi, H., Bloom, G.: Survey of automotive controller area network intrusion detection systems. In: IEEE Design & Test. IEEE (2019)
9. Kang, M.-J., Kang, J.-W.: Intrusion detection system using deep neural network for in-vehicle network security. PLoS ONE 11(6), e0155781 (2016)
10. Shone, N., Ngoc, T.N., Phai, V.D., Shi, Q.: A deep learning approach to network intrusion detection. IEEE Trans. Emerg. Top. Comput. Intell. 2(1), 41–50 (2018)
11. Kim, J., Kim, J., Thu, H.L.T., Kim, H.: Long short term memory recurrent neural network classifier for intrusion detection. In: 2016 International Conference on Platform Technology and Service (PlatCon), Jeju, pp. 1–5 (2016)
12. Faker, O., Dogdu, E.: Intrusion detection using big data and deep learning techniques. In: Proceedings of the 2019 ACM Southeast Conference, pp. 86–93. ACM, April 2019
13. Raza, S., Wallgren, L., Voigt, T.: SVELTE: Real-time intrusion detection in the Internet of Things. Ad Hoc Netw. 11(8), 2661–2674 (2013)
14. Lai, L., Suda, N., Chandra, V.: CMSIS-NN: Efficient Neural Network Kernels for Arm Cortex-M CPUs (2018). arXiv preprint arXiv:1801.06601
15. ARM NN SDK. https://developer.arm.com/products/processors/machine-learning/arm-nn
16. Renesas e-AI solution. https://www.renesas.com/en-in/solutions/key-technology/e-ai.html
17. Tensorflow Micro. https://www.tensorflow.org/lite/microcontrollers/overview
18. Cup, K.D.D.: Dataset (1999). http://kdd.ics.uci.edu/databases/kddcup99/kddcup99
19. Sharafaldin, I., Lashkari, A.H., Ghorbani, A.A.: Toward generating a new intrusion detection dataset and intrusion traffic characterization. In: 4th International Conference on Information Systems Security and Privacy (ICISSP), Portugal, January 2018

6D Pose Estimation for Industrial Applications

Federico Cunico[1], Marco Carletti[1(✉)], Marco Cristani[1,2], Fabio Masci[3], and Davide Conigliaro[4]

[1] Department of Computer Science, University of Verona, Verona, Italy
marco.carletti@univr.it
[2] Istituto Italiano di Tecnologia (IIT), Genova, Italy
[3] The Edge Company, Srl, Rimini, Italy
[4] Humatics, Srl, Verona, Italy
https://www.theedgecompany.net
http://www.humatics.it

Abstract. Object pose estimation is important for systems and robots to interact with the environment where the main challenge of this task is the complexity of the scene caused by occlusions and clutters. A key challenge is performing pose estimation leveraging on both RGB and depth information: prior works either extract information from the RGB image and depth separately or use costly post-processing steps, limiting their performances in highly cluttered scenes and real-time applications. Traditionally, the pose estimation problem is tackled by matching feature points between 3D models and images. However, these methods require rich textured models. In recent years, the raising of deep learning has offered an increasing number of methods based on neural networks, such as DSAC++, PoseCNN, DenseFusion and SingleShotPose. In this work, we present a comparison between two recent algorithms, DSAC++ and DenseFusion, focusing on computational cost, performance and applicability in the industry.

Keywords: Pose estimation · Deep learning

1 Introduction

Estimating the 6D pose of an object is an important task for many applications, such as the interaction of a robot with the real world [35], automotive [9,22], augmented and virtual reality for both entertainment and remote maintenance and training [20,21]. Ideally, a solution should deal with objects of varying shape and texture, show robustness towards heavy occlusion, sensor noise, and changing lighting conditions, while achieving the speed requirement of real-time tasks. Due to the constraints of such applications, it becomes mandatory providing accurate and fast algorithms that are robust to acquisition noise and occlusions.

In recent years, the scientific community has proposed an increasing number of approaches to face the pose estimation problem, with a particular focus

© Springer Nature Switzerland AG 2019
M. Cristani et al. (Eds.): ICIAP 2019 Workshops, LNCS 11808, pp. 374–384, 2019.
https://doi.org/10.1007/978-3-030-30754-7_37

on neural network based methods [14,34]. Deep learning allows to infer the pose without a complete scene description, reducing the information to store and process. Strict space and computational requirements need to be solved on wearable devices [16] and augmented and virtual reality systems [15,32] where energy consumption is a crucial aspect to optimize.

The advent of cheap RGB-D sensors has enabled methods that infer poses of low-textured objects even in poorly-lighted environments more accurately than RGB-only methods: prior works either extract information from the RGB image and depth separately or use costly post-processing steps, limiting their performances in highly cluttered scenes and real-time applications [12]. Nonetheless, precise depth sensors are usually energy consuming while RGB cameras are cheap, lightweight and perfectly fit the demands of mobile and wearable technologies.

Fig. 1. 3D printed model of the electronic component used in the comparisons.

In this paper, we present a comparison among state of the art methods on 6D pose estimation. Our purpose is to find those techniques that are suitable for real and industrial applications. Hence, we selected and tested efficient algorithms which code is publicly available: DSAC++ [4] and DenseFusion [31]. The decision was led by their promising results on different datasets, their efficiency and reproducibility. We investigate the performances of those methods by generating a synthetic dataset in order to estimate the 6D pose of an electronic component of a control panel (see Fig. 1).

The structure of the paper is as follow. In Sect. 2 a brief review of the literature is presented, with an in depth and technical description of DSAC++ and DenseFusion frameworks. Then, we provide qualitative analysis of those methods in Sect. 3. In the last section, we discuss the results.

2   State of the Art

Object pose estimation and the complementary problem of camera localization are open problems in computer vision with many practical applications that could benefit from their resolution, such as robot manipulation [35], autonomous vehicles [33], wearable devices [16] and virtual and augmented reality [15,32]. All these applications usually need lightweight, fast and robust localization systems that are reliable in cluttered scenes and under heavy object occlusions.

RGB Based. Classical methods rely on detecting and matching keypoints with known object models [1,19] while other methods address the problem by learning how to predict the 2D keypoints [23]. Such methods are not reliable when the system is fed with low resolution images or poor texture information. Despite many attempts provide interesting results, primarily based on neural architectures [27], the lack of depth information prevent reaching precise results.

Depth or Point Cloud Based. Working on 3D information is another way to tackle the pose estimation problem. Recent studies proposed a discretization of the space through voxelization [28] and 3D convolutions [24]. Despite the effective geometrical representation of the data, storing voxels is often prohibitively expensive [29]. Many alternatives have been proposed, working on point cloud data [34] representing urban driving environments. In such cases, depth information is usually enough to retrieve all the geometrical properties of the scene but in indoor tasks (i.e. small object pose estimation), appearance information should be taken into account. In [31] a 2D-3D sensor fusion architecture is proposed and described in the next sections.

RGB-D Based. Cheap depth cameras has spawned many RGB-D pose estimators [2,5,6]. The approaches that fuse both appearance and geometrical information (i.e. RGB and depth) often rely on 3D reconstruction of the scene [13], giving grouping hypothesis that are later validated [2]. Newer methods such as PoseCNN [34] directly estimate 6D poses from image frames where depth is later fused [18] as additional modules in the network architecture. Despite RGB-D based algorithms usually require expensive post-processing, they reach high accuracy and in general outperform RGB-only and depth-only methods.

In this work, we mainly focus on the following methods: DSAC++ [4] and DenseFusion [31], that we describe in details in the next subsections. For the sake of completeness, we also provide a brief description of other competitor, SingleShotPose [30]. We decided to compare those methods because of the following reasons: these are recent and good examples of state of the art approaches, results are promising for real applications, the source code is available and reasonably easy to adapt and run in near real-time on unseen scenarios.

2.1 DSAC++

DSAC++ is a new, fully differentiable camera localization pipeline which has only one learnable component, a fully convolutional neural network for scene coordinate regression. The authors proposed DSAC++ as an upgrade of their previous work DSAC [3]: they propose a probabilistic selection of the candidate

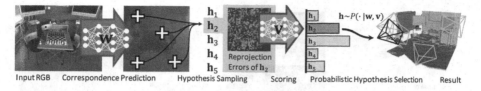

$\mathbf{h} \sim P(\cdot \,|\mathbf{w}, \mathbf{v})$

Input RGB   Correspondence Prediction   Hypothesis Sampling   Scoring   Probabilistic Hypothesis Selection   Result

Fig. 2. DSAC pipeline overview. The difference in DSAC++ pipeline is that the scoring is no more performed by a learnable component

poses in order to obtain a differentiable loss function instead of using the deterministic selection based on RANSAC [7]. DSAC was developed with two learnable components: one for regression and one for scoring. However, the scoring CNN tends to overfit and does not generalize well on unseen scenes. DSAC++ uses only one learnable component related to regression (Fig. 2).

The pipeline is the following:

- **Hypothesis generation by regression**: the regression module is used to estimate the depth information of the scene. A certain number of 3D points ($n = 4$) is selected to solve the PnP problem [8] in order to get an hypothesis $\mathbf{h}$ of the camera pose. This operation is performed m-times to obtain m different pose hypothesis.
- **Hypothesis selection**: each hypothesis is ranked through a function $s(\mathbf{h})$ to build a distribution of scores. Instead of selecting the best hypothesis, the system propagates the inlier poses distribution.
- **Pose refinement**: the hypothesis generation is repeated in order to refine the inlier distribution and the consequent pose estimation.

2.2 DenseFusion [31]

In this work, the authors propose an end-to-end deep learning approach for 6D object pose estimation from RGB-D inputs. The main idea is to fuse the extracted features from RGB and depth channels at per-pixel level. This per-pixel fusion scheme enables DenseFusion to explicitly reason about the local appearance and geometry information, enabling the system to handle occlusion. The pipeline of the method is shown in Fig. 3 and could be divided as follow:

- **Semantic segmentation**: the objects in the scene are segmented. The output of this step is a crop of the RGB frame and the corresponding point cloud extracted from the depth frame;
- **Features extraction**: RGB crop and point cloud are processed through a custom fully-convolutional network and a PointNet-based [24] architecture;
- **DenseFusion module**: color and depth embeddings are fused together and processed to generate global features of the selection;
- **Per-pixel pose estimation**: local (per-pixel) and global features are combined and fed into a pose predictor network which returns a per-pixel pose estimation;
- **6D pose estimation**: final pose is the argmax of the output of previous step.

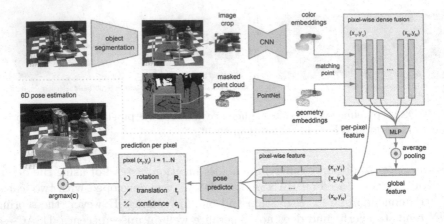

Fig. 3. Overview of DenseFusion. It generates object segmentation masks and bounding boxes from RGB images. The RGB colors and point cloud from the depth map are encoded into embeddings and fused at each corresponding pixel. The pose predictor produces a pose estimate for each pixel. Predictions are voted to generate the final 6D pose prediction of the object. Figure is taken from the original paper [31] (Color figure online)

2.3   SingleShotPose [30]

A state of the art method working on RGB frames is SingleShotPose [30]. The authors propose a single-shot deep CNN architecture based on YOLO [25,26] that takes a single RGB frame as input and directly detects the 2D projections of the 3D bounding box vertices of the objects. Given these 2D coordinates and the 3D ground control points of the bounding box corners, the 6D pose can be calculated algebraically with an efficient PnP algorithm [17]. Complete pipeline is shown in Fig. 4.

SingleShotPose pipeline could be divided in the following main steps:

- **Features extraction**: a single RGB image is processed with the fully-convolutional architecture in Fig. 4a;
- **2D prediction**: the features volume is subdivided into a 2D regular $S \times S$ grid (Fig. 4c) where each cell contains the predictions of 9 control points (the projection of the 3D bounding box and its centroid), the predicted class probabilities and a confidence value. During training, the model predicts the confidence of the bounding box projection according to Eq. 1:

$$c(x) = \begin{cases} e^{\alpha\left(1-\frac{D_T(x)}{d_{th}}\right)}, & \text{if } D_T(x) < d_{th} \\ 0, & \text{otherwise} \end{cases} \tag{1}$$

where $D_T(x)$ is the 2D Euclidean distance, in image space, between the predicted 2D point x and its ground truth; d_{th} is the cut-off threshold of the exponential decreasing function.

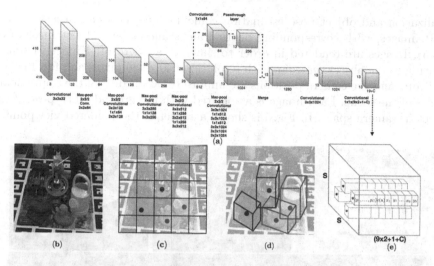

Fig. 4. Overview of SingleShotPose: (a) YOLO-based CNN architecture. (b) Example of input image. (c) The $S \times S$ grid showing cells responsible for detecting objects. (d) Each cell predicts 2D locations of the corners of the projected 3D bounding boxes in the image. (e) The 3D output tensor from our network. Figure is taken from the original paper [30].

- **Forward pass**: at run-time, the network returns the class prediction, its confidence and the 2D projections of the object 3D bounding box. For big objects, 2D coordinates are averaged on the occupied cells.
- **Pose estimation**: the PnP algorithm [17] is used to estimate the 6D pose from correspondences between the 2D and the 3D coordinates.

3   Experiments

We first describe how we create a dataset with ground-truth information followed by the experimental protocol. Then, we describe the setup and metrics we used to perform the evaluation. Qualitative and quantitative results are obtained on our synthetic dataset.

3.1   Dataset

In order to fairly compare the methods described in Sect. 2, we generated a new synthetic dataset in Unity[1] representing an electronic component of a control panel (see Fig. 1). We generated an office environment by modelling common furniture and objects (e.g. chairs, tables, monitor, keyboards): the target object is located on the central table in the world origin. Since in our data the world coordinate systems and the object pose are the same, the two problems of camera

---

[1] https://www.unity.com.

localization and object pose estimation coincide. The dataset consists of 7000 RGB images, with corresponding depth frames and binary object masks (see Fig. 5). Images are rendered in order to simulate a Microsoft Kinect v1 sensor pointing to the object centroid, with resolution 640 × 480 pixels and focal length of 26 mm, and the camera positions are uniformly sampled from the upper hemisphere of the scene. Each image is associated with the ground-truth pose of the object in camera space. In Fig. 5 is shown a subset of the rendered viewpoints.

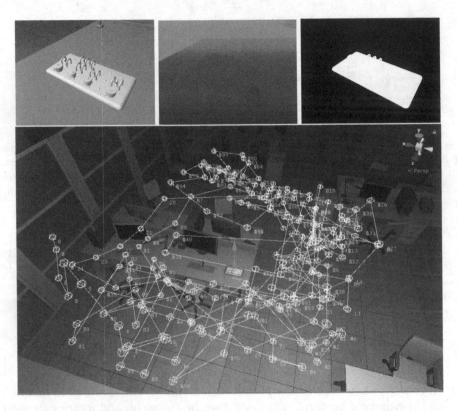

Fig. 5. Top: generated images for target object; from left to right: RGB, depth and binary mask frames. **Bottom**: overview of the scene with subset of visited viewpoints in white. (Color figure online)

3.2   Training

We run the experiments on a Linux machine with 16 GB of RAM, a NVidia RTX 2070 GPU (8 GB of vRAM) with NVidia CUDA 8.0 installed. We managed to run the original implementation and hyper-parameters of DSAC++ (C++, Lua 5.1) and DenseFusion (Python 3). Due to our hardware limitations, DSAC++ took roughly 5 days for training the complete model on our synthetic dataset. Testing runs at 200 ms per image. DenseFusion training converged in almost 3 days on the same machine. Testing is faster than DSAC++, requiring 50 ms per image.

3.3   Metrics

To compare the output poses of DSAC++ and DenseFusion, we compute the error of the rotation and translation components separately. We make use of the mean absolute error for both rotation (expressed as Euler angles, XYZ format) and the translation vector. Table 2 shows the averaged results on our synthetic dataset.

3.4   Evaluation

In our evaluation we have considered three state of the art methods: SingleShotPose, DSAC++ and DenseFusion. The decision was led by their promising results on different datasets and the availability of the source code. In Table 1 we give an overview of those methods. Before testing our dataset, we replicated the original results of all the methods: results have been successfully replicated on their datasets and same hyper-parameters. Tests on our data have been run by maintaining almost the same parameters of the original methods. We aim to train the models on a new domain and also to evaluate the robustness of the architectures by maintaining the same training settings.

Table 1. Main differences among the selected state of the art methods.

	Input data type	Output models	Trained on
SingleShotPose [30]	RGB	One per class	LINEMOD [11]
DSAC [3]	RGB, RGB-D	2	MS7S [10]
DSAC++ [4]	RGB, RGB-D	1	MS7S [10]
DenseFuion [31]	RGB-D	1	LINEMOD [11], YCB [34]

SingleShotPose. This method benefits of a RGB-based architecture which is capable to estimate the 6D pose of an object in the scene. Despite the promising results on the LINEMOD dataset [11], it quickly becomes clear that the training procedure is not simple to run: SingleShotPose needs a heavily annotated dataset, making very difficult to create one. Furthermore, it generates one model (CNN) for each class, occupying a significant amount of memory. This is a big limit in a scenario in which we want to minimize the energy and memory consumption, such as when using wearable devices. Since our goal is to simplify at most the training procedure and reduce the resource usage, we decided to focus on other methods and left SingleShotPose for future analysis.

DSAC++. It is a RGB-based camera localization method which exploits one single architecture to predict the camera pose. From a data generation point of view, the camera localization problem is simpler than the object pose estimation since it does not require any segmentation of the scene. Despite the training procedure is simple to prepare and run, it takes a long time to converge. Unfortunately, our tests demonstrated that the generalization capabilities of DSAC++ are limited: after training the model on our synthetic dataset, numerical results are higher than expected, showing high prediction errors both in rotation and translation (1.7 radiants and 2.6 m, respectively). Further experiments need to be run, with exhaustive cross-validation of both the dataset quality and hyper-parameters settings. We think the insufficient results are due to the poor texture information in our data: RGB-based methods are known to work well where high-frequency information is available, such as in presence of rich textures and geometrical details (when depth frames are usable). For the sake of completeness, we initially replicated the results of the DSAC++ method, starting with the datasets they proposed. We focused more on scenes representing small-scale contexts, so especially on the Microsoft 7-Scenes [10] RGB-D datasets. The results have been validated correctly, with a precision of camera pose estimation between 1.5 and 3 cm, and around 1° of rotation error.

DenseFusion. The last method we analyzed requires RGB and depth frames and the segmentation of the target object to train a single model for pose estimation. DenseFusion could be considered as a good compromise between space usage, time complexity and ease of training. Convergence of the new model on our dataset took several days. Nonetheless, pose estimations are quite accurate, reducing the average error up to 0.05 radiants on rotation and less than 4 cm on translation. As additional feature, DenseFusion runs in almost real-time (50 ms per image) while the competitors run up to 200 ms.

Table 2. Averaged rotation and translation errors of state of the art methods on our synthetic dataset. Rotation error is in radiants, while translation error is in meters. Standard deviation is in parenthesis.

	Rotation error (rad)	Translation error (m)
DSAC++	1.728 (0.253)	2.594 (1.176)
DenseFuion	0.054 (0.207)	0.038 (0.021)

4   Conclusions

We presented an overview of 6D pose estimation techniques and a comparison between some recent algorithms, DSAC++ and DenseFusion, focusing on performance, ease of training and robustness. Despite RGB-only and depth-only approaches usually need less information and less complex datasets, RGB-D methods demonstrated higher accuracy on average. DSAC++ proposes an intriguing pipeline but our tests demonstrated that its generalization capabilities are compromised if data is poorly textured (i.e. missing high frequency information) and parameters are not precisely tuned. On the other hand, DenseFusion showed stronger generalization, faster training and testing time. Results are also more encouraging without any specific parameter setting. In conclusion, after our evaluation, DenseFusion appears to be the best choice for 6D object pose estimation relying on RGB-D data. Its efficient implementation perfectly fits industrial and real application constraints, where space and time requirements are strict.

Acknowledge. We thank The Edge Company, Srl for the support to this research.

References

1. Bay, H., Tuytelaars, T., Van Gool, L.: SURF: speeded up robust features. In: Leonardis, A., Bischof, H., Pinz, A. (eds.) ECCV 2006. LNCS, vol. 3951, pp. 404–417. Springer, Heidelberg (2006). https://doi.org/10.1007/11744023_32
2. Brachmann, E., Krull, A., Michel, F., Gumhold, S., Shotton, J., Rother, C.: Learning 6D object pose estimation using 3D object coordinates. In: Fleet, D., Pajdla, T., Schiele, B., Tuytelaars, T. (eds.) ECCV 2014. LNCS, vol. 8690, pp. 536–551. Springer, Cham (2014). https://doi.org/10.1007/978-3-319-10605-2_35
3. Brachmann, E., et al.: DSAC - differentiable RANSAC for camera localization. In: CVPR (2017)
4. Brachmann, E., Rother, C.: 6D camera localization via 3D surface regression. In: CVPR (2018)
5. Choi, C., Christensenb, H.I.: 3D textureless object detection and tracking: an edge-based approach. In: IROS (2012)
6. Choi, C., Christensenb, H.I.: RGB-D object pose estimation in unstructured environments. RAS **75**, 595–613 (2016)
7. Fischler, M.A., Bolles, R.C.: Random sample consensus: a paradigm for model fitting with applications to image analysis and automated cartography. Commun. ACM **24**, 381–395 (1981)
8. Gao, X., Hou, X., Tang, J., Cheng, H.: Complete solution classification for the perspective-three-point problem. TPAMI **25**, 930–943 (2003)
9. Geiger, A., Lenz, P., Urtasun, R.: Are we ready for autonomous driving? The Kitti vision benchmark suite. In: CVPR (2012)
10. Glocker, B., Izadi, S., Shotton, J., Criminisi, A.: Real-time RGB-D camera relocalization. In: ISMAR (2013)
11. Hinterstoisser, S., et al.: Multimodal templates for real-time detection of textureless objects in heavily cluttered scenes. In: ICCV (2011)
12. Hinterstoisser, S., et al.: Model based training, detection and pose estimation of texture-less 3D objects in heavily cluttered scenes. In: Lee, K.M., Matsushita, Y., Rehg, J.M., Hu, Z. (eds.) ACCV 2012. LNCS, vol. 7724, pp. 548–562. Springer, Heidelberg (2013). https://doi.org/10.1007/978-3-642-37331-2_42
13. Kehl, W., Milletari, F., Tombari, F., Ilic, S., Navab, N.: Deep learning of local RGB-D patches for 3D object detection and 6D pose estimation. In: Leibe, B., Matas, J., Sebe, N., Welling, M. (eds.) ECCV 2016. LNCS, vol. 9907, pp. 205–220. Springer, Cham (2016). https://doi.org/10.1007/978-3-319-46487-9_13
14. Kendall, A., Grimes, M., Cipolla, R.: PoseNet: a convolutional network for real-time 6-DOF camera relocalization. In: ICCV (2015)
15. Lee, K.: Augmented reality in education and training. TechTrends **56**, 13–21 (2012)

16. Lee, Y.H., Medioni, G.: Wearable RGBD indoor navigation system for the blind. In: Agapito, L., Bronstein, M.M., Rother, C. (eds.) ECCV 2014. LNCS, vol. 8927, pp. 493–508. Springer, Cham (2015). https://doi.org/10.1007/978-3-319-16199-0_35

17. Lepetit, V., Moreno-Noguer, F., Fua, P.: EPnP: an accurate O(n) solution to the PnP problem. IJCV **81**, 155 (2009)

18. Li, C., Bai, J., Hager, G.D.: A unified framework for multi-view multi-class object pose estimation. In: Ferrari, V., Hebert, M., Sminchisescu, C., Weiss, Y. (eds.) ECCV 2018. LNCS, vol. 11220, pp. 263–281. Springer, Cham (2018). https://doi.org/10.1007/978-3-030-01270-0_16

19. Lowe, D.G.: Object recognition from local scale-invariant features. In: ICCV (1999)

20. Marchand, E., Uchiyama, H., Spindler, F.: Pose estimation for augmented reality: a hands-on survey. TVCG **22**, 2633–2651 (2015)

21. Marder-Eppstein, E.: Project tango. In: SIGGRAPH (2016)

22. Menze, M., Geiger, A.: Object scene flow for autonomous vehicles. In: CVPR (2015)

23. Pavlakos, G., Zhou, X., Chan, A., Derpanis, K.G., Daniilidis, K.: 6-DOF object pose from semantic keypoints. In: ICRA (2017)

24. Qi, C.R., Su, H., Mo, K., Guibas, L.J.: PointNet: deep learning on point sets for 3D classification and segmentation. In: CVPR (2017)

25. Redmon, J., Divvala, S., Girshick, R., Farhadi, A.: You only look once: unified, real-time object detection. In: CVPR (2016)

26. Redmon, J., Farhadi, A.: Yolo9000: better, faster, stronger. In: CVPR (2017)

27. Schwarz, M., Schulz, H., Behnke, S.: RGB-D object recognition and pose estimation based on pre-trained convolutional neural network features. In: ICRA (2015)

28. Song, S., Xiao, J.: Sliding shapes for 3D object detection in depth images. In: Fleet, D., Pajdla, T., Schiele, B., Tuytelaars, T. (eds.) ECCV 2014. LNCS, vol. 8694, pp. 634–651. Springer, Cham (2014). https://doi.org/10.1007/978-3-319-10599-4_41

29. Song, S., Xiao, J.: Deep sliding shapes for amodal 3D object detection in RGB-D images. In: CVPR (2016)

30. Tekin, B., Sinha, S.N., Fua, P.: Real-time seamless single shot 6D object pose prediction. In: CVPR (2018)

31. Wang, C., et al.: DenseFusion: 6D object pose estimation by iterative dense fusion. CoRR abs/1901.04780 (2019)

32. Webel, S., Bockholt, U., Engelke, T., Gavish, N., Olbrich, M., Preusche, C.: An augmented reality training platform for assembly and maintenance skills. RAS **61**, 398–403 (2013)

33. Weiss, S., Achtelik, M.W., Chli, M., Siegwart, R.: Versatile distributed pose estimation and sensor self-calibration for an autonomous MAV. In: ICRA (2012)

34. Xiang, Y., Schmidt, T., Narayanan, V., Fox, D.: PoseCNN: a convolutional neural network for 6D object pose estimation in cluttered scenes. RSS (2018)

35. Zhu, M., et al.: Single image 3D object detection and pose estimation for grasping. In: ICRA (2014)

Grain Segmentation in Atomic Force Microscopy for Thin-Film Deposition Quality Control

Nicolò Lanza$^{(\boxtimes)}$, Alessandro Romeo🄳, Marco Cristani🄳, and Francesco Setti🄳

Department of Computer Science, University of Verona, Verona, Italy
{nicolo.lanza,alessandro.romeo,marco.cristani,francesco.setti}@univr.it

Abstract. In this paper we propose an image segmentation method specifically designed to detect crystalline grains in microscopic images. We build on the watershed segmentation approach; we propose a preprocessing pipeline to generate a topographic map exploiting the physical nature of the incoming data (i.e. Atomic Force Microscopy) to emphasize grain boundaries and generate seeds for basins. Experimental results show the effectiveness of the proposed method against grain segmentation implementations available in commercial software on a new labelled dataset with an average improvement of over 20% in precision and recall over the standard implementation of watershed segmentation.

Keywords: Atomic Force Microscopy · Watershed segmentation · Visual inspection · Industrial quality control

1 Introduction

Atomic Force Microscopy (AFM) has evolved into a useful tool for direct measurements of intermolecular forces with atomic-resolution characterization that can be employed in a wide spectrum of applications such as electronics, semiconductors, materials and manufacturing, polymers, biology and biomaterials. With respect to other microscopic methods, AFM offers additional capabilities and superior performances in studies of surfaces and micro-structures, including superior resolution, 3D measurements, little or no sample/substrate preparation, and operation in ambient air or fluid. In particular, AFM can provide reliable measurements at the nanometer scale [9], which is a unique feature of great relevance for developing new alloys and for quality control in manufacturing processes.

This work has been partially supported by the project of the Italian Ministry of Education, Universities and Research (MIUR) "Dipartimenti di Eccellenza 2018-2022", and has been partially supported by the POR FESR 2014-2020 Work Program (Action 1.1.4, project No.10066183).

© Springer Nature Switzerland AG 2019
M. Cristani et al. (Eds.): ICIAP 2019 Workshops, LNCS 11808, pp. 385–394, 2019.
https://doi.org/10.1007/978-3-030-30754-7_38

In the field of surface analysis the purpose of AFM is usually the characterization of the surface topography in order to investigate the microscopic and nanoscopic structure that is for many applications of crucial importance. The ISO 25178-2 standard offers a total of 30 parameters for 3D areal surface characterization categorized in five groups: height parameters, spatial parameters, hybrid parameters, functional parameters and parameters related to segmentation. In practice the height parameters (*e.g.* the surface roughness) are the most commonly used as a typical measure of mechanical surface properties due to their influence on many phenomena like wettability [20], friction and wear [21], thermal conductance and radiation [22], etc.

In this work we focus on the geometrical analysis of surfaces in thin films. Thin film polycrystalline materials are semiconductors that can be deposited as coatings on glass or metals for many different applications. In our specific case, thin film CdTe material is deposited by vacuum evaporation for photovoltaic applications. CdTe solar cells are made by depositing different layers on a glass substrates, in our case front contact is deposited first on glass and consists of SnO_2: In (ITO) and ZnO, subsequently CdS (the n-part of the junction) and CdTe (the absorber and p-part of the junction) are deposited by vacuum evaporation. Finished cells have a Cu/Au back contact.

CdTe has the main task of absorbing light and by doing so generating electron-hole pairs. The structure of CdTe is very important since to large grain size generally corresponds higher efficiencies: the reduction of grain boundaries limits the recombination of carriers through the device. This is one of the reasons why CdTe is recrystallized by a specific treatment for enlarging the grain size up to one order of magnitude. AFM reveals the structural properties of this material and the deep analysis of the single grains can identify and optimize the best recrystallization treatment, mentioned above. More generally the structural features of thin films semiconductors are strongly affecting the electrical properties of these layers.

The main contributions of this paper are threefold:

– a new initialization strategy for watershed segmentation specifically designed for AFM images that allows for an improvement of 20% over the standard watershed segmentation implementations adopted by commercial software [13, 16];
– a publicly available MATLAB toolkit that implements the grain segmentation procedure described in this paper[1];
– a new dataset of fully annotated AFM images to be used as benchmark for grain segmentation algorithms

The remainder of this paper is structured as follows. In Sect. 2 we present an overview on the state-of-the-art in segmentation of crystalline grains in AFM images. The proposed method is detailed in Sect. 3 and experimental results are reported in Sect. 4. Finally, we draw conclusions in Sect. 5.

---

[1] http://vips.sci.univr.it/dataset/grainseg.

2   Related Work

There exist several software that help users to analyse microscopy images, including both proprietary software usually sold with instrumentation (like NT-MDT Nova[2], SPIP from Image Metrology[3], Mipar[4], MountainsMap SPM[5]) and open source projects (like Gwyddion[6], ImageJ[7]). All these software include several statistical analysis tools and some grain segmentation algorithms, mostly variants of adaptive thresholds and watershed transform. The implementations used in these commercial programs require many parameters to be tuned and nevertheless perform quite poorly when the sample conditions are challenging (*e.g.* when the surface is flat due to a corrosion process).

While in principle any existing image segmentation method –such as region growing [8,12], graph cuts [14] and deep learning based algorithms [1]– can be used to automate the grain segmentation task, in practice these methods, designed for ordinary images, are not appropriate for grain segmentation because of the intrinsic properties of these data. In particular, AFM images have no texture, since the data are depth maps; moreover, the curvature of target surfaces can vary a lot, spanning from smooth blobs (Sample C in Fig. 4) to sharp structures (Sample A in Fig. 4) to furrowed flat regions (Sample B in Fig. 4).

Image segmentation methods designed for AFM imaging can be divided into two groups. One group focuses on finding the boundaries between two grains by analyzing gray value differences of neighboring pixels, i.e. gradients on a local scale. A popular approach falling into the first group is the watershed transform, which often needs proper pre-processing of the data to provide food results. Several approaches have been proposed throughout the years, making use of anisotropic diffusion filters [2] or employing genetic algorithms for clustering pixels [17]. To overcome the main drawbacks of watershed transform, [3] proposes a digital cutting method where each boundary pixel of an object in a binarized image is tested whether it is a common boundary pixel of two neighboring grains. Automatic boundaries detection using a cellular automata approach is then described in [7]. All these methods can easily fall into over-segmentation, and in practical applications results have to be post-processed manually, making these methods not suitable for industrial automated applications.

A complementary group of methods minimizes a global energy function for partitioning an image into segments. Most of the methods proposed in the literature are based on region growing approaches [18,19] or level sets [15]. These methods are usually performing well in foreground/background segmentation, and are suitable for those cases in which few grains have to be segmented from an homogeneous substrate, but they suffer when the density of grains is high since they are not able to precisely detect the boundaries, e.g. when two grains

---

[2] www.ntmdt-si.com.
[3] www.imagemet.com/products/spip.
[4] www.mipar.us.
[5] www.digitalsurf.com.
[6] gwyddion.net.
[7] imagej.nih.gov/ij.

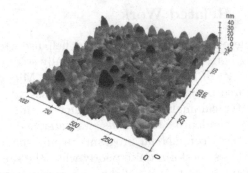

Fig. 1. An example of AFM scan in 2D and 3D.

are in contact. A step further is presented in [12]; here the authors adopt a region competition method for grain boundary detection, which combines local pixel and region statistics for minimizing an energy function on an image scale.

More sophisticated approaches are based on feature representation. In [10] a two steps method is proposed: in the first step an initial superpixels is produces; in the second step, multiple features are extracted for comprehensive description of the superpixels, and dissimilarities between superpixels are used to drive a merging strategy. The same authors then extended their work in [11] by substituting the feature extraction module with a convolutional neural network and including a fuzzy clustering algorithm to merge the over-segmented superpixels into mineral grains.

In this paper we will leverage the power of watershed transform in detecting boundaries to perform image segmentation. We start from the observation that carefully initializing seeds of iterative clustering methods is beneficial both in terms of speed and performances, and we propose a novel image pre-processing stage to provide both good seeds and sharpen boundaries for watershed segmentation procedure.

3   Our Method

In this paper we propose a grain segmentation algorithm that builds on the well grounded theory of watershed transform [16] and strongly improves performances by adopting a smart procedure to initialize seeds and magnify gradients in boundary regions.

AFM images are 3D representations of a surface that map each point $(x, y)_i$ in the scanning range to the height z_i. A sample AFM image in its 2D and 3D representation is shown in Fig. 1. We assume the surface is aligned with the xy-plane in the world reference frame; if this is not the case, standard PCA can be used to align the target to the previous case. We also allow the user to set a lower bound for z values: all the sample points under this threshold will be forced as background; this is not needed but can be helpful to prevent artifacts due to the mechanical structure of the scanning probe [5].

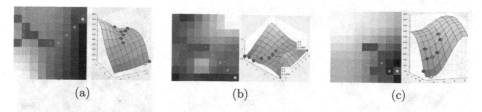

(a)   (b)   (c)

Fig. 2. Connection of open boundaries. (a) connection of two endpoints next to each other; (b) path from an endpoint to a local minimum; (c) closed loop generated by a path growing backwards.

In theory, the a AFM image is already a topographic map, and simply inverting the z values would be sufficient to run the segmentation algorithm [13]. In practice, edges between different grains are usually too smooth to be recognized as watershed ridge lines and this can easily lead commercial software to under-segmentation, as shown in the experimental section. Here we propose a two steps procedure to generate a topographic map which accounts for the physical nature of the target image. We start our procedure by detecting all the bound-aries between two grains; then we build a topographic image which is suitable to be handled by watershed algorithm.

3.1 Grain Boundaries Detection

While in general any edge detection algorithm can be applied –e.g. Sobel or Canny–, standard algorithms tend to underestimate grain boundaries. Instead, we propose a simple yet effective method to accomplish this task. We scan each row of the image by looking for local minima in the one dimensional space. We actually look for the local maxima of the inverted image, and we leverage on the concept of *prominence*, i.e. how much the peak stands out with respect to the lowest point that separates that peak from another (higher) peak. As a result, a low isolated peak can be more prominent than one that is higher but is an otherwise unremarkable member of a tall range. This is a common concept in topography as well as in our daily lives; for instance, we do not consider a small peak on the slopes of Mount Everest as the second highest mountain in the world.

We repeat this operation four times, considering directions every 45° apart. The output of this detection is a binary mask $\mathcal{B}$ that is quite noisy and edges are rarely connected. We first operate morphological cleaning to remove isolated points, and then close the gaps between edges with an iterative procedure. We localize endpoints of open branches in the binary mask $\mathcal{B}$, then we start from each endpoint (e_i) and analyse a 13×13 patch $\mathcal{N}$ centered in that e_i; we call this patch $\mathcal{N}(e_i)$. Two possible cases can arise: (i) if the patch contains another endpoint e_j –the endpoint of another open branch– we consider this second endpoint as target point $t_i = e_j$, or (ii) if the patch does not contain any other endpoint, we consider the pixel with lowest value as target point $t_i = \arg\min_{(x,y)\in\mathcal{N}(e_i)} z(x,y)$.

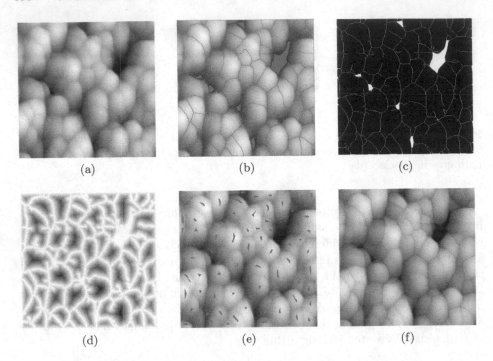

Fig. 3. The whole pipeline to segment grains from the original AFM scan. (a) AFM map of the target surface, (b) and (c) first detection of grain boundaries, (d) pixel-to-boundary distance map, (e) watershed seeds for growing catchment basins, and (f) segmented grains.

In both cases we use *shortest path* algorithm [6] to connect e_i and t_i by building an indirect graph where each pixel is a vertex, edges link pixels connected to each other – i.e. within the 8-neighbours – and weights are the sum of z coordinates of the two connected vertices. Figure 2(a) and (b) show a graphical explanation of both cases. The process iterates until all the endpoints are either connected or the shortest path generates a closed loop, see Fig. 2(c). In this case we drop the last growing step and we ignore the endpoint in future iterations.

3.2   Topographic Map

We build the topographic map $\mathcal{T}$ directly from the binary boundary mask $\mathcal{B}$ by associating each pixel with the additive inverse of the distance to the closest boundary pixel in the map. In this way, pixels belonging to boundaries have always value 0, while pixels in the center of grains are associated with high negative values. To further promote the selection of few seeds, and thus prevent oversegmentation, we impose all the pixels close to the local minima to $-\infty$. We used an adaptive threshold value which is 70% of the minimum value in each segment. The centroids of these flat regions are then used as seeds for growing the catchment basins. Please note that one segment can generate several seeds

(a) Sample A   (b) Sample B   (c) Sample C   (d) Sample D

Fig. 4. Four samples in the AFM dataset.

according to its shape. This is what we expect since boundary detection is not accurate and stable enough to separate all the grains, and this is why we need a second step of watershed segmentation.

The final stage is to run the standard watershed algorithm [16] to obtain a segmented image where each segment represents a crystalline grain. Figure 3 reports all the processing steps from the original image (a) to the segmented grains (e).

4 Experiments

We tested our method against two popular methods available in the commercial softwares: adaptive threshold [4] and standard watershed [13] used in Gwyddion.

For benchmarking, we present here a labelled dataset composed by four AFM images representing different materials and surface finishing. Images are shown in Fig. 4. The first two samples are a 6µm layer of Cadmium Telluride on substrates of CdS/ZnO/ITO deposited at 6–10mbar at 350 °C. *Sample A* is the standard result of the deposition process, while *Sample B* has been treated with a recrystallization process that increase the grain size, followed by a chemical etching that flattened the grains. The other two images (*Sample C* and *Sample D*) are nanowires of Zinc Oxide observed at different scales. This material is very interesting in the solar energy industry since it is possible to deposit it on substrates of CdS and CdTe increasing the area of the photovoltaic cell and thus the absorbed light and current density. Images have been manually annotated generating ground-truth boundary masks for each sample. The dataset is publicly available for research purposes[8].

Figure 5 shows qualitative results with the proposed method on the four samples of our dataset. Our method consistently outperforms the competitors over all the samples. Adaptive thresholding is very sensitive to noise, and many grains are lost because they are associated with background. Watershed instead has a high tendency to undersegment objects, i.e. to merge grains together into bigger regions; this is particularly evident in sample C.

We also report a quantitative analysis of the three methods. We compare all the predicted grains with the annotated ones, and we use Hungarian algorithm

---

[8] http://vips.sci.univr.it/dataset/grainseg.

Sample A   Sample B   Sample C   Sample D

Adaptive
threshold [4]

Watershed [13]

Our method

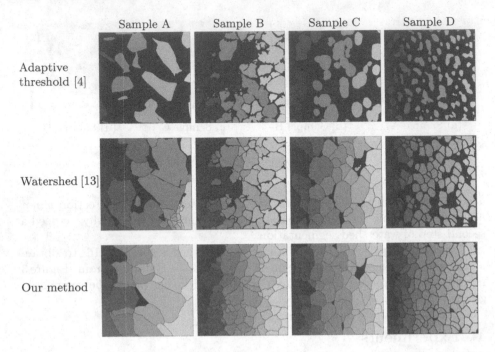

Fig. 5. Qualitative results with the proposed method on the four samples in the AFM dataset.

to find the optimal match between the two sets. We use the Intersection Over Union (IOU) ratio (i.e. the number of pixels belonging to both predicted and labelled grains over the total area spanned by the two grains) as a correspondance measure. All pairs of grains with IOU lower than 0.5 has been forced to 0. Within all the pairs returned by the matching algorithm we consider a grain correctly estimated (TP) if the IOU ratio is higher than 0.5, wrong otherwise. All mismatched grains are considered false positives (FP) if they have been predicted by the segmentation method or false negatives (FN) if they are labelled instances. In Table 1 we report for all the samples and all the methods standard classification scores: precision ($\frac{TP}{TP+FP}$), recall ($\frac{TP}{TP+FN}$) and average IOU ratio accounting only for the TPs.

Quantitative results confirm that the proposed method outperforms the competitors both in terms of precision/recall and average IOU ratio. This means that our method is not only able to correctly identify more grains than the competitors, but is also more accurate in detecting the boundaries between adjacent grains, which is very important for all the subsequent analysis required by phisicists.

Table 1. Quantitative results on the proposed dataset with our method and two commercial software alternatives.

	Adaptive threshold [4]			Watershed [13]			Our		
	Precision	Recall	Avg. IOU	Precision	Recall	Avg. IOU	Precision	Recall	Avg. IOU
Sample A	0.20	0.09	0.535	0.34	0.39	0.690	0.87	0.64	0.828
Sample B	0.27	0.26	0.673	0.59	0.57	0.797	0.73	0.72	0.813
Sample C	0.17	0.05	0.597	0.69	0.43	0.763	0.86	0.71	0.831
Sample D	0.06	0.04	0.533	0.62	0.55	0.653	0.74	0.69	0.728
Average	0.18	0.11	0.585	0.56	0.49	0.726	**0.80**	**0.69**	**0.800**

5   Conclusions

In this paper we presented a method to improve grain segmentation in AFM images by enhancing standard watershed segmentation technique with a preprocessing phase specifically designed for this kind of topological data. We compared results on a newly proposed dataset with commercial softwares and we show an average improvements of about 20% in precision and recall metrics. We are now working on a Graphical User Interface (GUI) and an implementation of our algorithm inside the open-source software Gwyddyon to allow users all across the world to use this method.

References

1. Badrinarayanan, V., Kendall, A., Cipolla, R.: SegNet: a deep convolutional encoder-decoder architecture for image segmentation. IEEE Trans. Pattern Anal. Mach. Intell. **39**(12), 2481–2495 (2017)
2. Barraud, J.: The use of watershed segmentation and GIS software for textural analysis of thin sections. J. Volcanol. Geoth. Res. **154**(1–2), 17–33 (2006)
3. Van den Berg, E.H., Meesters, A.G.C.A., Kenter, J.A.M., Schlager, W.: Automated separation of touching grains in digital images of thin sections. Comput. Geosci. **28**(2), 179–190 (2002)
4. Bradley, D., Roth, G.: Adaptive thresholding using the integral image. J. Graph. Tools **12**(2), 13–21 (2007)
5. Croft, D., Shedd, G., Devasia, S.: Creep, hysteresis, and vibration compensation for piezoactuators: atomic force microscopy application. In: American Control Conference (ACC), vol. 3, pp. 2123–2128. IEEE (2000)
6. Dijkstra, E.W.: A note on two problems in connection with graphs. Numer. Math. **1**(1), 269–271 (1959). https://doi.org/10.1007/BF01386390
7. Gorsevski, P.V., Onasch, C.M., Farver, J.R., Ye, X.: Detecting grain boundaries in deformed rocks using a cellular automata approach. Comput. Geosci. **42**, 136–142 (2012). https://doi.org/10.1016/j.cageo.2011.09.008
8. Izadi, H., Sadri, J., Mehran, N.A.: A new intelligent method for minerals segmentation in thin sections based on a novel incremental color clustering. Comput. Geosci. **81**, 38–52 (2015). https://doi.org/10.1016/j.cageo.2015.04.008
9. Jalili, N., Laxminarayana, K.: A review of atomic force microscopy imaging systems: application to molecular metrology and biological sciences. Mechatronics **14**(8), 907–945 (2004). https://doi.org/10.1016/j.mechatronics.2004.04.005

10. Jiang, F., Gu, Q., Hao, H., Li, N.: Grain segmentation of multi-angle petrographic thin section microscopic images. In: IEEE International Conference on Image Processing (ICIP) (2017). https://doi.org/10.1109/ICIP.2017.8297009
11. Jiang, F., Gu, Q., Hao, H., Li, N., Wang, B., Hu, X.: A method for automatic grain segmentation of multi-angle cross-polarized microscopic images of sandstone. Comput. Geosci. **115**, 143–153 (2018). https://doi.org/10.1016/j.cageo.2018.03.010
12. Jungmann, M., Pape, H., Wißkirchen, P., Clauser, C., Berlage, T.: Segmentation of thin section images for grain size analysis using region competition and edge-weighted region merging. Comput. Geosci. **72**, 33–48 (2014). https://doi.org/10.1016/j.cageo.2014.07.002
13. Klapetek, P., et al.: Atomic force microscopy characterization of ZnTe epitaxial films. Acta Physica Slovaca **53**, 223–230 (2003)
14. Ladicky, L., Russell, C., Kohli, P., Torr, P.H.S.: Graph cut based inference with co-occurrence statistics. In: Daniilidis, K., Maragos, P., Paragios, N. (eds.) ECCV 2010. LNCS, vol. 6315, pp. 239–253. Springer, Heidelberg (2010). https://doi.org/10.1007/978-3-642-15555-0_18
15. Lu, B., Cui, M., Liu, Q., Wang, Y.: Automated grain boundary detection using the level set method. Comput. Geosci. **35**(2), 267–275 (2009)
16. Meyer, F.: Topographic distance and watershed lines. Sig. Process. **38**, 113–125 (1994)
17. Ross, B.J., Fueten, F., Yashkir, D.Y.: Edge detection of petrographic images using genetic programming. In: Annual Conference on Genetic and Evolutionary Computation (2000)
18. Yesiloglu-Gultekin, N., Keceli, A.S., Sezer, E.A., Can, A.B., Gokceoglu, C., Bayhan, H.: A computer program (TSecSoft) to determine mineral percentages using photographs obtained from thin sections. Comput. Geosci. **46**, 310–316 (2012)
19. Zhou, Y., Starkey, J., Mansinha, L.: Segmentation of petrographic images by integrating edge detection and region growing. Comput. Geosci. **30**(8), 817–831 (2004)
20. Xia, W., Ni, C., Xie, G.: The influence of surface roughness on wettability of natural/gold-coated ultra-low ash coal particles. Powder Technol. **288**, 286–290 (2016). https://doi.org/10.1016/j.powtec.2015.11.029
21. Rahaman, M.L., Zhang, L., Liu, M., Liu, W.: Surface roughness effect on the friction and wear of bulk metallic glasses. In: 20th International Conference on Wear of Materials. Wear **332–333**, 1231–1237 (2015). https://doi.org/10.1016/j.wear.2014.11.030
22. Chen, Y., Xuan, Y.: The influence of surface roughness on nanoscale radiative heat flux between two objects. J. Quant. Spectrosc. Radiat. Transfer **158**, 52–60 (2015). https://doi.org/10.1016/j.jqsrt.2015.01.006

Advanced Moving Camera Object Detection

Giuseppe Spampinato[✉], Arcangelo Bruna, Salvatore Curti,
and Davide Giacalone

System Research and Application Group,
STMicroelectronics, Stradale Primosole 50, 95100 Catania, Italy
{giuseppe.spampinato,arcangelo.bruna,
salvatore.curti,davide.giacalone}@st.com

Abstract. Assuming a moving camera, detection of moving objects is a challenging task. This is mainly due to the difficulties to distinguish between objects motion and background motion, introduced by the camera. The proposed real time system, based on previous work without camera movement, is able to discriminate well the two kind of motions, thanks to a robust global motion vector removal, which preserves objects identified in the previous steps. The system reaches high performances just using input Optical Flow, without any assumptions about environmental conditions and camera motion.

Keywords: Optical flow · Object detection · Motion Estimation ·
Motion compensation · Clustering · Real time

1 Introduction

Independently moving object (IMO) detection is an important motion perception capability of a mobile observatory system. Changes in a scene may be due to either the motion of the camera (ego-motion) or the motion of objects, so IMO detection can be considered in two flavors for the dynamic nature of the camera and world setup, i.e. stationary camera with moving objects (SCMO) and moving camera with moving objects (MCMO).

In dynamic scene analysis, a variety of methods to detect moving objects in static scenes has been proposed in several research works [1]. SCMO can be analyzed by mainly using two approaches: region based and boundary based. The most popular and recent region based approaches is background subtraction [2–5], while recent boundary based approaches use edge based optical flow [6–9].

MCMO is extremely challenging as related to dynamic scene analysis. The difficulty of detecting moving objects with a moving camera is due to the overlap of two different types of movement, but lately this challenging task has been largely increased thanks to the usage of computer vision techniques in mobile platforms, such as Unmanned Aerial Vehicles (UAVs), automatic vehicles and mobile robots. This work refers to this specific area of research.

The key step in IMO detection in MCMO is camera motion compensation. A variety of methods to compensate for the ego-motion has been proposed. In particular, two main approaches have been suggested: visual feature based and motion based.

M. Cristani et al. (Eds.): ICIAP 2019 Workshops, LNCS 11808, pp. 395–404, 2019.
https://doi.org/10.1007/978-3-030-30754-7_39

Visual feature based approaches usually consider colors [10, 11], corners [12, 13], edges [14, 15] or shapes [16]. In general, these approaches are not computationally efficient, since image information are needed for the processing.

Different motion-based MCMO approaches have been also proposed, such as spatio-temporal background modeling [17], grid-based modeling [18] and feature clustering [19], but these methods are computationally heavy as well. Another MCMO method falling in this category, but computationally lighter, is based on Optical Flow (OF). Optical flow estimation gives a two-dimensional motion vector (MV), which represents the movement of some points of an image from one frame to the other. The basic idea is to calculate a background movement model, which is subtracted from the current frame to eliminate global camera movement. In this way, only foreground movements are retained in the current frame and can be clustered to correctly identify moving objects [20, 21].

We focused our attention in the last approach, which allows to reduce the overall complexity of the system, since entirely based on optical flow. Moreover, it works without any assumption about the camera motion and the environmental conditions and allows to obtain a real time application with good performances.

This paper is structured as follows: in the Sect. 2 the proposed global motion vector removal system is described, then the experimental results are shown in Sect. 3, followed by the conclusion in the Sect. 4.

2 Proposed System

The proposed advanced low cost moving camera object detection system is shown in Fig. 1. Briefly, the input optical flow OF (generated by any kind of algorithm) is filtered by the proposed *Global Motion Vector Removal* (GMVR) algorithm to eliminate global background motion. The obtained optical flow set OF_7, containing only the object movement motion vectors, MVs, is then used by the *Clustering* step [22], to obtain the moving object Bounding Box (BB) List for this frame. This BB List will be preserved for the next frame elaboration, avoiding to lose moving objects previously identified.

The *Global Motion Vector Removal* main block is detailed shown in Fig. 2. Briefly, the input optical flow OF is filtered by a *Pre-filtering* step, to eliminate noisy and out-of-range MVs, obtaining a new optical flow set OF_1. An Optimized Random Sample Consensus (RANSAC) is then applied to OF_1 obtaining two subsets: the inlier set OF_2, which should contain MVs related to global camera motion; the outlier set OF_3, which should contain only MVs related to local objects motion. At this point, the inlier set OF_2 contributes to obtain global motion parameters (x-shift, y-shift, rotation, zoom) through a simple *Motion Model Estimation*, while the outlier set OF_3 is adjusted by *Refinement Filter*, depending on distance metrics, obtaining the outlier set OF_4. A *Temporal Clustering* avoids to eliminate objects detected in previous frames. After that, depending on MVs occupied area, the *Global Check* determines if OF_5 can really contain MVs related to local objects motion. If *Global Check* condition is not met, OF_5 is discarded and then the final output OF_7 set will be emptied, so that no objects BB will be identified in this frame. Otherwise *Vectors Compensation* is applied to OF_5, obtaining the compensated outlier set OF_6. Finally, after the application of the *Post-filtering* step, which works in a similar manner of *Pre-filtering* step, the final output set, OF_7, will be obtained.

In the following subparagraphs, the aforementioned steps will be described in detail.

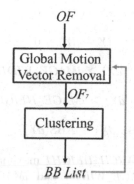

Fig. 1. Functional block diagram of the proposed solution

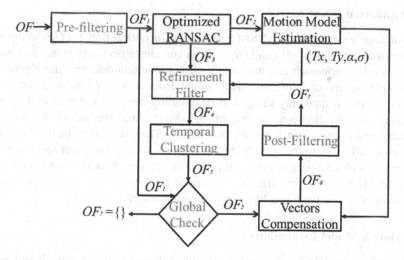

Fig. 2. Functional block diagram of the Global Motion Vector Removal.

2.1 Pre-filtering

The *Pre-filtering* step works on the input optical flow set OF, obtained with a general algorithm, and gives as output a new reduced optical flow set OF_1. Let us consider the MV composed by the parameters (X, Y, dX, dY), where X and Y are the position in the image and dX and dY are the displacement between the region of the current image versus the previous image. This step eliminates from *OF* the MV if at least one the following condition is met:

$$ABS(dX) > SEARCH\_WIDTH \tag{1}$$

$$ABS(dY) > SEARCH\_HEIGHT \tag{2}$$

$$(X + dX) < 0 \tag{3}$$

$$(Y + dY) < 0 \tag{4}$$

$$(X + dX) \geq IMAGE\_WIDTH \tag{5}$$

$$(Y + dY) \geq IMAGE\_HEIGHT \tag{6}$$

$$(ABS(dX) + ABS(dY)) \leq 1 \tag{7}$$

with *SEARCH_WIDTH* and *SEARCH_HEIGHT* maximum object movement between two adjacent frames and *IMAGE_WIDTH* and *IMAGE_HEIGHT* equal to frame dimensions. In particular: (1) and (2) deal with out of range MVs; (3), (4), (5) and (6) exclude out of frame MVs; (7) eliminates noisy MVs.

2.2 Optimized RANSAC

Random Sample consensus (RANSAC) [23] takes the optical flow set OF_1 as input and generates the two subsets, OF_2 and OF_3, which contain respectively inliers and outliers MVs. It is robust approach and the most used iterative non-deterministic algorithm to estimate parameters of a mathematical model from a set of observed data which contains outliers. It randomly samples corresponding matches and tries to fit them by calculating an error between the rest of the samples and the model. It produces a reasonable result only with a certain probability. The probability increases as more iterations are allowed. In this way the best consensus set (e.g. the inlier set) is obtained.

A model with four parameters (x-shift, y-shift, rotation, zoom) is used in this paper and RANSAC has been optimized in both error and probability calculation, with the elimination of heavy functions like pow(), log() and sqrt().

2.3 Motion Model Estimation

In order to compensate for the camera motion, a homography matrix should be calculated for each consecutive frame. This matrix relates the transformation between incoming and previous frames. A model with four parameters (x-shift, y-shift, rotation, zoom) is used. Starting from inlier optical flow set OF_2 gives the parameters (Tx, Ty, α, σ), which can be considered as the global camera motion [24].

2.4   Refinement Filter

This step takes as input the outlier optical flow set OF_3, to obtain a reduced outlier optical flow set OF_4. In particular, considering a motion vector MV in set OF_3, the moto-compensated vector MV' is calculated. MV' is obtained by applying to MV the parameters (Tx, Ty, α, σ), calculated in previous *Motion Estimation* step. At this point, MV is discarded if the following two conditions are satisfied:

$$SAD(MV, MV') < TRESHMV \tag{8}$$

$$ABS(\beta(MV) - \beta(MV')) < TRESH\beta \tag{9}$$

where SAD is the *Sum of Absolute Difference* $(|X - X'| + |Y - Y'|)$, the function β provides the orientation of the respective motion vector MV and MV' (e.g. with respect to the horizontal direction/axis of the image), while $TRESHMV$ and $TRESH\beta$ are thresholds opportunely calculated as percentage of the difference between maximum and minimum orientation lying around the considered MV.

2.5   Temporal Clustering

This step takes as input the outlier refined optical flow set OF_4 and the previous frame *BB List* to obtain a new outlier optical flow set OF_5. The motion vectors contained inside the *BB List* are preserved, to avoid eliminating moving object previously identified. Of course, these MVs can be motion-compensated, assuming, for example, a constant speed in the scene. It is a vital step. In fact, motion vectors of clusters going out of the scene in all directions can be easily confused with motion vectors to be eliminated, mainly due to camera movement. Introducing *Temporal Clustering* step, we overcome this problem, assuming that objects going out of the scene have been identified by previous *Clustering* step.

2.6   Global Check

Once a final optical flow set OF_5 is obtained, the *Global Check* step decides if OF_5 is valid and pass it to the next *Vectors Compensation* step; otherwise the OF_5 is refused otherwise and then no moving object will be identified for the current frame. OF_5 can be refused for two reasons: OF_5 contains just MVs related to global movement and not related to moving objects; OF_5 contains too few vectors. The main idea is that MVs of the background are more scattered than those of the moving objects, so background area is bigger than moving objects area.

In particular, to be accepted by *Global Check*, the set OF_5 should pass the following four conditions:

$$card(OF_5)/card(OF1) < TH1 \tag{10}$$

$$LenghtX(OF_5)/LenghtX(OF_1) < TH2 \tag{11}$$

$$LenghtY(OF_5)/LenghtY(OF_1) < TH3 \tag{12}$$

$$Area(OF_5)/Area(OF_1) < TH4 \tag{13}$$

with:

$$Area(OF) = LenghtX(OF) * LenghtY(OF) \tag{14}$$

where $card(OF)$ is the cardinality of the set OF, i.e. the number of elements of OF; $LenghtX(OF)$ and $LenghtY(OF)$ are the horizontal and vertical lengths occupied by all MVs in OF. In particular, the function $LengthX(OF)$ provides the difference between the maximum horizontal position and the minimum horizontal position of the motion vectors in OF and the function $LengthY(OF)$ provides the difference between the maximum vertical position and the minimum vertical position of the motion vectors in OF.

2.7   Vectors Compensation

Once a final optical flow set OF_5 passed the *Global Check* step, the parameters (Tx, Ty, α, σ) (obtained by *Motion Model Estimation* Step) are directly applied to the set OF_5, obtaining the final moto-compensated set OF_6. This step assumes that different distances among objects and camera will not have a big influence on the final results. A more sophisticated model can be applied taking this aspect into account.

2.8   Post-filtering

Post-filtering step purges from optical flow set OF_6 the noisy and out of range *MVs*, obtaining new optical flow set OF_7. This filter is the same as *Pre-filtering* step, but applied after *Vectors Compensation*.

2.9   Clustering

Clustering step obtains the *BB* List (that is the list of identified moving objects) from optical flow set OF_7. MVs are grouped into a *clusters* according to similarity measures. Each *cluster* corresponds to a single moving object. The *Clustering* step is the same described in [21] and, as mentioned, it relies only on optical flow analysis.

3   Experimental Results

Lots of tests have been executed with different scenarios and different cameras at different resolutions, with both linear and fish-eye lenses, obtaining really good visual results.

An aerial view example obtained with linear camera is shown in Figs. 3 and 4. In this case, the output of just Clustering system [22] (Fig. 3) shows different *BBs* on the ground, since the camera is moving; while applying the proposed *Global Motion Vector Removal* (GMVR) before the Clustering system (Fig. 4) these *BBs* are removed, since the related *MVs* are correctly identified and removed.

The example shown in Figs. 5 and 6 have the same scenario of Figs. 3 and 4, but in this case there is a moving vehicle. In this case, the Clustering system (Fig. 5) correctly identify the moving vehicle, but also shows different *BBs* on the ground, since the

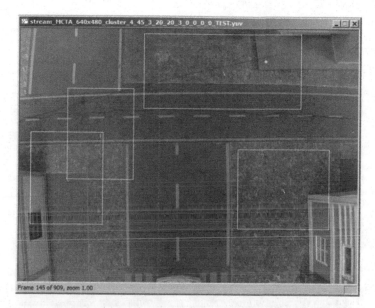

Fig. 3. Output of clustering system without moving objects in the scene.

Fig. 4. Output of clustering system (without moving objects), after GMVR application.

camera is moving; while applying the proposed *Global Motion Vector Removal* (GMVR) before the Clustering system (Fig. 6) only the *BBs* on the ground are correctly removed and the *BB* on the moving car is correctly maintained, indicating that the algorithm is able to well discriminate moving objects from moving background.

Fig. 5. Output of clustering system with moving objects in the scene.

Fig. 6. Output of clustering system with moving objects, after GMVR application.

4 Conclusion

The proposed system has been experimentally tested on a representative dataset obtaining convincing results in terms of accuracy. It is a very reliable and low complexity IMO detection system for MCMO. It makes use of optical flow of two consecutive frames only, without any assumption about camera movement and environmental conditions. It is flexible, so it can be used with any optical flow and clustering algorithm, without compromising the efficacy of the proposed system.

References

1. Yazdy, M., Bouwmans, T.: New trends on moving object detection in video images captured by a moving camera: a survey. Comput. Sci. Rev. **28**, 157–177 (2018)
2. Panda, D.K., Meher, S.: Detection of moving objects using fuzzy color difference histogram based background subtraction. IEEE Signal Process. Lett. **23**, 45–49 (2016)
3. Anandhalli, M., Baligar, V.P.: Improvised approach using background subtraction for vehicle detection. In: IEEE International Advance Computing Conference (IACC) (2015)
4. Harrouss, O.E., Moujahid, D., Tairi, H.: Motion detection based on the combining of the background subtraction and spatial color information. In: Intelligent Systems and Computer Vision (ISCV) 2015
5. Huynh-The, T., Banos, O., Lee, S., Kang, B.H., Kim, E., Le-Tien, T.: NIC: a robust background extraction algorithm for foreground detection in dynamic scenes. IEEE Trans. Circ. Syst. Video Technol. **27**, 1478–1490 (2016)
6. Huang, C., Hung, M.: Target motion compensation with optical flow clustering during visual tracking. In: IEEE 11th International Conference on Networking, Sensing and Control (ICNSC) (2014)
7. Wong, C., Siu, W.C., Barnes, S., Jennings, P., Fong, B.: Shared-use motion vector algorithm for moving objects detection for automobiles. In: IEEE International Conference on Consumer Electronics (ICCE) (2016)
8. Hariyono, J., Jo, K.: Detection of pedestrian crossing road. In: IEEE International Conference on Image Processing (ICIP) (2015)
9. Liang, C., Juang, C.: Moving object classification using a combination of static appearance features and spatial and temporal entropy values of optical flows. IEEE Trans. Intell. Transp. Syst. **16**, 3453–3464 (2015)
10. Hsu-Yung, C., Chih-Chia, W., Yi-Ying, C.: Vehicle detection in aerial surveillance using dynamic Bayesian networks. IEEE Trans. Image Process. **21**, 2152–2159 (2012)
11. Chen, L., Jiang, Z., Yang, J., Ma, Y.: A coarse-to-fine approach for vehicles detection from aerial images. In: International Conference on Computer Vision in Remote Sensing (CVRS) (2012)
12. Cheraghi, S.A., Sheikh, U.U.: Moving object detection using image registration for a moving camera platform. In: IEEE International Conference on Control System, Computing and Engineering (ICCSCE) (2012)
13. Gleason, J., Nefian, A.V., Bouyssounousse, X., Fong, T., Bebis, G.: Vehicle detection from aerial imagery. In: IEEE International Conference on Robotics and Automation (2011)
14. Zheng, Z., Wang, X., Zhou, G., Jiang, L.: Vehicle detection based on morphology from highway aerial images. In: IEEE International Geoscience and Remote Sensing Symposium (IGARSS) (2012)

15. Kembhavi, A., Harwood, D., Davis, L.S.: Vehicle detection using partial least squares. IEEE Trans. Pattern Anal. Mach. Intell. **33**, 1250–1265 (2011)
16. Sadeghi-Tehran, P., Angelov, P.: ATDT: autonomous template-based detection and tracking of objects from airborne camera. In: Filev, D., et al. (eds.) Intelligent Systems'2014. AISC, vol. 323, pp. 555–565. Springer, Cham (2015). https://doi.org/10.1007/978-3-319-11310-4_48
17. Kim, S.W., Yun, K., Yi, K.M., Kim, S.J., Choi, J.Y.: Detection of moving objects with a moving camera using non-panoramic background model. Mach. Vis. Appl. **25**, 1015–1028 (2012)
18. Yi, K.M., Yun, K., Kim, S.W., Chang, H.J., Jeong, H., Choi, J.Y.: Detection of moving objects with non-stationary cameras in 5.8 ms: bringing motion detection to your mobile device. In: Computer Vision and Pattern Recognition Workshops (CVPRW) (2013)
19. Kim, J., Wang, X., Wang, H., Zhu, C., Kim, D.: Fast moving object detection with non-stationary background. Multimedia Tools Appl. **67**(1), 311–335 (2013)
20. Sadeghi-Tehran, P., Clarke, C., Angelov, P.: A real-time approach for autonomous detection and tracking of moving objects from UAV. In: IEEE Symposium on Evolving and Autonomous Learning Systems (EALS) (2014)
21. Kim, J., Ye, G., Kim, D.: Moving object detection under free-moving camera. In: Proceedings of IEEE International Conference on Image Processing (ICIP) (2010)
22. Spampinato, G., Bruna, A., Curti, S., D'Alto, V.: Advanced low cost clustering system. In: 6th International Conference on Image Processing Theory, Tools and Applications (IPTA) (2016)
23. Fischler, M.A., Bolles, R.C.: Random sample consensus: a paradigm for model fitting with applications to image analysis and automated cartography. Commun. ACM **24**(11), 381–395 (1981)
24. Spampinato, G., Bruna, A., Farinella, G.M., Battiato, S., Puglisi, G.: Fast and Low Power Consumption Outliers Removal for Motion Vector Estimation. In: Battiato, S., Blanc-Talon, J., Gallo, G., Philips, W., Popescu, D., Scheunders, P. (eds.) ACIVS 2015. LNCS, vol. 9386, pp. 70–80. Springer, Cham (2015). https://doi.org/10.1007/978-3-319-25903-1_7

Author Index

Printed in the United States
By Bookmasters